CHRISTIAN HERITAGE COLLEGE

2100 Greenfield Dr.

El Cajon, CA 92021

LONG-TERM TREATMENTS OF PSYCHOTIC STATES

Psychiatry Series

Retreat from Sanity: The Structure of Emerging Psychosis
M.B. Bowers, Jr., M.D.

Strategic Intervention in Schizophrenia: Current Developments in Treatment
R. Cancro, M.D., N. Fox, and L. Shapiro, M.D.

The Behavioral Treatment of Psychotic Illness: Advances in Theory and Technique
W. DiScipio, Ph.D.

Overload: The New Human Condition
L. Bellak, M.D.

Psychiatry in Broad Perspective
R.R. Grinker, Sr., M.D.

Long-Term Treatments of Psychotic States
C. Chiland, M.D., Ph.D.

The Psychotic Animal: A Psychiatrist's Study of Human Delusion
W.J. Garre, M.D.

LONG-TERM TREATMENTS
OF PSYCHOTIC STATES

Colette Chiland, M.D., Ph.D.
with editorial assistance from Paul Bequart

 **HUMAN SCIENCES PRESS**
Formerly *BEHAVIORAL PUBLICATIONS INC.*
72 FIFTH AVENUE, NEW YORK, N.Y.   10011

This book is a translation of *Traitements au long cours des états psychotiques,* published in French by Privat, Toulouse, 1974. The editorial presentation is completely new.

Library of Congress Catalog Number 76-46582

ISBN: 0-87705-252-2

Copyright © 1977 by Human Sciences Press
72 Fifth Avenue, New York, New York 10011

Printed in the United States of America
789 987654321
Library of Congress Cataloging in Publication Data

Library of Congress Cataloging in Publication Data
Main entry under title:

Long-term treatments of psychotic states.

   Translation of Traitements au long cours de états psychotiques.
   Includes index.
   1. Psychoses—Congresses.   2. Psychotherapy—Congresses.   I. Chiland, Colette.   II. Béquart, Paul.
RC512.T713   616.8'914   76-46582
ISBN 0-87705-252-2

CONTENTS*

*Texts marked with an asterisk were originally written in English. The others were written in French and translated into English by Maev-Ann de la Guardia.

ACKNOWLEDGMENTS

This book is based on the Proceedings of a Symposium and could therefore not have been produced without all those who made the Symposium possible.

We thank first of all the members of the Scientific Committee who established the program: Juan de Ajuriaguerra, René Angelergues, Hélène Chaigneau, René Diatkine, André Green, Philippe Koechlin, Jean-Louis Lang, Roger Misès, Paul-Claude Racamier; and the members of the Organizing Committee: Conseiller d'Etat R. Grégoire, Serge Lebovici, and the late Philippe Paumelle, whose recent death has been a sad blow to us.

We thank the French Ministry of Health and Social Security for their sponsorship, and are grateful for the material assistance provided by the Laboratories of Berthier-Derol, Bouchara, Chabre, Dausse, Delagrange, and Specia, and most particularly the Solac and Squibb Laboratories, whose help was decisive.

It is a pleasure to acknowledge the unwavering devotion of the staff of the 13th District Mental Health Association in Paris, and especially M. Menteur and his team, and Mme. Tanet and her colleagues.

For the excellent simultaneous interpretation at the Symposium we thank Mr. Elles and his team of interpreters, and for the translation of the texts originally written in French we are grateful to Mme. Maev-Ann de la Guardia, whose meticulous professional work will be appreciated by the reader.

We should also like to express our gratitude to our publishers in both France and the United States for their help and kind consideration.

Finally, we are greatly indebted to the approximately 1200 participants of the Symposium, whose presence, questions, and intense enthusiasm forced speakers and discussants to probe the final implications of their positions, and who thus helped to guide the editorial work on this book.

Colette Chiland
Paul Béquart

CONTRIBUTORS

Juan de Ajuriaguerra, M.D.
  Professor of Psychiatry, University of Geneva.

Arthur Amyot, M.D.
  Director, Institut Albert Prévost, Montreal.

Teodoro Ayllon, Ph.D.
  Professor of Psychology, Georgia State University, Atlanta,
  Georgia.

Guy Baillon, M.D.
  C.T.R.S., Hôpital Psychiatrique de Ville-Evrard, Neuilly-sur-Marne,
  France.

Claude Balier, M.D.
  Deputy Director, 13th District Mental Health Association, Paris.

Leopold Bellak, M.D.
  Research Professor of Psychology, New York University, New York
  City; Clinical Professor of Psychiatry, George Washington University, Washington D.C.; Visiting Professor of Psychiatry, Albert Einstein School of Medicine, New York City.

11

Paul Béquart, M.D.
 Deputy Director, 13th District Mental Health Association, Paris.

Anne-Marie Bodenheimer, M.D.
 13th District Mental Health Association, Paris.

Léopold Carretier, M.D.
 13th District Mental Health Association, Foyer La Velotte, Besançon.

Hélène Chaigneau, M.D.
 C.T.R.S. Hôpital Psychiatrique de Ville-Evrard, Neuilly-sur-Marne, France.

Colette Chiland, M.D., Ph.D.
 13th District Mental Health Association, Paris; Professor of Clinical Psychology, University René Descartes, Paris.

Henri Collomb, M.D.
 Professor of Psychiatry, University of Dakar, Senegal.

Pierre Deniker, M.D.
 Professor of Psychiatry, University of Paris.

René Diatkine, M.D.
 Deputy Director, 13th District Mental Health Association, Paris. Professor of Psychiatry, University of Geneva.

Pierre Doucet, M.D.
 Institut Albert-Prévost, Montreal.

Jack R. Ewalt, M.D.
 Massachusetts Mental Health Center, Boston, Massachusetts.

Henri Ey, M.D.
 Former Director, Psychiatric Hospital of Bonneval, France.

Sylvia Faure-Dayant, M.D.
 13th District Mental Health Association, Paris.

Ronald B. Feldman, M.D.
 Director Child Psychiatry, Jewish General Hospital, Montreal.

Lester Grinspoon, M.D.
 Associate Clinical Professor of Psychiatry, Harvard Medical School; Director of Psychiatry (Research), Massachusetts Mental Health Center, Boston, Massachusetts.

André Green, M.D.
13th District Mental Health Association, Paris; Vice-President of the International Psychoanalytical Association.

Jean Guyotat, M.D.
Professor of Psychiatry, University of Lyon.

Jacques Hochmann, M.D.
Centre de Santé Mentale, Villeurbanne, France.

Louis Julou, D.V.M.
Director of Pharmaceutic Research, Société des Usines Rhône-Poulenc, Vitry-sur-Seine, France.

Dimitri Karavokyros, M.D.
C.T.R.S., Hôpital Psychiatrique de Ville-Evrard, Neuilly-sur-Marne, France.

Otto F. Kernberg, M.D.
Former Director, C. F. Menninger Memorial Hospital, Topeka, Kansas; Director, General Clinical Service, New York State Psychiatric Institute, New York; Professor of Clinical Psychiatry, College of Physicians and Surgeons, Columbia University, New York Training and Supervising Analyst, Columbia University Psychoanalytical Clinic for Training and Research, New York.

Evelyne Kestemberg, M.A.
Past President, Psychoanalytical Society of Paris.

Jean Kestenberg, M.D.
13th District Mental Health Association, Paris.

Philippe Koechlin, M.D.
Hôpital Charcot, Plaisir.

Pierre-Albert Lambert, M.D.
Hôpital Psychiatrique de Bassens, Chambéry, France.

Jean-Louis Lang, M.D.
Externat Médico-Pédagogique, Jouy-en-Josas, France.

Jean Laplanche, M.D., Ph.D.
Professor of Psychoanalysis, University of Paris.

Serge Lebovici, M.D.
Director, 13th District Mental Health Association, Paris. Professor of Child Psychiatry, University of Paris; President of the International Psychoanalytical Association.

Denise L'Ecuyer, I.L.P.
   Psychiatric Nurse, Institut Albert-Prévost, Montreal.

Gilbert F. Lelord, M.D., Ph.D.
   Director, Child Psychiatry; Professor of Physiology, University of
   Tours.

Philippe Meyer, M.A.
   Sociologist, 13th District Mental Health Association, Paris.

Marc Midenet, M.D.
   Hôpital Psychiatrique de Bassens, Chambéry, France.

Roger Misès, M.D.
   Director, Child Psychiatry, Fondation Vallée, Gentilly, France.

Christian Müller, M.D.
   Professor of Psychiatry, University of Lausanne, Switzerland.

Henry B. M. Murphy, M.D., Ph.D.
   Professor of Psychiatry, McGill University, Montreal.

Diego Napolitani, M.D.
   Director, Center of Sociotherapy "Villa Serena," Therapeutic Community "Omega," Milan.

Philippe Paumelle, M.D.
   Director, 13th District Mental Health Association, Paris.

Ping-Nie Pao, M.D.
   Director of Psychotherapy, Chestnut Lodge, Rockville, Maryland.

Paul-Claude Racamier, M.D.
   13th District Mental Health Association, Paris; Foyer La Velotte,
   Besançon; Director, Institute of Psychoanalysis, Paris.

Herbert A. Rosenfeld, M.D.
   British Psychoanalytical Society, London.

Harold F. Searles, M.D.
   American Psychoanalytic Association, Washington D.C.

Hanna Segal, M.B., Ch.B.
   British Psychoanalytical Society, London.

Richard I. Shader, M.D.
   Massachusetts Mental Health Center, Boston, Massachusetts.

René Tissot, M.D.
    Professor of Psychiatry, University of Geneva, Switzerland.

Pierre Vincent, M.D.
    Hôpital Saint-Michel-Archange, Quebec.

Hector Warnes, M.D.
    Assistant Professor of Psychiatry, Mc Gill University, Montreal.

Eva Weil, M.A.
    Psychologist, 13th District Mental Health Association, Paris, France.

Otto Allen Will, Jr., M.D.
    Clinical Professor of Psychiatry, Cornell University Medical School; Medical Director, Austen Riggs Center, Stockbridge, Massachusetts.

Israel Zwerling, M.D., Ph.D.
    Chairman, The Hahnemann Medical College and Hospital of Philadelphia, Pennsylvania.

PREFACE

This book presents a collection of papers dealing with long-term treatments of psychotic states. Although there is some discussion of general problems, especially in Part I, the emphasis is on the examination and comparison of actual concrete experiences. Working in different countries and under varying conditions, with divergent and sometimes even contradictory viewpoints, the contributors were at complete liberty to select and define their theme, but all were asked to make a contribution drawn from their own professional experience.

Some of these contributors had already met in Montreal in November 1969, where, at the invitation of the Albert-Prévost Institute on the occasion of its 50th anniversary, they worked and had discussions together on the *Problems of Psychosis*.[1] They met again in Paris in February 1972, on the invitation of the 13th District Mental Health Association of Paris which was celebrating, albeit a few months late, its 13th anniversary.

It might be useful to say a few words here about the 13th District Mental Health Association. Founded in 1958 by Philippe Paumelle, who was director of the General Psychiatry Department, and Serge Lebovici and René Diatkine in charge of the Child Psychiatry Department, this Association carried out one of the first "area psychiatry" studies in France. This undertaking comprised an original element in relation to its North American counterparts, in that while the Association directed its efforts toward the creation of all the psychiatric services required to respond to the needs of the population of a specific catchment area, it was also concerned with working within the community itself. The Association operates with only the very limited financial resources characteristic of all the public services. A high proportion of the psychiatrists who work there have had psychoanalytical training.

This volume is divided into four parts.

Part I deals with general problems of psychosis as seen from the point of view of long-term treatment. Does the experience acquired through the long-term treatment of patients labeled as "psychotics" lead to any modification or new definition of the concept of psychosis? The fact that Kraepelin gave the name of "Dementia Praecox" to what is, since Bleuler, called "schizophrenia," is due to his consideration of the *terminal state* reached by patients cared for in conditions far different from those we are trying to promote today. The psychiatric institution is a constant and problematical source of controversy; on this point psychiatrists with any awareness whatsoever feel "antipsychiatric," even though they take a stand against the antipsychiatrists in reaffirming the reality of mental sickness. However, although they have not yet acquired the therapeutic omnipotence the patient expects of the doctor and which public opinion attributes hopefully to the therapist, nor even a therapeutic power which those who provide treatment

would like to possess in order to bring relief to their patients, the psychiatrist and his team nonetheless no longer
find themselves in the same state of therapeutic powerlessness as former generations did. The role of drugs can still
be argued—effectiveness, wishful thinking, abuse of power,
harmfulness, etc.—but the fact remains that anyone who
has known a given psychiatric service before and after the
introduction of neuroleptics will have observed that they
have transformed the whole atmosphere of that service.
Chemical straitjacket? The point is debatable. The positive
development is that along with the feeling of impotence,
fear of the mental patient—of the "insane"—has also diminished; the day-to-day life of psychiatric services has
been reorganized on a different basis, and different relationships can be established between staff and patients.
Whatever the limitations of psychoanalytical therapy may
be in the field of psychosis, psychoanalysis has had a part
to play in this transformation. Freud's assertion of the absence of any qualitative difference between the normal and
the pathological did away with the gap that separated patients from those who looked after them; the patient is no
longer a "lunatic" and "alienus," even though legal texts
and institutions still reflect traces of this; he is no longer a
strange and incomprehensible creature. There are pathological mechanisms and moments in each one of us, and the
understanding of dreams has opened the way to the understanding of delusion.

Part II, which is the longest, comprises accounts of a
range of experiences so wide and diverse that it is rare to
find them all grouped together at any one time. The editors
of this book, like most of the French, have a less eclectic
concept of therapy than the Americans. Anyone French
finds it difficult to imagine that one and the same person
can practice both psychoanalysis and behavior therapy.
Perhaps the French, influenced by their philosophical tradition, are more concerned with theoretical coherence and

have an outlook which is more doctrinal than pragmatic. As readers, however, everyone will be interested to get a sample view of experiences shaped by a variety of therapeutic options, evaluated by different methodologies of research, and carried out in the context of institutions of different types and orientations.

Part III of the book deals with the problem of the fate of psychotics, seen from the viewpoint of epidemiology, chronicity and old age, and also in the light of differences between various cultures.

In Part IV we turn to the community with and in which the psychiatrist has to work if he wishes to prevent the psychotic from being rejected and maintained in a status of chronic impairment and alienation.

C. Chiland.

NOTES

1. See Doucet, Pierre and Laurin, Camille (1971), *Problems of Psychosis*. Amsterdam: Excerpta Medica Foundation, VIII, 451 pp.

Part I

GENERAL PROBLEMS

INTRODUCTION

To talk of "psychosis" is a simplification of the multifaceted reality of the problem of the psychoses. When talking about "madness" one is often caught up in a discourse whose poetry is rivaled only by its generosity of feeling, and which is divorced from both everyday reality and any attempt at scientific elaboration.

If we put the antipsychiatrists at one end of the entire range of possible attitudes, we find Henri Ey at the other. Over a period covering the years between the 1930s and his recent retirement, the teachings of this French psychiatrist have left their stamp on several generations of psychiatrists, mainly through his "organodynamic" theory, which follows the same lines as the concept of Jackson.

While one might very well part company with his trenchant position, his reminder of the harsh reality of mental sickness will nonetheless be useful. Henri Ey affirms the existence of mental illness and that by and large the notion of mental illness is making progress, that is, medical recognition of mental disease has dissociated the madman from "evil and sin" and made him accessible to therapeutic hope. Delusion, which is the disruption of the subject's contact with reality, still remains the central fact of psychosis.

Henri Ey advocates making a clear distinction between neurosis and psychosis (and also between neurosis and normality). He furthermore attributes a similar position to psychoanalysts, which, as will be seen in Chap. 4 of Part I, is by no means necessarily correct. It is true of Jacques Lacan with his "foreclosure" (*Verwerfung*), and of Jean Laplanche, who states the existence in psychosis of a "defect in some key element in the symbolic field." It cannot be said of Herbert Rosenfeld or Hanna Segal. Nor is it obviously the case as far as Freud himself is concerned.

Leopold Bellak shows the incidence of therapeutic modalities upon the concept of psychoses, with the example of the discovery of the effectiveness of lithium in the treatment of manic-depressive psychoses, which resulted in a sharp increase in their diagnosis. In a subtler vein, the effectiveness of a particular drug can lead to a more clear-cut classification of disorders, while a more accurate diagnosis will help to avoid the use of ineffective or even harmful drugs. Effective therapy has turned psychoses into a social problem, for the patient is no longer confined to the asylum and the community is involved in his fate.

Whereas Bellak attempts to cover the entire field of present knowledge of psychoses, Harold Searles opts for a less eclectic view and aims at an in-depth understanding of the psychotic where we are directly implicated. What we experience in the countertransference seems to Searles as vitally important to the diagnosis as to the therapy, while he expresses anxiety at the way in which medication can be used.

The problem of drugs is taken up by Juan de Ajuriaguerra, who emphasizes the fact that there are schizophrenics who are resistant to all forms of medication. René Tissot's exhaustive review of the literature on the subject shows the complexity of the matter, even though he deals solely with the problem of schizophrenic psychoses and leaves aside, in particular, the manic-depressive psychoses. It is remarkable to note that Tissot, who is one of those most familiar with the mode of action of drugs, or at least who can make a clear distinction between what is certain and what is unknown in this field, himself questions the utility and even the harmfulness of medication.

The introduction of neuroleptics in 1954 brought about a sharp change from 1955 onward (accentuating an evolution already begun by shock therapies which—especially electroshock therapy—should not be eliminated entirely today), namely, reduction of the psychiatric hospital population and of the length of stay, and lessening of chronic impairment. Nonetheless, Tissot feels that there is no evidence to warrant any categorical assessment of the role of neuroleptics: is it a specifically pharmacological role, or is it that of a "mediator of an active psychoergotherapeutic policy," one of whose efficiency factors is the time the doctor spends in the ward?

The clinical forms of psychoses have unquestionably undergone a change. Here again, Tissot shows how difficult it is to determine the extent of the direct pharmacological effects of drugs. Catatonic forms have given way to hebephrenic and particularly paranoid forms, that is, schizophrenia is no longer continuous as much as intermittent in its manifestation. The positive symptoms are receding, while inertia and the lack of initiative remain.

Perhaps the contradictory results of research on the effectiveness of neuroleptics are best accounted for by the problems of dosage and continuity or intermittency of treatment, which have to be settled in different ways according to the age of the patient and the type of treatment, whether outpatient or hospital treatment. A certain consensus emerges as to the predominantly sedative action of the aliphatic phenothiazines (chlorpromazine, levomepromazine) and the piperidine phenothiazines (thioridazine), and with regard to the major "antipsychotic" action on deficiency symptoms by the piperazine phenothiazines and the butyrophenones. With regard to a very widespread practice, we have to emphasize Tissot's discussion of drug combinations, some of which may present more disadvantages than benefit.

Tissot advises the greatest caution in handling delayed-action neuroleptics, particularly in outpatient therapy, where, when the patient attributes his discomforts to his drug medication, his only possible course of action is to eliminate the "correctors" (we should have delayed-action "correctors"). Serious accidents are still frequent.

Louis Julou gives some fuller pharmacological information on long-acting injectable neuroleptics, in which Pierre-Albert Lambert and Marc Midenet are interested from the point of view of the psychiatrist who has to care for a large population without sufficient psychotherapeutic means at his disposal. Apart from the advantages and disadvantages to the patient, they want to find out of what use this type of drug can be to the physician in his relations with a patient which can go on for decades.

Present knowledge concerning the mode of action of neuroleptics sheds little light on the physiopathological mechanisms of psychoses. Neuroleptics would seem to be no more than "symptomatic medication which do not interfere with the fundamental mechanisms responsible for psychotic disorders." Tissot takes issue with the position of those who, like Pierre Deniker, consider that the extrapyramidal syndromes can constitute a privileged experience susceptible to psychotherapeutic elaboration. For him they are "a particularly trying experience which the patient should be spared whenever possible." Emphasis must be laid on one of the conclusions of Tissot's text on drug action: "No drug therapy is without its disadvantages. . . . Drug treatment is only one single element, of greater or lesser importance according to the individual case."

Harold Searles, in the Chestnut Lodge tradition, feels that the psychoanalytic approach can constitute the sole individual therapy, in conjunction with the therapeutic milieu provided by the institution while the patient is hospitalized. He therefore excludes drug treatment entirely for patients who are, admittedly deliberately selected on the grounds of their probable receptiveness of psychoanalytic treatment and also on the basis of financial criteria, given the high cost of treatment in a private establishment such as Chestnut Lodge. In the view of Herbert Rosenfeld, Hanna Segal, and Evelyne Kestemberg, the psychoanalytic treatment of psychotics considered likely to benefit from it not only does not exclude other therapeutic approaches, but even necessitates the use of a "safety net." The psychoanalytic treatment of psychotics cannot be undertaken without ensuring the provision of a suitable framework of existence for him, a place he can be taken to, especially during the acute phases (Marion Milner also emphasizes this problem in *The Hands of the Living God*[1], of a "care" organization as Racamier puts it, in order for continued treatment to be possible). These authors by no means reject the support of drug medication.

At the other end of the scale of psychoanalysts, Jean Laplanche denounces the foolhardiness of those who undertake the psychoanalysis of psychotics; in his view, they are wasting their time and talent in dealing with patients who require so much attention. He considers that Freud discovered psychoanalysis in the field of neurosis, and he refers to Lacan to illustrate that it is folly to attempt to use it outside that context.

The thread of other disagreements among psychoanalysts runs through the various chapters. Some adopt standpoints akin to those of the antipsychiatrists in attributing an all-powerful etiological role to the family; these positions could equally well be considered antipsychoanalytic in the scotomization of the subject's own role and the original organization of his fantasies and defences against his drives, anxiety, and depression. Rosenfeld, Segal, and Kestemberg all take very careful positions avoiding any systematically negative attitude towards their patients' families.

A further split separates those who see a clear-cut distinction between psychotic and neurotic structure, and those who see no fundamental discontinuity between them. Rosenfeld speaks of latent psychosis in severe neurotics, and also mentions the nonpsychotic part of the personality of a psychotic. This has nothing in common with Laplanche's position on the matter. Everyone will have food for thought here in the light of his or her own experience. Our own falls in line with Rosenfeld's position and not with Laplanche's.

Whatever the limitations of psychoanalysis of psychotics—limitations with regard to the selection of patients as well as in the results obtained (one is often astonished at the facility with which certain authors on both sides of the Atlantic talk about patients being "cured")—the treatment of psychotics by psychoanalysts is a matter which goes far beyond consideration of a few individual cases, and throws a new light on the understanding of psychosis and the overall range of therapeutic problems it raises, particularly in the institutions. This is amply borne out by the work done in the United States in a number of especially privileged places, such as the Menninger Foundation, toward reaching an understanding of the articulations of milieu therapy and psychoanalytically oriented psychotherapies, and in France with, for example, the book *Le Psychanalyste sans divan*[2] by Paul-Claude Racamier and associates.

C. C.

NOTES

1. London: The Hogarth Press and the Institute of Psychoanalysis, 1969, XXXI-444pp.
2. Paris: Payot, 1970, 422 pp.

Chapter 1

REFLECTIONS ON PSYCHOSIS

Henri Ey, M.D.

This chapter presents the basic reflections which the very concept of psychoses necessarily provokes in everyone who finds his or her vocation in their recognition, treatment, and cure.

I think that even though it is called by a different name, the phenomenon of "delusion" has never ceased to be the central point of the theoretical, practical, moral, and social problems of psychiatry. The word "psychosis" has retained for us all the significance and mystery of the key words which have enlivened all psychiatric discussion and given rise to all psychiatric institutions. These words are "insanity" and "delusion." And there is no reason for us to hide the fact that when we practice psychiatry or, as we like to emphasize the dialectic of our action by saying that we hold a "psychiatric discourse," the constant subject of reference is still "the insane."

These sick people—and I use the word "sick" quite deliberately—constitute the nucleus of the field of psychiatry. Psychiatry, condemned to the "heavy," "asylum-oriented" approach (which is itself alienating or repressive), has not as its sole object the mental pathology of the highly delusional, or "psychotics" (who could be called "the insane par excellence"), but simply because our knowledge can only be organized in relation to what constitutes the most unquestionable form of "mental illness." In other words, it corresponds to the innermost *understanding* of this concept, and can-not be defined, as some people have done, via the periphery of its abusive *extension*, that is, to dissolve it entirely. Now psychosis, delusion, and alienation, in the truest sense, are the finally irrefutable psychopathological facts. If we ask what is psychosis, then we are asking what it is that constitutes the essence of mental illness, or in other words, what is its reality. One could of course quite easily say that there is not, or even cannot be, any such thing as mental illness. This tendency to scotomization of psychic pathology inherent in the forms of archaic societies has been, and still is, too strong to be ignored.

For a long time, and in many civilizations today, it has been said that there is no such thing as "illness." This is because the notion of illness, or of "anomalies in the natural organization of man" has been very difficult to separate from the notion of sin and evil. Illness, as a natural phenomenon of physical disorganization, had to be manifested in its own right before medical science was founded. It was founded however, and is maintained by the cumulative knowledge which, in spite of all vicissitudes, contradictions, absurdities, or passing fashions, prejudices or sheer naiveté, nonetheless constitutes the pathology whose object is the failures and disorders of the human organism.

It is far more difficult to apply and clarify the concept in regard to "mental illness," which is the disorganization not merely of man's vitality, but of his very "humanity" (the word used by the great clinician Boerhaave). Nonetheless, it is through the idea of an *organizational illness* as a natural and not a cultural illness that mental illness was *incorporated* into medicine to become the object of psychiatry. In fact all the work, all the knowledge which—in spite of and not because of the miserable asylum institutions—has developed from the first psychiatrists of the Renaissance up to the end of the 19th century, consisted of describing with more apparent than real accuracy the forms of major mental illnesses, the "psychoses" which were for so long the sole object of psychiatry and its hospital-legal institutions for disastrously excessive segregation; this, in fact, is the object of "heavy psychiatry."

But of this "heaviness," of this "solidity", or if you like, this "solidification" of psychosis there remains one feature which it is unfortunately impossible for anyone to eliminate with a stroke of the pen, or make disappear by an ostrich-like refusal to see it. This "factitiousness" constitutes the mass of alienation found in the human species because of the pathological anomalies of man's psychic organization. Indeed, the fact that some people are altered or even alienated in their modes of existence as human beings (that is, in the organization of the system of relationships linking them to others and to the environment in which they live and without which they cannot live), does not depend upon you or me, nor upon any sociopolitical or "event" structure, nor on society as a whole or the idea we have of things when we give them a name.

The reality of mental illness has always been a live subject and cannot be otherwise, since psychiatry is a response to its exigencies; and this reality of mental illness is more clearly defined in psychosis than in neurosis. It is precisely by taking psychosis as the starting point that we must come to an understanding of neurosis and, consequently, what loss from the natural organization of man impairs his psychic health.

THE NORMAL AND THE PATHOLOGICAL IN HUMAN EXISTENCE

Rest assured, I shall sin by omission here rather than by excess, referring you to what I have so often said and written on this fundamental problem, and asking you to reflect upon it yourselves after reading the three basic works on the subject by Hollingworth,[1] Canguilhem,[2] and Duyckaerts.[3] I myself find that this latter work—perhaps because, although I have not met the author, his thoughts come very close to meeting mine—gives the most clear and lucid outline of the psychic "norm," or "normativity" rather, which is apparent in:

1. the integration of behavior (in the least "behaviorist" sense of the word, of course), in its "molar" sense, that is to say, in its conscious directed purposiveness;
2. autonomy of "determination," inasmuch as these are determined by a choice (even if the choice is that of dependence), or, in other words, the subordination of means to end; and
3. adaptation, to the extent that this is creative, curative, and not simply a matter of conditioning.

Psychic "normativity" cannot be measured on the basis of average frequency (Quetelet), and demands more thoughtful criteria. In other words, being normal does not mean being a fool, a mediocre person, a "uomo qualumque"; it means being someone capable of managing his intentionality with the highest degree of efficiency. Hence, if being normal means being able to manage one's self, involving both the capacity of reality testing and making choices in line with one's own existential program, then the psychopathological person will, on the contrary, be the one who is incapable of reality testing and who is determined by forces which hinder the freedom of his choice or existential ideal. In other words, "mental illness" is a matter of pathology of reality and of organization of the psychic being. To understand this more fully, we must first consider the essential structure of psychosis, and then the essential structure of neurosis, inasmuch as both the one and the other diverge from psychic normality.

THE STRUCTURE OF PSYCHOSIS

Little is to be gained from calling something by another name. One speaks of "psychosis" today just as they spoke of "delusion" 19th century. The reference is still to that form of mental illness which alters or alienates the subject to the point of disturbing his relationship to reality. The reality of psychosis is that it is an illness of reality.[4] This phrase is not of my invention; everybody has said so and Freud in particular. Let us reread *The Loss of Reality in Neurosis and Psychosis* (1924).[5] In this work, which, of course, goes beyond his initial concept of the narcissistic psychosis of President Schreber,[6] psychosis is characterized by the "loss of reality" (*Realitätverlust*), which is more than just a simple "flight," regression, or protection; this process is not merely the expression of a need or a wish, but also a manifestation of powerlessness, as I have emphasized elsewhere (1957).[7] It tends to *substitute* (*Realitätersatzen*) another reality (let's say that of the autistic world) for common reality. This is what Freud means when he says that the psychotic represses reality under pressure from the unconscious (the id, that is). Since then the word "Verwerfung" (which Lacan translates by foreclosure "forclusion") has added the sense of a kind of *functional* rejection, an original obliteration of *desire*. It is easy to see what contradictions, what nonsense this "idealist" conception of a purely psychic "realität" can lead to. The usual way of getting around this difficulty of attaching unreality to delusion (of recognizing the reality of psychosis, in other words) by using an ingenious accumulation of arabesques and variations on the theme of the primal repression (*Urverdrängung*), its failure or inadequacy, foreclosure of the name of the father, that is to say the total lack of any law of communication insofar as it requires the symbolic and specular mediation of the "double bind," and so on and so forth. "Psychic reality," without the reality of the existence which nonetheless does envelope it, will never be able to solve nor even pose the problem of psychosis by itself. This is why Freud, and in fact all those who have since him tried at least to understand, if not to explain, the intrinsic breakdown of the system of reality which constitutes the structure of psychosis inevitably end up in the final analysis by emphasizing, as he wrote in his 1924 text, the alloplastic nature of the development of psychotic existence. Whether so many interpreters like it or not, Freud here agrees with the idea of processes of Bleuler and Jaspers when he insists—as I myself always have done within the perspective of a neo-Jacksonian psychopathology on positive manifestations—on the creation of the autistic world, that is, of a way of being unable to be part of the world of others because of being wrapped up in one's own "Eigenwelt." This, then, is psychosis, which, to the extent that it is pathology of reality, withdraws from communication with a world of common values. It is in this sense that it can be said, with Freud, that psychosis represses reality, or more exactly, that reality is no longer possible when the ego disappears and gets lost in the service of the id.

THE STRUCTURE OF NEUROSIS

The difference between neurosis and psychosis, which psychoanalysts (Freud first among them) have always wanted to be clear-cut, is blurred by the in-depth development of psychopathological structures and analytical psychotherapeutic methods.[8] The idea of a minor neurotic form of mental illness (represented by the paradigm of psychosis) comes naturally to all clinicians. With Breuer and Freud, psychoanalysis (at the level of hysteria and then obsessions and phobia) brought to light a "mechanism" of repression of unconscious childhood memories by the vigilant attention of the conscious, which is careful to suppress the suffering they can cause. From this stems all the dialectic of infantile libido, oedipal guilt, defense mechanisms, and so on. Thus it is that neurosis appears to be structured first of all according to the regressions or fixations which derive their significance from their position in the fundamental oedipal triangulation of the object choice, and from the tactical tricks (defenses, substitutions, camouflage) through which they are manifested in their consent or compromise. Thus the more the neurotic is shrouded in these defenses (superego), the more neurotic he appears. Like a hedgehog whose spikes are turned inwards, the neurotic is hence presented as someone entirely or partially occupied with repressing his unconscious. This amounts to triumphing in his conflict against the id over the danger of falling —as in psychosis—under its complete domination. (Psychosis then appears as a decompensation of neurotic defenses, and neurosis as a good resistance to unconscious drives). This "economic" or heuristic—and optimistic— point of view, whereby neurosis is seen as the victory (just as psychosis, as Laing would have it, is a "break-through," some kind of wonderful and metanoic revelation), does not stand up to analysis, which forbids abandonment to the dizzy temptation of a fatal reversal of the values of reality. It would be better to put some order into the chaos of the illness which, in fact, cannot be reduced to a pure and simple matter of disorder. Now in mental pathology, putting things back in order means first of all considering neurosis as not simply the effect of unconscious repression. Freud—to come back to the text to which I referred above, or to his 1927 study on fetishism[9]—found he had to recognize in the structure of neurosis a disturbance deeper than that of repression by the unconscious, which is normal enough, after all, as we shall see at the end. To Freud, in fact, in neurosis the ego is dealing with a piece of reality (psychic reality, of course; *ein Stück der Realität*). Neurosis depends precisely upon this, a piece of "reality," inasmuch as in its defense against it, it never stops denying (*Verleugnung*), "erasing" or avoiding it. When, in 1927, and again in 1938, he came back to the idea of a "splitting" of the ego in psychosis, insisting (as he does in his *Neurosis,* 1924[5]) upon the fact that in psychosis just as in perversion or phobia, this splitting divides reality rather than destroys it, I think that here he is really obviating the constantly affirmed difference between psychosis and neurosis. Perhaps it would be better to say that the modification of the *Realität* (psychic reality) and the ego, in other words, the relationship between the ego and its world makes neurosis, just like psychosis, an illness of reality; but that neuroses are illnesses of psychic reality which do not change—or do so only to a minor degree—the overall system of communications with common reality, while psychoses radically alter the relationship of the ego with its world. Neurosis is aimed at a symbolic reality whose "objects" are perceived, in the artificial form of fantasies, as internal objects. Psychosis substitutes for reality an autistic reality whose objects are perceived as those of a world controlled solely by the id, by the principle of desire.

In other words, neurosis is not a healthy defense against psychosis; it is the initial phase or a first degree of the plunge into psychosis.

Psychosis is essentially a *pathology of reality* which suppresses all freedom, all normative autonomy of the ego, and neurosis is essentially a *pathology of freedom.*

Such is the field of psychopathology that it is essentially a pathology of freedom which can extend to a pathology of reality. Obviously, there is less difference between the neurotic and psychiatric forms of this psychopathology than between psychopathology and psychic "normativity." But this concept would be purely verbal if it were not supported by the consistence of a hypothesis, that of an organization of the "psychic body."

THE "PSYCHIC BODY" AND ITS PSYCHOTIC DISORGANIZATION

It is not psychotic mechanisms which have to be traced back to psychogenic mechanisms, the psychodynamics of neurosis and particularly, the fantastic geometry of the oedipal space. On the contrary, it is neurosis which has to be traced back to the deeper disturbances of loss of freedom and reality in psychoses. Let us state this once again: mental illnesses (with their neurotic and psychotic aspects) are quite different from the normal variations of psychic life and psychic "normativity," which appear as the capacity of the normative structure for integration, direction, and freedom of existence, and in particular act as a counteragent to the disintegration, inertia, and determinism of pathological forms of existence.

The great mistake which distorts all contemporary psychopathology, or, to be more precise, the "apsychopathology" of modern times, is the idea that since the unconscious is pathogenic, and all human beings act under the direction of their unconscious mind, they can equally well and equally arbitrarily be considered normal or abnormal.

To my mind, the psychic norm is, on the contrary, organically contained in the architectonics of the "psychic body." It is because the principles of psychiatry have never been able to go beyond the parallelistic antinomy of the organic and the psychic, or the psychiatricide dilemma which abolishes the concept of "mental illness" by reducing it either to a physical illness first like any other or to an extranatural variation (supernatural or cultural) which is not an illness at all; it is because no model of a psychic body incorporated in the living body has ever been established that psychiatry has no solid basis. This is particularly apparent in the case of the neuroses. But the organodynamic model of the organization of the psychic body can be best understood and built up from the starting point of the psychoses, as I have tried to do.

The psychic body is essentially organized as a means of ensuring the integration of the unconscious in the conscious being, in other words, to go beyond the id and the dynamics of the hostile forces which constitute it. It is organized in order to build for itself the instrument of reality, of its relationships with its world and the freedom of its self-determination. My *Traité des Hallucinations* (Treatise on Hallucinations) is the study of the reality of these illnesses of reality of which the delusional and hallucinatory psychoses are the ultimate form. It may perhaps one day convince some people that without the idea of an ontology of the psychic body there is no such thing possible as mental illness. For in fact, only a concept of this kind permits escape from the two dangers which logically and polemically (I was about to say politically) threaten psychiatry, namely, the idea that psychiatry is a pathology of the organs and vital functions (that schizophrenia is like cyrrhosis of the liver), and the notion that it is not a pathology within the framework of the natural sciences, but purely a matter of sociology.

The study of the psychoses can be intensified and their long-term treatment seriously envisaged only on the basis of a concept which validates the reality of illness and defines the prescriptions, the possibilities, and the risks of therapeutic methods. I am certain that the moment has not yet come for the theoretical model—whose essential points I have just outlined, as I had intended to do in Montreal— to be taken into consideration by the majority of you, for I am well aware of the whirlwinds which drag most psychiatrists, lacking a solid doctrine and in reaction to a naive organicism, into the labyrinths of interminable (or more precisely, infinite, *unendliche*) analyses or into the round of more or less serious parlor games.

Far be it from me, however, to cast anathema even upon what seems to be subject for derision, in that it seems to belong to a primary ideology or be based on superficial knowledge. These contradictions, illusions, and even utopias have to intersect and collide upon the winding road of the "search for truth," a truth which has to be difficult to discover if it is to have a chance of lasting. For me there is no such thing as a psychiatric dogma, for this would represent the end of psychiatry. But it does seem necessary for the discourse of the psychiatrist to be as coherent as possible. I have tried to introduce this coherence in the knowledge of incoherence. Knowledge aimed at cure, for I have only too often observed the havoc wrought by psychosis to think that it must be respected, in all its glory, as a work of art. ... Psychiatric medicine is the only field where illness appears so clearly as an ill in which the sick displace and sometimes invert the suffering. This is particularly so in the psychoses. But it is our duty not to allow ourselves to be seduced by their delusions. At a time when some people think, say, and write that the delirant is right, that his irrationality is more precious than his reason, we must remember that mental illness is a real illness, that it is incumbent upon us physicians and those who help us in our work, to cure the dreamers and wake them out of their sleep, even if they were willing victims to the desire to abandon their existence.

Perhaps because, deep down, I have never been able

to get away from that irony which measures the distance between our knowledge and our illusions, let me remind you that we are here to know, recognize, and cure psychoses, and at the end of this homily, allow me to say "So be it." Not the gentle or simpleminded "amen" of vague assent, but the imperative form imposed by our knowledge and our duty.

NOTES

1. Hollingworth (1931), *Outline of Abnormal Psychology*. London.
2. Canguilhem, G. (1943), *Essai sur quelques problèmes concernant le normal et le pathologique*. Paris: Société d'Editions Les Belles-Lettres.
3. Duyckaerts, F. (1954), *La notion de normal et de pathologique*. Paris: Kron.
4. It seems that the problem of reality does not arise. . . . It is true that it is not present in the illusion which turns existence into a dream and the world into the impossible fulfilment of wish . . . But it arises all the time even to those who adhere to this profession of bad faith. As I look over this text again after having read the work of A. de Waelhens, I see—p. 174—that even to those who laugh in derision at people who confront the problem of psychosis and delusion with that of reality, a return to the natural attitude, a return to reality "is above and beyond all possible dispute." Of course it is! [Waehlens, A. de (1972), *La Psychose*. Louvain-Paris: Naeuve Caerts.]
5. Freud, S. (1924), The loss of reality in neurosis and psychosis. *Standard Edition*, 19:183–187. London: Hogarth Press, 1962.

6. Or his "Oedipal collapse," as it has more recently been called by Deleuze and Guattari. [Deleuze, G. and Guattari, F. (1972), *L'Anti-Oedipe*. Paris: Les Editions de Minuit.]

7. Ey, H. (1957), Fournées de Bonneval sur les schizophrenies. *L'Evolution Psychiatrique,* 1958: 143–199.

8. I noted this point some years ago in an article published in *Acta Psychotherapeutica* in 1954 (pp. 193–210).

9. Freud, S. (1927), *Standard Edition,* 21:152–157. London: Hogarth Press, 1962.

Chapter 2

THE CONCEPT OF PSYCHOSES AS A RESULT AND IN THE CONTEXT OF THE LONG-TERM TREATMENT MODALITIES

Leopold Bellak, M.D.

Diagnostic concepts are not only heuristic hypotheses with regard to possible etiology, they are also the basic propositions upon which rational treatment plans and prognostic statements must be based.[7] It is essential for the long-term treatment of psychoses to be predicated on concepts, as clearly formulated as possible, of the psychoses involved. If this is not so, the underlying theory of treatment is essentially not logically or experimentally testable and consists of little more than guesswork and biased hunches.

Scientific progress, however, does not always follow a straight deductive path. In medicine in general, and psychiatry in particular, therapeutic success is often followed by attempts to find etiological or taxonomic concepts to fit the treatment, rather than the other way around. Cerletti and Bini contributed a valuable technique when they originated electroconvulsive treatment (ECT). Cerletti attempted to postulate acroaginins to explain, alas unsuccessfully, the effect of ECT. Sackel did not fare much better in finding a rational concept for the effect of insulin coma and its relation to schizophrenic etiology.

Not all attempts to derive relationships to the concept of psychoses from their treatment have been as ill-fated, but some are amusing. It is well known that manic-depressive psychosis was rarely diagnosed in American hospitals, as compared, say, to British diagnostic fashions. No sooner was lithium established as the treatment of choice (originally suggested in 1949 by the Australian, Cade), than there was, to quote an American psychiatrist, nearly an epidemic of manic-depressive psychoses. Whereas only eight or nine patients a year had previously been diagnosed as manic in one New York hospital, 50 were so designated in the first year of lithium treatment. Obviously, the availability of a potent therapy affected the diagnostic concepts of psychiatrists.

CHEMOTHERAPY AND THE CONCEPT OF PSYCHOSES

The viewpoint of those who feel that progress in the somatic treatment of affective disorders has been made and, in turn, led to an elucidation of the diagnostic and pathogenic conceptualization of these disorders, has been clearly stated by Lipton:[21]

> Not only has clinical treatment improved to the point where management of the affective disorders is among the most gratifying aspects of clinical practice, but also basic and clinical research has revealed some common biological substrates upon which such apparently diverse somatic treatments as ECT, monoamine oxidase inhibitors, the tricyclic antidepressants and lithium act. These all appear to influence the synthesis, disposition, and metabolism of the biogenic amines, a group of compounds including noradrenaline, serotonin, dopamine, and perhaps others derived from the essential dietary amino acids phenylalanine and

tryptophane and produced mostly by cells whose nuclei lie largely in the brain stem and whose axons descend into the spinal cord and ascend by means of the median forebrain bundle to innervate the midbrain, cerebellum, and cerebral cortex.

These compounds seem to serve as neural transmitters or modulators. Since the pharmacological agents that ameliorate depression and mania appear to act upon and alter the concentration and metabolism of the biogenic amines in what are presumably corrective directions, *it may be inferred that in the affective disorders there exists a chemical pathology related to these compounds.* [1,31]

As you see, Lipton makes references from possible denominations in treatment modalities with regard to the concept of psychosis. He then continues to enumerate a number of problems which still remain. For instance, response to lithium treatment may eventually lead to a sounder taxonomy and a better formulation of etiology and pathogenesis. So far, however, we do not have any inkling why affective disorders occur and are so often cyclic. A host of other conceptual and clinical issues also remains unanswered.

Lithium has certainly encouraged a trend toward more careful attempts at differential diagnosis between manic and schizophrenic disorders. In the hope of thus increasing drug efficacy, Hekimian et al.[17] have designed diagnostic scales at Bellevue Hospital in New York City. Their usefulness in leading to increased therapeutic response remains to be demonstrated by other investigators.

What holds true for lithium holds true for other drug treatments. There have been widespread attempts to differentiate the multifaceted depressive syndrome into subgroups by virtue of the response to imipramine, to monoamineoxidase (MAO) inhibitors, and into those groups of patients who do best with a combination of tranquilizer and antidepressant. If further we should find a clear-cut subgroup of patients who never respond to antidepressants but do respond to ECT, as it sometimes seems, we should be much closer to some vital answers.

The facts, however, are far from clear as yet. Wittenborn[29] found in 1967 that imipramine was more effective in reactive depressions than in patients with manic-depressive disorder. Lapolla and Jones,[18] on the other hand, thought they could differentiate endogenous depressions from reactive depressions by virtue of the observation that the endogenous ones reacted favorably to imipramine (as compared to a placebo) as early as the fifth day of administration, while there was no difference in response to imipramine and placebo among reactive depressions.

Sargant[25] claims that MAO inhibitors are especially effective in atypical depressions, suggesting a yet different subgroup of depression.

A small study by Bellak and Rosenberg[5] suggested that patients treated with imipramine (Tofranil, a non-MAO inhibitor) produced Rorschach responses and behavior as rated on the Global Ego Strength Scale consistent with the hypothesis that this drug *inhibits affect*.

These patients fared better than those treated with phenalzine (Nardil, an MAO inhibitor) who responded both on the Rorschach and in terms of ratings on the Global Ego Strength Scale in a manner supporting the hypothesis that this drug produces its results by *increasing affect*.

In the field of schizophrenia, psychopharmacology has led similarly to attempts to extrapolate etiology and pathogenesis from therapeutic response, and also to subgroup the syndrome on the basis of therapeutic results.

Goldberg and Mattsson[14] suggested findings that schizophrenics with insight did not improve on active drugs but did so on placebos, while those without insight reacted the other way around. This suggests the possibility of two different nosological groups.

Although it is generally agreed that phenothiazines are effective in some way in the care of schizophrenics,[23] long-term treatment has made it clear that we need to know more about which subgroups are especially responsive to one drug rather than to another and which subgroups of schizophrenics are adversely affected in their natural restitutive process by the administration of drugs.

Goldstein[16] carefully studied the differential effect of phenothiazines on different schizophrenics. His most interesting finding is that patients with a good premorbid adjustment did better on placebo than on phenothiazine. A subgroup with poor premorbid history did significantly better on phenothiazine. The inference must be made that patients with some resources improved in response to the hospital milieu, and that phenothiazines interfere with their spontaneous ability to improve. This experimental result fits some clinical impression that patients with an ability for insight often seem to find the drug effect a source of disturbance on the sense of self.

In some patients the drugs interfered with the problem solving involved in some psychotic processes. It would therefore seem extremely important not to administer psychotropic drugs indiscriminately or exclusively. For instance, in distinction to the heavy emphasis some American workers put on the role of psychotropic drugs alone, May,[23] Schulsinger and Achte[27] report from Denmark and Finland that a combination of somatic and psychosocial treatment led to only 5 percent of schizophrenics being readmitted to the hospital within five years as compared to the 15 or 20 percent readmitted in the United States.

Lehmann[19] reviews a number of studies relevant to the relationship of nosology and treatment. Among other valuable points, he mentions that the advent of pharmacotherapy has led to the undesirable practice of medicating patients before an adequate diagnosis has been made. In that way, inappropriate pharmacotherapy compares to the masking of abdominal symptoms by too early administration of morphine. The enthusiasm for another modern treatment modality, community psychiatric approach, has similarly often led to some current tendency towards diagnostic nihilism. Overenthusiasm in any field tends to lead to overgeneralization and lack of discrimination—be it in gastronomy or medicine.

COMMUNITY PSYCHIATRY'S EFFECT ON THE CONCEPT OF PSYCHOSES

The field of community psychiatric treatment is as responsible for the revamping of the concept of the psychoses as drugs are. One must include here the concept of the open ward, the therapeutic community in and out of the ward, prompt treatment of acute conditions in psychiatric departments of general hospitals and in the community, half-way houses, industrial therapy,[12] and the general decrease of chronic psychoses and long-lasting hospitalization as a result thereof. Pioneers such as Querido, Duncan McMillan, Maxwell Jones, Cameron, Ey, Lebovici, Bierer, and others come easily to mind. Naturally, this community psychiatric approach has been interdependent with the drug therapies, as much of this activity would not have been possible without them.

One important effect of these changes in the treatment approach has been to show that some of what we considered typical chronic features of psychoses were probably iatrogenic, that is, if not *directly* physician-induced, then certainly induced as secondary phenomena to locking patients into wards away from human contact, and with no use for their higher faculties. The resultant deep regressions were due to a condition almost resembling perceptual isolation. Lack of intellectual stimulation, poor diet, and lack of any meaningful human interaction were responsible for most of the chronic features of schizophrenia described in the classical textbooks. In that respect, dementia in the sense of "Verblödung," trichotillomania, and coprophagia were often no more intrinsic features of schizophrenia than the tubercle bacillus which used to be so prevalent in schizophrenics that Loewenstein and others believed for many years that a micrococcus tuberculosis was responsible for schizophrenia.[22]

Scheidt's cyanotic syndrome and sudden death in catatonic or manic excitement were once a serious problem, one also considered an intrinsic aspect of psychoses. Since we understand it now as a result of a disturbance of the electrolyte metabolism due to exhaustion (rather than due to the psychosis per se) a full-blown or fatal case is virtually unheard of.

Community psychiatry contributes a specific change in the concept of psychoses by its special concern with treatment of the patient as *one social unit within the matrix of the social unit of his family and his community.* Young psychiatrists now go into the homes of their patients to treat them and to observe the interaction with the family members. Whatever else the etiology of one or another of the psychoses should turn out to be—genogenic, psychogenic, chemogenic, or neurophysiological, no one worth the name of psychiatrist doubts that the somatic features interact with the social matrix of the patient. The work of Lidz, and Cornelison,[20] Waxler,[28] and Wynne and Singer[30] illustrate these interactions. Speaking of the latter, a concept of psychoses predicated upon the style of verbal interaction plays a major role. The assumption is not necessarily one of a causal relationship in a primary etiological way. The work of Schopler and Loftin[26] showed that the same pathological style of communication existed between parent and schizophrenic offspring, but did not exist in the parent when the interview involved a healthy offspring. It suggests that the parents need *not* engage in the pathological forms of communication which exist between them and their ill off-spring, but in some way it underlines even more the importance of the vicious cycle of interaction that does exist between them and the ill one.

In that sense the concept of psychoses as a form of social interaction—earlier promulgated by Bateson and Ruesch[1] in the form of the double-bind hypothesis, emerges from the treatment of the patient in the community and contributes to it.

PSYCHOSES AS SOCIOECONOMIC-POLITICAL PROBLEMS

One other conceptual effect of modern treatment has been increasing awareness that functional psychosis (of which schizophrenia constitutes 80 percent in the United States) is a *social and economic problem* and has to be considered and solved on that basis.

The direct and indirect annual cost of two to three million Americans carrying the diagnosis schizophrenia, is estimated as 14 billion dollars a year.

Modern treatment has decreased the number of patients in hospitals at any given time by 30 percent in the last 15 years and not necessarily as a function of psychotropic drugs. At the same time, admission figures have risen correspondingly. Long-term treatment subsequently led to a decrease in hospital stay of any given patient and possibly to a decrease in chronicity. It has, however, also led to the "revolving door" policy of discharging patients and readmitting them. In the United States, the probability of readmission within two years is between 40 and 60 percent; between 15 and 20 percent of patients are eventually readmitted for continued long-time care.

Thus one effect of modern treatment on the concept of psychoses is that it had to be seen as *a social problem:* how to reintegrate the large number of patients discharged and readmitted to hospitals and discharged again into the modern community.

Modern long-range treatment has made solutions other than long-term hospital stay possible and essential and has led to a concept of psychoses as something to live with, within a family, within a community. What effect this will have on psychotics, their families, and communities remains as yet to be seen, and not necessarily with equanimity.

If there are iatrogenic aspects of the major psychoses, one could also speak of *socioeconomically induced psychoses.* The greater longevity of the general population is reflected not only in the longer life of psychotics, but also in an increase in the problems of the *psychoses of old age.*

The longer life expectancy of our culture has provided ample clinical evidence that *social disuse atrophy* is largely responsible for a vast percentage of patients so diagnosed. Rob older people of a useful social function by enforced retirement, prevent them from using their adaptive capacities, and they are likely to show psychotic phenomena.

The "disuse psychoses of old age," as I would like to call them, are a concept born of our cultural climate and greater longevity brought about by general medical progress. They are and will be an increasing socioeconomic problem, as well as a personal one, and will need prevention rather than treatment. The voting power of the aged will constitute an increasing political power, and therefore their care will become an increasingly political issue.

PSYCHOTHERAPEUTIC AND PSYCHODYNAMIC CONTRIBUTIONS TO THE CHANGING CONCEPT OF PSYCHOSES

Psychodynamics, especially in the form of psychoanalysis, is the grandfather among the long-term treatments. Armed with Freud's insights and treatment concepts, pioneers like Tausk, Federn, the Burghölzli group, and later Sullivan, Fromm-Reichmann, and nowadays, Arieti, John Rosen, Will, Searles, Rosenfeld, Bychowski, Lebovici, Semrad, Sechehaye, Schwind, and many others who deserve equal mention have watched, treated, and formulated ideas as they tried to heal in their own way.

Existentialists—Ey and Benedetti, for instance—have specifically contributed to the changing concept of psychoses by relating the problems of the self and identity to general human experience and to the crises of our time. As I had occasion to point out elsewhere,[6] in this respect, existentialists and psychoanalysts of all persuasions seem to have arrived at some agreement in giving the sense of identity priority in the problems of psychoses. On that point, such otherwise diverse analytic viewpoints as those of Edith Jacobson, Arieti, and Rosenfeld, on the one side, agree with each other and with Laing, as an extreme on the existential side.

Among the many who have worked over long periods with schizophrenics, Freeman, Cameron, and McGhie[13] derived their particular concept from Federn's concern with the self. Freeman et al. specifically hold that a disturbance of ego boundaries is the crucial one in schizophrenics. From this they deduce the disturbance in thought processes, the delusions and hallucinations, and the rest of the pathology. Their treatment and their concept of schizophrenia are logically interwoven with a texture of the hospital milieu in which the patient is given a chance to find his own identity through identification figures and his boundaries in relation to the environment.

We have already mentioned that the social matrix of the child plays a role in the development of schizophrenia.

Specifically focusing upon the long-term treatment and study of childhood schizophrenia, Goldfarb[15] believes that he can differentiate these children into neurologically determined and environmentally psychologically determined groups. Neurologically normal schizophrenic children come from abnormal family situations while neurologically abnormal schizophrenic children come from substantially better adjusted families. Thus, Goldfarb belongs to those in the many different areas of investigation who find at least two distinctly different groups of schizophrenics, in his case, among children i.e., some in whom neurological factors seem to play the primary role and others where the family pathology seems significant.

DISCUSSION

The most recent *Special Report on Schizophrenia in the United States* by the National Institute of Mental Health states that the "prevailing opinion favors 'multiple entities within the disorder' as the most likely explanation [of schizophrenia]." The research quoted concerning affective disorders tends in the same direction.[24]

At various times over the years, I have formulated my own impression from therapeutic work with psychoses as a multifactorial (somatic and psychological) concept of affective and schizophrenic psychoses.[2,3,6,9–11]

Experimental work of my research colleagues and myself over the past five years, as well as long-term treatment, have tended to bear out the clinical impression previously gained in the rehabilitation of chronic psychotics[4] that the phenotype commonly diagnosed as schizophrenia should be called the "schizophrenic syndrome" and considered to consist of several subgroups of probably quite different etiology and pathogenesis.

The pathway we have chosen in our research to attempt to establish this concept has been by the way of the study of 12 ego functions: reality testing, judgment, sense of reality, regulation and control of drives, object relations, thought processes, adaptive regression in the service of the ego (ARISE), defensive functioning, stimulus barrier, autonomous functioning, synthetic-integrative functioning, and competence of mastery.

The concept of schizophrenia—and psychoses in general—which our study seems to confirm, in my opinion, is *that psychoses are quantitative variations of adaptive functioning,* and that overall very poor adaptive functioning is their only common denominator. With the group of psychoses, different ego functions are more or less affected, allowing for the highly varied picture that can lead to clinically differentiated subgroups.

These subgroups may, however, start out with different etiology and pathogenesis but tend to merge into similar or identical epiphenomena, as they become chronic or at the very least very pronounced.

SUMMARY

Young psychiatrists in countries with high medical standards are not likely nowadays to see many patients with typical cerea flexibilitas in catatonics or become experienced in tube feedings, or see as many chronic psychotics as we saw 25 years ago. Our therapies have met with some success.

The concept of the psychoses that emerges from modern long-term treatments is a complex and not a simple one. To the extent that psychodynamics, psychopharmacology, and other somatic treatments, as well as many different facets of community psychiatry, contribute their treatment approaches to the modern concept of psychoses, it almost of necessity emerges as a multifactorial protean syndrome, whatever its more specific label may be. Whatever the ultimate specific etiologies and pathogeneses of subgroups of the schizophrenic syndrome, of the affective disorders, involutional and puerperal psychoses, and even those disturbances of old age (which I largely see as social disuse atrophy) might be, the concept of man and his psychotic manifestations emerges more clearly than ever as multifaceted interactions of environmental and biological conditions. The concept of psychoses emerges as an integral and indivisible part of the complex human condition. Many agree to this—few act on it either in their therapies or in their research.

There are diehards and bigots in all fields, and some of them would have man be but an assortment of reflexes or muscle jerks, and others can only see biochemistry or the tyranny of genes; some would only see social conditions, and others are so preoccupied with their psychodynamic microscopes that they miss the rest of the world in which they and their patient live.

The fact appears, nevertheless, that the modern concept of psychoses, attained by hard work and long-term care, involves the *whole spectrum of man.* In that sense, psychiatry has come a long way in the last 25 years. If we will guard against retrogression by selective overenthusiasm, we are almost automatically on the way toward increasingly better concepts and better therapy in steady interaction.

NOTES

1. Bateson, G. & Ruesch, J. (1956), Toward a theory of schizophrenia. *Behav. Science,* 1:251–264.

2. Bellak, L. (1949), A multiple-factor psychosomatic theory of schizophrenia. *Psychiat. Quart.,* 23:738–755.

3. Bellak, L. (1952), *Manic-Depressive Psychosis and Allied Disorders.* New York: Grune & Stratton.

4. Bellak, L., Black, B., Lurie, A., & Miller, J. (1956), Rehabilitation of the mentally ill through controlled transitional employment. *Amer. J. Orthopsychiat.,* 26:285–296.

5. Bellak, L., & Rosenberg, S. (1966), Effects of antidepressant drugs on psychodynamics, *Psychosomatics.* 7:Mar.–Apr.

6. Bellak, L., & Loeb, L. (1969), *The Schizophrenic Syndrome.* New York: Grune & Stratton.

7. Bellak, L. (1970), The validity and usefulness of the concept of the schizophrenic syndrome. In: *The Schizophrenic Reactions,* ed. R. Cancro. New York: Brunner/Mazel.

8. Bellak, L., Hurvich, M., Gediman, H., & Crawford, P. (1970), Study of ego functions in the schizophrenic syndrome. *Arch. Gen. Psychiat.,* 23:326–336.

9.   Bellak, L., & Berneman, N. (1971), A systematic view of depression, *Amer. J. Psychother.*, 21(3): 385–393, July.

10.   Bellak, L., Chassan, J., Gediman, H., & Hurvich, M., Intensive design study of Valium effect on ego functions. To be published.

11.   Bellak, L., Hurvich, M., & Gediman, H., Ego functions in schizophrenics, neurotics, and normals. To be published.

12.   Black B. (1970), *Principles of Industrial Therapy for the Mentally Ill.* New York: Grune & Stratton.

13.   Freeman, T., Cameron, J., & McGhie, A. (1957), The state of the ego in chronic schizophrenia. *Brit. J. Med. Psychol.*, 30:9–18.

14.   Goldberg, S. & Mattsson, N. (1968), Schizophrenic subtypes defined by response to drugs and placebo. *Dis. Nerv. Syst.*, 29:153.

15.   Goldfarb, W. (1971), Division into neurologically determined and environmentally determined groups, MH5753, Growth and Family Patterns in Childhood Schizophrenia, Henry Ittleson Center for Child Research, New York. Special Report: *Schizophrenia.* NIMH Center for Studies of Schizophrenia.

16.   Goldstein, M. (1970), Premorbid adjustment, paranoid status, and patterns of response to a phenothiazine in acute schizophrenia, *Mental Health Digest,* condensed from *Schizophrenia Bull.,* 3. Washington, D.C.: NIMH.

17.   Hekimian, L., Gershon, S., Hardesty, A., & Burdock, E. (1969), Drug efficacy and diagnostic specificity in manic depressive illness and schizophrenia. *Dis. Nerv. System.*, 30:1.

18.   Lapolla, A. & Jones, H. (1970), Placebo-control evaluation of desipramine in depression. *Amer. J. Psychiat.*, 127:3, September.

19.   Lehmann, H. (1969), The impact of the therapeutic revolution on nosology. In: *The Schizophrenic Syndrome, an Annual Review,* ed. R. Cancro. New York: Brunner/Mazel, 1971; reprinted from *Problématique de la psychose,* eds. Pierre Doucet and Camille Laurin. New York: Excerpta Medica Foundation, 1969.

20.   Lidz, T., Fleck, S., & Cornelison, A. (1965), *Schizophrenia and the Family.* New York: International Universities Press.

21.   Lipton, M. (1970), Affective disorders: progress, but some unresolved questions remain. *Amer. J. Psychiat.*, 127:3.

22.   Loewenstein, E. (1931), Tuberculosis bacteremia as cause of schizophrenia. *Psychiat-neurol. Wochschr.*, 33:379–381.

23.   May, P. (1968), *Treatment of Schizophrenia: A Comparative Study of Five Treatment Methods*. New York: Science House.

24.   Mosher, L. & Feinsilver, D. (1971), Special Report: *Schizophrenia*. NIMH Center for Studies of Schizophrenia.

25.   Sargant, W. (1962), The treatment of anxiety states and atypical depressions by the monoamine oxidase inhibitor drugs. *J. Neuropsychiat.*, 3(Suppl.):96.

26.   Schopler, E. & Loftin, J., Thought disorders in parents of psychotic children. *Arch. Gen. Psychiat.*, 20(2):174–181.

27.   Schulsinger, F. & Achté, K. (1971), Decreased recidivism in Denmark and Finland. Special Report: *Schizophrenia*. NIMH Center for Studies of Schizophrenia.

28.   Waxler, N. (1971), Unresponsive family interaction. Controlling parental behavior does not differentiate patient from sibling, MH18341, An Experimental Study of Families with Schizophrenics, Harvard University Medical School, Boston, Massachusetts, Special Report: *Schizophrenia*. NIMH Center for Studies of Schizophrenia.

29.   Wittenborn, J. R. (1967), Diagnostic classification and response to imipramine. *Folia Neuropsychiat.* (Lecce), 10:69.

30.   Wynne, L. & Singer, M. (1971), Communication deviance scores in families of schizophrenics, NIMH Intramural Research Program. Special Report: *Schizophrenia*. NIMH Center for Studies of Schizophrenia.

31.   Italics mine.

Harold F. Searles, M.D.

Dr. Bellak has carried out his assignment for the opening of this conference in a manner which shows remarkable mastery of the several highly diverse areas of his topic. I personally have learned much from his informative address, and could easily limit myself to appreciative comments upon the various ideas and bodies of data which he has provided us. To cite but a few examples, I greatly admire his discussion of community psychiatry and his emphasis upon the iatrogenic, hospitalization, or otherwise disuse-based origin of many features of chronic schizophrenia and the psychoses of old age.

But because my background and major interests in this field are very different from his, and because I am convinced that our conference will benefit most from the frank comparison of different viewpoints, I choose mainly to take issue with him on what is for me a most fundamental matter.

My experience in this field consists in nearly 15 years

on the staff at Chestnut Lodge, working on psychoanalytic psychotherapy with chronically psychotic patients who were not on psychotropic drugs; 12 years as a consultant to Wynne's research team at The National Institute of Mental Health, working as a cotherapist with him in the family therapy of schizophrenia, largely without resort to drugs; and, during the past 9 years, conducting single interviews at a dozen different hospitals, for teaching purposes, with many hundreds of psychotic—mostly, of course, schizo-phrenic—patients, a high percentage of whom have been on one or more of such drugs. I have supervised more than a hundred young therapists in their work with psychotic patients, most of whom have been on these drugs.

Dr. Bellak's paper gives the impression that, beyond his faithfully carrying out his assigned task here, his own major interest and emphasis is in drug and diagnostic stud-ies. This emphasis far overrides his pleasantly moderate mention, concerning Goldstein's experimental results, "In some patients the drugs interfered with the problem solv-ing involved in some psychotic processes. It would seem therefore extremely important not to administer psycho-tropic drugs indiscriminately or exclusively." His paper gives psychodynamics short shrift, indeed.

Where he leads into his announced subject by a lengthy discussion of many drug and diagnostic studies, I approach this whole admittedly difficult subject in a way that seems to me to offer a more essentially human orienta-tion, basically in opposition to the relatively nonhuman orientation represented by a psychiatry which would main-tain its focus primarily upon diagnosis and the dispensing of drugs in accord with diagnostic subcategories.

In my experience, the central problem in schizophre-nia, which Dr. Bellak reports to comprise 80 percent of functional psychoses, is the patient's having failed to achieve—or in more dynamic terms—having rejected tena-ciously at an unconscious level, a durable identity as an individual human being. While it clearly would be folly for us to rule out the possibility that genetic inheritance contributes significantly to this difficulty, a most formidable body of data, gained over the past approximately three decades primarily from individual psychoanalytic psychotherapy and family studies, attests that interpersonal processes are for all practical treatment purposes the major, and quite sufficient, etiological source of this impairment of humanization. The most solidly reliable data emerges from the unfolding, the evolution, of the patient's transferences to the therapist. The therapist is given to know, from the reality of his own feeling responses to the patient's unconscious transference reactions to him as being, for example, the mother or father of the patient's childhood, what really were the most warping elements in the emotional climate of the patient's crucial earliest years, years in which the healthy human infant and child ordinarily first becomes a truly human individual. All this, far from being merely impressionistic work on the part of an array of idiosyncratic therapists, is meaningfully validatable among them and is teachable to younger generations of therapists. Such data from psychoanalytic psychotherapy, steadily and firmly developing over the years, are providing a far more genuinely scientific foundation for dealing with schizophrenia than is provided by the vastly more numerous and heavily financed drug studies. In the impressive trappings of our more traditional biologically oriented sciences, these studies—with large numbers of patients, control groups, much attention to possible external variables, and with therapeutic intuition regarded mainly as a contaminant, produce, year after year, dozens of apparently exciting new findings. These findings usually suggest some inherent, inborn qualitative difference, setting schizophrenic persons unbridgeably apart from their fellow men, including, of course, the investigators themselves, findings that prove ephemeral and are soon replaced by other findings that in turn, seem momentarily revolutionary, only to be similarly quickly invalidated.

Several years ago, I put forward the hypothesis that to the extent that one is healthy, one's sense of personal identity is one's most reliable perceptual organ in dealing with the subtle data of interpersonal relations.[1] It follows that, in our endeavor to diagnose our patients' difficulties, what we find happening to our sense of identity in reacting with the patient should not be assumed to consist in unwanted and unscientific intrusions of countertransference phenomena but regarded, rather, as potentially priceless, highly scientific data, as to what is going on at an unconscious level in the patient. One of the surest criteria I have discovered, by which to know that a patient is schizophrenic, is my finding that I tend to experience myself as being nonhuman in relation to him—to feel, for example, that I emerge, in relation to him, as being so inhumanly callous or sadistic, or so filled with weird fantasies within myself, as to place me well outside the realm of human beings. I have not attempted to identify possible other kinds of diagnostically typical subjective experience of one's own personal identity when interviewing patients of various diagnoses other than schizophrenia; but I suggest that research money spent on such projects as this would be well allocated.

The one main point I wish to make here is to caution against our taking refuge, collectively, in an orientation toward our patients which seems to me largely epitomized by Dr. Bellak's paper. In this orientation we tend to think of psychotic patients primarily in terms of objectifying them for diagnostic purposes—trying to discern wherein they differ from their fellow men including, of course, ourselves—and in which we attempt to select this or that drug with the hoped-for magical power to reach the patient and affect his thinking and his feeling, without our own selves, our own feelings and private thinking becoming involved. In our ceaseless search for specifically powerful, but inescapably nonhuman, drugs we depart more and more widely from the possibility of access to the specifically therapeutic power within our human selves, the power inherent in intense and highly personal emotions, such as Winnicott, for example, helped us to reach in his pioneering paper entitled, "Hate in the Counter-Transference."[3]

What I am doing here is no mere tilting at windmills, for my observations of younger therapists' work has clearly shown me that although the psychotropic drugs are at times used with discretion in a manner which fosters genuinely human relatedness between the patient and his therapist and other persons around, all too often they are resorted to too soon, or in too heavy dosage, or too long, primarily for providing the therapist, the nursing and supporting personnel with a refuge from the therapeutically necessary emotional involvement with the patient, involvement which tends so powerfully to assault one's own sense of humaneness. With the best medical intentions, the therapist is unconsciously choosing to remain a diagnostician and dispenser of drugs, and to limit the so-called "psychotherapy" to a pro forma basis, rather than risk his partially becoming, in terms of his own experience of himself, the transference object whom the patient needs. Such a transference object would feel within himself, to some appreciable degree, the kinds of disturbances in various of the twelve ego functions which Dr. Bellak and his research team have found diagnostic for various types of psychosis.

I emphatically do not mean that, in order to function effectively as therapist for the schizophrenic person, one needs to become crazy, or partially crazy, along with him. What I mean is that, while keeping in touch with one's own individual identity, one must become able to experience within oneself, in a manageable degree, the intense and conflicting emotions which he must unconsciously defend against with his craziness. This process provides the necessary therapeutic context for the patient's coming to explore and understand the meanings of his psychosis, which is being projected upon the therapist as the transference personification of the crazinesses in the parents, and provides the foundation, also, for the patient's coming to accept and integrate his own human emotions, partially through identification with the therapist whose humaneness has been able to cope with and integrate this projected schizophrenic onslaught.[1]

I should like very much to share Dr. Bellak's hopefulness about the future; but his own paper, with its heavy emphasis upon drug and diagnostic studies, highlights my main concern about the future of our profession and our patients. If the present avalanche of drug use continues unchecked, there will inevitably result not only a congealing of our psychotic patients' struggle to become genuinely human, but also a dehumanization within our psychiatric culture itself—a loss of humaneness within ourselves personally.

On our overpopulated, pollution-ridden planet where the quality of human existence becomes steadily more degraded, psychiatry is a profession which inherently tends to pioneer in man's new ways of thinking about himself. Dr. Bellak and I come from a country where the overuse or misuse of various drugs influencing mind and emotions are among our most ravaging social ills—where, for example, there are 9 million problem drinkers of alcohol, and where heroin is a leading, if not the leading, cause of death among young men in some of our large cities. In such a nationwide social context, I am troubled about an American psychiatry which itself is relying more and more heavily upon psychotropic drugs, for it seems to me that such a psychiatry tends mainly to pioneer man's increasing alienation from himself. I have no quarrel with such drugs when they are used to help the patient to gain access to, and to integrate, his human emotions. But far too often, antidepressant drugs are used to dull a healthy grief, and sedative drugs are used to lull anxiety and fear in a patient who needs desperately to become more part of a human world where such emotions are realistic indeed.

NOTES

1. Searles, H. F. (1965), *Collected Papers on Schizophrenia and Related Subjects.* London: The Hogarth Press and The Institute of Psycho-Analysis; New York: International Universities Press.

2. Searles, H. F. (1965), The Sense of identity as a perceptual organ. Presented as part of the Scientific Day Program at The Sheppard and Enoch Pratt Hospital, Towson, Maryland, May 29, 1965. Included subsequently in: Concerning the Development of An Identity, *Psychoanal. Rev.* 53:507–530, Winter 1966–67.

3. Winnicott, D. W. (1947), Hate in the counter-transference. *Int. J. Psycho-Analysis* 30:69–74.

Juan de Ajuriaguerra, M.D.

The Scope of the Notion of Psychoses

The notion of psychosis is used in psychiatry today particularly in reference to schizophrenic psychosis. It must nevertheless be pointed out that, although throughout the history of psychiatry there has always been an effort to separate neuroses from psychoses, within the framework of psychosis itself the melancholia of dementia praecox has been set apart (in both Kraepelinian and psychoanalytical classifications) by Freud and also by Melanie Klein in her definition of two essential positions: the paranoid-schizoid on the one hand, and the depressive position on the other. In spite of the fact that in almost all countries we find a clear distinction between entities known as "manic-depressive psychosis" and "schizophrenic psychosis," we must nonetheless observe that the importance given to schizophrenia is less in some areas, whereas in others schizophrenia has become "The Mental Illness." Virtually exclusive from the nosographic standpoint, it is the prototypical entity of a structure whose general framework, once defined, is divided into subgroups each with its own particular characteristics. This explains how, as Bellak points out, the diagnosis of manic-depressive psychosis is more frequent in Great Britain than in the United States, and its frequency is also higher in France, as well as the fact that in Switzerland the notion of schizophrenia is more limited in the French-speaking areas than in the German-speaking regions. The emphasis placed upon one or the other of these diagnoses depends on a number of factors: the extension of the notion of schizophrenia on the basis of E. Bleuler's contribution introducing the idea of primary and secondary symptomatology, which partially breaks away from the notion of pure endogenesis of the illness in its totality and introduces psychodynamic components; the subsequent development of analytical theories on the notion of psychoses; and the importance given later to sociogenetic theories in the genesis of this illness. In other countries, on the contrary, the importance attributed to genetic and constitutional factors in both of these conditions (mostly in German- or French-speaking countries), the resistance to psychoanalytic contributions, the basic formal organicism of the major German and French schools (even when they accepted a psychogenesis of the content), all explain the persistence from the clinical viewpoint of the manic-depressive-schizophrenia dichotomy in which neither eliminates or eclipses the other. Each of us, even those who hold an antinosographic attitude, uses a certain type of taxonomy which enables us to orient our medical attitude within the field of a particular kind of comprehension or forecast. Even if we accept A. Green's identification of two types of nosography—a catalogue-nosography and a compass-nosography (the latter providing cardinal points from which to get our bearings)—our point of view is usually based on the characteristics presented by the patient and a certain theoretical model, which together suggest the idea of a particular structure and give us a basis for calculating at least partially the characteristics of the evolution of the condition and its probable duration. We must beware, however, of becoming a slave to our model in the face of modifications which may arise. We have to maintain a certain degree of flexibility to enable ourselves to evaluate not only the apparent symptomatology but also the modifications of the symptomatology in relation to the patient's personal dynamics. The significance of the symptom (even what is known as primary symptomatology) can have a particular value in itself and in relation to the individual, according to our concept of the illness and sometimes of its genesis. The modifications, which sometimes seem to correspond to a worsening or an improvement, can be evaluated only in relation to a whole. This must not be compared with a general and specific normativity without reference to the economic value of certain symptoms which are a positive necessity in the framework of the time evolution of the personalized illness.

Since this is a discussion on the long-term evolution of psychoses, we will not go into the problems of organogenesis, psychogenesis or sociogenesis, or the issue of causality, which have already been dealt with at the Montreal meeting.

THE MODIFICATION OF SCHIZOPHRENIC PSYCHOSES FROM THE HISTORICAL VIEWPOINT

All experienced psychiatrists have observed changes in the characteristics of the psychoses. In our opinion, it is highly unlikely that a certain transmutation of clinical pictures could be the result of pure chance rather than of changes in the psychiatrist's view of illness and of his therapeutic and relational attitudes. Everyone has noticed the decrease in conditions of chronic agitation, particular types of motor behavior and accepted passivity—conditions which were self-perpetuating, since they were accepted at face value and served as real culture media. For theoretical reasons and because of a need for reassurance, nosography created conditions, or at least perpetuated the idea of chronicity. Entomologists of behavior, we accepted illness as it was handed down to us, and often found something satisfying in the spectacle, with a kind of indulgence towards delusional dysmorphia or in the richness of the imaginary. Patients are more aware than the psychiatrist whether the latter is fascinated by illness or is determined to fight it, and whether the psychiatrist finds a source of satisfaction in the configuration presented by the patient, or if he is trying in spite of their mutual defenses to grasp or understand the hidden meanings. Some conditions have become long-term illnesses through the respective inertia of the patient and the psychiatrist. When the psychiatrist introduces the notion of chronicity he often becomes the author of a chronologically prolonged illness. The initial significance of the illness loses its sense; the patient's experiences and his inner experience of them can also gradually lose a certain indispensable creative resilience; in the same way their repetitions and our indifference blunt their sharpness and muffle their resonance.

It is an indisputable fact that with the evolution of drug treatment, psychotherapeutic activities, and other means of assistance, mental illness has taken on a different appearance. It is difficult to assign any given value to one or another of these changes. For the moment it is fashionable to decry drug treatment on the grounds that the mechanism of this action is not always clearly understood. Nevertheless, it is unfair to criticize the action because it does not reveal the intimate mechanisms of the illness. The action of mercury was effective long before the cause of syphilis was known, and the effects of neuroleptics cannot be denied simply because their means of action is not always evident and often appears to us as no more than a cover mechanism or a simple modification of certain manifestations (such as aggressivity, anxiety, etc.) which does not in itself explain the overall organization of the illness, or because they act as agents for a subsequently restructuring regression.

CHARACTERISTICS OF THE EVOLUTION OF THE IDEA OF MANIC DEPRESSION

In cases of manic depression it is equally unjust not to take into account drug treatment as a factor of diagnostic orientation, as Bellak points out. Manic-depressive psychosis (in its typical form of alternating melancholia and manic states or in the form of intermittent manic or melancholic psychosis) falls within a framework which is difficult not to associate with a certain type of biological disorganization, although this by no means implies the elimination of phenomenological or psychoanalytical explanations from the clinical pictures as such. Here it is a matter of disordered biological rhythms in which the depressant element is improved by imipramine or the monoamine oxydase inhibitors which appear to have at least a relatively specific action. Action through antimanic drug treatment is less clear, and here one wonders to what extent this simply affects states of excitement. We may have exhausted the possibilities of treatment of melancholia and mania, but what has obviously been missing is an attempt to interrupt the biological cycle. Research on lithium seems to offer this possibility, although its action on the biological clockwork of dysthymia is not yet clear. It is furthermore evident that apart from typical manic-depressive psychosis, the other forms of depression, reactive or neurotic, may well be explicable in terms of the same biological phenomenon. Neither does drug treatment give us any information as to how far involutional melancholia falls within the framework of the manic-depressive, when often there is either no history of crisis at all, or there has been only a single crisis in previous years. Nonetheless, the effect of such therapies is often excellent; here these drugs probably do not have any quasi-specific action (although this could be the case in all forms of depression in the young and in adults, and even in the case of tardive depressions which are sometimes of existential origin), but if this is so, it might be asked whether in fact their effect is not more likely to be of the energizing type and not specific at all.

Polymorphism of Schizophrenic Psychoses and Their Long-Term Evolution

Speaking of the treatment of schizophrenic psychoses, Bellak quite rightly asks himself whether, within this polymorphous framework, there might not be certain types of drugs which are more effective in particular cases. Even more interesting seems to be the problem presented by schizophrenics who resist all therapeutic activity, hebephrenics as well as chronic hallucinatory psychotics. From 1952 onward it was observed that certain schizophrenics failed to respond to drug treatment (there were about fifty of them at the Bel-Air Clinic in 1952). The number has decreased with the discovery of new drugs, but we still have in our department five patients who have shown no change whatsoever in response to any of these drugs. This prevents any social reintegration because of the persistence of florid delusion, attacks of anxiety, states of depersonalization, and autistic withdrawals. It was thought for some time that the action was ineffective because the treatment began too late. But there are some among our present patients who have received treatment from the outset with the same results. In the context of schizophrenic polymorphism, we intend to undertake a specially intensive study of these drug-resistant forms in order to determine whether their common factors correspond to a particular structure.

If we study the long-term evolution of schizophrenic syndromes we can under no circumstances consider schizophrenia as an immutable syndrome necessarily evolving toward a given type of deterioration. Some people have placed special emphasis on the importance of the heredity factor (which has recently been challenged sharply by M. Bleuler) or the morphophysical elements which (following the lead of Kretschmer and Mauz) have been of particular interest to a number of authors under German influence. We ourselves, however, feel that their importance is subject to question, given the fixed value implied by classic genetics which does not seem to be demonstrated by the type of response to drugs. Many authors hold the view that two factors seem to play a role, premorbid personality and age. This traditional classification within the framework of schizophrenia and the subgroups does not seem to be sufficiently precise for us to predict whether these will be long-term patients or if an improvement is likely to appear during the course of a more or less lengthy evolution. We know that Klaesi bases his prognosis on the character of the patient, that is, on his former personality, rather than on the clinical form of the illness. Many authors, with whom J. Wirsch seems to agree, have laid considerable stress upon the links between character and "tendency to cure."

The term "tendency" becomes for M. Muller "cure mechanism," which proves that tendency is something creative and active, and has nothing to do with the mechanical development of the process.

The present trend is to accept a multifactorial concept, and authors such as Bellak feel that phenotypes commonly diagnosed as "schizophrenic" should be called "schizophrenic syndrome" and be considered as consisting of a number of subgroups with completely different etiologies and pathogeneses. In the same way, Arieti wonders if schizophrenia might not be the result of the combination of several different factors. Indeed, can we possibly attribute identical pathogeneses to Kanner's infantile autism, with its extremely variable evolution on the one hand and on the other the so-called "schizophrenic psychoses" appearing at a later stage (during the latency period or in preadolescence) and which frequently evolve toward a deficiency form, if not to dementia, or adolescent hebephrenic forms and the systematized delusional states which the French school entitles "chronic hallucinatory psychoses," which have a different evolution, in spite of their apparent schizophrenic structure? Furthermore, can we consider as the same illness certain types of acute schizophrenia (called "acute delusional psychosis" or "delusional crisis" by the French school) and can they be included, by virtue of their symptomatology, which is equivalent to that of classic schizophrenia, in the same nosographic and prognostic framework? While we would go along with Henri Ey in supposing the existence of a clinical reality of a passage from "temporary insanity" to "insanity of an existence," we agree with J. Laboucarié that in the contemporary therapeutic situation—whatever their initial clinical aspects—acute delusional psychoses in young people are more likely to have a favorable outcome than to develop into secondary chronic schizophrenia.

"DETERIORATING" EVOLUTIONS

In the view of the public and a fair number of psychiatrists, a schizophrenic diagnosis is inevitably accompanied by an unfavorable prognosis. E. Bleuler admitted that 25 percent of schizophrenics evolve toward a state of autistic dementia; 25 percent toward a state of deficiency virtually incompatible with social life; and 50 percent show no deterioration other than some traces of deficiency. An epidemiological study carried out in Geneva by F. Jaeggi shows that the evolution of schizophrenics, even severe cases, does not correspond to the notion that this process is inevitable, an assumption of classical teaching. When we go into the problem of long-term psychoses, we enter the framework of a favorite subject of discussion for German authors in particular, namely, defective states and terminal states of schizophrenia. But are we dealing here with an evolution in the course of which the process subsides and is stabilized for a certain length of time, or a progressive picture evolving toward "dementia"? We now know, in the light of the action of new therapies, that drugs can have different results: either complete disappearance of the clinical picture, which can be considered as a kind of cure, or else a persistence of certain disorders where one can speak of "social cure," and reintegration into the former milieu is possible. In spite of the persistence of a hallucinatory syndrome in some of our patients, they have managed to detach themselves sufficiently for valid reintegration to be possible, whereas for others, as we have already mentioned, drug action has no effect whatsoever. This lack of effect can take two forms: one, where the dissociative and delusional syndromes persist without any deficiency state of the demential type, and the other, where there is progressive deterioration. It must also be pointed out that occasionally, and in some cases for a long time, drug action can make the schizophrenic condition worse. Obviously, when we speak of a "state of dementia," we are by no means able to compare all cases of deficiency schizophrenia with organic types of dementia, and many of them in fact present what E. Bleuler called "affective dementia" or Minkowski calls a "pragmatic deficit." Psychosis causes the loss of a certain number of reference points; these processes can result from the demands and impositions of the milieu of a socioaffective disafferentation. The capacity of these patients for carrying out activities and forming relationships is diminished for a variety of reasons: loss of flexibility in modes of thought and action; and lack of appetency and loss or deterioration of cathexis. It is important to differentiate between disorders involving dissociation or debility and incapacities for functional utilization with loss of learning powers, leading to efficiency disorders in which efficiency can itself be affected by the absence of motivation, deficit of afferentation, lack of participation by a rigid hospital structure, or lack of contribution and exchange within the social milieu. But with reference to break-off of relations, it could be asked, as Wirsch does, which symptoms are determined by the illness, and which are determined by the patient himself? Henri Ey says that the forms of organization of one's being in the schizophrenic catastrophe depend less on the specificity of the process than on the ups and downs of its psychodynamics.

What exactly is meant by the word deterioration? Despite all that has been written, Arieti insists on the fact that the cognitive aspect of the individual has been neglected both by psychoanalysis and general psychiatry. If we study the primary process when the patient enters a state of psychosis, he acquires habits which have not been taught to him, which are not imitated and which constitute his schizophrenic way of seeing the world and himself. According to Arieti, this primary process does not consist of mere chaos, but is a chance-based mixture of disparate elements. It is a less-differentiated cognitive system which has its own principles and its own mechanisms. The subject enters into a phase of active concretization. He has not lost the capacity to conceive of an abstraction, but he is unable to cope with it, and when it gives rise to too much anxiety he must immediately transform it unconsciously into a concrete representation. Furthermore, still according to the same author, whereas the normal individual only accepts the notion of identity on the basis of identical subjects, the schizophrenic can accept it on the basis of identical predicates.

A great variety of procedures has been used in an attempt to understand the cognitive difficulties of the schizophrenic character.

In our current research, of which we have the initial results here, the Bel-Air Clinic team (E. Schmid-Kitsikis, Y. Burnand, M.-L. Zutter, J.-J. Burgermeister, R. Tissot, and J. de Ajuriaguerra) has tried to study, by the Piaget-Inhelder method, the cognitive functions in adult schizophrenics who have undergone normal schooling, in order to see if there exists an equivalent spectrum of deterioration in different subjects and if there is overall deterioration, or if only certain aspects of reasoning are affected.

With this end in view we have used the tests developed by Piaget during his research on the genesis of intelligence and also the Wechsler Adult Intelligence Scale (WAIS). These two types of tests should give us complementary information: on the one hand the Piaget tests put the operative structures in evidence and permit the analysis of thought processes; on the other hand, the WAIS provides a basis for assessment of intellectual efficiency in tests with a strong sociocultural component. The Piaget tests were chosen for studying the notions of conservation, elementary logic, formal logic (induction processes and notion of probability, and the notion of causality), and finally, the problems of construction of projective and euclidean space and mental images (in all, about 20 tests).

The population under study at present comprises two groups. The main group consists of:

1. Four young patients (26 to 30 years old) suffering from a dissociative form of schizophrenia with or without catatonic elements; and 2. old patients, whose dissociative-form psychosis, with or without catatonic elements,

appeared prematurely (at about the age of 20)—five subjects; or whose illness appeared during early adulthood (at age about 30)—four subjects.

The second group consists of four subjects suffering from systematized chronic delusion (one subject of 29 years old and three between 40 and 50).

In Table 2.1 we try to show in detail the degrees of deterioration.

Table 2.1.   Degrees of deterioration

Categories	Number of cases	Deterioration: structural logical and preservation		Space	Mental image
young patients	4	0		2 0 2 ±	2 0 2 ±
Dissociation type schizophrenia	5 early onset (20)	1 1 2 1	0 + ∓ ++	0	0
old patients	4 adult onset (30)	3 1	0 ++	+	+
Systematized chronic delusions	4	0		0 (projective space ±)	0

1. From a structural point of view (through tests of logic and conservation);
2. in some more specific fields (euclidean space and mental image); and
3. of mental functioning.

Analysis of Mental Functioning

The same kind of difficulties are found at different genetic levels in all cases of schizophrenia where dissociation is the predominant feature.

Among others, the following points appear most clearly:

1. We find that the possibility of anticipating a classification or a spatial transformation is better than the effective realization of the anticipation, whether by manipulation or graphic realization.

2. In an activity whose successful completion requires coordination of a series of operations, there are tremendous difficulties of anticipation and feedback.

Wechsler Adult Intelligence Scale

A comparison of the results obtained in the operative reasoning tests and those of the WAIS test shows that the operative tests indicate an intellectual potential higher than the WAIS results might lead one to expect.

In studies undertaken with our colleagues (B. Inhelder, S. Roth, and M. Stirlin) on the problem of intelligence in psychotic children between 10 and 15 years of age, we found characteristics such as the inability to understand and assimilate aleatory phenomena and the refusal to reason in probabilistic terms, even in children who manage to develop the initial formal operations and whose reasoning gives evidence of complete integration of concrete operations. Even though the psychotic child is unable to envisage aleatory functions, he often attributes a magical, or at least a hidden cause to events. His concept of the physical world is stamped by animism and his thinking frequently falls back into primitive forms of dualism. Intelligent children explicitly eliminate the element of chance; others substitute for it a series of processes which, although not deducible, are not aleatory. We also find a frozen aspect of the symbolic function, for the psychotic child has difficulty in decentration and seeing things from someone else's viewpoint. Furthermore, it is not easy for him to see the relationship between the signifier and the signified, and he finds it difficult to grasp the idea that symbols are not the reality itself, but that they simply denote the reality. The disturbances observed are manifested either by reduced decentration ability, or by instability in the differentiation between the ego and the external world, or else by various forms of confusion between symbols and signs on the one hand and reality on the other. One has the impression that these disorders correspond to a particular mode of exchanges (difficulty of direct, nondeforming grasp of reality) and relationships with the world of objects. It is hardly surprising, then, that these distorted functionings throw out of joint the organization of the cognitive structures and, in some cases, the organization of coherent operative structures. Our own research has demonstrated that the child has difficulty in seeing himself from the outside as having an autonomous existence and to place himself in the world of objects recognized as being external to himself. Some cognitive areas are particularly fragile, especially those which can only be controlled by the ability to get one's bearings and see oneself from the outside, which call for a relative autonomy lacking in children to an extent which varies according to the cathexes effected and the difficulties they have been able to overcome. However, there are evolutive differences according to the subjects, and also a certain variability. Some present an efficiency level constantly within weak norms throughout their entire evolution, while others improve upon a level which was relatively good in the first place, and others yet "weaken" quite markedly. A certain number of child psychoses have a general appearance of an encysted organization, with very limited mobility, while in other cases there is a certain degree of mobility together with functioning capacity but with poor thinking in general. In other cases, in spite of some difficulty in thought mobility, instead of withdrawal of cathexis we find partial or overall cognitive hypercathexis, notwithstanding the usual absence of adequate social thinking. We know that knowledge can be translated into functioning only when the child manages to assume a certain reality. In the psychotic child the object of knowledge or the function itself can often be considered dangerous. Furthermore, the break with reality can be accompanied by either incapacity for fantasy formation, annulment, or inability to form images, or else by fantasy formation which, although apparently rich, is in fact disturbed. In both cases this distorts the developing human being's apperception of the external world, the fixity of the object or its permanence; this being so, the child places himself outside the phenomenal world or within an animistic or transitivistic framework, and this causes the disorganization of the evolution of discovery of reality or the distortion of concept formations. These few facts on psychotic children are an attempt to demonstrate that in these subjects knowledge of cognitive disorders cannot be studied in a static manner, or by means of a numerical methodology of a classic psychometric type. On the other hand, operative examinations seem to yield a great deal of information because they require considerable involvement of the child's personality; the child is constantly obliged to take a stand, to question himself, and to determine step by step the direction of his thoughts. If by "thought" we mean a totalizing process, comprising all the psychotic symptoms (such as the irruption of primary processes in ideational activity, magical thought, psychotic anxiety and the difficulties of socially referenced symbolization), we find a common factor in these children, namely, the distorted and subjective assimilation of reality. We cannot outline here all the variants we have found in the different forms of child psychoses, but we have observed the fact that there are various types of evolution that do not appear to depend directly upon the seriousness of the disturbances, or upon intellectual levels at the outset, or upon the therapies applied.

What we have presented here is not weighted in favor of an organogenesis or of a psychogenesis, but demonstrates a certain diversity of thought organization corresponding to our patients' personality changes and not necessarily adhering to the traditional classifications or subgroups.

It is not appropriate here to discuss all the forms of therapeutic action on schizophrenic patients, but we can emphasize some of the aims we wish to attain, leaving aside any pathogenetic theory, and avoiding any global, all-explanatory and sometimes omnipotent concept of schizophrenia. In the foggy light of our present knowledge of the biology and psychogenesis of an entity known as schizophrenia, we are groping for a means of action to apply when confronted with our schizophrenic patients; for, as Arieti says, if schizophrenia is the result of a combination of a number of different elements, there is no necessity to eliminate all of them; the removal of a certain number, or even a single one, can avoid psychosis. This is why some therapeutic methods, whether physiological or psychological, could be used to arrest the development of the illness or to cure it, even though they may not have been based upon adequate knowledge of the etiology of schizophrenia. What we are aiming for is to prevent the permanent installation of floating elements, to prevent what is burning from drying up altogether, what is mobile from becoming static and irreversible; we are attempting to enable the dissociated conscious to find by the most appropriate paths an ego sufficiently strong to confront reality and to create, even with contradictions, a certain coherence of existence, and sufficient cathexis to be able to establish object rela-

tions in which attachment finds both its echo and its complementarity in other people. This is where our role lies. It
is during what is frequently a long exchange that we can
find the weak point, a crack through which at the critical
moments we can awaken illuminating experiences which
help in the discovery of identity. Our knowledge of etiopa-
thogenesis is still too hazy for us to use any single therapeutic approach. Each clinician has to make his own choice, not
at random, but through his assessment of the most appropriate method at any given moment of the evolution of the
condition. There is no such thing as a consistently "good"
or "bad" therapy, and there has to be a decision involved
to maintain the balance between the act itself and the moment at which the act can be effective. As Benedetti says,
what is important in therapy is anything and everything that
reinforces the ego; the reality of medical considerations is
no less important than the analysis of the transference; the
symbolic transformation of the present carries no greater
weight than the abandonment of the insecurity of the past.
What is more important is that our new means of assistance
should be articulated within the framework of a new detailed understanding of the patient's psychodynamics, and
that this should be translated into our interpretation.

It is obvious that institutions, which so often function
along completely sterotyped lines, are likely to be bad
ground for the self-realization of the individual. But one
has to be wary of the mirage of outpatient wards as a value
in themselves if in fact they retain the same institutional
formulas, for in this case the subject runs the risk, in different forms, of again finding himself immobilized, manipulated, or, in other words, alienated.

Rigidity is however by no means confined to the organizational framework, and can be found just as much in the
choice of univocal therapies applied in a way which is itself
stereotyped and insufficiently individualized for each type
of disturbed person. Making a clinical choice adapted to

each case within the context of the time and space of its evolution, and having the courage to apply differentiated and even different therapies according to the evolutive stages of the subject—who, apart from his structural and historical unity, presents particular values at any given moment—means changing attitudes. It is not a matter of clinging to one form of therapy or another, but of finding the right balance between our action and the patient's accessibility to it.

This requires a firm belief in mobility and consideration of more than the negative aspects of the disease; it also necessitates a departure from what is often a contemplative or solely interpretative attitude on our part, from which only too often the physician gains more than the patient does.

Chapter 3

LONG-TERM DRUG THERAPY IN PSYCHOSES

René Tissot, M.D.

INTRODUCTION

On the occasion of this symposium, whose theme is "the notion of psychosis," I should be tempted, like Daumezon,[42] "to cry shame at the use of the word psychosis in the singular: the result of the reductive abrasion introduced by analytic terrorism. . .". But it would be an impossible undertaking to try to deal with the long therapy of psychoses in the time and space allotted to us here. I shall, therefore, give rein to my own form of terrorism: I shall leave aside the treatment of manic-depressive psychoses and confine myself to that of the clinical forms of the so-called "schizophrenic psychoses" whose unity, if it exists at all, is of a genetic order.[76] Since, if the diagnosis is rigorous, we are dealing with psychoses whose evolution is from the outset enmeshed with the patient's life, the expression "long-term therapy" is no more than a manner of speaking. It would be more accurate to make the distinction between therapeutic methods at the onset and during the evolution of psychoses. We shall, therefore, confine our attention to these.

One has to ask the question: are drugs useful? The idea may seem absurd if one considers that according to Brill[20] in 1966 the pharmaceutical industry's sales of phenothiazines alone came to more than 38 million dollars. This would, however, implicitly accept the argument of Cawley,[31] the paragon of English neopositive scepticism, according to whom even if there is nothing to establish the efficacy of drugs in schizophrenia beyond doubt, it has nonetheless to be admitted that they are useful in one way or another, since they are used by virtually all practitioners. One also has to consider the corollary to the first question: do drugs have a harmful effect in schizophrenia? Nowadays there is no shortage of authors—and some of them are by no means to be dismissed lightly—who would willingly propose a reversal of the roles and have schizophrenics make the psychiatrist and the rest of the so-called "normal population" swallow the drugs intended for the schizophrenics themselves. As early as 1959, Balvet[11] considered the possibility that phenothiazines might actually provoke the conditions which lead the patient into "hospitalism." Although this development thrives particularly in the hospital milieu, it is not exorcised simply by the patient's discharge. While I cannot share the view of a colleague (who was one of our neighbours at the time, and whom we had invited to instruct our staff) according to whom the only use for neuroleptics in his ward was to fatten the hog while making him impotent, it is difficult to agree with Delay and Deniker[50] when they state that schizophrenic passivity exists in spite of neuroleptics and not because of them. Passivity is a psychotic symptom, but it can be intensified by neuroleptics and even created by them where it does not exist. It is enough to observe a few laboratory experiments to be convinced of this. It is quite probable that Balvet has protected a considerable number of French-speaking psychotics from a serious aggravation of their condition and a fair amount of complications which would have in all likelihood been anything but benign.

This being said, can we, without aiming at any absolute statement, try to make an objective assessment of the contribution of drugs to the therapy of schizophrenic psychoses? The weightiest arguments seem to fall within the epidemiological sphere.

EPIDEMIOLOGICAL DATA

Evolution of the Psychiatric Hospital Population in General and of Schizophrenics in Particular

The total number of hospitalized patients in American psychiatric hospitals fell from 558,000 in 1955 to 400,000 in 1968. In New York State there were 66,500 in 1969 as compared to 93,000 in 1955. The onset of this evolution was as sudden as it was unexpected, and immediately followed the introduction of new psychiatric drugs, according to Brill[19-21] (see Fig. 3.1). It was obvious that American hospitals were overpopulated, however—6 and even up to 10 percent of the total number of residents in certain urban areas. With or without the aid of drugs, the fact of caring for these patients at all was bound to improve the situation. Could it be that chlorpromazine was simply the mediator of a new psychiatric policy? Brill retorts that in England and in France the psychiatric revolution got under way during and immediately after World war II and that even so, it was only in 1954, with the introduction of chlorpromazine, that the hospital population began to decrease; in 1954 it was 152,194, and in 1968 it was 120,000. And yet there was no evidence of overpopulation, since the figure never exceeded 3 percent.

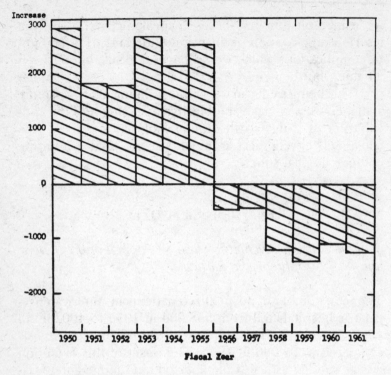

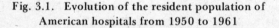

Source: Brill, H. (1962), *Amer. J. Psychiat.*, 119:20–30.

Fig. 3.1.   **Evolution of the resident population of**
American hospitals from 1950 to 1961

Although the general population of psychiatric hospitals in other countries has not invariably followed the same
evolution, that of hospitalized schizophrenics has decreased virtually everywhere, regardless of the number of
admissions. In order to judge the hospitalization prognosis, Wing[197] bases his calculations on the following major
surveys which, after cross-checking the results, seem to him
to be valid. Perhaps you will allow us to add to them our
own series from the Bel-Air Clinic relating to the period
1965–1968 (see Table 3.1).

Table 3.1. Hospital prognosis for schizophrenia

	Satisfactory social adjustment on discharge	Discharged	Permanently hospitalized
Before 1930			
Kraepelin	20%	20%	80%
Mayer-Gross [141a]	35%	40%	60%
After electro-shock insulin Harris et al. [97]			
1945–1950	45%	66%	34%
After neuroleptics Brown et al.[25]			
1956–1961	56%	89%	11%
Bel-Air Clinic 1965–1968			
Admitted in 1965 (after 3 years)		97.9%	2.1%
Admitted in 1966 (after 2 years)		95.4%	4.6%
Admitted in 1967 (after 1 year)		96.3%	3.7%

Without confusing discharge prognosis and prognosis of the illness, there is an indisputably favorable evolution. At the very least, 90 percent of schizophrenics today are protected against hospitalism in the hospital milieu. It is difficult to imagine that the introduction of biological therapies after 1930 and of neuroleptics from 1954 onwards, did not play a role in the successive jumps in frequency of hospital discharges. But as to what this part may be, whether in quantitative or qualitative terms (pharmacological, placebo function, intermediary of an active psycho-ergo-sociotherapeutic policy) there is no foundation to form any objective judgment. Any assessment has to be based on an intuitive appreciation, which permits statements all the more categorical for being poorly supported by the evidence. Thus in the view of Goldman[84] it can be categorically stated that the changes observed in American psychiatry over the last 12 years are due to the intensive application of pharmacological treatments in the therapy of psychoses and, in particular, the use of phenothiazines.

Length of Hospital Stays of Schizophrenics

If the number of hospital beds occupied by schizophrenics is decreasing with no corresponding decrease in the number of admissions for schizophrenia, then it follows that the length of these patients' stay must also be diminishing. Curiously enough, however, opinions are divided on this point. It is impossible to make an inventory of all the work done on the subject, but among those who have compared the duration of hospitalization before and after the era of neuroleptics and have found no change for the better, let us consider the work of Achté & Apo.[3] They compare two groups of hospitalized schizophrenics in the same hospital in Finland, between 1950–1952 and 1957–1959. During the first period the average stay was 106 days, as opposed to 162 days during the second period, which shows a high increase. Now this increase is linked to the reduction of the use of electroshock therapy. If patients under this therapy are excluded from the series, the difference is eliminated. Given the innocuousness of this treatment, it would be a mistake to drop it entirely in favor of pharmacotherapy.

Among the numerous studies where a decrease in the duration of hospitalization since the introduction of neuroleptics has been observed, we shall quote only Röder,[166] who gives the position of Scandinavian literature on the subject, and who has the merit of having compared over successive years the length of stay of all the schizophrenics (310) discharged from the same ward between 1951 and 1960, and 1955 marking the introduction of neuroleptics. Discharges before and after 1955 can be grouped according to length of stay under three months or between three months and two years. Thus, the first series of patients were not given neuroleptics, while the second series did receive this treatment. Let us leave aside for the moment patients whose stay in hospital exceeded two years:

	Patients dismissed	
Length of stay	*Before neuroleptics* 1951–1954	*After neuroleptics* 1955–1960
< 3 months	22	55
3 months 2 years	64	47

$$p < 0.0005$$

It could, of course, be objected that if the same statistics were established over another decade the same observations might well result. We can try to get around that difficulty by comparing the evolution during the four years preceding neuroleptics and the six years following their introduction:

	Patients dismissed			
Length of stay	1951–52/1953–54		1955–56/1958–60	
< 3 months	13	9	22	25
3 months 1 year	27	37	27	28
	NS	$p < 0.01$	NS	

To make things even clearer, we can make another comparison of the periods 1951–1954 and 1955–1960:

	Patients dismissed			
Length of stay	1951–1954		1955–1960	
< 3 months	7	3	8	10
3 months				
2 years	15	20	13	9
	NS	$p < 0.2$	NS	

There was therefore no change within the periods preceding and following neuroleptics, while there is a significant change between the period 1953–1954, two years before neuroleptics, and the period 1955–1965, two years after neuroleptics. If we leave aside 1955, a year during which patients discharged after a stay of over three months were unlikely to have received neuroleptics for more than a very short time, and we compare 1953–1954 with 1956–1957, we get the following tabulation:

	Patients dismissed	
Length of stay	1953–1954	1956–1957
< 3 months	9	20
3 months	37	12
2 years		
	$p < 0.0005$	

In other words, there is an undeniable break linked to the introduction of neuroleptics.

The prescription of neuroleptics has shortened the length of stay of schizophrenics in hospitals. Is this because of their direct pharmacological action or some other modification of the cure factors which they bring about through their pharmacological action, or independently of their pharmacological action? Once again, the answers given to this question are based on subjective intuition.

We ourselves have no statistics of such univocal signifi-

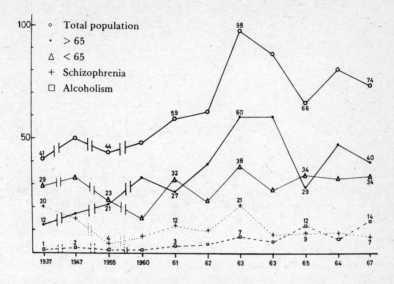

Fig. 3.2. Evolution of the "minor sediment" (cf. text) at the Bel-Air Clinic

cance. But de Meuron[142a] has studied for the control years —1934, before insulin and electroshock; 1947, after insulin and electroshock; 1955, immediately following the introduction of neuroleptics; and 1964, after 10 years of neuroleptics—the changes in duration of stays in hospital, through the constitution of what he calls the "minor sediment," that is, patients admitted during the control year and still in hospital at the end of the following year; and the "major sediment," that is, patients admitted during the control year and remaining in hospital throughout that year (Figs. 3.2 and 3.3 and Table 3.1a).

Discharge of Patients after Prolonged Hospitalization

In his extensive review of literature on the subject, Brown[25] clearly shows that between 1900 and 1960 the curve indicating frequency of discharge invariably went down after

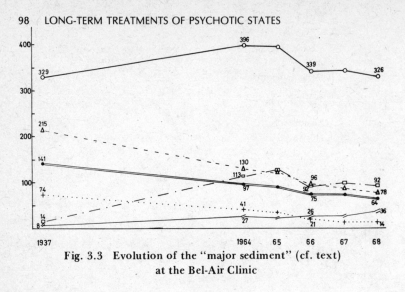

Fig. 3.3   Evolution of the "major sediment" (cf. text)
at the Bel-Air Clinic

○ Total population   = Alcoholism
+ Systematized delusions   ☐ Senile dementiae
· Schizophrenics

two years of hospitalization (Fig. 4). After that point the schizophrenic's chances of being discharged went down to no more than 6–7 percent. In the light of this well-established fact, let us examine the results of some of the studies of the postneuroleptic period.

Table 3.1a. Development of "Sediment"

Control year	"Minor sediment"	"Major sediment"	Number of admissions
1937	20	215	
1947	15	—	
1955	4	—	
1964	8	130	147
1965	9	123	143
1966	9	96	151
1967	7	87	191
1968	—	78	203

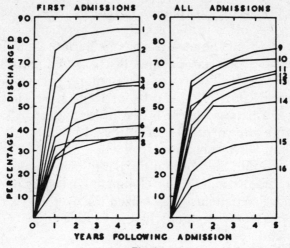

Fig. 1.

Source	Nos. Patients	Date Admission	Place
1. F. Freyhan (1958)	216	1948–50	Delaware, U.S.
2. F. Freyhan (1958)	313	1940–47	Delaware, U.S.
3. M. Kramer et al. (1956)	1,271	1936–45	Warren State, U.S.
4. B. Malzberg (1952)	2,949	1943–44	New York
5. M. Kramer (1956)	658	1926–35	Warren State, U.S.
6. R. Fuller (1930)	1,200	1909–11	New York
7. A. Harris (1955)	357	1930	London
8. F. Freyhan (1958)	129	1900–07	Delaware, U.S.
9. G. Brown (unpublished)	350	1950–51	London
10. J. Wing (unpublished)	160	1950	London
11. V. Norris (1959)	2,279	1947–49	London
12. J. Drasgow (1952)	100	1950	Buffalo, U.S.
13. M. Shepherd (1957)	179	1945–47	Hertford, England
14. G. Brown (cf. Fig. 3)	50	1945–46	London
15. L. Danziger (1946)	18,000	1933	U.S.
16. G. Brown (cf. Fig. 3)	387	1943–49	London (Polish Army patients)

Source: Brown, G. W. (1960), *Acta Psychiat. Scand.*, 35:414-430.

Fig. 3.4.   Evolution of schizophrenic discharge rates in relation to length of hospital stay

To go back first to Röder's study, the variation of frequency of discharge for patients hospitalized for two to five, five to 10, and more than 10 years is highly significant.

In the preneuroleptic period 1951–1954, 10 patients with over two years' stay in hospitals were discharged, as compared to 48 for the postneuroleptic period 1955–1960. If we consider only the patients discharged after a 10-year hospital stay, the difference is even more striking: none for the period 1951–1954, and 18 for 1955–1960. Here again we have a perfectly clear break in the pattern. 1954: one discharge after over 10 years; 1955: 15.

Quite obviously, the introduction of neuroleptics has made possible the hospital discharge of a number of encysted patients, and this development is a lasting one, since in 1960, five patients hospitalized for over 10 years were discharged, whereas none had been able to leave during the period 1951–1954.

Ekblom & Lassenius[59] examine the development of patients who had been in hospital for three years at the time of the introduction of neuroleptics. Of those treated with these drugs, 30 percent were discharged after three years, as opposed to 18 percent of those who were not so treated. Within the same population, 45 percent of women under neuroleptic treatment for five years were discharged, while 31 percent of men who had been receiving neuroleptics for only 2 years were able to leave. The authors feel they can justifiably deduce that long-term treatment with neuroleptics is an important factor. Whatever the case may be, this is a far cry from the 6–7 percent likelihood of discharge for the preneuroleptic period.

In a large-scale series of more than 1000 subjects, Goldman[85] observes that the rate of discharge between three and seven years remains virtually identical, varying between 32 and 36 percent.

It can therefore be accepted that in recent years long-term hospitalization has been eliminated to a large extent. This does not imply that the evolution of the illness has been fundamentally changed in itself. The conclusions which can be drawn relate only to the natural history of

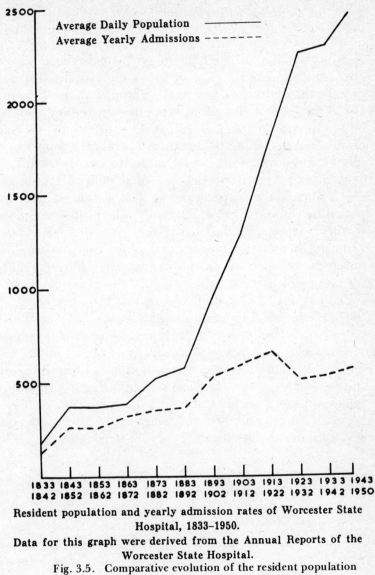

Resident population and yearly admission rates of Worcester State
Hospital, 1833–1950.
Data for this graph were derived from the Annual Reports of the
Worcester State Hospital.
Fig. 3.5.   Comparative evolution of the resident population
and admissions at the Worcester State Hospital

Source: Brown, G. W. (1960), *Acta Psychiat. Scand.*, 35:414–430.

schizophrenia in the hospital milieu and demonstrate that patients more and more frequently escape the affliction of hospitalism within the hospital. It is difficult to deny that neuroleptics have something to do with this fact. Their appearance marked a clear break in the evolution of the population of hospitalized schizophrenics and the associated parameters (length of hospital stay, sedimentation, and frequency of discharge). It is nonetheless just as well established that these parameters depend on a number of other conditions besides, and in particular, on what the English and Americans call "hospital policy." Although this is outside the scope of our subject, it is impossible to pass it by without a glance. Brown[25] follows the evolution of the resident population of Worcester State Hospital from its foundation onward, and notes the catastrophic influence which seems to have been exercised by a certain form of medical treatment during the first half of this century[25] (see Fig. 3.5). Gurel[93] shows that the mere transfer from one hospital to another is followed by a definite increase in the frequency of discharge of patients hospitalized for over two years. We ourselves have observed an analogous phenomenon in a neighboring canton, although the competence of the medical staff in question cannot be queried. Linn[137] in his study of discharges from 12 state hospitals notes that between the number of discharges and several other factors there is:

1. a significant positive correlation of
    0.54 with the number of attendants, but not with that of nursing staff,
    0.54 with the number of therapeutic programs,
    0.75 with the time spent by the doctors in the wards,
    0.55 with the frequency of patient/attendant relationships,

0.52 with the frequency of patient/patient relationships,
0.51 with the frequency of visits from outside,
0.57 with normal patient activity;

2. a positive but nonsignificant correlation of
0.46 with the number of patients in ergotherapy;

3. a negative significant correlation of
0.51 with the number of hospital beds,
0.77 with inadequate patient activity;

4. a negative nonsignificant correlation of
0.45 with the number of disciplinary controls exercised upon patients; and

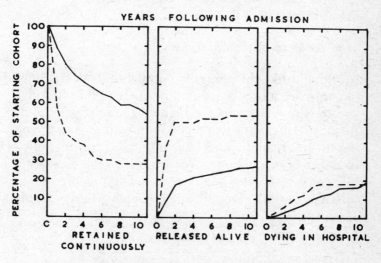

Fig. 3.6. Proportion of hospitalized schizophrenics leaving
(discharged or on death) Long Grove Hospital
over a 10-year period

Key:

―――― Polish patients admitted between 1943 and 1949
- - - - English patients admitted between 1945 and 1946.

Source: Brown, G. W. (1960), *Acta Psychiat. Scand.*, 35:414–430.

5. no correlation with
   a. the comfort of the hospital,
   b. the esthetic surroundings of the hospital,
   c. freedom to leave the hospital at will, freedom to go to work, and
   d. the possibility of keeping personal objects.

The author concludes that while hospital comfort and freedom from controls have relatively little bearing upon the reduction of the length of hospital stay, understanding staff-patient relationships, the presence of the medical team, sufficiently varied activities, and also contacts with the outside world are basic requirements for any such decrease (see Fig. 3.6).

The Problem of Readmissions

Although the schizophrenic population is decreasing, discharges are more frequent, and the length of hospital stay shorter, readmissions are higher. There is general agreement on this point that since the beginning of the neuroleptic era, readmissions have increased considerably. The number of readmissions, particularly in the case of schizophrenics, appears to be directly related to the number of discharges (Odegard,[147b] and is higher where ward mobil-

Table 3.2 Admissions and readmissions of schizophrenics at the Bel-Air Clinic

Control year	Total no. of schizophrenic admissions	First admissions		Readmissions	
1947	90	51	56.7%	39	43.3%
1964	147	72	49 %	75	51 %
1968	203	97	47.8%	106	52.2%
	NS	p < 0.8			

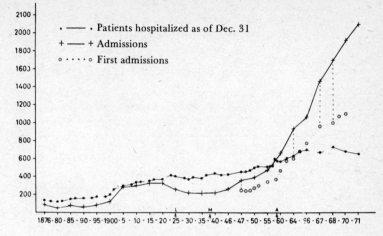

Fig. 3.7. Evolution of the resident population and admissions at the Bel-Air Clinic from 1876 to 1971

ity is greater. There seems to be a tendency for over 50 percent of hospitalized patients to be readmitted [Achté & Apo,[3] 47 percent; Auch,[62] men: 50 percent, women: 67 percent]. For our own observations, see Table 3.2 and Fig. 3.7.

What may be of even greater importance, however, is the fact that, given similar hospital policy conditions, readmissions for schizophrenia are decreasing as a percentage of total readmissions (Burgermeister[27a]); see Table 3.3 for our own data.

Table 3.3 Schizophrenics as percentage of total readmissions at the Bel-Air Clinic

Control year	Total no. of readmissions	Readmissions of schizophrenics	Percent of total
1947	90	39	43.3
1964	296	75	25.3
1968	655	106	16.2
		$p < 0.001$	

Table 3.4. Length of stay of subjects admitted for the first
time in 1968 as opposed to that of subjects readmitted
in that year

	0–1 month	1–3 months	3–6 months	6–9 months	Not discharged during the year	Total
First admission	36	22	11	1	27	97
Return	30	42	8	1	35	106
	p < 0.01	NS		p < 0.05	NS	

Brown[26] considers it evident that the length of stay on readmission increases with each new admission (see Table 3.4). This phenomenon does not seem to us—or to Battegay & Gehring[13] or Röder[166]—to be of particular importance. It applies only to stays of less than one month and those of between one and three months.

Although few authors have paid attention to the length of time elapsing between successive admissions, there are some highly contradictory views on the subject.[156] According to Apo & Achté (1967)[3] the average interval before readmission was shorter in 1957–1959 (15.9 months) than in 1950–1952 (18.5 months). We have reached the same conclusions with Frogel (results not published) in comparing readmissions between 1948 and 1952 with those between 1957 and 1961. Before neuroleptics, the length of time between hospital stays, which were themselves infrequent (33) was on average more than three years; after neuroleptics they were much more frequent (104) and on average of a duration of less than two years. Rasmussen[161a] finds that the number of patients not readmitted three years after discharge is no higher for 1955–1960 than for 1950–1954, but Röder[166] finds that as the percentage of total discharges went up from 24 to 50 percent. These facts are worth clarifying, for if after a certain level of mobility is attained a reduction in the length of hospital stays is accompanied by compulsory readmissions, there is as yet little hope of seeing any decrease in the number of hospital beds occupied by schizophrenics, and the value of such a policy could well be held up to scrutiny.

It would be of vital importance to determine if frequency of readmission is linked to the patient's continued medical supervision after discharge. Much more work has been done in this area, but results and conclusions are contradictory. In a review of literature on the subject, Orlinsky and d'Elia[148] mention almost as many papers arguing the beneficial effect of aftercare on the readmission rate as those with negative or ambiguous results.[61,108,142,144,188] Yet experiments relating to patients divided at random into two groups, of which one was followed up and the other not, showed Free et al.[73] and Katz et al.[115] that only 14.6 percent of the first group were rehospitalized during the length of the experiment, as opposed to 35.1 percent in the group which was not followed up. The same type of experiment relating to the parameter of aftercare with or without neuroleptics would also be favorable to the latter group. The study carried out by Orlinsky and d'Elia[148] deals with the catamnesis of 2132 patients of whom 1336 received aftercare and 796 did not. No distinction was made as to the quality and type of postcure involved, but the vast majority of patients who were followed up received neuroleptics (see Table 3.5).

These differences are significant. But, as the authors themselves point out, since the patients receiving aftercare did so voluntarily it is possible that their more favorable rehospitalization rate may be due to their nosognosis, their desire for treatment, just as much as to the aftercare itself.

At the present time a hospitalized schizophrenic has a very good chance of rapid, or fairly rapid discharge, and is

Table 3.5. Study of catamnesis

Length of time after discharge	Of 1336 patients receiving aftercare, percent not rehospitalized	Of 796 patients not receiving aftercare, percent not rehospitalized
3 months	95.0	85.0
6 months	87.9	68.7
1 year	74.3	54.3
2 years	59.4	46.6
	$p < 0.05$	

also highly likely to be readmitted several times, although the frequency of return will be lower if he receives outpatient treatment. But what is the patient's fate once he leaves the hospital? According to Wing,[197] who refers to Brown (1966), patients who are socially ill-adjusted on discharge run just as high a risk of "hospitalism" in society as in the hospital. They remain totally inactive during 30 percent of their waking time, as compared with 21, 26, and 43 percent, respectively, in the three hospitals from which they were discharged.

In a recent paper, Paerregaard[150,157] studies the subsequent life of 270 schizophrenic women hospitalized between 1955 and 1963 in Copenhagen (see Table 3.6).

Ten years after admission, a little over 10 percent of these patients remain in the hospital, which coincides with the statistics quoted, but at least 57, or 20 percent, remain attached to an institution of some kind. As far as their socioprofessional catamnesis is concerned, the picture is as follows: whereas only one was pensioned prior to hospitalization in 1969, 162—over 67 percent—were pensioned without having reached retirement age. Although the hospital outlook for schizophrenics is brighter today, their future as human beings still remains very gloomy.[97,102,104,135,136]

Table 3.6. Subsequent developments in 270 schizophrenic
women hospitalized in Copenhagen between 1955 and 1963

	1963	1965	1969	Readmissions from 1965–1969
Prolonged hospitalization	69	61	32	2
Temporary hospitalization	30	20	10	10
Outpatient treatment	18	26	21	11
Nonhospital private institution	7	15	26	9
Self-discharge	48	46	59	31
Disappeared	54	42	29	5
Dead	10	17	37	4
Change of address	34	43	56	5

CHANGES IN THE CLINICAL FORMS OF PSYCHOSES

Most authors agree, apart from some divergence on detail, that there have been changes in the clinical forms of psychoses since the era of neuroleptics.[157] Deniker[56] and his group have described these changes time and again. But has sufficient attention been paid to the significance of these changes, which is by no means univocal?

It is common practice to credit the neuroleptics with the virtual "disappearance in hospitals of clearly catatonic forms of schizophrenia" (Peron-Magnan[152]). To the practitioner who is still relatively young but old enough to have known mental hospitals just before the neuroleptic era, and therefore has a clear idea of the clinical picture of that time, this simplification of facts is disturbing. There were already very few cases of catatonic schizophrenia by that time—in the wards I worked in, at any rate. Achté's work[2] on the evolution of schizophrenia in Finland between 1933 and 1955 provides categorical confirmation of this. Catatonia, which was present in 37 percent of cases in 1933 was absent in all but 11 percent of cases in 1955. It has yet to be proven that this was due to the effect of electroshock treatment and insulin comas. We would be much more readily inclined to consider the disappearance of catatonia as a sociocultural problem, like the virtual disappearance of major hysteria crises. Both were encouraged by the combination of patients' sociocultural development and medical complacency. The joint effects of Babinski on the one hand, and medical services upon the other, in conjunction with sociocultural factors, have banished both. Cannot both be observed even independently of any pathological situation, in other parts of the world? And finally, is it possible to become catatonic when immobilized by an extrapyramidal syndrome?

Before neuroleptics, as Achté states, the decrease in catatonic forms was accompanied by a corresponding increase in hebephrenic, and to an even greater extent, paranoid forms. The reverse situation apparent today is probably due to the use of neuroleptics. Indeed, paranoid traits are fine target symptoms for pharmacotherapy. It is quite likely that the decline of hebephrenia itself is also the result of the direct pharmacological action of neuroleptics. As Brill says (after many others, but in a much simpler way), drugs act upon the positive symptoms of schizophrenia; they do not remove the inertia, the inability to work or the lack of constructive initiative necessary for regular occupation. Even the discordance and incoherence are considerably attenuated. Neuroleptics level off schizophrenia and leave us faced with Guiraud's nucleus[92]—perplexity and athymhormia.

As for the favorable evolution of less severely affected subjects toward pseudoneurotic and pseudopsychopathic forms (Peron-Magnan[152]), we also wonder if this might not have a great deal to do with the cultural setting, including the psychotherapeutic environment. And that is not meant as a derogatory remark!

Finally, by transforming schizophrenia from a continual-expression syndrome, which was most frequently the case, into an intermittently expressed syndrome—by this fact alone and independently of their direct pharmacological action—drugs bring about its fundamental modification. A number of vicious circles are broken and dismantled. Impenetrability to the external world is no longer constant. The other is no longer invariably the initiator of a unilateral relationship. It becomes possible for previous acquirement to be put into effect intermittently, and the possibility of new acquirements is not excluded. The noxious continuity of the psychopathological process is broken. "Chronic" hallucinatory psychoses, which are still so called even though they are not only intermittent, provide easily observable examples of this. Their delusions are no longer systematized, as in classic manifestations. Is this not held up to question and often challenged for months at a time? Hallucinations, although they have not lost the characteristics described by Clérembault, are less frequently categorically confirmed as authentic, and they are less readily attributed to fixed characters. The externalization and attribution of hallucinations, even if they retain the same esthesic character, are more difficult when one bears in mind the fact that a year before these were simply voices, produced by the disorder.

All in all, it seems presumptuous, in view of the changes we are witnessing in the clinical forms of psychoses, to try to assess the relative importance of (1) direct pharmacological effects of drugs (the target symptoms of the English and Americans); (2) the sui-generis secondary evolution of the psychopathological process divested of a certain number of its manifestations, either intermittently or long term; (3) the repercussions of these initial effects upon the patient's milieu and on hospital policy—repercussions which rebound upon the patient himself; and (4) changes of a more general sociocultural order, including changes in hospital policy. Here we need no double-blind procedure to declare ourselves nonstarters.

SHORT- AND MEDIUM-TERM CLINICAL TESTS

We have a curious situation before us here. There is hardly any special number of a journal dealing with psychopharmacology, hardly any symposium on the subject, where a general review by some famous author demonstrating that the antipsychotic action of neuroleptics is impossible to prove scientifically, is not accompanied by numerous articles based on some unchallengeable scientific methodology (random samples, double-blind technique, etc.), establishing the superiority of the antipsychotic action of preparation X as opposed to preparation Y. This is the false dialectic of two different breeds of psychiatrists: those who prescribe drugs, or have them prescribed by others, but pride themselves on having no faith in them; and those who prescribe drugs while continuing the care of their patient, but claim with false modesty to be simple pill-pushers "just like any other doctor."

Perhaps under these circumstances, it would be preferable to leave the paradox unelucidated. Ruskin et al.[172] put 555 depressive patients under "controlled" administration of 600 mg of chlorpromazine, imipramine, or placebo. After five weeks, when the test was terminated with all subjects being put onto placebos, the majority of the patients who had received imipramine deteriorated, while the majority of those who had received chlorpromazine appeared to emerge from their lethargy and even showed a considerable improvement upon their state before the treatment, although this improvement turned out to be only temporary. Hence, even if neuroleptics have no positive effect on psychoses, they do at least have negative effects in the majority of depressive cases, as is clearly demonstrated by withdrawal of therapy. Greenberg et al.[87] divided schizophrenics who had been on chlorpromazine for at least 8 months into two groups. The first underwent gradual withdrawal of treatment over a period of eight weeks, and the second abrupt withdrawal at the end of eight weeks. The patients in the second group suffered from insomnia, sometimes to a severe degree, necessitating the administration of soporifics. They became extremely hyperactive and bulimic, and externalized a number of neurovegetative signs. It can therefore be deduced that chlorpromazine has a pharmacological effect. Who would contradict this? But in the case of patients convinced of the magical properties of little colored pills, this aspecific effect acts as an intermediary for the doctor's psychotherapeutic action. Why should a relatively specific and positive effect not play exactly the same role? Whatever the case may be, Glick[80] attempts to assess the repercussions by its effects on the patient's attitude towards the drug before its prescription. Twenty subjects received placebos for two weeks and perphenazine for four weeks, with the usual methodological precautions. The patients' improvement shows no correlation with their positive or negative attitude concerning the drug $(r = 0.02)$. There is a correlation with the gravity of the patient's symptomatology $(r = 0.38, p < 0.01)$. Mistrust of the drug is in correlation with the gravity of the illness $(r = 0.24, p < 0.07)$. In other words, the more willingly the patient accepts, or even requests the drug, the less benefit he gains from it. The more serious his illness and the more he tries to avoid it, the greater the benefit. This may seem obvious, I grant you! The fact is perfectly well known to the pharmaceutical industry, which has been known to put on the market a virtually inactive drug which will be prescribed and ingurgitated in vast quantities. It is also a fact which should more frequently be borne in mind by the outpatient department physician who, in his dialectic of transference, is inclined to doubt the efficacity of his action if it is not actively requested or at least willingly accepted.

Let us remain within the semiparadox. The above-mentioned study of the withdrawal process shows that whether the break is abrupt or gradual, it is nevertheless followed by a 50 percent relapse rate after a period of 12 weeks. According to Paerregaard's study, which, you will remember, deals with the catamneses of 270 schizophrenics, more than 50 percent of rehospitalizations (40 out of 77) are linked time-wise to the termination, diminution, or change of drugs. In our work with Frogel on the rehospitalization of psychoses at Bel-Air between 1957 and 1961 (there were 174), we observed 130 relapses, of which 75 percent occurred in patients who had not received outpatient treatment at all or after an interruption of this treatment of at least two weeks, and 44 (25 percent) in patients under drugs or concomitantly with the withdrawal of drugs. Greenberg & Roth[88] have collected the results of a number of studies on the length of time before relapse after termination of drug treatment (see Table 3.7).

There are countless studies whose results demonstrate either the positive or the negative action or else the absence of action of neuroleptics in psychoses, but we shall simply quote or evoke some of the major series. Goldman,[84] for example, relating to 1600 patients under treatment for periods of between three and seven years. According to this author, the prescription of neuroleptics for schizophrenics whose hospital stay is longer than three years enables about 35 to 45 percent of these patients to leave the hospital each year, a total of 1044 in seven years. Then we have the results of the National Institute of Mental Health collaborative study on 400 schizophrenics,[146] which concludes that drugs are effective. Considerable clinical improvement is observed in 51 percent of these cases, moderate or distinct improvement in 75 percent, as opposed to 23 percent in the placebo group. The subjects were treated in the same hospitals and within the same environment.

But now let us quote Letemendia et al.[133] who, in a rural annex of a clinic, virtually abandoned as far as medical

Table 3.7. Percentage of patients remaining drug-free
in ten studies[87]

Study	Percent of patients drug-free in week, number									
	1	2	3	4	8	12	16	20	24	48
Greenberg and Roth (present study)										
Abrupt termination group	94	94	94	94	65	41	29	24	24	18
Gradual termination group	95	95	95	95	81	48	38	38	38	14
Diamond and Marks; Good, Sterling, and Holtzman						a			b	
Caffey and associates										
Drug group				98	97	95	95			
Drug (three days a week) group				98	95	93	85			
Placebo group				90	80	65	55			
Olson and Peterson										
Abrupt termination group				70	55	45	38	33	25	
Drug group									95	
Rothstein							78		78[c]	
Shawver and associates					b					
Wilcox										
Abrupt termination group	67	55		45	35		25		20	
Group terminated in one week without psychotherapy	80	70		60	50		40		35	
Group terminated in one week with psychotherapy				66	64		62		60	
Ray, Ragland, and Clark					a	b				

[a]No significant differences between control and experimental groups.
[b]Significant differences between control and experimental groups.
[c]Including 17 percent with "moderate" regressive symptoms.

who had been hospitalized continually for more than five years without treatment. A perfectly orthodox test, with placebo and 300 mg of chlorpromazine, gives no indication of any difference between placebo and chlorpromazine, apart from the fact that under the latter treatment delusions flare up more acutely. One might wonder if this rural clinic could have "had a hog to fatten . . ." It is true that among 77 schizophrenics, of whom 37 were transferred to an open ward and underwent an intensive program of community therapy, these same authors find no difference be-
treatment was concerned, observed 65 male schizophrenics

tween the latter and the rest of the group, apart from a detrioration of their personal habits (cleanliness, dress, eating).

We should also bear in mind the study carried out by Follin et al.[66] in which the termination of neuroleptics for nine months in a ward was followed by an improvement in the vast majority of cases of schizophrenia, and aggravation in only two cases.

Should one come to the conclusion then, as many already have, that in the final analysis empirical methods constitute the most valid judgement criteria? Whatever the case may be, the prescription of neuroleptics in psychoses is practically universal.

CONDITIONS OF APPLICATION OF NEUROLEPTICS

Dosage

The introduction of chlorpromazine brought with it the problem of posology of neuroleptics. Is this determined by the psychiatric syndrome, which motivates the administration of drugs, or by the common characteristics of the patients regardless of their psychiatric symptomatology, their age, length of sickness or hospitalization, or again by strictly personal tolerance? The accumulation of studies on the subject has not been followed by any accumulation of certainties about it. But perhaps the problem is not presented properly here either. To take the example of chlorpromazine, the dominant pharmacological properties of this drug depend upon the dosage. Administered in very small doses, like imipramine, it increases the effects of noradrenaline. We have all had to admit that the brilliant results obtained with chlorpromazine in depressive syndromes shortly after 1953 were the expression of well-meaning illusions. But could this not be related to the doses administered at that time? In medium doses of 1–2 mg/kg, chlorpromazine develops, especially in animals, above all a sedative effect, with diminution of conditioned responses to external stimuli. Although it has not been proven, there are many arguments to support the idea that in these quantities chlorpromazine acts mainly upon the noradrenergic receptors. In higher doses, and particularly in repeated higher doses, it tends mainly to induce cataleptic states, probably connected with its antidopaminergic action. In such circumstances it would be surprising if in humans the variation of dosage were to produce only quantitative differences in the drug's action. These concepts may be clearer in the study of the relative specifity of the action and indications of the different neuroleptics.

Whatever the case may be, and in spite of the confusion which reigns in this field, the discussion of the posology of neuroleptics has become of greater interest with the observation of tardive complications—skin-eye syndrome and cardiac and neurological side-effects—which are regularly caused by the long-term administration of high doses of phenothiazines.

The most interesting and the best study, although perhaps somewhat biased in its premises for the reasons outlined above, is that carried out by Prien et al.[159-161] This study covered 800 chronic schizophrenics in a number of different hospitals; all of the patients, whose ages ranged from 19 to 55, had been hospitalized for more than two years (up to 34 years), and all had received neuroleptics previously. The chlorpromazine doses selected were, respectively, 2000 and 300 mg per day, and those of trifluoperazine 80 and 15 mg per day. According to the table of equivalences generally used by American authors, this means that if the dose of chlorpromazine = 1, then trifluoperazine (Stelazine) = 1/25, fluphenazine = 1/100, thioridazine = 1, and perphenazine (Trilafon) = 1/12. No significant difference was observed in these patients as a whole, apart from a deterioration in those receiving placebo. There is, however, one group of patients to whom high doses of chlorpromazine were clearly beneficial: those under 40 years of age, hospitalized for less than 15 years, and who had previously received chlorpromazine in lower doses. With trifluoperazine, patients older than 40 years being excluded from this experiment, high doses were useful for patients hospitalized for less than 15 years and who had previously received piperazine phenothiazines in lower doses.

Side effects are all far more numerous and more severe in patients over 40, and appear to be responsible for the failure of high doses of chlorpromazine in this group. Compared with younger patients, unsatisfactory results from the psychiatric point of view, when drugs were continued, are of much the same order—11 as opposed to 7 percent. In patients over 40 failures related to intolerance of high doses were as high as 40 percent, compared with 16 percent in younger subjects. This sensitivity which appears in the 5th decade can have, among others, two types of explanations. According to Heyck,[100] in equal doses, phenothiazines do not perturb the cerebral energic metabolism of patients under 50 years of age, whereas from 50 up there is a reduction of the cerebral vascular flow of 38.0 ± 3.3 cc/min/100 g, of O_2 consumption of 1.73 ± 0.33; glucose: 2.85 ± 0.51 mg/min/100g, together with increased cerebral vascular resistance: 3.3 mm/Hg. The technique used is a reliable one (n-20, Kety and Schmidt[116a]) but the determinations are made only after neuroleptics. According to Gottfries et al.[85] the level of HVA (homovanillic acid) in the human brain diminishes with age and, in particular, with senility. This lowering of the main metabolite of dopamine would derive from a diminution of the catecholamine metabolism and may explain the ease with which these patients present Parkinson-type extrapyramidal syndromes under phenothiazine.

There still remains the curious fact of the specificity of

the responses, that is, the patients who benefit from high dosages of each of the two drugs are those who had previously received them in smaller quantities. The authors advance the following hypothesis: for these patients, who had been receiving treatment for a considerable length of time, the drug best suited to them had been found empirically; it had been administered in sufficiently high dosages to produce a certain degree of improvement in the symptomatology, but not the optimum degree.

They conclude as follows: from the age of 40 on high-dosage phenothiazines are more dangerous than useful. All treatments must be initially administered in low or medium dosages. In the event of a distinct but insufficient improvement, no change of drug should be made before higher dosages of the same drug have been tried. However, there remain to be weighed the respective risks of less than satisfactory psychiatric results and phenothiazine-induced complications.

Continuous or Intermittent Prescription

Whether it is the total dosage or the continuity of administration of phenothiazines which plays the major role in determining the complications to which they lead, it would be preferable to use intermittent prescriptions. The answer to this question will depend upon the risk of relapse in the event of withdrawal of the drug. Opinion is divided on this point also. However, there are very few authors who agree with Goldman[84] that termination of neuroleptics is followed by relapses within the following month. As Greenberg[87] reminds us, such precocious relapses could be linked to the withdrawal itself, which, if carried out abruptly, frequently leads to a rather perturbing kind of rebound. Greenberg collected and compared studies, shown in Table 3.7, and finds that relapses generally appear between the 8th and 12th week. It is by no means easy to explain the reason for this particular lapse of time. A number of disputed facts seem to indicate a progressive accumulation of phenothiazines, at a rate varying greatly from one subject to another. We ourselves would be inclined to think that since neuroleptics do not constitute a specific therapy of psychoses (they often require a considerable length of time before permitting any reorganization of behavior if environmental circumstances are favorable), such a reorganization can continue for a more or less prolonged length of time after termination of drug treatment. In this hypothesis it is easier to understand the fact that in outpatient practice we usually find the cycle so well summarized by Wing:[196] increase in family tension or that of the receiving milieu; a period of severe distress culminating in a "social crisis" (police intervention, etc.); followed by rehospitalization.

Independently of their interpretation, the above facts should indicate the necessity for different attitudes according to each individual case. In the hospital setting, including outpatient services, it would be highly desirable to interrupt neuroleptics more frequently for a short length of time, although the optimum duration of the break has yet to be determined. In outpatient treatment, this should only be undertaken with patients who can be kept under regular attention. This practice may have the advantage of giving increased responsibility to nonhospital teams and constituting a remedy to Wing's observation[196] that virtually all patients consult a doctor or a social service during the periods between hospital stays, but truly effective preventative measures are taken very rarely indeed.

RELATIVE SPECIFICITY OF ACTION OF NEUROLEPTICS

Classic Neuroleptics

Although there are very few works assembling large-scale series of studies of patients observed and treated over long periods, there seems to be a relative consensus in the French school concerning the specificity of action of neuroleptics.

The aliphatic phenothiazines (chlorpromazine, levopromazine) and the piperidine phenothiazines (thioridazine) develop primarily a sedative action, accompanied by somnolence, indifference to internal and external stimuli, and affective indifference and even passivity. As such, they are indicated for acute psychotic crises with agitation rather than in forms evolving over the long term, and in productive rather than deficient forms.

While the piperazine phenothiazines and the butyrophenones, still known as major neuroleptics, have equal or even greater action upon productive symptoms, they appear to act far more effectively on deficiency symptoms. This latter action usually seems to become apparent only after fairly long drug treatment. Hence, the major neuroleptics appear to be the drugs par excellence for the long-term psychoses, whether they are deficient from the start, or have become so during their intrinsic evolution, or under the influence of long hospitalization, or under the effect of minor neuroleptics. Some go so far as to suggest that only the major neuroleptics are worthy of consideration as antipsychotic drugs, all the others being no more than powerful sedatives. This attitude seems to us to be based on a conceptualization of the notion of psychosis which, all things considered, comes pretty close to Bleulerian metaphysics. According to this author, after all, autism is both the deficiency core of psychosis and its "essence." From this angle, it is perfectly natural to consider that the major neuroleptics are the "essential" antipsychotic drugs.

At first sight there seems to reign the greatest confusion in the English and American literature.[120] There are probably as many articles detailing the differences between the aliphatic and piperazine phenothiazines as there are to deny their specificity altogether. A craze for fluphenazine

(Goldman[84]) has been followed by the development of a definite reaction in favor of the rehabilitation of chlorpromazine, first of all partially (Goldberg[81–83]), and then completely (Galbrecht,[78] Hollister[106]). Thus, Goldberg[82] considers that chlorpromazine acts primarily upon the schizophrenic core. In fact, if one reads between the lines and makes a slight departure from the base line of regression, it seems to us that a number of these works describe the facts of the matter very closely. Of the sedative phenothiazines, thioridazine is the one most often used by American authors, who claim that it helps patients in states of agitation or logomania, possibly suffering from an impression of unreality, but without a schizophrenic core or paranoid element.

Chlorpromazine is beneficial to patients who hear voices, present a persecution syndrome, whether they are agitated, slowed down, indifferent, or hardly participate at all in social activities, are no longer able to see to their own personal needs, or have feelings of unreality. They must not, however, show feelings of uselessness nor marked incoherence. Hallucinations must be predominantly auditory. It is easy enough to recognize here the paranoid forms with a greater or lesser degree of autism described by German authors, and the systematized delusions and paranoid schizophrenia of the French classification.

Fluphenazine has demonstrated its usefulness in patients whose dominant characteristic is indifference, feelings of uselessness or of unreality, who refuse participation in social activities or who no longer attend to their personal needs. These are the hebephrenics.

Finally, Cawley,[31] who doubts the possibility of establishing the slightest objective difference between one neuroleptic and another, nonetheless quotes the results of an opinion poll among 80 psychiatrists. In syndromes dominated by apathy and inertia, the great majority selected a

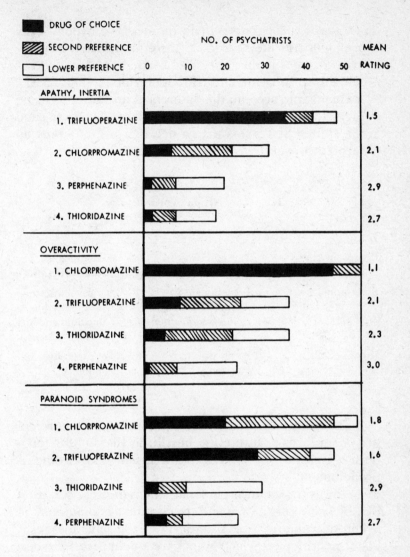

Fig. 3.8. Use of phenothiazines by 80 English psychiatrists according to the symptomatology of schizophrenics

Source: Cawley, R. H. (1967), *Recent Developments in Schizophrenia,* Royal Medico-Psychological Association, Coppen A. Walk.

piperazine neuroleptic; in syndromes where hyperactivity is predominant, they chose chlorpromazine; and in paranoid syndromes their choice was fairly evenly divided between chlorpromazine and trifluoperazine (see Fig. 3.8).

Taking into account the differences in chlorpromazine dosages (2000 mg representing a dosage frequently used in the United States less than a decade ago), opinions on the whole converge, as summarized in Table 3.8.

Table 3.8. Action of neuroleptics

	Europe	United States
Levopromazine Thioridazine	Predominant sedative action	Predominant sedative action
Chlorpromazine	Predominant sedative action (low and medium dosages)	Antipsychotic and sedative action (medium and high dosages)
Major neuroleptics	Antipsychotic action	Antipsychotic action

This consensus demonstates that the major neuroleptics do in fact constitute the best drug therapy for long-term psychoses in which the deficiency syndrome is predominant.

However, our own personal experience concurs with that of Laboucarié[124,125] and the Scandinavian authors.[166] When athymhormia persists despite sufficient dosage by major neuroleptics, electroshock treatment is still the best way to break the vicious circle, however ignorant we may be of how it acts. During electroshock cure the patient is already intensively mobilized, and this mobilization will continue after the return to major neuroleptics.

Drug Combinations

It remains to be asked whether it is wise to resort to drug combinations. Both opinions have their advocates (Hollister,[106] Kurland[123]).

In France, the combination of major and sedative neuroleptics, thioproperazine and levomepromazine,[128] for example, is quite common. Our long use of this combination leads us to feel that the data of Freeman's survey[74] are accurate: the long-term results are no better than those obtained by the major neuroleptic alone. But, as Colmart[35] has already pointed out, the cure is easier and there are far fewer side effects.

On the other hand, the combination of minor tranquillizers with major neuroleptics, whether these are incisive or sedative, seems to us, as it does to Kurland,[123] to have more disadvantages than advantages. In particular, and with more than negligible frequency, it produces confusional syndromes.

For a long time, antidepressants were thought to make the psychotic syndrome and delusions in particular, flare up. This opinion seems exaggerated, to say the least.[54,119] Some recommend combination with imipramine, in spite of the use of major neuroleptics, in cases of persistent athymhormia. According to Kurland[123] and Freeman,[74] amitriptyline is the best antidepressant in combination with major neuroleptics. One might well wonder, however, if the contributive factors here may not be the sedative properties of amitriptyline rather than its antidepressant action.

The fact remains that we do not know how two combined products are absorbed, and how they act upon each other in their metabolism. Thus, since we have been able to control the chlorpromazine plasma level by methods sensitive to the nonogramme, Curry et al.[41] have shown that a phenobarbital combination lowers it by half. It is not impossible that the decrease in the neurodysleptic effects of major neuroleptics brought about by minor neuroleptics might bear the same explanation.

Delayed-Action Neuroleptics

The therapeutic efficacy of fluphenazine derivatives or Rp 550 (pipotiazine) no longer needs any demonstration. For obvious reasons, their use in long-term psychoses is particularly effective, and the more so since (for the time being at least) these are major neuroleptics.[129,139] Nonetheless, some reservations must be expressed. In our experience the majority of patients (approximately two out of three) present "acute akineto-hypertonic dyskinetic extrapyramidal syndromes" so intense that it is absolutely necessary to administer daily doses of anticholinergic drugs. In outpatient treatment, when the patient rightly or wrongly attributes part of his symptomatology to drugs, he can only take action by refusing to take his anti-Parkinson correctors, which can lead to serious accidents. In our own small-scale series we have observed two cases of malignant syndromes, of which one was fatal. We are prepared to admit the possibility that these dangerous complications may partly be the result of our own lack of experience, that they may not have been inevitable, and that in the future it will be possible to avoid them entirely. Although relatively frequent when major neuroleptics (majeptil, haloperidol) were first introduced, these complications are rarely observed today. It is nonetheless essential to be aware of the threat to patients, for whom termination of the therapy can only be carried out gradually over a long period of time.

Under delayed-action neuroleptics some patients very quickly present the "persistent tardive dyskinesia" syndrome. It is too soon to be able to state whether these dyskinesias are really persistent or not, but it is unfortunately highly likely. In one case, where they had practically disappeared six months after termination of the therapy, they began again, with greater intensity, after a few days of thioridazine. And yet this was a young patient, who had received only very little classic neuroleptic treatment previously.

Finally, Rp 550 (pipotiazine) derivatives, which are highly active in athymhormia, and which can even produce minor syndromes of agitation with euphoria, in some cases, as Lempérière[131] has already pointed out, seem to intensify the delusional component of the syndrome.

Some Aspects of Neuroleptic Action Mechanisms

Uptake and Topical Distribution in the CNS

Phenothiazines easily pass through the blood-brain barrier and traces can be found in the CNS (by autoradiography in particular) five minutes after injection and for several hours, even several days, afterwards.[30] There is some difference of opinion as to their distribution. Some[191] consider that phenothiazines are distributed almost homogeneously throughout the grey matter, while the majority, holds that their concentration varies considerably with brain structure.[94,111,190] However, cartographies coincide only partially. This can possibly be explained by the very different kinetics of metabolism of phenothiozines in the different areas. It seems certain that 5 minutes after the injection the sites with highest uptakes are:

1. the nuclei of brain stem and bulb (locus niger);
2. the corpora quadrigemina;
3. the thalamus;
4. the corpus mamillare; and
5. the neocortex.

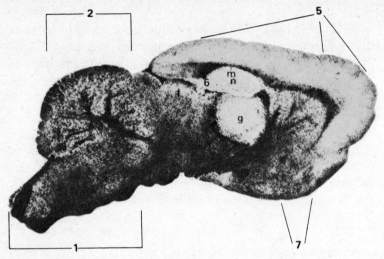

Fig. 3.9. Rat brain, sagittal cross-section. Enlarged three times. Autoradiogram, 1 hour after intravenous injection of thioridazine-^{14}C

1: Rhombencephalon; 2: cerebellum, c:cortical area, d: nuclei; 3: mesencephalon; e: posterior corpora quadrigemina, f: anterior corpora quadrigemina; diencephalon; G: thalamus, k: globus pallidus; 5: neocortex; 6: Hippocampus; m: molecular stratum of the horn of Ammon and the dentate gyrus; n: dentate gyrus; 7: Paleocortex; 8: white matter.
Source: Eckert, H. & Hopf, A. (1970), *Int. Pharmacopsychiat.,* 4:98-116.

The hypothalamus and the horns of Ammon show practically no traces at all. After some time, radioactivity in some of the above sites decreases, but it appears or increases in the horns of Ammon, the neocortex, and the thalamus, particularly in the frontal area.[58] Radioactivity in the extrapyramidal structures remains average (see Fig. 3.9). Contradictions appear, particularly as far as the hypothalamus is concerned. Although Wase et al.[190] (who admittedly give injections over a four-day period) and Guth[94] find a strong concentration in the hypothalamus, other authors are struck by its vacuity after 24 hours. Guth[94] is the only author to report different localizations according to the type of neuroleptic injected. A piperazine-phenothiazine combination is distinguishable from chlorpromazine by its greater accumulation at the level of the paleocerebellum. Whatever the case may be, it seems difficult to find any correlation between these preferential localizations and the neuropharmacological actions of phenothiazines. At most one might be tempted to see in the modification of their gradient in relation to time from the stem toward the telencephalon a link first of all more marked with the cell bodies of the catecholamine neurons and secondly with their presynaptic endings.

Metabolism and Biochemical Action Mechanism

The metabolism of the phenothiazine drugs is far less well known than might be expected. Neither does it appear to provide the explanation of their pharmacological action. For, as Pletscher et al.[154] point out, among neuroleptics and tranquilizers there is as much similarity of metabolism as there is difference within each class. The very tardive and individual urinary elimination of chlorpromazine and its metabolites after prolonged treatment, observed by some authors,[68] might explain the mildness of withdrawal reactions and the long delay before relapse.[69]

In doses higher than those necessary for their effective pharmacological action, phenothiazines in vitro and in vivo interfere with the cellular energy metabolism.[200] This property very probably has nothing to do with their specific action.[165] It is pointed out, however, by Christensen et al.,[34] as an explanation of the definitive cell lesions which would account for the syndrome of "persistent tardive dyskenesias."

From the in-vitro biochemical standpoint, what differentiates neuroleptics from the minor tranquilizers is their effect on the transport of monoamines by the membranes. After administration of neuroleptics the penetra-

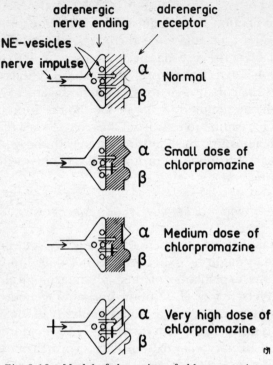

Fig. 3.10. Model of the action of chlorpromazine on
peripheral adrenergic nerve endings

Source: Pletscher, A. (1967), in *Neuropsychopharmacology*, Excerpta Medica
Foundation.

tion of monoamines into the cells slows down. In vivo,
neuroleptics increase the concentration of the catecholamines and particularly that of their metabolites at the level
of the structures which retain them.[154] Anden et al.[4a] observe after haloperidol as well as after chlorpromazine, increased pericaryonal fluorescence in neurons rich in
noradrenaline and dopamine. After inhibitors of catecholamine synthesis, renewal of the presynaptic reserves of
dopamine and noradrenaline is slowed down. Under the
influence of these drugs, the same phenomenon is ob-

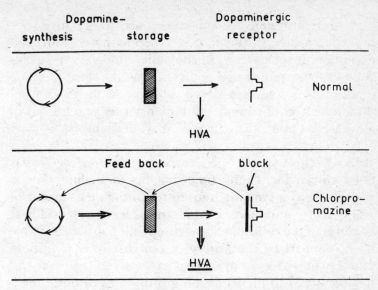

Fig. 3.11. Tentative scheme on the mechanism of action of chlorpromazine on the cerebral dopamine metabolism

Source: Pletscher, A. (1967), in *Neuropsychopharmacology,* Excerpta Medica Foundation.

served after inhibition of dopa-β-hydroxylase, but only at the level of the noradrenaline synapses. The most likely explanation of these phenomena, which are corroborated by pharmacology, is that chlorpromazine and haloperidol block the catecholaminergic receptors (see Fig. 3.10[154a]). A compensatory teleonomic mechanism probably intensifies catecholamine synthesis by means of a positive feedback system whose precise nature is not known[154a] (see Fig. 3.11).

Some Parameters of Behavior and Neurophysiological Action

PERIPHERAL MECHANISMS.   To the extent that they block the peripheral catecholamine receptors, neuroleptics produce a great number of well-known neurovegetative phenomena, which we shall not describe here, with one exception. It seems that catecholamines increase the excitability of the sensory receptors.[4] It is therefore possible that neuroleptics might already at this peripheral level reduce the effect of stimuli upon the nervous system. It is in any case no more than an accessory mechanism.

CENTRAL MECHANISMS.   1. *Lowering of Alertness Level.* It has been known for a long time that noradrenaline plays a major role as a synaptic transmitter in the mechanisms of maintenance and increase of alertness levels, especially at the level of the reticulated mesencephalic substance.[185] We have summarized the history of this discovery elsewhere and the controversies to which it gave rise.[185] If anyone still has doubts as to the stimulating properties of noradrenaline, the latest work done by the Scandinavian school[36]

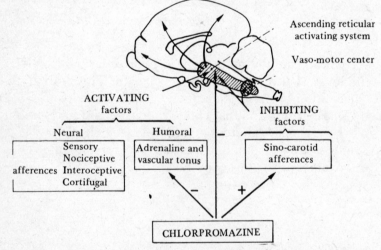

Fig. 3.12. Schematic representation of chlorpromazine action on the ascending reticular system

Source: Hiebel, G. (1954), *Sem. Hop.,* 30:1–7.

should dispel them entirely. After inhibition of dopa-β-hydroxylase, the enzyme of the final stage of noradrenaline synthesis, both L-Dopa and the MAO inhibitors lose their ability to stimulate activity in animals.

The sedative effect of neuroleptics can therefore be attributed either wholly or in part to their ability to block the noradrenergic receptors (see Fig. 3.12[100b]). But their action on the Moruzzi and Magoun arousal system is complicated. They raise only very slightly the threshold of the arousal response produced by electrical stimulation of the reticulated mesencephalic substance, while on the other

Key:

  • • Controls

  ▲ Chlorpromazine

  + LSD

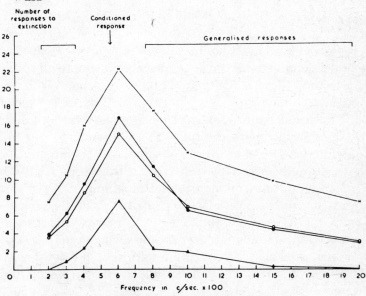

Fig. 3.13.   Effects of chlorpromazine and LSD on extinction and generalization of a negative-reinforced conditioned response

hand they raise considerably the thresholds of response to sensory stimuli.[100a] Bradley and Key[17,18] find that neuroleptics inhibit the effects of the collaterals of the specific afferents upon the reticular system. In contrast to LSD, which increases this effect, prevents habituation of arousal responses to repeated sensory stimuli, and increases the generalization of conditioned responses, neuroleptics facilitate habituation of arousal reactions to repeated sensory stimuli, and decrease generalization of conditioned responses[117,118] (see Fig. 3.13). We concur with Bovet[186] in finding that habituation of the rhythm response to extinction is facilitated by chlorpromazine and haloperidol in human beings. Now it is known that the slowing down of habituation phenomena, whether the alpha response to extinction[112] or multiple neurovegetative responses, is one of the only constant neurophysiological factors observed in psychoses of the schizophrenic type.[175] This loss of habituation capacity bears a curious resemblance to the Pavlovian external inhibition phenomenon.[113] As the LSD model demonstrates, giving equal significance to all stimuli leads to a type of desafferentation by overarousal with concomitant loss of the capacity for sensory selection, which is the main mechanism for selection and processing of information according to the subject's requirements. It is precisely this loss of the capacity for habituation in schizophrenics which seems to reduce their ability to distinguish significant from nonsignificant stimuli.[116] This interpretation of the facts makes it possible to understand the advantage of neuroleptics to the psychotic. By restoring his capacity for habituation they should enable him to recover an increased ability to integrate information from the outside world, and perhaps even information from his own inner world.[184] However, if the sedative effect of the neuroleptic is overdone, it reduces all the reaction thresholds of the subject to that of the habituated nonsignificant signals, and again, produces a kind of desafferentation. Seen in this light, it is easier to understand the relationship between the clinical pictures produced by classic sensory deprivation, by the administration of hallucinogenic substances such as LSD, and by the paradoxical effects of neuroleptics emphasized by Lambert,[128] particularly with overdoses of sedative neuroleptics.

2. *Alteration of conditioned responses.* The deconditioning activity of neuroleptics was one of the first pharmacological parameters ever discovered.[37] Since then all effective neuroleptics have shown this property to a greater or lesser degree.[99] It is generally agreed that the more effective they are, the stronger their deconditioning activity. They affect passive conditioning just as much as "operative conditioning," positive reinforcement just as much as negative reinforcement conditioned responses. This direct impact on motivation differentiates them even from the minor tranquilizers which seem to affect only avoidance responses by reducing the emotional impact of negative reinforcements, thus enabling animals better to stand up to punishment to satisfy their needs (pressing the lever which gives them access to food pellets, even if they receive a painful shock at the same time by doing so[140,182]).

Conditioned responses are extremely complex behaviors involving the interplay of all the brain structures. However, it is known that the diffuse projection systems play an important part here, as do[145,176] the habituation phenomena. From here we come back to the problem of the control of alertness and the role played in this by noradrenaline. Nevertheless, since the work of Olds[147c] we know of the so-called "positive and negative motivation structures" running from the mesencephalon to the limbic system via the hypothalamus, and whose stimulation can replace positive and negative reinforcements in the establishment of conditioned reflexes. This problem is very well reviewed by Cardo.[29] The self-stimulation in animals, when a lever enables them to turn off the current of electrodes implanted

Key:

—— Controls

- - - - Animals under treatment

Source: Olds. J. (1959), in: *Neuropsychopharmacology,* Elsevier, pp. 20–34.

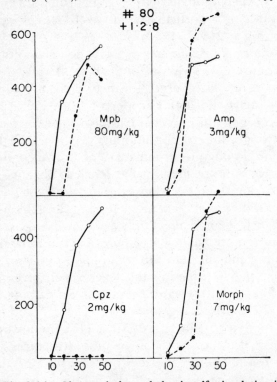

Fig. 3.14. Changes in hypothalamic self-stimulation in the
rat under the effects of various drugs,
including chlorpromazine

in their positive motivation structures, is amazing. It is generally preferred to any other kind of satisfaction, carried even to the point of death through starvation. It is well established that all the neuroleptics eliminate or heavily reduce self-stimulation (see Fig. 3.14).

Histochemical, biochemical, and neurophysiological

arguments seem to attribute an important role in these structures to the noradrenergic and serotoninergic mesencephalo-limbic pathways. Many authors, and Stein in particular,[182] consider that in the selection of behavior through positive reinforcement a predominant role is played by the noradrenergic pathway, which runs from the A-10 interpeduncular cell group to the rhinencephalus, via the central fasciculus of the telencephalon. This gives us a point of impact for neuroleptics which block the noradrenaline receptors, and at the same time provides a plausible explanation of passivity syndromes with exaggerated listlessness provoked by sedative neuroleptics. But major neuroleptics, which have little or no effect upon the noradrenaline receptors, but do block the dopamine receptors, have a deconditioning power at least equal to, if not greater than, that of sedative neuroleptics. For the time being this problem remains unsolved. It can nevertheless be noted that there also exists a dopaminergic mesencephalolimbic pathway whose exact function is not known[101] (see Fig. 3.15) Furthermore, while the dopaminergic nigrostriatal system is essentially involved in extrapyramidal motor control, the neostratum, in conjunction with the prefrontal lobe, plays an extremely important part in the acquisition of conditioned reflexes, and particularly in the inhibition of erroneous responses. There is a striking analogy between the behavior of animals with prefrontal lobe damage or lesions of the caudate nuclei and animals treated with neuroleptics. In both conditions they are known to lose the ability to acquire conditioned reflexes. However, in both cases such acquisition remains possible provided that the animal does not have to proceed by a method of trial and error.[169,183] The clinician here evokes a further connotation: the action of neuroleptics has often been characterized as a chemical frontal lobotomy.

3. *Central neurovegetative controls.* We shall deal very

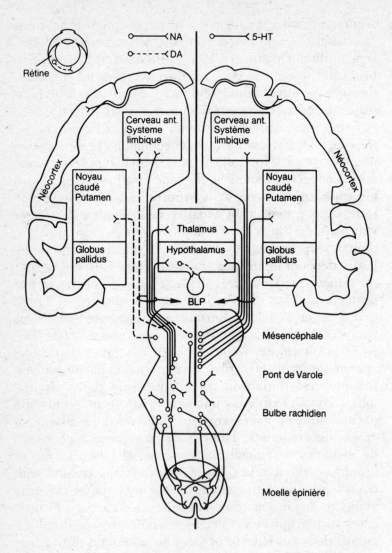

Fig. 3.15. Schematic hodology of main monoamine neuron systems in the central nervous system

Source: Amden, N. E. et al. (1966), *Acta Physiol. Scand.,* 67:255.

briefly with the subject of hypothalamo-hypophysial catecholaminergic regulation. Let it suffice to say that dopamine is here represented by a very isolated system whose
pericaryons lie in the nucleus arcuatus and terminals in the
median eminence. Its activity seems to increase particularly
the secretion of gonadotropic hormones and prolactin.
This system itself seems to be inhibited by terminations of
ascending noradrenergic fibres of bulbar origin. The latter
still appear to participate in the regulation of adrenocor-
ticotropic hormone secretion, osmotic pressure, and tem-
perature.[75,80] These initial indications therefore seem to
provide a valid substrate for galactorrhea, genital hormone
deficit, and difficulties of thermic regulation which can be
caused by neuroleptics.

4. *Blocking of dopamine receptors.* There remains to be
considered the question of the neurophysiological interpretations of the blocking of dopamine receptors which
characterizes major neuroleptics. Our knowledge here is
very limited indeed, apart from the role played by dopamine in the regulation of extrapyramidal motivity, and even
in this field there still remain a number of unknown factors.
Although it is certain that the dopaminergic nigrostriatal
pathway inhibits the action of the cholinergic striofugal
pathways, it is not yet known whether this leads to a hype-
rexcitability of both the static and the dynamic components
of the gamma system or even to a change in the excitability
of the alpha motor neurons.[155] Our knowledge is virtually
confined to the pharmacological side of the matter. Major
neuroleptics have a powerful antiapomorphine action, and
apomorphine is the most specific stimulant of the dopaminergic receptors. As you all know, there is a clear correlation
between antiapomorphine action and the production of
catalepsy in animals and extrapyramidal syndromes in humans.

CONCLUSION.   Contrary to the study of action mechanisms of antidepressants for manic and depressive syn-

dromes, however satisfactory studies on the modes of action of neuroleptics may be from the pharmacological point of view, they have offered very little concerning the physiopathological mechanisms of psychoses. They give clear grounds for supposing that neuroleptics are no more than symptomatic drugs which do not interfere with the fundamental mechanisms responsible for psychotic disorders, and they completely justify the attempt at classification carried out by Lambert et al.[126] The correlation between the minor/major neuroleptic bipole and the antinoradrenaline/antidopamine pharmacological bipole is quite obvious and provides the best possible synthesis for the present, with all due respect to those clinicians who consider it "erroneous in its basic postulates."[50]

Remarks on Metapharmacology

In the interpretation of the action of neuroleptics we find the same kind of thinking as in the case of convulsive therapy in depressive and manic syndromes. According to a long-standing principle of medical Manichaeanism, the positive effect of a drug is due to the development within the organism of a principle antithetic to the essence of the disorder. Convulsions are antithetical to depression. Extrapyramidal syndromes are the antithesis of dissociation-predominant psychosis. Seen from this point of view, the side effect—in this case the extrapyramidal reaction—is not merely inseparable from, but is a sine qua non of the therapeutic action.[181] When it is possible to correct secondary effects without impairing the effectiveness of the drug, the secondary effects themselves become the mediator in the therapeutic doctor-patient relationship.[201] The doctor cannot alleviate matters without first causing suffering, without initially doing harm. Even Deniker[56] writes that: extrapyramidal reactions can be "privileged experiences susceptible to psychotherapeutic elaboration." In our opinion they constitute a particularly trying experience which the patient should be spared whenever possible. I suggest that all metapharmacologists should give themselves a good dose of major neuroleptics; just let them go as far as akathisia, let alone the major oculocephalogyric crisis, and then let us talk about their "positive experience." Is it not strange that psychiatrists have to go into this kind of metaphysical consideration in order to justify some simple observations, namely, that no drug therapy is without its disadvantages, that drug treatment is only one single element, of greater or lesser importance according to the individual case.

COMPLICATIONS OF PROLONGED DRUG TREATMENT OF PSYCHOSES

There are several different types of complications, although the majority of them are fortunately rare.[8,107]

Malignant Neuroleptics Syndrome (Hypertonicity, Hyperthermia, Hypercrinia)

We shall not dwell upon this subject, for there is nothing to add to the description done by Vedrine et al.[189] and to the best of our knowledge its physiopathology is no better known now than it ever was.[7] It should be borne in mind, however, that this represents a real danger to patients receiving delayed-action neuroleptics and anticholinergic correctors, which are the only ones which can be withdrawn.

The Sudden Death Syndrome

Here the patient is found dead in his bed in the morning or dies suddenly in front of the attendants or the doctor, and reanimation is absolutely impossible. In a very few cases[130,164] the cause of death is brought to light by autopsy. It can be (a) pulmonary embolism arising from a venous thrombosis, a relatively frequent complication in deep-sleep cures. Locally, the thrombosis—most often of the distal veins in the lower limbs—was asymptomatic. Pulse acceleration and slight hyperthermia were so common in cures carried out with high dosages of chlorpromazine that they drew no attention at all; (b) asphyxia by aspiration, either secondary to difficulties of deglutition together with a lowering of alertness levels, or arising during the abatement phase of an epileptic seizure; (c) major myocardial infarctions whose cause-effect relationship to the neuroleptic cure is still a matter of conjecture; and (d) in the case of alcoholics, myocardial necrosis of the alcoholic cardiomyopathic type, whose development could be precipitated by phenothiazines.

It frequently happens, however, that no apparent cause of death is revealed by autopsy. The status, like the clinical history, is that of an irreversible collapse. These are usually subjects who have received high doses of phenothiazine over a long period of time. Richardson[163] points out that before the introduction of neuroleptics there were only two sudden deaths unexplained by autopsy over a period of 10 years in a 2000-bed hospital. Between 1957 and 1966, out of 87 patients who died while under phenothiazine, 21 died suddenly and with no apparent cause of death revealed by postmortem examination. Heart cross-sections done with the usual techniques showed no visible infarction, but after treatment with PAS (p-amino salicylic acid) or some other special colorants, there appeared tiny but numerous areas of myofibrillary degeneration in the subendothelial part of the cardiac muscle, particularly at the level of the papillary muscles and the bundle of his. The corresponding vessels presented no atheroma or classic sclerosis, but there was damage in the small arteries and the capillaries, which were thickened. Their walls contained and were surrounded by deposits of PAS-positive mucopolysaccharides. These lesions have been extremely difficult to reproduce in animals, and appeared in only one of several dogs given prolonged phenothiazine treatment. This one had reacted in a paradoxical manner and remained agitated. Phenothiazine plus stress can produce these lesions in rats, and they are obtained with greater regularity when the animals are protected against fatal injections of adrenaline and noradrenaline by chlorpromazine. The mechanism which causes this seems to be the blocking of the alpha-adrenergic receptors by phenothiazines, which cause inversion of catecholamine action.

Whatever the case may be, it is known that phenothiazines do cause ECG disturbances. These consist of the alteration of the repolarization phase, and are so frequent (50 percent of cases) that there seems no reason to attribute any prognostic value to them.[3,105,163] One must watch, however, for nonsinus rhythm disturbances (auricular and ventricular tachycardia), coupled rhythm, lengthening of the QRS complex and, of course, more serious conduction disorders, from bundle-branch block to complete auriculo-ventricular dissociation.

Skin-Eye Syndromes

The skin, the exoskeleton, and the eye all fix a large amount of phenothiazine.[67,94]

Pigmentary change in the fundus oculi (pigmentary retinitis) seems to be virtually exclusive to thioridazine, and this occurs only with doses equal to or exceeding 1000 mg per day, in any case, never with doses below 600 mg.[177] The first signs are subjective ones. Patients first of all complain of not seeing colors properly, and that colors look brownish and dirty; next comes the concentric reduction of the field of vision and impaired dark adaptation. At this stage a retinography would already show functional alterations.

Pigmentation of the fundus is tardive in relation to these functional alterations. If it is not very marked, it is reversible, but in most cases it is permanent.

Some authors attribute the other changes to chlorpromazine alone,[71,88] but they can probably be observed following all the phenothiazines,[6] and take a variety of forms. On the skin there appear depigmentations, especially a blue-grey hyperpigmentation, and less atypical hyperpigmentations on the uncovered parts of the body. In the eyeball the conjunctiva is sometimes pigmented opposite the palpebral cleft, but the most frequent change is the presence of axial opacity in the anterior layers of the crystalline lens and the posterior layers of the cornea.[51] Most authors are of the opinion that these are pigmentary deposits, but Rubin et al.[171] consider that they are polysaccharides. The skin-eye syndrome in general, and more particularly lens and corneal opacities, depend first and foremost on the total dose of chlorpromazine received without interruption. Buffaloe[27] gives the following statistics with 20 patients with lenticular and corneal opacities paired off with 20 patients of the same age, also treated with chlorpromazine but not affected in this respect:

Doses of chlorpromazine	Patients with opacity	Patients without opacity
1000–2400 g	9	1
300–999 g	9	9
0–299 g	2	10

$$p < 0.005$$

Theoretically, these opacities disappear after termination of the therapy. This underlines the desirability of discontinued cures wherever possible. Lenticular and corneal deposits only very rarely lead to impairment of sight. It is difficult to estimate their frequency because of the fact that in their initial stages they are easily confused with axial punctate opacities which are probably present in 6 to 7 percent of normal subjects below 40 years of age and in 11 percent of older subjects.[52] Although different authors give different estimates, they would seem to be present in between 10 and 20 percent of patients given prolonged chlorpromazine treatment.[51] According to Rubin,[171] chlorpromazine or one of its metabolites binds with melanine in the skin and the eye membranes, thus producing a compound which is no longer capable of inhibiting the retroactive regulatory mechanisms of pigment synthesis. In the cornea and the lens an analogous phenomenon of liaison is produced with polysaccharides. This hypothesis, which is supported by a number of facts, is an interesting one, for it would be of very general value. By perturbing the functions of tyrosine derivatives, chlorpromazine would appear to increase their synthesis by a mechanism of positive feedback.

According to Nicolson[147] and Greiner,[88] with the use of chelating agents such as penicillamine it is possible to avoid or reverse the skin-eye syndrome while at the same time having a beneficial effect upon the subjects' psychiatric symptomatology. These results, which were put forward as confirmation of the hypothesis of a primary disorder of the metabolism of tyrosine and its derivatives in schizophrenia, have not been confirmed.[1,15]

Persistent Neurological Syndromes

A distinction should be made between these tardive syndromes and the precocious syndromes described for the akineto-hypertonic syndrome akin to the Parkinsonian and hypertono-akatistic syndromes and the major neurodysleptic crises which bring to mind both the symptomatology of lethargic encephalitis and Charcot's major crises.[47–49] All of these precocious forms arising with a greater or lesser degree of rapidity during the course of treatment with major neuroleptics are sensitive to anticholinergics but do not respond to L-Dopa.[162]

In contrast, "persistent tardive dyskinesias" have the three following characteristics:[203]

1. They usually occur after lengthy drug therapy and are often only discovered when neuroleptic drug dosages are reduced or treatment terminated altogether. They do seem to appear only in the case of slightly hypertonic, normal, or hypotonic basic tonicity.

2. They have a very particular semiology with all the persistent abnormal movements described by G. Levy after the lethargic encephalitis epidermic under the name "excito-motor syndrome."

3. They are permanent or else regress only very slowly and reappear as soon as neuroleptics are administered.

SEMIOLOGY.   The main feature of persistent neurological syndromes is that they have the same characteristics as stereotyped movements. When they are not very marked, they can be misleading and can easily be mistaken for motor habits, such as finger-tapping, rubbing the thigh with the palm of the hand, alternate rotating movements with the inside and outside of the ball of the foot with the heel against the floor, rocking backwards and forwards on a chair, and so on. With a greater degree of intensity they become real stereotypes akin to those observed in degenerative, senile, or presenile dementia, and particularly in Pick's disease. Facial movements include a chewing motion which may or may not be accompanied by alternate backward and forward or lateral movements of the tongue. They can also include jutting out or diduction movements of the lower jaw, grimacing contractions of the facial platysma or masticatory muscles, protrusion of the lips and pursing of the mouth, etc. In upper-limb movements, patients clutch and unclutch their knees or a handkerchief, or cross and uncross their arms. At lower-limb level they resemble a very strong pseudoclonus, crossing and uncrossing of the legs, pedalling movements etc. In the axis of the body they affect in particular the upper part of the trunk and the scapular girdle, e.g., shrugging of the shoulders; less frequently there are movements or rotation or extension (torticollis, retrocollis) either confined to the neck or including the waist. In their maximum degree of intensity and in normal or hypotonic muscular tonicity, they take on the appearance of choreoathetosic movements which, although disordered, only very rarely show the jerky, spasmodic characteristics of real choreic movements.

It frequently happens, and more often in the case of a hypotonic musculature, that these involuntary movements are completely anosognosic. It is usually the families who complain rather than the patients themselves. This may explain why, after having been pointed out at a very early stage by French authors,[24,178] they were relatively long in arousing any further interest. In addition to their relationship with the postencephalitic excito-motor syndrome, particular emphasis must be placed on their extreme similarity, if not their complete identity, with the involuntary movements induced by L-Dopa in cases of Parkinsonism. In all three cases there occur the rare syndromes of respiratory dyskinesias with respiratory difficulties in normal breathing (Hunter[110]), pharyngitic and oesophagal dyskinesias with feelings of constriction and stoppage of the alimentary bolus (Sigwald[178]), attacks of hiccups or sneezing and a peculiar gait, where on one side of the body each step resembles the beginning of a genuflexion, like the Denny Brown peacock gait.

CONDITIONS OF APPEARANCE.   For a long time the reassuring thought was held that persistent tardive dyskinesias appeared only in subjects with preexistent brain lesions (Meyendorf[143]). Such lesions probably facilitate the appearance of dyskinesias, but they are by no means a necessary condition for it. In a general review of observations published in 1965, Wertheimer[193] estimated that over 50 percent of the subjects considered unmistakably had brain lesions before the prescription of phenothiazines. In the review by Crane[39] this appears with certainty in only one-third of cases. Faurbye,[63] for reasons which are not altogether convincing, also holds electroshocks responsible (no other author corroborates this). Age is also a predisposing factor, although, again, by no means a necessary condition. Crane[39] gives the following figures: out of 279 usable observations published, cases can be divided according to age groups: 20–29, 7; 30–39, 18; 40–49, 29; 50–59, 90; 60–69, 92; <70; 44.

It has been stated that there is a clearly marked predominance of the syndrome in women. The fact of the matter is that several authors interested in the syndrome ran services for female patients. Crane[39] finds no significant difference between the sexes. The length of phenothiazine treatment and the doses received are two basic elements, although from the very first cases reported (Sigwald[178]) some examples of persistent dyskinesias occurring very quickly and with low dosages were observed. Under high dosage (2000 mg of chlorpromazine, 80 mg of trifluphenazine) a 43 percent rate of dyskinesia was observed after six months. Degkwitz[45,46] compares two hospitals and finds that tardive dyskinesias are far less frequent in the one where phenothiazine doses are always kept to the minimum possible. The more effective the neuroleptic, the greater the risk, given equivalent doses, of the syndrome making its appearance. In 1965 Wertheimer[193] noted that dyskinesias quite often appear with the change from a sedative phenothiazine to a major neuroleptic. This observation may simply be the equivalent of the facts noted by Faurbye,[63] namely, that dyskinesias appear with the reduction of dosages or the termination of the neuroleptics which produced them. According to Crane,[38,40] neuroleptics applied over a long time cause tardive dyskinesias with the following frequency: piperazine phenothiazine 15 percent, chlorpromazine 13 percent, and thioridazine 6 percent. All authors agree in attributing particular responsibility to perphenazine (trilafon). All in all, advanced age, preexisting brain lesions, long-term application of high-dose neuroleptics and the choice of major neuroleptics are all factors which favor the appearance of persistent tardive dyskinesias, although none of them is absolutely determinant. There is still one point to be mentioned: in our own small series, incisive delayed-action neuroleptics very frequently seem to trigger this type of dyskinesia, and do so at an early stage. It is true that the majority of our patients had already been receiving classic neuroleptics for years, but we were particularly struck by one young patient who was an exception to this rule.

PHYSIOPATHOLOGY.   Postmortem examinations are still quite rare. Until the recent series done by Christensen et al.,[34] which deals with 28 cases, publications on isolated cases did not give very specific results.[202] Observations do agree on two points, however: discrete damage to the locus niger and former cellular degeneration in the striatum, in some cases more marked in the caudate nucleus and in others in the putamen and the globus pallidus. Christensen compares 28 brains of subjects suffering from tardive dyskinesia, mostly bucco-facio-lingual, with 28 brains of patients of similar age who had also received phenothiazines but who did not have involuntary movements. The only significant differences between these two series consist of moderate degeneration of the locus niger and gliosis of the brain stem. Most authors find it difficult to attribute dyskinesias to lesions of the locus niger, and therefore relate them to brainstem lesions. These facts should be compared with the diffusion of the lesions observed in postencephalitic Parkinsonism, precisely within which Levy describes the excitomotor syndrome. Escourolle[62] finds that alongside the depigmentation of the locus niger the lesions most frequently found in the postencephalitic Parkinson lie all along the mesencephalic reticular substance. They comprise atrophy with gliosis and neuronal disappearance. We ourselves, with Gauthier,[77] have demonstrated that L-Dopa most often induces abnormal movements in patients suffering from Parkinsonian tremor. Poirier,[155] however, finds that it is not possible to induce a postural tremor in animals without adding to disturbances of the nigrostriatal pathway mesencephalic lesions involving either the rubro-olivo-cerebello-rubral loop or the ascending serotoninergic pathways. It should also be pointed out that although we do not have any postmorten dosage of cerebral catecholamines in people with this syndrome, the level of HVA in their cephalo-rachidian fluid is normal, contrary to observations of Parkinsonians, and that it has a normal accumulation reaction to probenecid.[153]

What is the mechanism by which neuroleptics induce irreversible tardive dyskinesias? Christensen[34] suggests their interference with the energy metabolism of the neurons and attempts to explain the localization he has noted of lesions by the topical distribution of phenothiazine in the CNS. All other authors evoke the ability of neuroleptics to block the dopamine receptors. It remains to be understood why this usually reversible action should cause lesions or new permanent properties of the postsynaptic membranes. No feasible hypothesis has yet been proposed in the case of neuroleptic-induced tardive dyskinesias. On the other hand, two hypotheses have been formulated regarding identical but reversible dyskinesias which have so far been induced by L-Dopa. The Scandinavians (Steg[181a]) have observed stereotypes after apomorphine and amphetamine injections in animals with undamaged caudate nuclei, and hold the view that dyskinesias induced by L-Dopa in Parkinsonians may be the result of hypersensitivity of the desafferent dopamine receptors.[65] By blocking these same receptors, neuroleptic drugs create the equivalent of a desafferentation, as is borne out by an increase in dopamine synthesis. It is not yet known whether such a modification can become permanent. Yahr[199] has partially corrected

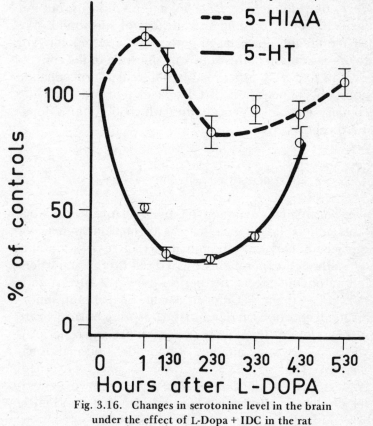

Fig. 3.16.   Changes in serotonine level in the brain under the effect of L-Dopa + IDC in the rat

Source: Bartholini, G., Da Prada, M., & Pletscher, A. (1968), *J. Pharm., Pharmacol.,* 20:228.

secondary L-Dopa dyskinesias by administering 5-HTP (5-hydroxytryptophane) before serotonin. We know that if high doses of L-Dopa penetrate the brain, the latter, in competition with decarboxylase, can reduce serotonin synthesis and, once transformed into dopamine, cause the displacement of serotonin[12] (see Fig. 3.16). It is difficult to imagine parallel mechanisms in the action of neuroleptics. Indeed, they do increase catecholamine synthesis, but not sufficiently for it to compete with that of serotonine. We shall indubitably have taken a tremendous step forward with the resolution of this annoying question of the convergence of action of processes as different as encephalitic lesions, the penetration of L-Dopa in the brain and the secondary effects of neuroleptics which block the dopamine receptors.

NEUROLEPTICS AND PREGNANCY

Unless we are mistaken, there has been relatively little work on this subject. It is known that chlorpromazine penetrates the placental barrier.[72] In animals, as Favre-Tissot points out,[64] although experiments carried out do not show definite teratogenic effects, neither do they give any grounds for excluding them.[170] Chlorpromazine provokes an abnormal rate of abortions in rats and the offspring born alive are underdeveloped.[32,132,167] In mice chlorpromazine produces a considerable number of abortions and malformations. As far as other neuroleptics are concerned, manufacturers quote experiments covering two generations of animals of different species, rats, dogs, and mice, where no malformation has been present.

Our long experience of chlorpromazine with humans seems to exclude the possibility of its being, at least in moderate doses, dangerous to pregnant women. According to surveys carried out, among others, by Sobel,[180]

Henne et al.,[98] Favre-Tissot et al.,[64] figures relating to miscarriages, stillborn or malformed children are not significantly higher than those for the population as a whole.[203] Studies on a smaller scale have produced similar conclusions for thioridazine,[23] prochlorpromazine, perphenazine,[96] and trifluoperazine.[174,174a]

NOTES

1. Abood, L. G. & Romanchek, L. (1957), The chemical constitution and biochemical effects of psychotherapeutic and structurally related agents. *Ann. N.Y. Acad. Sci.*, 66:812–824

2. Achté, K. A. (1961), Der Verlauf der Schizophrenien und der schizophreniformen Psychosen. *Acta Psychiat. Neur. Scand.*, Supp. 155, 273p. TP II, p. 23.

3. Achté, K. A. & Apo, M. (1967), Schizophrenic patients in 1950–1952 and 1957–1959. *Psychiat. Quart.*, 44:422–441.

4. Alcocer Cuarrin C. (1963), Aspectos funcionales de la actividad receptora sensorial. *Gaz. Med. Mexico*, 86:641–652.

4a. Anden, N.-E., Dahlstr°4m, A., Fuxe, K., & H°4kfelt, T. (1966), The effect of haloperidol and chlorpromazine on the amine levels of central monoamines neurons. *Acta Physiol. Scand.*, 67:255.

5. Ansell, G. B. & Dohmen, H. (1956), The depression of phospholipid turnover in brain tissue by CPZ. *J. Neurochem.*, 1:150–152.

6. Ardouin, M., Feunier, Y.-M., & Delattre, A. (1969), Manifestations oculaires au cours du traitement par des derivés de la phénothiazine. *Bull. Soc. Ophtal. France.*, 69:395–401.

6a. Auch, W. (1963), Beeinflusst die Psychopharmakotherapie die Aufnahmeentwicklung, die stationäre Behandlungdauer und den Verlauf endogener Psychosen? *Fortschr. Neurol. Psychiat.,* 31:548–565.

7. Ayd, F.-J. (1956), Fatal hyperpyrexia during chlorpromazine therapy. *J. Clin. Exper. Psychopathol.,* 17:189–192.

8. Ayd, F.-J (1968), Is psychiatry in a crisis because of the complications of the psychopharmaceuticals? *Dis. Nerv. Syst.,* 29 (Suppl.):23–25.

9. Azima, M. & Sarwer-Foner, G.-J. (1961), Psychoanalytic formulations of the effects of drugs in pharmacotherapy. In: *Système extrapyramidal et neuroleptiques,* (J.-M. Borderleau). Montreal: University of Montreal, Dept. of Psychiatry.

10. Baker, J. (1960), The effects of drugs on the foetus. *Pharmacol. Rev.,* 12:37.

11. Balvet, P. (1959), Activité du comportement de passivité. Son rapport avec les chimiothérapies. Journée de therapeutique psychiat. Hôp. Vinale, 1955. *J. Médecine Lyon,* Spec. No. 4:83–102.

12. Bartholini, G., Da Prada, M., & Pletscher, A. (1968), Decrease of cerebral 5-HT by L-Dopa after inhibition of extracerebral decarboxylase. *J. Pharm. Pharmacol.,* 20:228.

13. Battegay, R. & Gehring, A. (1969), Influences of neuroleptics on the course of the disease in schizophrenic patients. In: *Psychotropic drugs,* eds. Cerletti and Boré, International Congress Series, Excerpta Medica Foundation, Amsterdam, pp. 400–463.

14. Berger, M., Strecher, H.-J., & Waelsch, H. (1957), The biochemical effects of psychotherapeutic drugs. *Ann. N.Y. Acad. Sci.,* 66:806–811.

15. Bernsohn, J., Namajuska, I., & Boshes, B. (1956), The action of CPZ and reserpine on brain enzyme systems. *J. Neurochem.,* 1:145–149.

16. Brockhoren, J. S. (1956), Moral treatment in American psychiatry. *J. Nerv. Ment. Dis.,* 124–167, 292.

17. Bradley, P.-B. & Key, B.-J. (1958), The effect of drugs on arousal responses produced by electrical stimulation of the reticular formation in the cat. *EEG Clin. Neurophysiol.,* 10:97–110.

18. Bradley, P.-B. (1965), Neurophysiological mechanisms of pharmacological desafferentation. In: *Désafférentation expérimentale et clinique.* Masson, Paris: pp. 37–46.

19.   Brill, H. & Patton, R. E. (1957), Analysis of 1955–1956 population fall in N.Y. State mental hospitals in first year of large scale
use of tranquillizing drugs. *Amer. J. Psychiat.*, 114:509–516

20.   Brill, H. & Patton, R. E. (1962), Clinical statistical analysis of
population changes in N.Y. State Mental Hospitals since introduction of psychotropic drugs. *Amer. J. Psychiat.*, 119:20–30.

21.   Brill, H. (1969), Evolution de la population des hôpitaux psychiatriques américains. *Confrontations psychiatriques*, 4:167–186.

22.   Brody, Th. (1955), The uncoupling of oxidophosphorylation as
a mechanism of drug action. *Pharmacol. Rev.*, 7:335–363.

23.   Brougher, J. (1960), Treatment of emotional disorders in ob-
stetrics with thioridazine. *Quart. Rev. Surgery Obstet. Gynecol.*,
17:44–47.

24.   Broussole, P. & Rosier, Y. (1959), Evolution des symptômes
neurologiques dus aux neuroleptiques. *Ann. Med. Psychiat.*,
117:140–151.

25.   Brown, G.-W. (1960), Length of hospital stay and schizophrenia. A view of statistical studies. *Acta Psychiat. Scand.*, 35:414–
430.

26.   Brown, G.-W., Parkes, C.-M., & Wing, J.-K. (1961), Admissions
and readmissions to the London mental hospitals. *J. Ment. Sci.*,
107:1070–1077.

26a.   Brown, G.-W., Bone, M., Dalison, B., & Wing, J. K. (1966),
Schizophrenia and Social Care. London: Oxford University Press.

27.   Buffaloe, W., Johnson, A., & Sandifer, M. (1967), Total dosage
of chlorpromazine and ocular opacities. *Amer. J. Psychiat.*,
124:250–251.

28.   Burgermeister, J.-J. & Christin, M. (1967), Modification de la
population de l'Hôpital psychiatrique: incidence des réadmis-
sions. *Méd. hyg.*, 25:894–896.

29.   Cardo, B. (1970), Le comportement d'autostimulation. *Confrontations Psychiatriques*, 6:65–86.

30.   Cassano, C.-B., Sjöstrund, S. E., & Hanssen, F. (1965), Distribution of 35 S-chlorpromazine in cat brain. *Arch. Int. Pharmacodyn.*,
156:48.

31.   Cawley, R. H. (1967), The present status of physical method of
treatment of schizophrenia. In: *Recent Developments in Schizophrenia*, eds. A. Coppen and A. Walk. London: Royal Medico-Psychological Association, pp. 97–114.

32. Chambon, Y. (1955), Action of chlorpromazine on the evolution and prospect of the gestation in the female rat. *Ann. Endocrinol.*, 16:912.

33. Chassagne, P., Lechat, P., & Gerges Jand, L. (1965), Risques embryonnaires et néonataux liés aux traitements appliqués au cas de la grossesse. *Rev. Prat. Paris,* 15:1329.

34. Christensen, E. Moller, J.-E., & Faurbye, A. (1970), Neuropathological investigation of 28 brains from patients with dyskinesia. *Acta Psychiat. Scand.,* 46:1–23.

35. Colmart, C. H., Bridgman, F., & Girard, B. (1969), La thiopropérazine et la lévopromazine utilisées en association dans le traitement des psychoses chroniques. *Evol. Psychiat.,* 34:847–860.

36. Corodi, H., Fuxe, K., Ljungdahl, A., & Ögren, S.-O. (1970), Studies on the action of some psychoative drugs on central noradrenaline neurons after inhibition of dopamine-β-hydroxylase. *Brain Res.,* 24:451–470.

37. Courvoisier, S., Fournet, J., Ducrot, R., Cauchon, J., & Buisson, P. (1953), Propriétes pharmacodynamiques du chorhydrate de chloro-3-demethylamino-3-propyl-10 phenothiazine. *Arch. Int. Pharmacodyn.,* 92:305.

38. Crane, G.-E. (1967), Involuntary movements in a sample of chronic mental patients and their relation to the treatment with neuroleptics. *Int. J. Neuropsychiat.,* 3:286–291.

39. Crane, G.-E. (1968), Tardive dyskinesia in patients treated with major neuroleptics. A review of the literature. *Amer. J. Psychiat.,* 124(Supp):40–48.

40. Crane, G.-E. (1970), High doses of trifluoperazine and tardive dyskinesia. *Arch. Neurol.,* 22:176–180.

41. Curry, S.-H., Davis, J.-M., Janovsky, D.-S., & Marshall, J.-H.-L. (1970), Factors affecting chlorpromazine plasma level in psychiatric patients. *Arch. Gen. Psychiat.,* 22:209–215.

42. Daumezon, G. (1971), Le point de vue d'un psychiatre de service public. *L'évolution psychiatrique,* 36:501–509.

43. Decsi, L. (1961), Further studies on the metabolic background of tranquilizing drug action. *Psychopharmacologia,* 2:224–242.

44. Degkwitz, R. & Luxemburger, O. (1965), Das terminale extrapyramidale Insuffizienz, bzw. Defektsyndrom infolge chronischer Anwendung von Neurolepticis. *Nervenartz,* 36:173–175.

45. Degkwitz, R., Wenzel, W., Binsack, K. F., Herkert, H., & Luxemburger, O. (1966), Zum Problem des terminalen extrapyramidalen Hyperkinesen an Hand von 1600 langfristig mit Neuroleptika Behandelten. *Arzneimittel Forsch.*, 17:276–279.

46. Degkwitz, R. & Wenzel, W. (1967), Persistent extrapyramidal side effects after long-term application of neuroleptics. In: *Neuropsychopharmacology*, ed. H. Brill, International Congress Series No. 129. Excerpta Medica Foundation, Amsterdam, pp. 608–615.

47. Delay, J., Deniker, P., Bourguignon, A., & Lempérière, T. (1956), Complications d'allure extrapyramidale au cours des traitements par la CPZ it la réserpine. *Encéphale*, 45:1039–1098.

48. Delay, J., Deniker, P., Green, A., & Mordret, M. (1957), Le syndrome excito-moteur provoqué par les médicaments neuroleptiques. *Presse médicale*, 65:1771–1774.

49. Delay, J., Deniker, P., & Berges, J. (1960), Mimiques et neuroleptiques (analyse des modifications motrices et toniques de la face produites par la thioproperazine). *Presse médicale*, 68:2072–2074.

50. Delay, J. & Deniker, P. (1969), Lacunes et besoins en matière de neuroleptiques. In: *Psychotropic Drugs*, eds. Cerletti and Bové, International Congress Series, Vol. 22, Excerpta Medica Foundation, Amsterdam, pp. 139–144.

51. Delong, S. L. (1967), Chlorpromazine induced eye changes. In: *Neuropsychopharmacology*, ed. H. Brill, International Congress Series, No. 129. Excerpta Medica Foundation, Amsterdam, pp. 656–660.

52. Delong, S. L. (1968), Incidence and significance of chlorpromazine-induced eye changes. *Dis. Nerv. Syst.*, 29(Suppl.):19–22.

53. Dember, H. C. B. (1961), Psychodynamic effects of drug-induced extrapyramidal reaction on ward social structure. In: *Système extrapyramidal et neuroleptiques* (J.-M. Bordeleau). Montréal: University of Montreal, Dept. of Psychiatry.

54. Deniker, P.(1962), Monoamines, médicaments psychotropes et nosographie psychiatrique, In: *Monoamines et systèm nerveux central* ed. J. de Ajuriaguerra. Paris: Masson, pp. 215–231.

55. Deniker, P. & Gente, G. (1967), Effects secondaires et processus thérapeutique. In: *Neuropsychopharmacology*, ed. H. Brill, International Congress Series, No. 129. Excerpta Medica Foundation, Amsterdam, pp. 650–655.

56. Deniker, P., Peron-Magnan, P., Perier, M., & Dalle, B. (1967), Modifications de la séméologie et de l'évolution des psychoses sous l'influence des chimiothérapies. In: *Neuropsychopharmacology*, ed. H. Brill, International Congress Series, No. 129. Excerpta Medica Foundation, Amsterdam, pp. 942–947.

57. Druckman, R., Seelenger, D., & Thulin, B. (1962), Chronic involuntary movements induced by phenothiazines. *J. Nerv. Ment. Dis.*, 135:69–75.

58. Eckert, H. & Hopf, A. (1970), Autoradiographic studies on the distribution of psychiatric drugs in the rat brain. LV C14 Thioridazine. *Int. Pharmacopsychiat.*, 4:98–116.

59. Ekblom, B. & Lassenius, B. (1964), A follow-up examination of patients with chronic schizophrenia who were treated, during a long period with psychopharmacological drugs. *Acta Psychiat. Scand.*, 40:49–279.

60. Ekborn, K. (1966), Oral dyskinesia associated with phenothiazine therapy. *Psychiat. Neurol. Neurochir.*, 69:155–159.

61. Ellsworth, R. B. & Clayton, W. H. (1960), The effects of chemotherapy on length of stay and rate of return for psychiatrically hospitalized patients. *J. Consult. Psychol.*, 24:50

62. Escourolle, R., Recondo, J. de, & Gray, F. (1971), Etude anatomopathologique des syndromes parkinsoniens. In: *Monoamines et noyaux gris centraux*, eds. J. Ajuriaguerra and G. Gauthier. Paris: Masson, pp. 173–230.

63. Faurbye, A., Rasch, P. J., Bender-Petersen, P., Brandborg, G., & Pakkenberg, H. (1964), Neurological symptoms in pharmacotherapy of psychoses. *Acta Psychiat. Scand.*, 40:10–27.

64. Favre-Tissot, M. & Broussolle, P. (1967), Du pouvoir teratogène éventuel des produits psychopharmacologiques, In *Neuropsychopharmacology*, ed. H. Brill, International Congress Series, No. 129. Excerpta Medica Foundation, Amsterdam, pp. 683–689.

65. Foy, R.-L., Randrup, A., & Pakkenberg, H. (1969), Chlorpromazine and related neuroleptic drugs in relation to corpus striatum in rats. In: *Psychotropic drugs*, eds. Cerletti and Bové, International Congress Series. Excerpta Medica Foundation, Amsterdam.

66. Follin, S., Chanoit, P., Pilon, & Huchon (1961), Le remplacement du Largactil par des placebos dans un service psychiatrique. *Ann. Med. Psychol.*, 1:976–983.

67. Forrest, F. M., Forrest, I. S., & Roizin, L. (1963), Clinical bio-
     chemical and post mortem studies on a patient treated with
     chlorpromazine. *Rev. Agressol.,* 4:259–265.

68. Forrest, I. S., & Forrest, F. M. (1963), On the metabolism and
     action mechanism of the phenothiazine drugs. *Exp. Med. Surg.,*
     21:231.

69. Forrest, F. M., Gerter, C. W., Snow, H. L., & Steinbach, M.
     (1964), Drug maintenance problems of rehabilitated mental
     patients. The current drug dosage. *Amer. J. Psychiat.,* 121:33–
     40.

70. Forrest, F. M., Forrest, I. S., & Roizin, L. (1964), Clinical bio-
     chemical and post mortem studies on a patient treated with
     chlorpromazine. In: *Lectures in Psychopharmacology,* eds. W. G.
     Clark, and K. S. Ditman. Sepulveda.

71. Forrest, F. M. & Snow, H. L. (1968), Prognosis of eye complica-
     tions caused by phenothiazines. *Dis. Nerv. Syst.,* 29(suppl.).

72. Franchi, G. & Granni, A.-M. (1957), Chlorpromazine distribu-
     tion in maternal and fetal tissues and biological fluids. *Acta
     Anaesth. Padova,* 8:197.

73. Free, S. & Dodd, D. (1961), Aftercare for discharged mental
     patients. *Conference on a five state mental health study in Virginia.*
     1961, Vol. 11, No. 28.

74. Freeman, H. (1967), The therapeutic value of combinations of
     psychotropic drugs. *Psychopharm. Bull.,* 4(1):1–27.

75. Fuxe, R., & Hockfelt, T. (1970), Central monoaminergic system
     and hypothalamus function. In: *The Hypothalamus.* New York:
     Academic Press, pp. 123–138.

76. Garrone, G. (1962), Etude génétique et statistique de la schizo-
     phrénie à Genève. *J. de Génétique humaine,* 11:1–219.

77. Gauthier, G., Ajuriaguerra, J. de, Simona, B., Constantinidis, J.,
     Esenring, J. J., Krassoievitch, M., Yanniotis G., & Tissot, R.
     (1970), Thérapeutique du syndrome parkinsonien par L-Dopa
     associée à des inhibiteurs de la décarboxylase. *Rev. Neurol.,*
     123:297.

78. Galbrecht, C. R. & Klett, G. J. (1968), Predicting response to
     phenothiazines; the right drug for the right patient. *J. Nerv.
     Ment. Dis.,* 147:173–183.

79. Glick, B. S. (1968), Attitude toward drug and clinical outcome.
     Amer. J. Psychiat., Supp. 124:37–39.

80. Glowinski, J. (1970), Metabolism of catecholamines in the CNS and correlation with hypothalamic functions. In: The Hypothalamus. New York: Academic Press, pp. 139–152.

81. Goldberg, S. C., Mattsson, N.-B, Cole, J. O., & Kleiman, G. L. (1967), Differential prediction of improvement in acute schizophrenia under four phenothiazines. In: *Neuropsychopharmacology*, ed. H. Brill. International Congress Series, No. 129. Excerpta Medica Foundation, Amsterdam, p. 735.

82. Goldberg, S. C., Mattsson, N.-B., Cole, J. O., & Kleiman, G. L. (1967), Prediction of improvement in schizophrenia under four phenothiazines. *Arch Gen. Psychiat.*, 16:107–117.

83. Goldberg, S. C., Nils, & Mattsson, N.-B. (1968), Schizophrenic subtypes defined by response to drugs and placebo. *Dis. Nerv. Syst.*, 29(Suppl.):153–158.

84. Goldman, D. (1968) Prolonged treatment of psychotic states. Over 1600 patients treated continuously 3 to 7 years. *Dis. Nerv. Syst.*, 29(Suppl.):51–57.

85. Gottfries, C. G., Gottfries, I., & Roos, B. E. (1969), The investigation of HVA in the human brain and its correlation to senile dementia. *Brit. J. Psychiat.*, 115:563–574.

86. Gowdey, C. W. & Forster, K. S. (1961), Parkinsonism and the use of tranquilizers. *Canad. Psychiat. Assoc. J.*, 6:79–87.

87. Greenberg, L. M. & Roth, S. (1966), Differential effects of abrupt versus gradual withdrawal of chlorpromazine in hospitalized chronic schizophrenic patient. *Amer. J. Psychiat.*, 123:221–226.

88. Greiner, A. C. & Berry, K., (1964), Skin pigmentation and corneal and lens opacities with prolonged chlorpromazine therapy. *Canad. Med. Assoc. J.*, 90:663–665.

89. Greiner, A. C. (1968), Schizophrenia Melanosis. Iatrogenic-congenital defects? *Dis. Nerv. Syst.*, 29(Suppl.):14–15.

90. Gross, H. & Kallenback, E. (1969), Neuropathological findings in persistent hyperkinesia after neuroleptic long-term therapy. In: *Psychotropic Drugs,* ed. Cerletti and Bové, International Congress Series. Excerpta Medica Foundation, Amsterdam, pp. 474–476.

91. Grunthal, E. & Walther-Buel, H. (1960), Über Schädigung des oliva inferia durch chlorpromazin (Trilafon), *Psychiat. Neurol.*, 140:249–257.

92. Guiraud, P. (1968), Origine et évolution de la notion de schizo-phrénie. *Confrontations psychiatriques,* 2:9–29.

93. Gurel, L. (1966), Community stay in chronic schizophrenia. *Amer. J. Psychiat.,* 122:892–899.

94. Guth, P. S. & Spirles, M. A. (1964), The phenothiazine tranquilizers biochemical and biophysical actions. *Int. Rev. Neurobiol.* 7:231–272.

95. Hall, R. A., Jackson, R. B., & Swain, J. M. (1956), Neurotoxic reactions resulting from chlorpromazine administration. *JAMA.,* 161:214.

96. Harer, W. (1958), Tranquilizers in obstretics and gynecology studies with Trilafon. *Obstet. Gynecol.,* 11:273–279.

97. Harris, A., Linker, I., Norris, V., & Shepherd, M. (1956), Schizophrenia: a prognostic and social study. *Brit. J. Prev. Soc. Med.,* 10:107–114.

98. Henne, M., Tonnel, M., & Henne, S. (1961), Traitements neuroleptiques chez les femmes enceintes. *CR du Congès de psychiatrie et neurologie de langue française, Montpellier 1961.* Paris: Masson, pp. 375–383.

99. Herz, A. (1960), Drugs and the conditioned avoidance response. *Int. Rev. Neurobiol.,* 2:229–272.

100. Heyck, H. (1962), Der Einfluss hoch dosierter Dauerbehandlung mit phenothiazinen auf den Hirnstoffwechsel bei verschiedenen Altersgruppen. *Nervenarzt,* 33:66–70.

100a. Hiebel, G., Bonvallet, M., & Dell (1954), Action de la chlorpromazine au niveau du système nerveux central. *Sem. Hop.,* 50:2346–2353.

100b. Hiebel, G. et al. (1954), *Sem. Hop.,* 30:1–7.

101. Hillarp, M. A., Fuxe, K., & Dahlström, A. (1966), Demonstration and mapping of central neurons containing dopamine noradrenaline 5-HT and their reactions to psychopharmaca. *Pharmacol. Rev.,* 18:727–742.

102. Hoenig, J. (1967), The prognosis of schizophrenia. In: *Recent Developments in Schizophrenia,* eds. A. Coppen and A. Walk. London: Royal Medico-Psychological Association.

103. Hoff, H. & Hofman, G., (1967), Das persistierende extrapyramidale Syndrom bei Neurolepticatherapie. *Wiener Med. Wochenschr.,* 117:14–17.

104. Hollinghead, A. B. & Redlich, F. C. (1958), *Social Class and Mental Illness.* New York: Wiley.

105. Hollister, L. E. & Kosek, J. C. (1965), Sudden death during treatment with phenothiazine derivatives. *JAMA,* 192:1035–1038.

106. Hollister, L. E. (1970), Choice of antipsychotic drugs. *Amer. J. Psychiat.,* 127(2):186–190.

107. Hollister, L. E. (1968), General review of complications of psychotherapic drugs. In: *Neuropsychopharmacology,* ed. H. Brill, International Congress Series, No. 129. Excerpta Medica Foundation, Amsterdam, pp. 646–649.

108. Hornstra, R. & McPortland, T. (1963), Aspects of psychiatric aftercare. *Int. J. Soc. Psychiat.,* 9:135.

109. Hornykiewicz, O., Extrapyramidal side effects of neuropsychotropic drug. In: *Proceedings of the European Society for the study of drug toxicity.* International Congress Series, No. 118. Excerpta Medica Foundation, Amsterdam, p. 8.

110. Hunter, R., East, C. F., & Thernieroft, S. (1964), An apparently irreversible syndrome of abnormal movements following phenothiazines medications. *Royal Soc. Med. Proc.,* 57:758–762.

111. Jaramillo, G. A. V. & Guth, P. S. (1963), A study of the localization of phenothiazines in dog brain. *Biochem. Pharmacol.,* 12:525–532.

112. Jasper, H. & Shagass, C. (1941), Conditioning the occipital alpha rhythm in man. *J. Exp. Psychol.,* 28:373–388.

113. Jouvet, M. (1965), Mécanismes neurophysiologiques de l'habituation. In: *Désafférentation expérimentale et clinique,* ed. J. de Ajuriaguerra. Paris: Masson, pp. 15–36.

114. Kammerer, Th., Eblinger, R., & Bauer, J. P. (1965), Approche phénoménologique et psychodynamique des psychoses délirantes aiguës traitées par neuroleptiques majeurs. In: *La relation médecin-malade au cours des chimiothérapies psychiatriques,* ed. P. A. Lambert. Paris: Masson, pp. 17–40.

115. Katz, M. M. & Cole, J. O. (1962), Research on drugs and community cure. *Arch. gen. Psychiat.,* 7:345.

116. Kety, S. S. (1971), Commentary (on Shakow). *J. Nerv. Ment. Dis.,* 153:323–326.

116a.   Kety, S. S. & Schmidt, C. F. (1968), The nitrous oxide method for the quantitative determination of cerebral blood flow in man. *J. Clin. Invest.* 27:476–492.

117.   Key, B. J. & Bradley, B. J. (1960), The effects of drugs on conditioning and habituation to arousal stimuli in animals. *Psychopharmacol.*, 1:450–462.

118.   Key, B. J. (1961), The effect of drugs on discrimination and sensory generalization of auditory stimuli in cats. *Psychopharmacol.*, 2:352–363.

119.   Kielholz, P. & Labhardt, F. (1962), Déductions tirées de nos connaissances sur les IMAO par rapport à la classification des psychoses. In: *Monoamines et système nerveux central,* ed. J. de Ajuriaguerra. Paris: Masson, pp. 233–238.

120.   Klett, C. J. (1967), The right drug for the right schizophrenic patient. In: *Neuropsychopharmacology,* ed. H. Brill, International Congress Series, No. 129. Excerpta Medica Foundation, Amsterdam, pp. 732–734.

121.   Kornetsky, C. & Eliasson, M. (1969), Reticular stimulation and clorpromazine. An animal model for schizophrenic over arousal. *Science,* 165:1273.

122.   Kris, E. B. (1962), Children born to mothers maintained on pharmacotherapy during pregnancy and postparturi. *Recent Adv. Biol. Psychiat.,* 4:180.

123.   Kurland, A. A. & Hanlen, T. E. (1971), The use of psychotropic drug combinations. Comment and observations. *Neuropsychopharmacol.,* 4:297–307.

124.   Laboucarie, J. (1968), Valeur comparée des thérapeutiques biologiques et des psychothérapies en psychiatrie. *Presse Médicale,* 76:830.

125.   Laboucarie, J. (1968), Le devenir des psychoses délirantes aiguës et le risque de leur évolution schizophrénique secondaire. *Confrontations psychiatriques,* 2:31–52.

126.   Lambert, P.-A., Perrin, J., Revol, L., Archaintre, A., Balvet, P. M., Berthier, C., Broussole, P., & Requet, A. (1958), Essai de classification des neuroleptiques d'après leurs activités psychopharmacologiques et cliniques. *J. Neuropsychopharmacol.,* 618–624.

127.   Lambert, P.-A. (1964), Essai de systématisation des associations de neuroleptiques. *L'Encéphale,* 53:262–273.

128. Lambert, P.-A. (1965), A propos de la désafférentation médicamenteuse en psychiatrie. In: *Désafférentation expérimentale et clinique,* ed. J. de Ajuriaguerra. Paris: Masson, pp. 201–228.

129. Lambert, P.-A. & Marcou, G. (1970), Fluphenazine enanthate given to inpatients and outpatients. *Dis. Nerv. Syst.,* 31(9)(Suppl):63–65.

130. Leestma, J. & Koenig, K. (1968), Sudden death and phenothiazines. *Arch. Gen. Psychiat.,* 18:137–147.

131. Lempépière, T. (1971), Communication to Congress in Mexico, in press.

132. Lesinski, J. (1957), Data on effect of largactil on rat fetuses and extra-uterine development. *Ginek. Polska,* 28:669–672.

133. Letemendia, F. J. J. & Harris, A. D. (1967), Chlorpromazine and the untreated chronic schizophrenic. *Brit. J. Psychiat.,* 113:950–958.

134. Letemendia, F. J. J., Harris, A. D. & Willem, J. A. (1967), The clinical effects on a population of chronic schizophrenic patients of administrative changes in hospital. *Brit. J. Psychiat.,* 113:959–971.

135. Leyberg, J. T. (1965), A follow-up study on some schizophrenic patients. *Brit. J. Psychiat.,* 111:617–624.

136. Lindelius, R. (1970), A study of schizophrenia. *Acta Psychiat. Scand.,* Supp. 216: 125.

137. Linn, L. S. (1970), State hospital environment and rate of patient discharge. *Arch. Gen. Psychiat.,* 23:346–351.

138. Lortie, G. (1961), The importance and the meaning of drug-induced extrapyramidal reactions to the psychotic patient. In: *Système extrapyramidal et neuroleptiques* (J.-M. Bordeleau). Montréal: University of Montreal, Dept. of Psychiatry.

139. Malm, U. (1970), Intra-muscular long-acting fluphenazine in the treatment of schizophrenia. *Arch. Psychiat. Scand.,* 46:225–237.

140. Margules, D. L. & Stein, L. (1967), Neuroleptics vs tranquilizers. Evidence from animal behavior studies of mode and site of action. In:*Neuropsychopharmacology,* ed. H. Brill, International Congress Series, No. 129. Excerpta Medica Foundation, Amsterdam, pp. 108–123.

141. Mathalone, M. B. R. (1968), Ocular effects of phenothiazine derivatives and reversibility. *Dis. Nerv. Syst.,* 29 (Supp.):29–35.

141a.   Mayer-Gross (1932), Die Schizophrenie. In: *Handbuch der Geis-teskrankheiten*, Band IV. Berlin: Springer.

142.   Mendel, W. M. (1963), Outpatient treatment for chronic schizo-phrenic patients. *Arch. Gen. Psychiat.*, 8:190.

142a.   Meuron, M. de & Christin, M. (1967), Modification de la popu-lation de l'hôpital psychiatrique:contribution à l'étude de la "mobilité" et du "sédiment" dans un hôpital psychiatrique. *Méd. Hyg.*, 25:897–900.

143.   Meyendhorf, R. (1969), Extrapyramidale Hyperkinesen nach zerebraler Verschädigung und Langzeitbehandlung mit Neuro-leptica. *Schweiz. Arch. Neurol. Neurochir. Psychiat.*, 105(1):165–176.

144.   Michtom, J., Goldberg, N., Offenkrantz, W., & Whittier, J. (1957), Readmissions rates for state mental hospital patients discharged on maintenance ataractics. Findings with a matched control group and methodological considerations. *J. Nerv. Ment. Dis.*, 125:478.

145.   Morell., F. (1961), Electrophysiological contributions to the neural bases of learning. *Physiol. Rev.*, 41:443–94.

146.   National Institute of Mental Health, Psychopharmacology ser-vice center collaborative study group, (1969), Phenothiazine treatment in acute schizophrenia. *Arch. Gen. Psychiat.*, 10:246–261.

147.   Nicolson, G. A., Greiner, A. C., Mc Farlane, V. J. G. & Baker, R. A. (1966), Effect of penicillamine on schizophrenic patients. *Lancet*, I(1):344–347.

147a.   Nielsen, J., Friedrich, U. & Tsuboi, T. (1969), Chromosomes abnormalities in patients treated with chlorpromazine per-phenazine and lysergide. *Brit. Med. J.*, 3:534–636.

147b.   Odegard, O. (1969), Pattern of discharge from Norwegian psy-chiatric hospitals before and after introduction of the psycho-tropic drugs. *Amer. J. Psychiat.*, 120:772–778.

147c.   Olds, J. (1959), Studies of neuropharmacologicals by electrical and chemical manipulation of the brain in animals with chroni-cally implanted electrodes. In: *Neuropsychopharmacology*, Brad-ley, Deniker, Raducco Thomas Elsevier, 20–34.

148.   Orlinsky, N. & d'Elia, E. (1964), Rehospitalization in the schizo-phrenic patients. *Arch. Gen. Psychiat.*, 10:47–54.

149.   Ostow, M. (1960), The effects of neuroleptic drugs on psychic

functions. In: *The Dynamics of Psychiatric Drug Therapy,* ed. G. J. Sarwer-Foner. Springfield, Ill.

150. Paerregaard, G. (1969), The hospital requirement and the possibilities of occupation for schizophrenic women. *Acta Psychiat. Scand.,* 45:172–186.

151. Paerregaard, G. (1971), The significance of follow-up treatment for the hospital requirements of schizophrenic women. *Acta Psychiat. Scand.,* 47:217–222.

152. Peron-Magnan P. (1968), Chimiothérapie et évolution des schizophrènes. *Confrontations psychiatriques,* 2:125–127.

153. Pind, K. & Faurbye, A. (1970), Concentration of HVA and 5-HIAA in the CBF after treatment with probenecid in patients with drug induced tardive dyskinesia. *Acta Psychiat. Scand.,* 46(4):323–326.

154. Pletscher, A., Prada da, M. & Fogler, G. (1967), Differences between neuroleptics and tranquilizers regarding metabolism and biochemical effects. In: *Neuropsychopharmacology,* ed. H. Brill, International Congress Series, No. 129. Excerpta Medica Foundation, Amsterdam, pp. 101–107.

154a. Pletscher, A. (1967), Pharmacological and biochemical bases of some somatic side effects of psychotropic drugs. In: *Neuropsychopharmacology,* ed. Brill, International Congress Series, No. 129. Excerpta Medica Foundation, Amsterdam, pp. 571–577.

155. Poirier, L. Bouvier, G. , Bedart, P., Boucher, R., Larochette, L., Olivier, A., & Singh, P. (1969), Essai sur les circuits neuronaux impliqués dans le tremblement postural et l'hypokinésie. *Rev. Neurol.,* 120:15–40.

156. Pollack, B. (1958), The effect of chlorpromazine in reducing the relapse rate in 716 released patients. *Amer. J. Psychiat.,* 114:749.

157. Porot, M., Couadau, A. & Aubin, B. (1968), Aspects évolutifs actuels des schizophrènes. *Confrontations psychiatriques,* 2:53–75.

158. Poursines, Y., Allier, J., & Toga M., (1959), Syndrome parkinsonien consécutif à la prise prolongée de CPZ avec ictus mortel intercurrent. Aspect des lésions pallidales. *Rev. Neurol.,* 100:745–751.

159. Prien, R. F., Levine, J., & Cole, J. O. (1969), High dose trifluoperazine therapy in chronic schizophrenia. *Amer. J. Psychiat.,* 126:305–313.

160.   Prien, R. F., Levine, J., & Cole, J. O. (1970), Indications for high dose chlorpromazine therapy in chronic schizophrenia. *Dis. Nerv. Syst.*, 31(11):739–745.

161.   Prien, R. L. & Cole, J. O. (1968), High dose chlorpromazine in chronic schizophrenia. *Arch. Gen. Psychiat.*, 18:482–495.

161a.   Rasmussen, E. B. (1966), Admission and discharge of schizophrenic male patients 1950–1960. A Study from Sct. Hans Hospital. *Acta Psychiat. Scand.*, Suppl. 191:216–231.

162.   Rego, A. (1971), Effects de la L-Dopa et de l'inhibiteur Ro 1756 sur le Parkinson Médicamenteux. In: *Monoamines et noyaux gris centraux.* Paris: Masson, pp. 529–540.

163.   Richardson, H. L., Graupner, K. I., & Richardson, M. E. (1966), Intramyocardial lesions in patients dying suddenly and unexpectedly. *JAMA*, 195:254–260.

164.   Richardson, H. L., Richardson, M. E., & Graupner, K. I. (1967), Cardiac findings in sudden death after prolonged use of phenothiazines. In: *Neuropsychopharmacology*, ed. H. Brill, International Congress Series, No. 129. Excerpta Medica Foundation, Amsterdam, pp. 619–629.

165.   Richter, D. (1965), Mode of action of the phenothiazines. In: *The scientific bases of drug therapy in psychiatry*, eds. Marks and Pare. New York: Pergamon, pp. 63–69.

166.   Röder, E. (1970), A prognostic investigation of female schizophrenic patient discharged from Sct Hans Hospital, Department D, during the decade 1951–1960. *Acta Psychiat. Scand.*, 46:50–63.

167.   Roizin, L., True, C., & Knight, M. (1959), Structural effects of tranquillizers *Res. Nerv. Ment. Dis. Proc.*, 37:285.

168.   Roizin, L., Eros, G., Gold, G., Weinberg, F., Wodruska, T., & English, W. H. (1959), Histopathologic findings in the lever and central nerves system, following the administration of some tranquilizing drugs in humans. *J. Neuropathol. Exp. Neurol.*, 18:349–351.

169.   Rosvold, H. E., Szuarbart, M. V., Musky, A. F., & Mishkin, M. (1961), The effects of frontal lobe damage on delayed response performance in chimpanzee. *J. Comp. Physiol. Psychol.*, 54:368–374.

170.   Roux, C. (1959), Teratogenic action of prochlorpromazine. *Arch. franç. pédiat.*, 16:968–971.

171. Rubin, M. & Slonicki, A. (1967), A proposed mechanism for the skin eye syndrome. In: *Neuropsychopharmacology,* ed. H. Brill, International Congress Series, No. 129. Excerpta Medica Foundation, Amsterdam, pp. 661–679.

172. Ruskin, A., Schiltenbrandt, J. G., Realig, N., & Ms. Keen, J. J. (1970), Differential response to chlorpromazine imipramine and placebo. *Arch. Gen. Psychiat.,* 23:164–173.

173. Sawner-Foner, G. S. (1961), Some commands on the psychodynamic aspects of the extrapyramidal reactions. In: *Système extrapyramidal et neuroleptiques* (J.-M. Bordeleau). Montréal: University of Montreal, Dept. of Psychiatry.

174. Schire, T. (1963), Trifluoperazine and fetal abnormality. *Lancet,* 1:174.

174a. Shader, J. R. (1970), Pregnancy and psychotropic drugs. In: *Psychotropic drug side effects,* eds. J. R. Shader and A. Di Mascio. Baltimore: Williams and Wilkens.

175. Shakow, D. (1971), Some observations on the physiology (and some fewer on the biology) of schizophrenia. *J. Nerv. Ment. Dis.,* 153:300–316.

176. Sharpless, P. B. & Jasper, H. H. (1956), Habituation of the arousal reaction. *Brain,* 79:655–680.

177. Siddal, J. R. (1968), Ocular complication related to phenothiazines. *Dis. Nerv. Syst.,* 29(Suppl.):10–13.

178. Sigwald, J., Bouthier, D., & Raymondeaud, Piot, C. (1959), Quatre cas de dyskinésie facio-bucco-linguo-masticatrice à évolution prolongée secondaire à un traitement par les neuroleptiques. *Rev. Neurol.,* 100:751–755.

179. Sigwald, J., Boutheir, D., & Courvoisier, S. (1959), Les accidents neurologiques des médications neuroleptiques. *Rev. Neurol.* 100:553–595.

180. Sobel, D. E. (1960), Foetal damage due to ECT, insulin coma, chlorpromazine, reserpine. *Arch. Gen Psychiat.,* 2:606.

181. Steck, H. (1956), Le syndrome extrapyramidal dans les cures de CPZ et serpasil, sa symptomatologie clinique et son rôle thérapeutique. *Encéphale,* 45:1083–1089.

181a. Steg, G. (1971), Pathological aspects on L-Dopa hyperkinesia. In: *Monoamines et noyaux gris centraux.* Paris: Masson, pp. 275–276.

182. Stein, L. (1968), Chemistry of reward and punishment. In: *Psy-*

chopharmacology. A review of Progress, 1957–1967, ed. D. H. Effron. Washington: Public Health Service, p. 105.

183.   Terrace, H. S. (1963), Errorless descrimination learning in the pigeon: effects of chlorpromazine. *Science,* 140:318–319.

184.   Tissot, R. (1965), Desafférentation médicamenteuse; neuroleptiques et relaxants musculaires. In: *Desafférentation expérimentale et clinique,* ed. J. de Ajuriaguerra. Paris: Masson, pp. 229–246.

185.   Tissot, R. (1970), Monoamines et régulation thymique. *Confrontations psychiatriques,* 6:87–152.

186.   Tissot, R. & Bovet, J. (1967), Modifications de l'habituation de la réaction d'arrêt du rythme alpha chez l'homme sous l'effet de la chlorpromazine et du halopéridol. *Psychopharmacologia,* 10:298–307.

187.   Tuteur, W., Stiller, R., & Glotzer, J. (1959), Discharged mental hospital chlorpromazine patients. *Dis. Nerv. Syst.,* 114:749.

188.   Uhrbrand, L. & Faurbye, A. (1960), Reversible and unreversible dyskinesia after treatment with perphenazine, chlorpromazine, reserpine and EC. *Psychopharmacologia,* 1:408–418.

189.   Vedrine, J., Schott, B., & Chanoit, G. (1967), Les hyperthermies liées à l'administration des neuroleptiques. In: *Actualité du Thérapeutique psychiatrique,* ed. Lambert. Paris: Masson, pp. 332–350.

190.   Wase, A. W., Christensen, J., & Polley E. (1956), The accumulation of S35 chlorpromazine in brain. *Arch. Neurol. Psychiat.,* 75:54.

191.   Wechsler, M. B. Roizon, L. (1960), Tissue levels of chlorpromazine in experimental animal. *J. Ment. Sci.,* 106:1501–1505.

192.   Werbhoff, J. & Cottlieb, J. S. (1963), Drugs in pregnancy: behavioral teratology. *Obstet. Gynecol. Surv.,* 18:420.

193.   Wertheimer, J. (1965), Syndromes extrapyramidaux permanents consécutifs à l'administration prolongée de neuroleptiques. *Schweiz. Arch. Neurol. Neurochir. Psychiat.,* 95:120–173.

194.   Wet de Vorster (1965), Psychiatric drugs and treatment in pregnancy. *Brit. J. Psychiat,* 111:431.

195.   Williams, R., Walker, R. (1961), Schizophrenics at time of discharge. *Arch. Gen. Psychiat.,* 4:87

196.   Wing, J. R., Monck, E., Brown, G. W., & Custans, G. M. (1966), Morbidity in community of schizophrenic patients discharged

from London mental hospital in 1959. *Brit. J. Psychiat.,* 110:10–21.

197. Wing, J. R. (1968), L'évolution et le pronostic de la schizophrènie. *Confrontations psychiatriques,* 2:77–85.

198. Winkelman, W. J. (1959), Psychoanalytic study of phenothiazinic actions. In: *Psychopharmacology Frontiers,* Little Town Ed.

199. Yahr, M. D. (1970), *Abnormal Unvoluntary Movements induced by Dopa; Clinical Aspects,* ed. Barleau Mc Donnell. Philadelphia: Davis Company, pp. 101–108.

200. See notes 1, 5, 14, 15, 22, 43 and 95.

201. See notes 9, 53, 114, 138, 149, 173, and 198.

202. See notes 67, 70, 90, 91, 109, 159, and 168.

203. See notes 39, 44, 57, 60, 86, 103, 178, 188, 193, and 197.

204. See notes 33, 122, 192, and 194.

Pierre Deniker, M.D.

Professor Tissot must be given unqualified congratulations for his extremely important report which, like the rest of his work, is characterized by the scope of his view and his precision of argument. It is by no means an easy task to discuss this study, for the author has already anticipated the main possible objections and given the appropriate answers in advance.

No doubt he was right not to include manic-depressive psychosis in his very wide-ranging and concentrated report, but he has not made it clear whether he considers this problem as being solved. It could, in fact, be said—and we are talking about a psychosis here—that the progress made with a combination of electroshock therapy, neuroleptics, antidepressants, and lithium cure, have turned this into a disorder as accessible to therapy as, say, diabetes.

On the other hand, the author may have been rather too restrictive in confining himself to the framework of the schizophrenic psychoses, for the other forms of chronic delusions in the French nosography are also most instructive. Hence, the quasi-specific action of haloperidol in idiopathic delusional psychoses, the superficial effect of neuroleptics in interpretative delusions of persecution (where more satisfactory results are often obtained by the combination of antidepressants) and the virtual uselessness of biological treatments in imaginative or confabulatory delusions are worth looking at from the point of view of the interpretation of the action mechanism of chemotherapy.

However, we have to be grateful to Tissot for going straight to the heart of the problem in deliberately limiting his report to the action of neuroleptics in the schizophrenic psychoses and concentrating his work around a real "match"—neuroleptics versus schizophrenia—which he has refereed with consummate skill from both the quantitative and the qualitative angles.

What is there to be added to his virtually exhaustive analysis of available statistics concerning hospital populations, length of hospitalization, discharges after prolonged hospital stays, and the rhythm of readmissions? It could perhaps be pointed out that there is a contradiction between American data which show a deflation in psychiatric hospitalization in the state of New York, for example, and the INSERM[1] statistics which indicate the persistence of sedimentation in our hospitals during the same period in France. The "trend" was clearly and durably reversed in New York from 1954 onward, and this reversal has been attributed to the extensive use of new drugs. One might ask whether their use in our own country has been as widespread and determined, although some surveys give grounds for doubting this. A comparison of neuroleptic consumption in the two populations may well be a revealing exercise.

The main issue, in fact, is certainly whether or not any use of any agent is enough to diminish the incidence of schizophrenia. If there were any absolutely positive answer to this, our debate would have little purpose, but we agree with the speaker himself that the greatest importance must be attached to the conditions in which the various drugs are used and the relative specificity of their actions.

It has to be admitted that the matter of effective dosages still remains within the realm of a certain empiricism in which the doctor's experience and the patient's reactivity each have their part to play, and it is not simply the role of placebo. For any one compound some would be in favor of medium dosages and others would recommend high doses. It also happens that prolonged cures give results which could not be obtained with treatments of a few weeks duration. It is likely that in the future better knowledge of drug metabolism will enable us to understand—as is already the case with lithium—certain therapeutic resistances and a number of paradoxical actions. One fact can already be emphasized: in the case of long-acting neuroleptics, the dose injected for two, three, or four weeks is hardly any greater than the daily dosage necessary with the normal compound (nondelayed) and this is valid for fluphenazine as well as pipotiazine salts.

With regard to the question of the actions proper to the various compounds, and their classification according to these properties, we feel it necessary to go back to the oversimplified—and mistakenly bipolar—classification of "minor" and "major" neuroleptics. If one must have a linear classification, then it should be set up between *sedative* and *disinhibiting* (not to say "stimulant") compounds. In such a classification the right-hand end of the chain would terminate with sulpiride, which is certainly the least sedative of all. As we have often stressed, the activity of neuroleptics is extremely complicated. The most powerful compounds, such as haloperidol for example, have a sedative or antimanic action frequently as great as the so-called "antipsychotic" action upon delusions or hallucinations, which again is different from the disinhibiting action observed in hebephrenia. So here we have at least three parameters which have to be taken into consideration if the available agents are to be classified correctly, and these parameters have also to be compared with the neurological or neurovegetative "secondary" effects. Most important of all, a distinction can be made between the powerful compounds (the major neuroleptics) and those which are less powerful. Finally, the chemical structure is another factor to be reckoned with in classifying the existing groups: the dibenzothiazepines are related to the aliphatic phenothiazines, and the butyrophenones and the thioxanthens are related to the piperazine phenothiazines, while the piperidine compounds are in a position midway.

The variety of the different types of action of the compounds in current use justifies the therapeutic drug combinations, which will undoubtedly continue to develop along with greater knowledge of the workings of these combinations—those that correct side effects and those with synergic or cumulative effects. However, the development of therapeutic combinations is not confined to the intercombination of neuroleptics only. It has been observed for a long time now that the most satisfactory results obtained in chronic psychoses (results confirmed by permanent discharges) were brought about by means of the combination of neuroleptics and antidepressants, the former apparently acting mainly upon the productive delusional semiology and the latter upon the deficiency symptoms of schizophrenia. In more recent times the systematic use of lithium in resistant schizophrenia has enabled us to observe not only the reduction of the phases of incoercible agitation and dysthymia, but also more efficient neuroleptic action on residual hallucinatory or delusional activity.

Finally, emphasis has to be laid upon the possibilities offered by the combination of chemotherapy with shock treatment, such as insulin therapy, which seems to be the most disinhibiting treatment, and should be alternated in the deficiency forms with a combination of the sulpiride-clomipramine type; electroshocks can be useful in reducing the persistent aftermath of the repeated paranoid reactions which have been a frequent evolutive form of schizophrenia since the introduction of modern treatments.

To go back to Tissot's report, stress should be put on the particular interest of the section dealing with hypotheses concerning the action mechanisms of neuroleptics at the level of the central nervous system, a field in which the author has acquired a justified reputation.

Despite the considerable progress made in latter years in the biochemistry of the cerebral amines and in the chemistry of the brain, his endeavors were hampered from the start by the present lack of knowledge about the disorders caused by mental illnesses within a system where more is known about what goes on at the intraneuronal or inter-neuronal level than at the level of structures and functions. Hence, our object of interest is mainly the antithesis between the action of hallucinogenics (or possibly amphetamines) and that of neuroleptics.

Talking about the major psychic functions, Tissot concentrated on the alertness level, conditioned reflexes, and the integration of perception and information. One might regret, though, that he made no reference to mood control or perturbation of the dream-function which can be involved in the psychoses of particular interest to us.

The author took a somewhat caustic attitude to meta-pharmacology, a modern form of metaphysics which is a menace to us all, and myself in particular. However, it has to be admitted that one has to rack one's brain when confronted with some mysteries—and the process of improvement produced by chemotherapy in mental disturbances is just that—a mystery. The few studies on this subject, such as the theses of Bauer and Conté,[2] refer to the hypochondriac experience of side effects in the mechanism of the decrease of delusional disorders. It is to be hoped that specialists in psychodynamics will give rather more attention to what happens during the process of drug therapy.

Finally, Tissot coyly concludes with the "adverse" effects of the treatments he has very carefully put forward as worthy of recommendation. But is this not likely to scare those off completely who are hesitating to prescribe the treatment. Whatever the case may be, one has to recognize the fact that all active therapies have some disadvantages, which means that it is essential for patients, particularly chronic patients receiving relatively heavy treatment, to be under constant surveillance and followed up very closely.

I should just like to add a word on hyperkinesias, and choreiform syndromes persisting after neuroleptic cures carried out with compounds that have a high incidence of extrapyramidal reactions. In our own experience, the problem of treatment of these permanent disorders is generally solved only by means of a new neuroleptic treatment in sufficiently high doses, in combination with another drug; when reduction of hyperkinesia is eventually obtained it is usually permanent.

NOTES

1. Institute National de la Santé et de la Recherche Médicale.

2. Bauer, J. P. (1963), Aspects psychopathologiques des cures à la thiopropérazine. Thèse Strasbourg.

3. Conté, C. (1972), Contribution à l'analyse du processus thérapeutique réalisé par les neuroleptiques dans les psychoses dé lirantes. Thèse Paris.

4. Conté, C. (1963), Psychoses dé lirantes et neuroleptiques. Remarques sur le processus thérapeutique. *Encéphale,* 52: p. 46.

Louis Julou, D.V.M.

SOME NOTIONS ARISING FROM THE EXPERIMENTAL STUDY OF LONG-ACTING INJECTABLE NEUROLEPTICS

Professor Tissot's extremely well documented report gives us a picture of long-term drug therapy in psychoses seen from a great number of different angles, and where the rosy tints of optimism are offset by grey shades of pessimism.

Naturally, as a psychopharmacologist whose work is confined to experimental studies on animals, I am not in a position to give any authoritative opinion on the various clinical problems raised by Professor Tissot. With regard to the mechanism of the action of neuroleptics, I do agree with him that, as far as experimental work is concerned, for the time being the different hypotheses put forward "give only a very limited view of the physiopathological mechanisms of psychoses." However, to look at the problem from the opposite angle, I hope that despite the difficulty of this field of study, research will be developed particularly on the changes which may occur in the metabolism of the cerebral amines in psychotic states. The information obtained could be of vital importance in enabling us to take a more logical and safe approach in our research for new and more specific drugs for use in the treatment of psychoses.

Prf. Tissot states that "for obvious reasons the use of delayed-action neuroleptics in prolonged psychotic states would be particularly useful, especially since these are (for the time being at least) major neuroleptics."

Given my experience in the laboratory study of this new type of compounds, I should like to use these few minutes to give you as concise a summary as possible of the major conclusions emerging at present from experimental studies on long-acting injectable neuroleptics. Since the first experimental[4,6,10] and clinical studies on the enanthic ester of fluphenazine were published in the United States between 1962 and 1965 a number of other long-acting injectable neuroleptics have made their appearance, which has improved our knowledge concerning this type of compounds and the various problems involved in their experimental and clinical study and use.

A special session was devoted to compounds of this type during the *VIIth Congress of the Prague International Collegium Neuro-Psychopharmacologicum, August 1970,* and in a publication issued in early 1971,[11] Villeneuve and Simon, who chaired this session, outlined "the essentials of the communications and ideas exchanged on the subject of this new category of drugs." Finally, to mention only the most recent international meeting, at the *5th World Congress of Psychiatry, Mexico City, 29 November–4 December 1971,* there were about 50 communications on the subject of long-acting injectable neuroleptics.[2]

Table 3.9 shows the long-acting injectable neuroleptics clinically known at present, together with some data concerning the doses used and the frequency of injections; most of these data are taken from the paper by Villeneuve

Table 3.9. Long-acting injectable neuroleptics

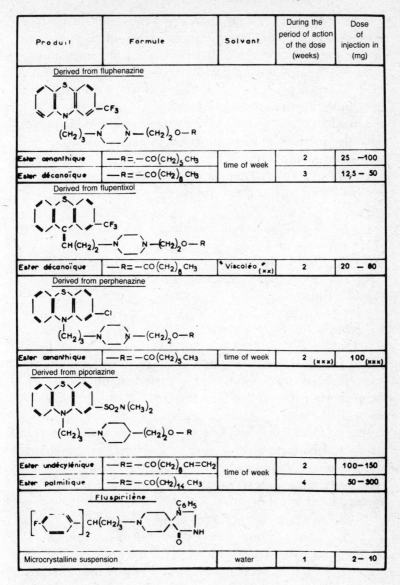

Produit	Formule	Solvant	During the period of action of the dose (weeks)	Dose of injection in (mg)
Derived from fluphenazine				
Ester œnanthique	$-R=,-CO(CH_2)_5 CH_3$	time of week	2	25 —100
Ester décanoïque	$-R=-CO(CH_2)_8 CH_3$		3	12,5 — 50
Derived from flupentixol				
Ester décanoïque	$-R=-CO(CH_2)_8 CH_3$	Viscoléo (××)	2	20 — 80
Derived from perphenazine				
Ester œnanthique	$-R=-CO(CH_2)_5 CH_3$	time of week	2 (×××)	100 (×××)
Derived from piporiazine				
Ester undécylénique	$-R=-CO(CH_2)_8 CH=CH_2$	time of week	2	100—150
Ester palmitique	$-R=-CO(CH_2)_{14} CH_3$		4	50 — 300
Fluspirilène				
Microcrystalline suspension		water	1	2— 10

[a] Villeneuve & Simon [11].
[b] Low-viscosity fraction of coconut oil.
[c] From Kempen (1971), *Psychopharmacologia*, 21:283–286.

and Simon.[11] At present, apart from the enanthic ester of fluphenazine,[12] only the decanoic esters of fluphenazine and flupentixol are available to the medical profession, at least in some countries, and have only been so recently. With the exception of fluspirilene, which is administered i.m., in the form of a microcrystalline suspension in water, the products are obtained by the esterification of fatty acids with the primary alcohol function of classic neuroleptics; they are administered by i.m. injection in solution in oil. We shall concentrate mainly on the latter type of product, and will deal with the two following points:

1. the demonstration of the prolonged action of esters, and
2. the study of the distribution and metabolism of esters and the mechanism of their prolonged action.

Demonstration of Prolonged Action

First of all, we have to emphasize the fact that although the experimental study of the classic neuroleptics has now been made relatively easy by the use of carefully chosen correlation tests, the same cannot be said for the long-acting injectable esters. The length of the prolonged action of these products after a single injection can be clearly demonstrated only by the use of highly sensitive tests.[3,9] The two following tests seem to us to be particularly satisfactory in this respect:

1. apomorphine induced emesis in the dog, which is usually particularly sensitive, and
2. amphetamine induced stereotypies in the rat, the value of which is generally recognized for the prediction of "antipsychotic" activity.

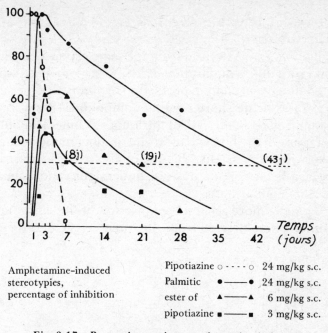

Amphetamine–induced
stereotypies,
percentage of inhibition

Pipotiazine	o - - - - o	24 mg/kg s.c.
Palmitic	•———•	24 mg/kg s.c.
ester of	▲———▲	6 mg/kg s.c.
pipotiazine	■———■	3 mg/kg s.c.

Fig. 3.17. Protection against amphetamine-induced
stereotypies (each dot represents the average
value for six rats)

Examination of the results leads to a number of ideas.
The intensity of the protective effect of any given long-
acting ester and the duration of its action increase with the
dose administered, at least within a certain range of doses.

Figure 3.17 shows clearly that against amphetamine
induced stereotypies in rats, the palmitic ester of pipotiazine in doses of 3, 6, and 24 mg/kg s.c., gives protection
of 30 percent or higher for a period of about 8, 19, and 43
days, respectively. However, only the 24 mg/kg, s.c. dose
can produce 100 percent protection for two or three days.
Of course, as Fig. 3.17 also shows, the duration of action
of a 24 mg/kg s.c. dose of palmitic ester of pipotiazine is
considerably longer than that of a similar dose of pipotia-

zine, whose protective effect falls below 30 percent after four or five days.

For two esters derived from the same classic neuroleptic and with different duration of action, a given dose—just enough to give maximum protection of almost 100 percent in the case of the shorter-acting compound—has a lower maximum effect in the case of the longer-acting compound.

Figure 3.18 shows that, in the amphetamine-induced stereotypies test in rats, this hypothesis is verified in the case of a 6 mg/kg s.c. dose of undecylenic and palmitic esters of pipotiazine.

To get a more accurate comparison of the duration of action of esters derived from the same classic neuroleptic

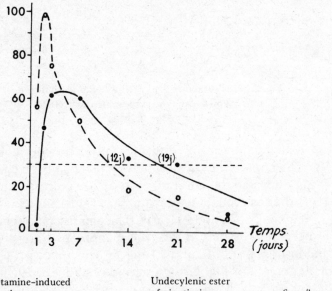

Amphetamine–induced stereotypies, percentage of inhibition

Undecylenic ester of pipotiazine   o - - - - o 6 mg/kg s.c.

Palmitic ester of pipotiazine   •———• 6 mg/kg s.c.

Fig. 3.18.   Protection against amphetamine-induced stereotypies (each dot represents the average value for six rats)

and, a fortiori, that of esters derived from two different neuroleptics, it is therefore useful to follow the time rate of evolution of their 50-percent effective doses which give the same level of protective activity in a selected test.

The results we recently submitted in detail in a general review[9] of long-acting injectable neuroleptics show that the peak effect of the 50-percent minimum effective doses appears, depending on the product, a few hours to several days after the injection; the delay seems to increase the longer the duration of the ester's action. On the other hand, in two esters derived from the same classic neuroleptic, the 50-percent minimum effective dose is higher the longer the duration of the ester's action.

On the other hand again, comparison of the experimental and clinical results obtained with different esters show that in general experimental studies can only be considered of limited value in predicting duration of action in the clinical situation. However, in the case of the esters derived from the same classic neuroleptic, the classification according to the duration of action observed in animals does seem to be satisfactory.

Study of the Distribution and Metabolism of Esters and the Mechanism of their Prolonged Action

The study of the distribution and metabolism of the classic neuroleptics presents thorny enough problems, but the study of the injectable esters is even more difficult, because the concentrations of these compounds and their metabolites found in the organs or the excreta is lower still. The use of labeled compounds is more necessary than ever. These methods, and particularly those using tritiated compounds with high specific activity, are the only ones which are sufficiently sensitive to reveal in the target organs amounts of around one hundredth of a part per thousand million, which are still biologically significant.

A number of notions emerge from the relatively few studies carried out so far.[5-9]

Obviously, given the purpose in view, long-acting injectable neuroleptics must be eliminated from the organism slowly.

Hence, in the rat, 45 days after injection of a 4.5 mg/kg i.m. dose of tritiated palmitic ester of pipotiazine, the cumulated urinary and fecal excretions (radioactivity of the ester itself and its metabolites) represent only about 65 percent of the radioactivity administered; moreover fecal excretion is around 10 times as strong as urinary excretion.[9]

Similar results have been obtained with rats by Ebert and Hess[6] with the enanthic ester of fluphenazine labeled with ^{14}C, and by Jörgensen et al.[7] with tritiated decanoic ester of flupentixol.

As is shown by Figure 3.19 the amounts of radioactivity present in the organism of the rat after injection of a 0.75 mg/kg i.m. dose of palmitic ester of pipotiazine further confirm that elimination of this compound is slow; however, 60 days after injection, only about 15 percent of the radioactivity administered is still present in the organism. It is essential, though, to emphasize the fact that, at any given moment during the 60 days of observation, about 95 percent of the total amount of radioactivity found in the organism is in the foot in which the injection has been given, with between 40 and 50 percent in the form of ester, and 5 to 8 percent in the form of "bioformed" pipotiazine.

It is therefore likely that, as with the case of esters of certain steroid hormones (see Ariëns[1]), the prolonged action of the esters of certain classic neuroleptics, after injection in oily solution, is essentially the result of an increase in the lipophile character of the compounds from which they are derived, which results in their slow liberation from the injection area outwards.

Esters were found in a number of tissues[6-9] and in

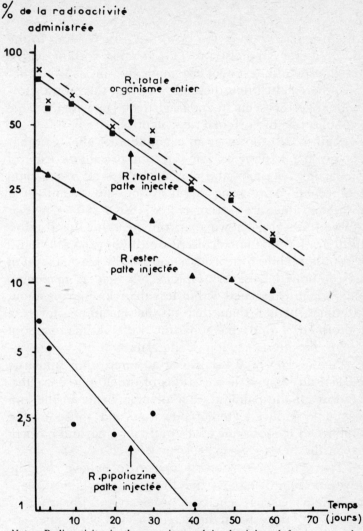

% de la radioactivité administrée

R. totale organisme entier

R. totale patte injectée

R. ester patte injectée

R. pipotiazine patte injectée

Temps (jours)

Note: Radioactivity in the organism and in the injected foot expressed as a percentage of radioactivity administered (dosages carried out in pooled samples of two rats at each time).

Source: Julou, L. (1972), *Actualités Pharmacologiques*, 25:23-59.

Fig. 3.19.   Injection of the rat with palmitic ester of pipotiazine (specific activity: 8 Ci/mM) in dose of 0.75 mg/kg i.m.

some cases[7–9] in the brain; however, in the various tissues of the organism (in varying proportions according to the different tissues in question[7,9]) but to an important degree overall, esters undergo an enzymatic hydrolysis which liberates the original neuroleptic,[6–9] so that the biotransformations of esters seem by and large to end up with the same metabolites as the original neuroleptics.

Figure 3.20 shows, as an example, that after a rat has been given a 0.75 mg/kg i.m. injection of palmitic ester of pipotiazine, plasma and brain levels of ester and "bioformed" pipotiazine diminish very slowly and their maximum values are extremely low (100 to 200 ng/liter or kg); we have also shown that, on the other hand, after injection of an equimolecular dose (0.5 mg/kg i.m. in oil solution) of pipotiazine itself in the rat, the plasma level of this compound falls very rapidly, but that its maximum value, which is reached within less than an hour, is about 100 times higher than that of the maximum level of "bioformed" pipotiazine apparent in the plasma on about the 7th day after injection of the ester.[9]

Finally, Fig. 3.20 brings out an interesting similarity between the time-scale variations of the 50-percent effective dose of the palmitic ester of pipotiazine in the amphetamine induced stereotypies test and those of the "bioformed" pipotiazine levels in the plasma, and particularly in the brain.

There is therefore every reason to believe that the active compound in the brain is the nonesterified neuroleptic which may have reached this organ after its liberation by hydrolysis of the ester in the neighborhood of the injection area or in other tissues, or which may be the result of hydrolysis in situ. (As Villeneuve and Simon[11] suggested, the presence of small quantities of esters in the brain could, however, lead to some slight qualitative differences between the activities of the esters and those of the original neuroleptics.)

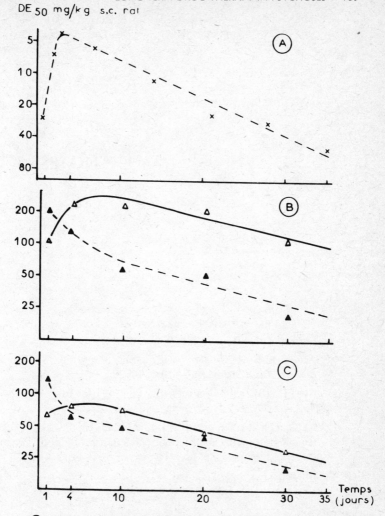

DE 50 mg/kg s.c. rat

Note: (A) variations of the 50 percent effective dose of palmitic ester of pipotiazine with time. (B) and (C) Variations of ester level (▲- - - -▲) and "bioformed" pipotiazine (△——△) in relation to time, in B in the brain, in C in the plasma (dosages carried out in pooled samples of two rats at each time; same rats for B and C).

Source: Julou, L. (1927), *Actualités Pharmacologique*, 25:23–59.

**Fig. 3.20. (A) Amphetamine induced stereotypies in the rat
(B) and (C) Injection of the ester (specific activity: 28 Ci/mM)**

NOTES

For more details, see Note 9.

1. Ariens, E. J. (1966), Molecular pharmacology, a basis for drug design. *Arzneimittel Fortsch.,* 10:429–529.

2. Ayd, J. (1972), Long-acting injectable neuroleptics. *Int. Drug Ther. Newsletter,* 7:1–8.

3. Boissier, J. R., Simon, P., & Lwoff, J. M. (1966), Etude pharmacologique d'un neuroleptique à action prolongée : l'énanthate de fluphénazine. *Med, Pharmacol. Exp.,* 14:435–442.

4. Burke, J. C., High, J. P., Laffan, R. J., & Ravaris, C. L. (1962), Depot action of fluphenazine enanthate in oil. *Fed. Proc.,* 21:339.

5. Dreyfuss, J., Ross, J. J., & Schreiber, E. C. (1971), Excretion and biotransformation of the enanthate ester of fluphenazine ^{14}C by the dog. *J. Pharm. Sci.,* 60:829–833.

6. Ebert, A. G. & Hess, S. M. (1965), The distribution and metabolism of fluphenazine enanthate. *J. Pharmacol.,* 148:412–421.

7. Jorgensen, A., Fredricson Overo, K., & Hansen, V. (1971), Metabolism, distribution and excretion of flupenthixol decanoate in dogs and rats. *Acta. Pharmacol. Toxicol.,* 29:339–358.

8. Julou, L., Bourat, G., Fournel, J., & Garret, C. (1971), Etude pharmacologique de deux esters de la pipotiazine, neuroleptiques injectables à longue durée d'action (19 551 R.P. et 19 552 R.P.). *5th World Congress of Psychiatry, Mexico City, 1971*, Abst. 359.

9. Julou, L. (1972), Etude expérimentale des neuroleptiques injectables à action prolongée. *Actualités Pharmacologiques*, 25:23–59.

10. Laffan, R. J., High, J. P., & Burke, J. C. (1965), The prolonged action of fluphenazine enanthate in oil after depot injection. *Int. J. Neuropsychiat.*, 1:300–306.

11. Villeneuve, A. & Simon, P. (1971), Les neuroleptiques à action prolongée. *Thérapeut.*, 2:3–16.

12. Available to the medical profession in Great Britain from 1966 on.

Pierre Albert Lambert, M.D.,
and Marc Midenet, M.D.

Professor Tissot has clearly shown to what a great extent the introduction of neuroleptics has changed the treatment and prognosis of chronic psychoses in general, and schizophrenias in particular.

From the clinical point of view, which is the only one we are qualified to talk about, we agree entirely. In order to remain within the framework of the subject under discussion, i.e., the long-term drug treatment of psychotic states, rather than go back over this paper, which deals more than adequately with the question, we prefer to add complementary observations in two fields: *the introduction of long-acting neuroleptics* which is one of the turning points of present-day psychopharmacology, and secondly, the *attitude of the doctor* prescribing long-term treatment for psychotics—a problem which will remain an open question for a long time.

To keep the daily aspect of our practice in mind, it must be pointed out that most psychiatrists, in France at least, do not have at their disposal the psychotherapeutic

Table 3.10. Chronic psychotic patients under treatment
with delayed-action neuroleptics: 69 hospitalized
patients (43 men and 26 women)

Length of care period, years	As from the first medical consultation		As from the beginning of treatment[a]	
	Men	Women	Men	Women
0 to 1	11	5	22	12
1 to 2	2	3	7	2
2 to 5	10	1	11 ⎫	3 ⎧
5 to 10	5	0	3 ⎬ 26	9 ⎨
More than 10	15 ⎫ 32	17	0	0

[a]Maximum six years.

means to enable each psychotic patient to develop on the basis of a privileged relationship, and that drugs are therefore seen as a bulwark against psychotic regression. The catchment-area experiment is considered the solution for these patients for a given length of time, with drugs playing a specific role for the psychotic core, and also that of a mediator for the medical team. It can also be said that any treatment is the result of an association of people and their means and possibilities, and that it would be a mistake to try at all costs to isolate drugs in this context.

Since they were first put into use in 1965, we have carried out 687 treatments with long-acting neuroleptics. Some patients were treated successively with two or several of these, as longer- and longer-acting neuroleptics became available. At the present time, 173 of our patients receive delayed-action neuroleptics, 69 of them in hospital, and 104 in aftercare. Tables 3.10 and 3.11 show the length of the care period, beginning with the initial medical intervention and also from the onset of treatment with delayed-action neuroleptics. Table 3.10 refers to hospitalized patients and Table 3.11 to outpatients.

Table 3.11. Chronic psychotic patients under treatment
with delayed-action neuroleptics: 104 patients in
aftercare (48 men and 56 women)

Length of care period, years	As from the first medical consultation		As from the beginning of treatment[a]	
	Men	Women	Men	Women
0 to 1	11	10	16	19
1 to 2	5	4	8	7
2 to 5	18	14	20 ⎫	6
5 to 10	13	7	12 ⎭ 54 ⎰	16
More than 10	9	13	0	0
		22		

[a]Maximum six years.

It must be pointed out that despite the hospital-vs.-
aftercare alternatives, which Tissot also uses, there are in
fact a number of other possibilities open to us: night or
daytime hospitalization, private nursing, and carefully controlled gradual social reintegration, for example.

All treatments were carried out with the neuroleptics
shown in Table 3.12.

We are also fortunate to be able to refer to the experience in this field of our colleagues at the Committee on
Therapeutic Research in Psychiatry, in Lyon who have car-

Table 3.12. Delayed-action neuroleptics used on
chronic psychotics

Compound	Number of cases
Fluphenazine enanthate	102
Fluphenazine decanoate	138
Undecylenate of pipotiazine	53
Palmitate of pipotiazine	122 personal
Pipotiazine undecylenate, palmitate	120 C.L.R.T.P.
Flupenthixol decanoate	81
Fluspirilene	71

ried out over 200 treatments with the undecylenate and the palmitate of pipotiazine over three years. The results obtained here also confirm those of French and foreign authors; that is, delayed-action neuroleptics have tremendous advantages; nonetheless, there remains the possibility of their leading to excitomotor syndromes which can even be permanent, as Tissot describes, as well as to some rare malignant syndromes and especially depressive states which it would be worth while to examine closely.

Treatments of chronic psychotics with delayed-action neuroleptics have the following advantages:

1. Delayed-action neuroleptics ensure that the drug is administered. The injection is given at regular intervals, usually every two, three, or four weeks. Local resorption is good and there is no concomitant pain or induration, even after several years.

2. Doses are far lower than when administered orally —10, 20, or even 30 times less is used to produce the comparable therapeutic activity.

3. The cost of such treatments is therefore generally lower.

4. They can provide no occasion for accidents involving the absorption of overdoses, either by children or in suicide attempts. They are less frequently held in reserve stock than orally administered neuroleptics, and therefore less often a source of wastage.

5. These treatments are acceptable to patients and their families; injections at regular intervals fit into other social rhythms (the basic time unit is usually a period of a week) and is more readily accepted than oral treatments following alimentary or daily patterns.

6. Because of this, however paradoxical it may seem in the light of considerations on the discontinuity of treatment with delayed-action neuroleptics, this inevitably imposes the observation of a continuity of attention which is

beneficial to the patient. Although there have as yet been too few works published on this subject, it is certain that there is a lower relapse rate among patients treated with these products than among those treated with oral neuroleptics.

7. It sometimes happens that in cures lasting anywhere between five and 15 years the physician gets weary of the repetitiveness of oral prescriptions. The paramedical system is ready—and sometimes with great enthusiasm—to take over the cure from him, and in the context of the enormous problem of organization of outpatient treatment of chronic psychotics, delayed-action neuroleptics make such a take over possible. The paramedical system takes advantage of the drug to get away from the hospital context, within which it had only a partial view of the patients' lives, and uses this as a stepping-stone for promoting its own desire for fuller development, the extension of its own professional role and to boost an advance in therapy which is likely to present the most favorable picture of the role of the nursing profession as well as of the outcome for the patient. Its members are quite happy to take the physician's place, although without removing him from the scene entirely. This is why we seem to see less frequently than in the past cases of those patients who, left to their own devices, used to wander from one sector to the next and find themselves assigned to one service after another. We are by no means alone in stressing the importance of the continuity of attention which is essential to psychotics whatever drug or psychotherapeutic treatment they may be undergoing.

8. Consequently, the question does not arise as to whether or not delayed-action neuroleptics make existing institutions work better or whether or not a sector adopts this new type of therapy. Nonetheless, it is obvious that unless great care is taken there is a danger of such an arrangement giving rise to new forms of alienation.

We shall come back to the role of the physician in long-term treatments, but first we have to mention the two complications most frequently observed in chronic psychotics: (1) chronic excitomotor disorders, and (2) depressive states. These complications appear under orally administered treatment, but to a lesser degree, particularly as far as *depressive states* are concerned. The reason for this is perfectly simple: depression intensifies the psychotic's loss of initiative, which leads him to abandon the oral treatment in order to alleviate the depressive state, even if this means a subsequent relapse into psychosis. If the delayed-action parenteral treatment is continued without competent supervision the depression can become worse. Our statistics show that, depending on the products used, depression is present in 10 to 20 percent of all cases, manifested either as depressive tendencies in which antidepressants are effective and need not always be continued indefinitely, or else as full-scale states of the melancholia type which necessitate suspension of the treatment. Be it said also that suicides in such cases are not rare (de Alarcon).

The *excitomotor syndromes,* described in such detail, seem to us to be frequent but not altogether inevitable. Tissot goes into two points in particular—age and posologies—to which we shall come back later. It is true that extrapyramidal disorders and tardive excitomotor syndromes are observed with delayed-action neuroleptics, but many authors have also noted that such disturbances are no more frequent here than with oral treatments. Posologies have to be taken into particular account. When chronic hyperkinetic phenomena appear, especially in subjects over 50 years of age, this is more often than not an indication that doses are too high, and possibly that the intervals at which they are administered may be too close. If doses are reduced and spaced out at longer intervals, with treatment suspended for a few months if necessary, there follows, first of all, a regression of the neurological disorder and secondly, the reappearance of the psychotic phenomena. This is quite marked, particularly in chronically delusional patients. This means that in most cases a small dose—sometimes as little as 10 mg every five or six weeks—is sufficient to ensure continued remission in chronically psychotic old people. By the same token, delayed-action neuroleptics require a type of surveillance of patients different from that necessary with oral neuroleptics, but no less constant or attentive. It is essential for the nursing staff relieving the doctor to be warned of the possibility of such disturbances and their detection must be a routine.

This leads us on to the therapeutic requirements of the prescribing doctor. Must the essential aim be the disappearance at all costs of delusion and hallucinations and even criticism of the morbid state? That was the case at the beginning of the neuroleptic era. In long-term treatments a great number of patients retain a residual mental symptomatology which has little or no adverse effect upon their social adjustment. Furthermore, the long-term treatment often acts as a bulwark against a state of depression and the small doses of neuroleptic prescribed give rise only to discreet excitomotor symptoms, a slight movement of the jaw or a rhythmic foot tapping, which are often hardly noticeable. Thus, it takes several months to determine the optimal posology, whereby adequate antipsychotic effects are obtained along with only slight or easily corrected neurological effects. There are some exceptional cases where permanent disorders arise; we ourselves have seen only three cases of such disorders still continuing a year after complete termination of neuroleptics. This is a proportion so low that it has no common measure with the immense benefit to the total population treated.

With regard to malignant hyperthermic syndromes, three cases published in the French literature on the subject can be added to the two reported by Tissot. Only two were fatal and, although there must also exist other unpublished cases, this complication appears to be relatively rare. We share Tissot's hope that it will become even less frequent as time goes by.

In the context of our work, we are analyzing observations on schizophrenics first hospitalized more than 10 years ago, at a time when the patients were under 35 years of age. After examining 30 files out of a hundred or so, we note that several patients made something like 60 dispensary visits in 10 to 12 years. In all, 23 of the 30 patients living outside the hospital accounted for 706 dispensary consultations.

Out of 30 patients (20 men, 10 women) followed over 10 years—at which time they were between 28 and 46 years old—two committed suicide, five remained in the hospital almost without interruption, and 23 are in postcure. (This patient sample has no statistical value.)

The 23 postcure patients were followed for the last 10 years, which led to the following observations: 706 outpatients' department consultations, with an average of 30 consultations per patient (a minimum of three consultations in 10 years, and a maximum of 65 consultations per patient); seven patients received antidepressants for depression; ten received delayed-action neuroleptics; all patients have been readmitted between two and twelve times.

Seeing the same patients for drug treatment over decades gives rise to a number of problems. Of course, as in any type of treatment, the doctor's own desire to restore health is obvious, and this desire is perceived by the patient through the prescription which is its expression in concrete form.

Deeper analysis of doctors' attitudes leads to the identification of a number of different types of prescribers. At the extreme end of the scale some have a greater fear of the therapeutic disturbance than of the psychosis itself, while others rationalize the prescription of heavy posologies.

The psychiatrist cannot escape from mental structures and as his prescription is made in the context of a given relationship and involves more than the symptoms alone, he cannot remain unaffected by his patient's anxiety whether it is expressed or otherwise. The drug response in turn supports a predominant fantasy which is generally shared by the personnel dealing with the patient. Because the drug and the way it is used set the tone for a particular mode of behavior of the group using it, it is often extremely difficult to identify its exact position in the therapeutic situation. It would be useful to make a study of psychiatrists' attitudes to drugs, just as one studies drugs in relation to the psychotic.

With regard to the patient, in a chronic illness, hence in long-term treatment, there is but little similarity between an organically sick and a psychotic patient. The latter forces the therapist into an identification, or perhaps simply an understanding which, once again, indicates psychiatry. As Tissot points out, all drug treatments are liable to increase passivity or apragmatism at the least. The degree of recovery gives rise to a variety of forms which have already been described by Bleuler, but whose diversity has been even further increased by present-day cure arrangements. Thus one finds former psychotics who have turned into hypochondriacs, neurotics, or asthenics, but behind whose complaints or symptoms is hidden another need—no longer a need for the drug, but for a relationship which cannot be given into entirely without running the risk of anxiety.

The most exemplary cases are probably those where the scar of the underlying psychosis, after the action of neuroleptics, breaks through in the form of relatively low-key erotomania directed at the physician. We all know what tact is required in dealing with such patients, the relationship has to be tolerated without getting too close or being too distant; the pregenital mother is scarcely concealed, and anyone who is careless enough to be misled by the appearances of this positive transfer is liable to let loose an agressivity which can only be muted by high doses of neuroleptics, or else to see his patient refuse to continue treatment and relapse.

Generally speaking the best distance to keep is at the point where the patient does us the favor of accepting the prescriptions. We are perfectly well aware that when the patient shows up at the outpatients' department or in the private consulting rooms, the purpose of the visit is not to receive the drug.

All the ambiguity, and at the same time the complicity of the relationship, between the psychiatrist and the psychotic resides in the fact that the patient expects a response to a question he never actually formulates, and that the physician knows quite well that drugs are not always the right answer even though in the present state of affairs they probably constitute the response which it is most urgent, or essential or useful to give. In the long run, however, the psychotic often remains the child who does not grow up. And that is how we get institutions, systems, teams of people, organizational structures, and so forth which, in conjunction with drugs showing a parallel increase in quantity, constitute both the instruments of a progress everyone approves of, but also those of intermediaries or mediators. We must not allow our tranquillity to be set against the price of partial eclipse or abandonment.

Chapter 4

NOTES ON THE PSYCHOANALYTIC TREATMENT OF PSYCHOTIC STATES

Herbert A. Rosenfeld, M.D.

The psychoanalytic approach to psychotic states was stimulated in England through the pioneer work of Melanie Klein who in the early 1930s reported on some successful work with psychotic children and also adults. She wrote that she found evidence, in early infantile development, that children went through phases in which they experienced anxieties which had much in common with the psychotic states of the adult. She concluded that the adult psychotic had never outgrown the psychotic anxieties of infancy and regressed to them when the psychotic state became manifest. Her papers, "A Contribution to the Psychogenesis of Manic-Depressive States," in 1935, and "Mourning and its Relation to Manic Depressive States," in 1940, described her detailed observations of the "infantile depressive position" and "manic defenses." A later paper, in 1946, on "Notes on Some Schizoid Mechanisms," described minute observation of psychotic anxieties and defenses originating in earliest infancy, a phase which she called the "paranoid-schizoid position." These papers had a powerful influence on British analysts and provided the basis for the psychoanalytic approach to manic-depressive and schizophrenic states. Clifford Scott reported in Paris in 1938 on a manic-depressive patient, and I read a paper on "A Schizophrenic State with Depersonalization," in 1947 to the British Psychoanalytical Society. In 1950 Dr. Segal was the first to treat a severely delusional schizophrenic in a mental hospital and a little later in 1953, Bion published his first important work with schizophrenic patients. Since then the number of analysts (Thorner, Meltzer, Sohn, Klein, Mason, and others) who have treated severely psychotic patients has increased but there are still comparatively few British analysts who have consistently accepted psychotic patients for analysis.

I shall try in the short time available to give you a condensed picture of some of the knowledge and experience which we have acquired so far. I have been asked to discuss, among other topics, first the kind of result that one may expect from the psychoanalytic treatment of psychotic patients, particularly if one adheres strictly to a purely psychoanalytic technique, and to define its limits; second, to discuss the value of other kinds of therapeutic help such as drug treatment, occupational therapy, and environmental aids such as allowing the patient to live in a therapeutic community, hostel, or hospital.

I shall first discuss the importance of diagnosis and management in psychoanalytic treatment of psychotic patients.

In selecting psychotic patients for psychoanalysis, the psychoanalytic consultant is interested, as is any other psychiatrist, to establish what kind of psychosis he is dealing with, the duration of the illness, and any previous treatment. He also inquires into the historical background and the precipitating causes. However, the main diagnostic task is to try and assess whether and why the previous treatments failed and whether the patient, even in severe psychotic hallucinated states, shows indications of any latent capacity to respond to analytic understanding and insight. By this I do not mean that it is necessary that from the beginning of treatment the ego of the psychotic patient should be able to establish the kind of therapeutic alliance with the analyst which was for Freud[3] the precondition for any psychoanalytic approach. This latent capacity of the psychotic, to make contact with an analyst, can sometimes be assessed by an experienced analyst in a lengthy interview, even in patients who appear mute or talk only in an apparently senseless incoherent manner. For example, I have occasionally had the experience of a severely psychotic patient who has not only failed to respond positively to drug treatment and shock therapy but even showed signs of deterioration in response to it, seeming to come temporarily alive in a psychoanalytically conducted diagnostic interview. In such an interview the patient's deep-seated but hopeless search for personal understanding and contact could be understood and interpreted to him in spite of his difficulties in verbal communication.

Another important aspect of the psychoanalytic consultation, particularly in severely neurotic patients, is the diagnosis of latent psychosis. I myself am doubtful about the reliability of the very detailed evaluations of some of the American institutions, which I was allowed a few times to observe, though probably in some cases such psychological testing has advantages. Severely phobic, obsessional, and also certain psychosomatic states, such as ulcerative colitis, often hide a psychotic state which is bound to become manifest during psychoanalytic treatment. An early diagnosis enables one to make arrangements for management, so that the treatment of the patient can be continued in the acute psychotic state.

This brings us to the importance of "management" in all chronic and acute psychotic states. If a psychosis is diag-

nosed or suspected, I always arrange for a psychiatric colleague with some knowledge of psychoanalysis, other than
the analyst treating the patient, to see the patient from time
to time, to assess his capacity to cope with his current life
situation, and to arrange for hospitalization or private nursing if this becomes necessary. This colleague also assesses
the patient's need for drugs, occupational therapy, or help
in finding occupational or social contacts. I do not object
to the use of drugs while I am treating psychotic patients,
so long as the drugs are only used to alleviate symptoms
such as sleeplessness, severe manic excitement, or violence
and unbearable anxiety. Certain drugs cut the patient off
from his feelings, and this of course interferes considerably
with psychoanalytic treatment. However, there are others
such as Serenace (Haloperidol) which seem to have a sedat-
ing effect both in schizophrenic and manic-depressive
states without interfering with the patient's capacity to keep
in contact with his feelings. I never rely, even in severe
depressive suicidal patients, on specific antidepressive
drugs, because it is in severe depressive states that analytic
understanding and interpretative work are frequently effective, and some of the antidepressive drugs not only do not
assist the treatment but actually work against it by helping
the patient to deny his anxiety and depression.

I regard effective management as an important background to the psychoanalytic treatment of all psychotic
patients, as many of the failures of analytic treatment can
be traced to a failure to arrange proper management or to
a failure in the management during the treatment of the
patient. It provides the patient with a holding environment
which takes into account his ego weakness and incapacity
to look after himself during the acute psychotic state. This
implies that I value cooperation with mental hospitals or
nursing homes where the nurses and consultants are supporting the analytic treatment and where occupational
therapy or a social background can be created for the pa-

tient until he is ready to leave the hospital. We have very few nurses available who are trained to cooperate with the analyst treating psychotic patients, but it is interesting to watch the stimulating effect of psychoanalytic treatment on the staff of a hospital ward which generally caters to severely regressed patients. The atmosphere of hopelessness previously dominating the ward gradually lessens, and the staff becomes interested to cooperate practically and also to learn (they may also ask for seminars.) It is important for the analyst to realize that all mistakes in management, such as allowing a too early discharge from the hospital or nursing home, severely interfere with the patient's relationship to the analyst. The patient makes the analyst responsible for all arrangements relating to the management and therefore attributes any difficulties to the analyst's hostility or his failure to understand. Thus the patient often becomes paranoid and refuses to continue treatment. It is therefore essential that the managing psychiatrist remains in close contact with the analyst. The cooperation of the family of the patient is, of course, important but only very few patients are able to provide a background for the psychoanalytic treatment of a severely psychotic patient, and even when parents are willing to do so it often fails. I myself therefore prefer a hospital or nursing-home environment while the patient is acutely psychotic.

THE FAMILY HISTORY IN PSYCHOTIC STATES

The family history of psychotic patients varies a great deal but there is often a history of a disturbed mother-infant relationship with feeding difficulties such as slowness in feeding or a rejection of the breast, but it is often stressed that the baby has been particularly quiet and good, never crying even for his food. Sometimes the mother is described as depressed or anxious. One sometimes hears of severe traumas in the history of these patients, such as the death of a parent or of a family breaking up, but often the family disturbances are much more subtle and hidden. I feel critical of those workers who state categorically that psychotic illness is always caused by the environment. They seem to forget that there is often a predisposition to psychotic reactions in children, and later adults, described by Mahler as "defects in infants in their ability to use the good mothering agency as distinct from the self." A fairly normal parent confronted with a psychotic child feels a failure and blames himself for apparently not being able to provide the environment needed for his child's normal development. This starts a vicious circle. There are always obvious interconnections between the psychotic child creating a disturbing influence on the parents who cannot manage and therefore feel rejected and rejecting, and the psychological, sometimes psychotic, disturbances of the parents who are too difficult and overwhelming for the child to deal with. It is clear to me from the study of many psychotic patients that they feel that their parents did not understand them, or that they could not communicate sufficiently with them, but they also fear that nobody ever will understand and bear their problems so that they feel isolated and rejected. It is this aspect of the infant-parent relationship that plays a central role in the transference situation of most psychotic and borderline psychotic patients.

The Therapeutic Function of the Analysis and the Analyst in Psychotic States

Acute psychotic patients are generally seen by the analyst six times a week. Ideally there should be no interruption of the treatment by holidays until the acute phase has subsided. The treatment often starts in a hospital or nursing home, and as soon as possible the patient comes, or is brought by a nurse, to the analyst's consulting room. Even during the acute phase the analytic situation is preserved insofar as the analyst uses an analytic interpretative technique as much as possible. During this phase the patient never lies on the couch. All the patient's verbal and nonverbal communications, including his behavior, are treated as analytic material.

In the treatment of psychotic patients it is essential that the analyst is particularly sensitive to the nonverbal aspects of the patient's communication because they generally contain the most important message of the patient even if he is able to talk. Nonverbal communication is based on a process of projection which originates in early infancy and it depends on the analyst's capacity to receive and to perceive consciously the patient's projections and his ability to translate them into verbal thinking, as to whether they can be used in analytic therapy and be interpreted to the patient in a meaningful way. Those projective mechanisms of communication of the psychotic, which Melanie Klein called "projective identification," seem to be a distortion or intensification of an aspect of the early infantile relationship based on nonverbal communication between infant and mother where the "good" mother is able instinctively to respond by containing the infant's anxiety and alleviating it by her behavior (Bion). Psychotic patients use both positive and negative aspects of projective identification in their communication with the analyst, and when the need and the capacity of the patient to communicate in this way predominates, even a seriously ill psychotic patient can respond well to analysis and the outlook is prognostically relatively good.

It is important here to realize that not only does the psychotic patient in the transference relationship repeat the relation which he had with his original objects, but he attempts to form, particularly by projective identification of his impulses and fantasies conveyed verbally and nonverbally, a relationship with the analyst which he rightly or wrongly believes that his parents rejected or were incapable of accepting. I have often heard the psychotic patient state: "I am nothing, I have no identity, I dare not be anybody because I am afraid. Only if I live in a world of my own do I feel safe." Detailed investigation shows that these patients are often afraid of their positive, or aggressive intrusions into their objects as they felt or believed in the past that their primary objects, the parents, were either unreceptive and detached or too anxious and therefore the patient felt rejected. In addition they are left with a notion that they are dangerous and ought to be rejected, and therefore they have to keep away from people. The patient's nonidentity is here a protection both against the powerful intrusion into their object which they believe is omnipotent, and also the paranoid anxieties of being intruded upon if they admit any relationship to objects. They often prefer complete isolation to the terror of pain which any relationship is bound to produce in them. In the analytic transference these patients gradually dare to express themselves by projecting their impulses and problems onto the analyst. It is the analyst's receptiveness and acceptance of these projective communications conveyed to the patient by verbal interpretations which forms the basis of the patient's beginning awareness that he can be understood and accepted by another person, which is often a completely new experience for him. The analyst's interpretations also have the function of making the patient's psychotic responses and feelings acceptable to a saner part of the self that has a capacity to perceive and think which the psychotic self is lacking. In this way the patient can begin to consider and assimilate experiences which were previously meaningless or too frightening for him. I do not agree with some American analysts, for example Fromm-

Reichmann, who believe that the psychotic patient is himself the best person to understand his psychotic experiences. I have gradually come to realize how little the psychotic patient understands his own communication and how great are his difficulties in connecting his many split-off experiences and thoughts in a meaningful way. It is also extremely difficult for him to introject and retain what he has learned; again and again any sense, meaning, and sanity which are gradually rescued during analysis are lost for long periods. At such times he seems almost entirely dependent on the analyst's mind to function as a container or auxiliary ego to retain memories and experiences which have to be preserved until *the patient's introjective processes,* which are essential for normal development, begin to function more effectively.

DIFFICULTIES AND LIMITATIONS OF THE ANALYTIC APPROACH

So far I have concentrated on the projective processes used for communication. There are, however, many psychotic patients who use projective processes predominantly for noncommunication or destructive attacks on the analyst's capacity to function. Those patients are difficult to treat and they arouse very complex countertransference reactions such as mental blocking in some analysts whose unconscious problems are stirred up by the psychotic patient. However, analysis or often self-analysis enables the analyst to use his countertransference constructively to diagnose and understand the patient's hidden projected attack so that the treatment can proceed. Some psychotic patients use projective identification for releasing their impulses, anxieties, and internal objects into many different objects in the external world, leading to a complete denial of psychic reality and to mental emptiness. This produces in the patient a preoccupation with hypochondriacal sensations and a tendency to turn from the analyst to physical treatments, often in collusion with psychiatrists who are antidynamically oriented.

Occasionally a very destructive psychotic patient may form an omnipotent controlling parasitical relationship with the analyst, where the attacks on the analyst are acted out in a way which may have a paralyzing effect on both the analysis and the analyst, even though the analyst understands the meaning of this behavior and is able to verbalize it. In such cases, the patient often experiences the analyst as having been changed from omnipotence into a empty, dead, or paralyzed figure, and as a result the analyst's interpretations are felt to be lifeless or lacking in sense and meaning. Analytic work can then progress only extremely slowly and is often only of limited value. I have continued work with some of these patients for a number of years, in order to see how far such states are reversible. It is the detailed research into some of these cases which led me to the notion of a destructive narcissistic structure which kept such negative processes going. As a result of my findings, analysis did eventually make some impact on these patients, but the improvement or recovery would depend on how far it was possible to change the basic destructive narcissistic organization.

In order to understand how destructive narcissism operates, it is at first important to differentiate in the psychotic patient between the psychotic and the non-psychotic part of his personality, concepts which were first touched upon by Freud[4] when he discussed the splitting of the ego in psychosis, and were developed further by Katan[6] and particularly by Bion.[1] I have been able to observe in many psychotic patients that there is a struggle between a destructive narcissistic omnipotent part of the self which represents death and a libidinal dependent part of the self which is object-related and represents life. The destructive narcissistic parts of the self mainly attack the libidinal dependent sane parts of the self and try to destroy its object ties. As a result of this omnipotent attack there is a danger that the sane part of the self is experienced as lost or destroyed, which means that the pull towards death is almost unopposed. This situation occurs frequently in severe suicidal states where all desire to live has been lost. Analytic interpretations usually help the patient to find the lost libidinal self, which for the time being lessens the suicidal danger, but detailed analytic work is necessary to analyze the basic conflict between the positive and aggressive impulses directed against primary objects. In the schizophrenics the destructive narcissism is more organized and tries to lure the sane dependent self away from any object relatedness by false premises in order to entrap and imprison it inside the psychotic narcissistic structure. This exerts a powerful paralyzing suggestive influence on the sane parts of the self which then become entirely dominated and tied to the delusional psychotic processes. They can no longer function on their own and seem to have forgotten all good experiences of object-relatedness. Donald Meltzer has studied this process in some detail. The patient is generally not aware of the deathly power of the psychotic destructive narcissistic self which may be hidden behind a very benevolent lifesaving cover which completely deceives the psychotic patient. When the analyst gradually succeeds in exposing the destructiveness of the psychotic self, the sane ego makes some attempts to free itself from the psychotic world. But benevolent persuasiveness changes quickly into deathly threats when the patient attempts to choose health. Then the sane parts of the patient feel terrorized and are generally too weak to challenge the psychotic destructive self and so submit again for appeasement's sake. This process often completely paralyzes the analysis, and I have seen a number of psychotic patients where this structure remained dominant and unchanging despite many years of analysis. Progress in understanding these processes has opened up possibilities of helping these patients. One such patient, who had about 14 years psychotherapeutic treatment and psychoanalysis before coming to me, is making considerable progress after three and a half years of analysis using the methods and theories which I have described in this paper.

Psychoanalytic research has recently uncovered other important factors relating to the origin and function of those psychotic structures that are dominant during the acute psychotic state and are a constant threat to mental health if they remain latent or split off. Not only is time too short to report on this work, but the amount of work that is going on is still very limited. I have supervised and followed closely the analytic treatment of approximately 25 patients apart from about 15 patients whom I treated myself. Some of the analysts have been more successful than others but one can observe permanent improvements—even in cases with long hospitalization and apparent deterioration—in 40 to 80 percent of cases being treated by individual analysts. By improvement I mean that the patient appears sufficiently restored to normal functioning to be able to work, and considerably improved in social relations. Twenty years ago I suggested that all sound psychoanalytic treatment of psychotic patients would improve our understanding of the processes involved, even in cases in which we failed. But we need more facilities and funds for work with patients who cannot afford private fees, and we need more analysts trained to work with psychotics. We cannot, of course, guarantee success in any way, but I certainly feel that our results in this field have been much more successful in the last five years. This success has been due not to any change of our behavior toward our psychotic patients but to an increase of knowledge and understanding of the psychopathology of psychosis, which our more classical psychoanalytic technique gradually revealed.

This has led to improvements in our capacity to interpret psychotic material and thus to greater effectiveness of our work with psychotic patients.

NOTES

1. Bion, W. R. (1957), Differentiation of the psychotic from the non-psychotic personalities. *Int. J. Psycho-Analysis,* 38; and in *Second Thoughts.* London: Heineman.

2. Bion, W. R. (1962), *Learning from Experience.* London: Heinemann.

3. Freud, S. (1937), Analysis terminable and interminable. *Standard Edition,* 23:216–253. London: Hogarth Press, 1964.

4. Freud, S. (1940), An outline of psycho-analysis. *Standard Edition,* 23:141–207. London: Hogarth Press, 1964.

5. Fromm-Reichmann, F. (1948), Notes on the development of treatment of schizophrenics by psychoanalytic therapy. In: *Psychoanalysis and Psychotherapy,* ed. D. M.Eullard. Chicago: Univ. of Chicago Press, 1959.

6. Katan, M. (1954), The Importance of a non-psychotic part in schizophrenia. *Int. J. Psycho-Analysis,* 35.

7. Klein, M. (1935), A contribution to the psychogenesis of manic-depressive states. *Int. J. Psycho-Analysis,* 16: 16:145–174.

8. Klein, M. (1940), Mourning and its relations to manic-depressive states. In: *Contributions to Psychoanalysis (1921–1945),* ed. M. Klein. London: Hogarth, 1948.

9.   Mahler, M. S. (1969), Perturbances of symbiosis and individuation in the development of the psychotic ego. In: *Problems of Psychosis,* eds. P. Doucet and C. Laurin. Amsterdam: Excerpta Medica Foundation, pp. 188–195.

10. Rosenfeld, H. A. (1947), Analysis of a schizophrenic state with depersonalisation. *Int. J. Psycho-Analysis,* 28:130–139.

11. Rosenfeld, H. A. (1959), An Investigation into the Psychoanalytic Theory of Depression. *Int. J. Psycho-Analysis,* 60:105–129.

12. Rosenfeld, H. A. (1964), Object relations of an acute schizophrenic patient in the transference situation. In: *Recent Research on Schizophrenia.* Psychiatric Research Reports of the American Psychiatric Association, Washington, D.C.

13. Rosenfeld, H. A. (1969), *The Negative Therapeutic Reaction.* In: *Tactics and Technique in Psychoanalytic Therapy,* ed. Peter L. Giovacchini, Vol. II. London: Hogarth Press, 1975, pp. 214–228.

14. Rosenfeld, H.A. (1969), Contribution to the psychopathology of psychotic states. The importance of projective identification in the ego structure and the object relations of the psychotic patient. In: *Problems of Psychosis,* eds. P. Doucet and C. Laurin. Amsterdam: Excerpta Medica Foundation, pp. 115–128.

15. Rosenfeld, H. A. (1971), A clinical approach to the psycholanalytic theory of the life and death instincts: an investigation into the aggressive aspects of narcissism. *Int. J. Psycho-Analysis,* 52:169–178.

16. Scott, W. C. M. (1947), On the intense affects in treating a severe manic-depressive disorder. *Int. J. Psycho-Analysis,* 28:139–165. (The original paper was presented to the Congress in Paris, 1938).

17. Segal, H. (1950), Some aspects of the analysis of a schizophrenic. *Int. J. Psycho-Analysis,* 31:268–278.

18. Thorner, H. (1955), Three defences against inner persecution. In *New Directions in Psychoanalysis,* ed. M. Klein et al. London: Tavistock.

19. Winnicott, D. W. (1945), Primitive emotional development. In *Collected Papers.* London: Tavistock, 1958.

20. Meltzer, D. (1963), A Contribution to the Metapsychology of Cyclothymic States. *Int. J. Psycho-Analysis,* 44:83–96.

Hanna Segal, M.B., Ch.B.

As my own work has the same roots and the same theoretical bases as Dr. Rosenfeld's, my contribution will probably be a matter of going into finer detail on certain problems raised in his report rather than an actual discussion of it.

Since time is limited, I shall confine my comments to three points in particular:

1. the external framework of analysis, which we call "management";
2. the internal framework of analysis, or the "analytical setting"; and
3. the particular importance of psychotic attacks against what we call "sanity," whether that of the analyst or that of the patient's own ego, or that of the healthy part of the patient projected into the analyst and attacked in him.

To begin with the problem of management of the environment, I entirely agree with Dr. Rosenfeld that this has to be arranged with extreme care. I think the reputation of psychoanalysis of psychotics has suffered great damage because of overoptimism on the part of certain analysts who have undertaken analyses of psychotics without first ensuring that the analysis is backed up by an environment in which continuity of psychoanalytic treatment is feasible. To take a very basic example, they failed to make sure at the outset that someone could accompany the patient to his consultation if he were unable to come alone. I should just like to add a word to what Dr. Rosenfeld said about the danger of hospitals which are too "good." I am extremely wary of institutions, hospitals, therapeutic communities, and so on which have ambitions of providing analytical or pseudoanalytical therapies, as an environment for patients undergoing psychoanalysis. I feel that the psychoanalyst's own psychoanalytical intervention is adversely affected by the interference of what are invariably confused pseudoanalytical interventions upon the patient. A recent experience of mine in the United States made me reflect a great deal on the matter. I saw a borderline case, a young girl, who was undergoing psychoanalytic treatment (or analytical psychotherapy, depending on what one calls "analysis") in a therapeutic community; in the space of two days she had one session with her therapist, one group session, one session of psychodrama, interpretations from her young resident, a nurse, an attendant, and at least four other patients. This girl's symptom was depersonalization, and I shall leave to you to imagine the effect these various interventions must have had on the depersonalization symptom. What I, as an analyst, would want in the way of management and environment for a psychotic patient in analysis with me is a minimum of physical security and, if possible, an understanding environment capable of providing support and human warmth, an environment which would be analytically neutral and not one where there is any attempt made to mobilize or interpret the patient's unconscious. Obviously, it is up to the analyst to see to this. I am not referring here to the effect of psychotherapeutic communities on patients who are not in analysis, because this is a different problem entirely.

Once this external framework is organized, it is the analyst's job to provide an analytical environment within which the analysis can be carried out, or what I term the "internal framework."

Naturally, we are all familiar with the formal elements of an analytical framework, such as the regular frequency and length of sessions, the various elements in the consulting room, which must always remain unchanged, and so forth. But possibly the most important element of all in the analytical setting is provided by the analyst's own behavior. I refer particularly here to the manner in which the analyst offers himself as a container, a framework for the patient's projective identifications. Bion and Rosenfeld have gone into great detail on this function, and I shall simply add a remark concerning the role of verbal interpretation as a necessary element in holding together the analytical framework itself. Last year I presented in London and Los Angeles a paper on a psychotic or chronic borderline patient who had done some major acting out. After a period of five years there was an important change in the content of his material and in his behavior. In both London and Los Angeles a number of colleagues observed that this change could be attributed to my own patience, the length of treatment, my friendliness, my lack of irritability, and so on. This very kindly view of my personality was of course most flattering, but I am nonetheless convinced that the comment was beside the point. This would be like saying that an operation was a success because the surgeon had two hands or did not suffer from blindness. His two hands and two eyes are a sine qua non of the operation, because you cannot become a surgeon if you are one-armed or blind; and I sincerely hope that no one becomes an analyst—and especially one who treats psychotics—if they are going to be short-tempered or irritable with their patients. In the same way as a surgeon has to use his hands to make something happen, the analyst has to use his own personality to bring something about in analysis.

From the point of view of the framework of the analysis as a container for the patient's projective identification, I think that interpretation plays a very important role here; especially because in order to maintain his omnipotence the psychotic patient makes incessant attacks upon the analytical framework itself and also upon the analyst's capacity to function. Now unless his attacks are understood and interpreted, the patient does not feel understood or contained. For example, if the patient projects a great deal of anxiety and hostility through his behavior and the analyst remains calm and friendly but fails to grasp what is happening, the patient is likely to have the impression that the analyst is a wall. In many cases this repeats what the patients felt about their parents—that the parents did not understand what was going on. Very often in this situation the attacks are intensified and can become very dangerous if the analyst fails to understand and does not interpret. The patient may react in the following way: "If the analyst does not understand the aggression contained in verbal expression, then I shall have to smash the windows to make him understand anything!" Furthermore, the patient's fantasy of omnipotence can make him feel that the analyst's capacity to function is completely destroyed, or imagine that the analyst is laughing at him, and so on. The analyst's calm and friendliness can be seen as a form of mockery or as a counterattack. Hence, whatever the analyst's behavior, the depressive and persecution fantasies multiply. The interpretation is the means whereby the patient is given the feeling that his projection has been received, contained, and understood. The more accurate and complete the interpretation is, the more the patient feels that his projected parts are contained and containable. The interpretation then enables him to reintegrate the parts of himself and of internal objects which have become more acceptable through the functioning of the analyst.

Among the various types of attacks upon the analyst's capacity to function and upon the sane part of the ego involved in the psychotic process, I only want to deal with one extremely important category; namely, the attacks made by the patient's psychotic element against the saner parts and the ego function. This emerges in particular when the saner part of the ego begins to assert itself as a result of the psychoanalytic cure. At that point the patient is in a very painful situation, and it is the saner part of the ego, the ego apparatus whose perceptions are most intact, which is affected by the depressive suffering in the psychotic patient. Furthermore, there is also the special pain involved in recognizing the fact that one is psychotic, and the awareness of all the internal—and often external—destruction brought about by the psychosis. I think it was in 1940 that I presented a paper on "Depression in the Schizophrenic," where I describe how a young schizophrenic girl as she approached the depressive position identified with Ophelia and, in a moment of lucidity, made her first comment with insight by saying sadly "But Ophelia was mad, wasn't she." Threatened by this insight and the suffering entailed by it, she attacked her ego, fragmenting it entirely, in that moment. At times one sees in psychotics a real hatred mobilized against everything that represents sanity. The word "sanity" is charged with emotion; some patients say "I hate my sanity" because their "sanity is what causes all the suffering."

Let me tell you here a borderline patient's dream which, I think, will give a simple illustration of this point. This is not one of my own patients, but a case I am supervising. This patient frequently has psychotic episodes and moments of violence. Her violent episodes are more or less contained in analysis, but almost every Saturday there is an incident of one kind or another; she might smash the analyst's windows, break her watch, take a dangerous overdose of sleeping pills just outside the analyst's consulting room, or try to set fire to the analyst's couch, and so on. One Saturday after a week of very significant work, she left without any psychotic act having taken place, and on the following Monday the analysis began in a neurotic stance with associations. She said that she had not been feeling well during the weekend, and that she felt as though her head did not belong to her at all; she could remember nothing about the previous Saturday's analytic session. She had been unable to drive her car because (the phrase is important because it recurs in the dream) "she could not take notice of anything"; she had also felt very irritable toward Robert, a friend of hers, and had been unable to speak to him. Then she recounted a dream. In the dream she was in the analyst's waiting room with some other people, among them Mary. She went into the consulting room but found that she was not alone with the analyst; leaning against the analyst in a very friendly way, there was a secretary at work taking notes; the patient was furious at this presence in her analysis. First of all she attacked the secretary verbally, but as the latter remained quite untroubled and continued to take notes and do her work, the patient, carried away in a frenzy of rage, vomited on both the analyst and the secretary, and tried to force the vomit into the secretary's mouth "to make her break down." The associations to this dream mostly concerned Mary, a friend of hers at primary school when she was five or six years old; this Mary seemed to her a very enviable person because she was full of self-confidence, was good at her schoolwork, was gay, fairly aggressive, and had many friends. At that time the patient herself was quite the opposite; she never spoke and lived in constant, paralyzing fear of death. She always felt that she was in a state of mortal sin and went to confession every day, although this did her precious little good because she was convinced that eating or breathing was a mortal sin. The analyst's interpretation was that the secretary represented a part of the patient as it had been the previous week, and which rather resembled Mary, capable of friendship and of independence, leaning in a familiar way against the analyst, dependent upon him, and able to "take notice," to remember things, and to work. It is this part of herself, these ego functions of retention and "taking notice," the capacity to establish relations, that she hates and attacks as much as the analyst. This is what made her unable to perceive, to take note, to remember, and to have any relations with her friends over the weekend. Just as in her childhood she forbade herself to eat and breathe.

I mention this scrap of material to draw attention to the importance of the moments when the patient comes closer to sanity and, feeling this improvement as a danger, attacks the sane parts and often provokes serious negative therapeutic reactions. In my view, the understanding and interpretation of this reaction at the time it is produced is abolutely essential and indispensable in maintaining progress in the analysis of psychotics.

Jean Laplanche, M.D., Ph.D.

This symposium lies directly in the path of a previous confrontation of ideas in Montreal in 1969. Would it be asking too much to hope that interest can still be given to the general subject of the contributions, communications, and discussions, which was the overall problem of psychosis? Even though the present Symposium concerns the treatment of psychosis, I think it has to be put into perspective on the basic question which has always put psychoanalysis to the test right from the start and which still remains unchanged: should psychosis be considered homogeneous to the field of psychoneuroses of defense so masterfully explored by Freud, or should we try to find a specific and completely heterogeneous mechanism for it; or perhaps not even a mechanism, but rather a rift, a defect, a fundamental lack? The communications by Green and Rosolato on this point will be reread with great interest. The school of Melanie Klein, to which Mr. Rosenfeld belongs, leans as far as possible in the direction of homogeneity, since it even goes so far as to reverse the terms and make the paranoid-schizoid and depressive positions the fundamental common lot of all human beings, with both neurotic symptomatology and normality itself as nothing but more or less successful modes of overcoming psychotic positions. This is not without direct influence upon technique, since the Kleinians are the most determined supporters of a classic psychoanalytical technique for psychotics. After all, psychoanalytical technique would not have to conquer psychosis since from the start and for all time there has never been a departure from it.

"Long-term treatments of psychotic states." The title of this symposium—whose French translation would be "long-haul" treatment—merits reflection. For if psychosis is a common potentiality overcome to a greater or lesser degree according to each case, if psychosis is *homogeneous* with other psychic and psychopathological manifestations, then the *length* of treatment becomes a purely quantitative matter. The more serious the case the more difficult, and therefore the longer, the treatment will be.

However, if psychosis is in fact heterogeneous, qualitatively different, and marked by a hiatus, then one might object to the marine metaphor "long-haul" which irresistibly evokes its ironical complement in the final phrase of a well-known article by Lacan: "using the technique instituted by Freud outside of the experience to which it applies". . . is like "laboring at the oars when the boat is on the sand."

If one is convinced of the psychotic *defect,* then "long-term" treatment can only have three possible meanings: the most pessimistic is that it will never be possible to remedy the defect; the two others are that either the object of the search has not yet been found and the quest is still going on, or else the lengthy duration of this prolonged treatment offers a possibility of some day stumbling by pure chance over the lever that will bring the whole structure down.

I shall mention only as a reminder the problems of countertransference entailed in the unlimited commitment involved in dealing with a psychotic—it is often stressed that this commitment should ideally constitute a veritable alienation of the psychoanalyst, of his time, his leisure, his autonomy, and of his whole being. But let us go back to the heterogeneity, to the qualitative hiatus of psychosis, of which there are so many instances of proof that it seems both banal and anachronistic to recall a few of them. For example:

1. The phenomena of spontaneous and abrupt recoveries in schizophrenias following a traumatic event or an intercurrent affection, in which Freud saw an indication of a process of sudden renarcissisation.

2. Shock cures, and particularly insulin shock treatment. What a condemnation of our shortsighted empiricism it is to see the major *theoretical* interest of these treatments suddenly vanish, on the pretext that they are being abandoned in practice and perhaps for reasons of mere convenience!

This heterogeneity of psychosis is borne out, particularly for a Kleinian such as Rosenfeld, by the idea that the analyst of a psychotic must act as a sort of reservoir or archivist of the analysis, because of the patient's own inability to register subjectively, to memorize, to metabolize what is interpreted. A most interesting idea which brings us back to a discussion between Lebovici and Leclaire in Montreal. For we know that the process of subjectivization in analysis is inseparable from a certain dialectical concept of temporality, which, with Freud, we call "deferred action" and which refers to the very particular modality of human symbolization. This is not the place to deal with that matter, but it should nevertheless be asked:

1. What are the basic conditions for "deferred action" to take place?
2. Are these conditions partially lacking in psychosis?
3. Would it not be preferable to concentrate our efforts on the restoration of the capacity to integrate or symbolize rather than to provide a thousand times over material for symbolization in the hope that perhaps just once it will work, without quite knowing how?

If we decide in favor of this "heterogeneous" concept of psychosis, there are two lines of thought, Freudian and postFreudian at the same time, concerning the nature of the defect in question:

1. a defect in ego formation and coherence; and
2. a defect in some key element in the symbolic field

Ego defect. This idea appears with Freud's Project for a Scientific Psychology and continues through Federn, Pankow, or Widlöcher in his communication in Montreal. Here the "ego" has to be taken in its Freudian sense, not as a functional and rational centre, but as an identificatory element subject to cathexis or withdrawal of cathexis, "Gestalt" in the image of a body acting in any and every way possible on the primary process it inhibits. Hence hallucinations are never diminished through any amount of learning or training; they are liberated or inhibited by an overall effect for which Widlöcher would like to bring back the term of "sense of reality," the "intimate feeling of a familiarity between the ego and reality," which has nothing to do with the reality principle conceived as a principle of adaptation, detour, and rationality.

With regard to the *defect in a key element in symbolization,* let us bear in mind that its explicit origin lies in Freud's incessant efforts to define the mode of "defence" proper to psychosis. Rejection of a piece of reality, repression of reality, disavowal *(Verleugnung)* of reality, are all conceptual stages of Freud's obstinate searching. In "disavowal of reality" the word "reality" should not be misconstrued if it is understood that what Freud generally saw the psychotic disavow was a very strange "reality," the symbolic organizer of reality but never positively perceptible : castration. I shall not dwell here on the differences between the Freudian disavowal of castration, the Lacanian foreclosure of the "Name of the Father" or the defective triangulation invoked by others, but rather upon the designation of a field of deficiency—a deficiency within the oedipal framework, which, as Rosolato pointed out, does not exclude the fact that the Oedipus complex appears in the negative throughout the psychotic universe.

Are these two defects, that of the ego and that of symbolization articulated together, are they dependent on each other, and how? Should we go along with Green in saying that it is triangulation which makes the acquisition of identity possible, or can we maintain the contrary? Can one not conceive of a relative independence between the defect of symbolization and the failure of the ego image, with these two elements of psychotic deficiency rejoining each other in different combinations and different dialectics, which would account, for example, for the schizophrenic's inability to stabilize his "object of narcissistic projection," which the paranoiac is able to do?

Whatever the case may be, these and no others are the fundamental questions, and it is these questions rather than any empirical considerations which should determine the initiation and the management of any cure. I shall list a few practical questions which become meaningful only when placed in the correct perspective:

1. The role of the extrinsic anamnesis, of recourse to the environment, to the family. Here we oscillate between two extremes, i.e., from systematic recourse, to exclusion and violent condemnation;

2. the role of the psychiatric colleague;

3. the role of therapy with two or more psychotherapists;

4. the role of institutions inasmuch as they can be the conveyors of a "law." One must be wary, however, of any inclination to establish a law artificially on a semiplayful register;

5. the role of shock therapies;

6. the frequency and rhythm of consultations, where there will sooner or later have to come up an examination of the subjective motivations of the dependence into which some analysts fall headlong; and

7. the role to be attributed to the imaginary, or simply the image, in the relation, namely, the image of the other in face-to-face confrontation, objects of projection and narcissistic structuration, modeling, drawing, and so on.

Yes, it can quite truly be said that until these options are systematically discussed in their theoretical fundamentals, the treatment of psychotics will be no more than tales of individual adventures, expeditions into a "terra incognita" where no one looks for, or even imagines meeting up with, the experience, the discoveries, and the hypotheses of another explorer.

Evelyne Kestemberg, M.A.

After the theoretical considerations presented by Dr. Laplanche, I shall now try to keep to the role of discussant, which leads me to put a certain number of questions to Dr. Rosenfeld. Perhaps somewhere along the line we will rejoin some of the theoretical aspects mentioned a moment ago.

First of all, I should like to tell Dr. Rosenfeld that I was struck by a certain number of points of agreement between us. It is interesting to note that the lessons of clinical experience have led many of us to adopt fairly similar attitudes on techniques in spite of our theoretical differences. Indeed, it looks as though genuine attention to the discourse of psychotic patients inevitably leads to certain technical options upon which it is up to us to theorize subsequently.

Hence I want to start at the outside and work inward, and begin by emphasizing the points of agreement. I myself am very much aware of the importance, stressed by Dr. Rosenfeld, of the selection of psychotic patients for analysis and also that of diagnosis in discerning what he calls "latent psychosis." I would be tempted to say: a psychotic structure predominant in certain phobic, obsessional, psychosomatic states, and others, which to all appearances seem to belong to a neurotic-type organization. I feel that this is extremely important and here perhaps I fall in line, to a certain extent, with what Laplanche just said. I do not think that *all* psychotic patients are capable of coping with the new orientation of the psychoanalytical experience and gaining some benefit from it. Their capacity for it should be assessed during their interviews with the analyst and should be weighed with the greatest caution with a view to proposing analysis to some, but also recognizing the necessity of abandoning the idea for others. As Rosenfeld points out, this aptitude must be evaluated not according to the request—which is being rather dinned into our ears at the moment, and which is a "catch-all" word—but especially by means of the patient's experience during the initial meetings with the analyst. This shows firstly that the patient wants to be recognized for himself as he is, and secondly that he understands what the analyst says, however discreet the latter's intervention may be, and even if he gives no explicit response to it. This implicit response and its various modalities are nonetheless perceptible, for the patient's manner changes during these sessions. I cannot expound upon this at length and give illustrations, but I think that it has something in common with what Dr. Rosenfeld says, even though I am by no means sure that the theorization involved is quite the same.

A second point of agreement with Dr. Rosenfeld concerns the use of a psychiatric colleague parallel to the analysis. This seems to me absolutely essential for severely psychotic patients, for a number of reasons. In the first place the patient has to be able to bear his suffering without doing any irreversible acting out; in this respect psychiatric attention is an indispensable aid without which in a great many cases the analyst's work could not continue. Furthermore, the double-sided care of the patient is necessary to the analyst himself, from the countertransference point of view. First of all it gives him a degree of security, and secondly it attenuates the feeling of being all-powerful which seems to me particularly dangerous when dealing with psychotic patients and which is often present in the mothering referred to by Laplanche, as well, no doubt, as in the desire to treat psychotics. Long experience has convinced me that cooperation with a psychiatrist or an institution is particularly fruitful. One condition of working in this way is that each one knows exactly what he has to do and does it; for example, the institution must not take over the role of the analyst and produce interpretations, while the psychiatrist must not go back over the work of the analyst and the analyst must, in turn, not lose sight of the fact that during his interviews with the patient or in the course of the analysis the effects of the respective functions of the psychiatrist and the institution have to be taken up and if necessary interpreted. To give a rough illustration, it seems to me that an analyst cannot ignore the Oedipal constellation organized at the outset when he treats patients who are also "managed" by a psychiatrist or an institution. This creates for the patient a sort of "forcing" into a confrontation with the unconscious Oedipal experience whose impact has to be assessed with the finest degree of accuracy possible by the analyst. To my mind, this does not imply that the interpretation has to be formulated immediately in every case.

In the third place, I go along with Dr. Rosenfeld entirely not only with regard to the difficulty of being able to count on the cooperation of the family but also in his evaluation of the role of the family environment in both the genesis of the mental disturbance and its effect on the course of the evolution of the psychosis. I am as critical as Rosenfeld is of the maternal psychogenesis as it is so often described. Although it is easy to demonstrate that psychotic patients have families—and especially mothers—whose

structural characteristics and behavior have been the subject of careful study, it is also easy to demonstrate that
mothers with these characteristics do not always produce
psychotic children. Furthermore, there can also be
psychotic children in families with very different characteristics. In actual fact, what can be observed is the enormous
variety of family backgrounds, and even life histories of
psychotics. As for the importance of the mother's libidinal
contribution at the outset of life, there are a number of far
more detailed studies which can enlarge our knowledge
concerning its importance and its quality and flexibility in
the organization of the psychical apparatus and in its evolution. At this level Winnicott and others have opened a door
which gives us a glimpse of rich prospects, although without leading us to what would be a facile and mechanistic
psychogenesis.

On the other hand, I do think that the fact of having
a psychotic child in the family creates a situation, a way of
existence which has such a changing effect, and produces
such alterations in the psychic economy of each member of
the family that it creates a vicious circle whose pernicious
effects are worth careful assessment and lengthy consideration.

To continue my way "from the outside working inwards," I should now like to dwell for a moment on the
"analytical setting" Hanna Segal spoke about. I did notice
a rather guilty smile on the faces of some of my colleagues
when Dr. Rosenfeld said that "acute psychotic patients are
generally seen by the analyst six times a week" and that
"there should be no interruption of the treatment by holidays" when necessary. We are aware that this frequency of
sessions is very often desirable, but we also know that despite all kinds of difficulties, a valid psychotherapeutic, and
even psychoanalytic treatment can be carried out according
to a different rhythm. In any event, it seems necessary to
me to stress that one cannot consider the frequency of

sessions as a sine qua non condition of the analytical process. All the same, I think that Dr. Rosenfeld and I do agree on this too.

I think the moment has come now to put to him several questions raised by his interesting report. With regard to the "face to face" consultation, it would be extremely useful to hear him explain in greater detail why he recommends this technique for acute psychotic states and some psychosomatic cases, particularly so since our attitudes are again in line with each other here. It would be most interesting to all of us to hear Dr. Rosenfeld's theorization on this point, as well as his point of view and an outline of his technique concerning the methods of interpretation of nonverbal material. I should be very glad if he would explain how he thinks this extremely valuable nonverbal material should be reintegrated so as to avoid the risk of damage which can be involved in interpretations of behaviour.

Now I should like to get away from techniques and their theoretical underpinnings and concentrate on some theoretical considerations which seem to me worthy of further clarification. Here I refer first of all to the two facets of projective identification. As a rule we see the negative aspect of such an identificatory process, namely, that what is bad is projected onto or into the analyst. Now, as Dr. Rosenfeld emphasizes, Kleinian texts underline a beneficial aspect which I think should be given very careful attention in the interpretation of the projective identification; the introjective retrieval of what the subject has himself emptied out through projection on or into the analyst.

If you will forgive me for going back a little, I should like to say a word in passing about the feeling of nonidentity Dr. Rosenfeld mentioned, and which I feel must not be taken too literally. It seems to me that when the patient experiences a feeling of nonidentity, this should be understood not only as a bid for recognition, as Rosenfeld states implicitly, but also as a feeling of the impossibility of identification. This feeling could represent the present state of the patient's internal economy whose drives have been defused and whose images are differentiated badly or not at all, because the organizing Oedipus complex has been dismantled or disorganized within the present topic and economic regression.

To come back to projective identification, there is another aspect which seems worthy of consideration. I was impressed, as most of you probably were, by the fact that Kleinian texts, and Dr. Rosenfeld's in particular, say "project into" and not "project on to." This formulation of interpretation brings into play the notions of "container" and "contained." I do not think that this is just a matter of verbal form, and it would be useful to try and grasp the deeper significance of the words. It seems to me that verbalization of the interpretation in the terms "you project into me the bad side of yourself" implies the analyst's own introjection of what is projected by the patient. This means that the interpretation proposes the substitution of an introjective process—that of the analyst—for the patient's projective process, thus modifying the balance of the patient's economy at the time. If the analyst introjects the "bad" elements projected into him by the patient and remains undestroyed by it, could it not be said that he thereby reduces the splitting between the good and the bad object and opens the way, through identification, to a more accessible introjection? Can we not discern here a passage towards the mobilization of the patient's introjective processes in the first place, and subsequently toward evolutive identificatory processes? Is this not perhaps the beginning of the ability to identify with the analyst's analytic function, or in other words, with the analyst's ego? Is this one of the aspects of the auxiliary ego constituted by the analyst, such as Rosenfeld describes? If so, this could possibly imply the feasibility of renewed symbolic functioning of the ego, either lost or destructured in the psychosis or not yet reached in the case of an extremely severe psychotic evolution, such as infantile autism. Furthermore, the advantage of such a formulation seems to be that it involves the body in the process of introjection and therefore in that of interpretation. It could be suggested that this explicit reference to the projection-receiving body of the analyst might in some fortunate cases help to bolster up their own body fantasy and a more explicit reference to the oral and anal erogenous zones in particular—a propping up necessary for the gradual installation of Oedipal identifications via dissimilar bodies for each of the differentiated parental images, integrating the castration fantasy.

I was speaking there of the more fortunate cases, which are relatively few in comparison with the others, as Dr. Rosenfeld pointed out. With regard to the latter he proposes the notion of a destructive, deathly narcissism, an absolutely fundamental concept which should be brought under discussion. It seems to me that destructive narcissism, as seen by Dr. Rosenfeld, somehow takes the place of the "biological bedrock" evoked by Freud, which includes castration.

This is not, of course, the right place for an in-depth discussion of the concept, even if time allowed, but it might nonetheless be appropriate to outline here what I consider to be its importance and its limitations.

With regard to its importance, its descriptive value is certain when it is put for patients in terms of a "disturbed part" (that which is organized by the narcissistic encystment) opposing recovery, or the sane, healthy part turned toward objectal ties. From the theoretical viewpoint, however, things look more complicated: the invalidation of therapeutic attempts by the deathly aspect of narcissism was, as we know, put forward by Freud in his division of psychoneuroses into two categories, that is the narcissistic neuroses (including the psychoses) inaccessible to transference, and the transference psychoneuroses. However, Freud later laid greater stress on the negative therapeutic reaction based precisely upon castration anxiety—the "biological bedrock." Now Dr. Rosenfeld's theorization seems to substitute for castration anxiety and its underlying Oedipal organization, the complete division, even a splitting between the subject's good part (accessible to objectal ties) and the bad part, which emanates from this deathly narcissistic core. It seems rather dangerous to me to dismiss from our own conceptualization the organizing value of the Oedipus, within the regressions it entails, and of which, in my view, the narcissistic withdrawal is the final and most perilous phase. Also, such a conceptualization of the splitting between good and bad, sane and disturbed, the objectal and the narcissistic, seems to ignore the economic factor in the diachronic and synchronic organization of the psychism.

Perhaps it would be better to speak of the tremendous prevalence of narcissistic cathexes, which can go so far as to stifle the interplay of object-cathexes, that involved a lethal aspect or even the deathly fascination of megalomanic omnipotence which effaces the object in favour of hallucinatory satisfaction. Finally, it may be that in the above-mentioned dichotomy there is a risk of neglecting the beneficial aspect of secondary narcissistic cathexes which, as we well know, are powerful props in the evolution of identificatory movements during the course of treatment.

I am sorry they have had to be so cursory, but these are just a few of the reflections raised in my mind by Dr. Rosenfeld's most interesting work and which I wanted to put to you.

Part II

THERAPEUTIC EXPERIENCES AND EXPERIMENTS

INTRODUCTION

A very wide and varied range of experiences is presented here. They were carried out by teams working in different geographical situations and administrative, financial and material conditions. These teams were furthermore made up by people of different age groups and professional training. It might appear somewhat surprising to be presented with contributions from the high places of research on psychiatric therapy, such as Chestnut Lodge, the Menninger Foundation, the Massachusetts Mental Health Center, and the Austen Riggs Center, at the same time as with papers written by youthful teams like the Laval catchment area team in Quebec, and hear accounts of relatively recent experiments such as the La Velotte Home or the therapeutic communities in Milan. However, these experiments are not very far removed from their initial stages and the difficulties encountered are therefore still fresh in mind, so that any reader who is about to embark upon a new experiment will find a guide here to help, a mediation between his own first halting steps and the ideal or idealized models provided by the successes of the above-mentioned major institutions.

The experiences presented relate either simultaneously or alternately to institutions and their functioning, and therapeutic methods and research concerning the evaluation of therapeutic outcome.

A group of French child psychiatrists (René Diatkine, Serge Lebovici, Jean-Louis Lang, and Roger Misès), with between 20 and 30 years of practice in the treatment of psychotic children, met to compare experiences. A summary of their discussion is presented by Roger Misès.

These authors—all psychoanalysts—avoid the trap of a discussion opposing organogenesis and psychogenesis; in this they follow thefootsteps of Freud, who proposes an "aetiological equation"[1] in which, to culminate in the same disturbance, the fewer biological "predispositions" there are the more external events there have to be and vice versa.[2] There are undeniably some neurobiological factors involved, but child psychoses are of extreme etiological, symptomatic, and evolutive complexity. The multidimensional therapeutic approach leaves a wide margin for relational factors.

The course of evolution runs more frequently to character disorders than towards adult schizophrenia, which rarely occurs. The major problem remains the existence of a deficiency syndrome, in the functional, not the organic sense of the term. This syndrome, consisting of alterations of speech, motricity, temporospatial organization, etc. is often the more marked the earlier the onset of the psychosis.

Are there grounds for pessimism or for optimism? Statistics published fail to take into sufficient consideration the great amount of information provided by longitudinal studies covering long periods of time. All of them include children whose evolution was favorable enough to justify all the energy put into the therapeutic endeavor, conditional upon the availability of a gamut of different therapies for appropriate use according to the various stages of evolution.

Behavior therapy, which is one of the possible therapeutic techniques, is as yet little used in France; those who are now beginning to use it are opponents of psychoanalysis, and not themselves psychoanalysts as Ronald Feldman is.

As Feldman points out, behavior therapy lends itself better than other psychotherapies to an objective evaluation of outcome. It is easy to understand its attraction to researchers trained in the mold of experimental psychology methods.

These methods can certainly be applied to the most unpromising cases where direct psychoanalytical therapy is out of the question, even though psychoanalytic understanding is likely to be able to enlighten the caring staff.

Thus, for example, the cases treated at the Orthogenic School were very carefully selected by Bettelheim; individual psychotherapy is only one facet of therapy whose major aspects consist of therapy through the milieu and the counsellors' considerable cathexis of the children. In his philosophy this therapy is diametrically opposed to behavior therapy of any kind; it is far preferable to allow for a movement of regression in which to get rid of all the conditionings that have imprisoned the child and prevented him from being able to feel, express or fulfill his wishes, or to become the subject of his instincts, to attain any internal autonomy.

However distant it may seem from the theoretical conceptions of psychoanalysis, behavior therapy has the merit of proposing something for the most hopeless cases. We are perfectly within our rights to disagree with it, but in that case it is up to us to provide an alternative proposition.

One thing that should also be added, and which is

more apparent in the accounts given by Feldman than in Ayllon's, is that much more can happen in behavior therapy than is contained in its theoretical description. It provides an opportunity for contacts with the patient and the possibility of establishing an extremely important relationship between the latter and the caring staff. If "something can be done," then there is something codified to alleviate the anxiety of the caring staff when confronted by what were until then hopeless cases. In other words, there are other interpretations of the therapeutic process and results than those put forward by the behavior therapists. *Mutatis mutandis,* the behavior therapists could give an interpretation of the action of psychoanalysis which would consider the psychoanalyst's interventions as reinforcements of certain forms of verbal conduct. Despite the benefits Ayllon attributes to the token economy, one remains rather perplexed by the generalization of this point of view and eager for exchanges at another level. The development of the symbolic function in the higher apes gives them access to this token economy, as has been common knowledge for a very long time.

True, in operant conditioning experiments there are electroencephalographic differences between normal and psychotic children, such as those presented by Lelord, but we are nevertheless tempted to join Ajuriaguerra in adding "I do not believe at all that psychic illness occurs solely in the brain. I think it happens through the brain, and that nothing goes on in the aureola!"

The antipsychiatrists, even those who originally had psychoanalytical training, simultaneously reject the idea of the biological substrate of psychosis and the internal instinctual, fantasy, and defensive organization. From the alienating disturbance of communication within a family, to which psychosis is traced—that eventually turns the sick member into a provisional "identified patient," a favorite theme of family psychotherapy—they go straight to the accusation and condemnation of society as a whole. There is a certain amount of confusion here: although one might say that society is mad just as we say the psychotic is mad, it cannot be said that society is psychotic.

André Green's paper is a thorough examination of the theoretical positions adopted by the English antipsychiatrists. Philippe Paumelle agrees with André Green that there is an antipsychiatrist in every psychiatrist who criticizes certain intolerable situations. Fortunately for psychiatry, psychiatrists, nursing staff, and patients have raised their voices in protest at various points throughout its history. But this is quite a different thing from decrying violence *in* psychiatry and the violence *of* psychiatry.

If we go beyond the theory and take a look at antipsychiatric "practice" we find no fewer problems than at the theoretical level. The antipsychiatric experiments, such as Kingsley Hall for example, have also dealt with selected cases and failed to avoid the rejection of those who proved unable to integrate themselves into these particular communities. The lack of concern for the caring staff puts them in a very distressing position when faced with the mortal aggressiveness, the deathly narcissism of psychotics.

Ping-Nie Pao's paper reveals the quality of the work done at Chestnut Lodge, which was founded in 1910. In structure and conditions of treatment, the patients of whom he writes are placed at the opposite end of the scale from Ayllon's. One can appreciate not only the standard of training and supervision given at Chestnut Lodge, but also the honesty, authenticity, and depth of the commitment on the part of the therapists, of whom Searles is another example in this symposium.

The reader will also be able to see the quality of the work carried out at the C.F. Menninger Memorial Hospital. Like much of his work, the text presented by Otto Kernberg concentrates on the distinction between borderline and chronic schizophrenics. Both treatment modalities and prognosis are different for each of these two groups of patients, which points out the utility of diagnostic criteria. Kernberg proposes a combination of intensive psychoanalytical psychotherapy, highly structured milieu therapy, and drug medication.

In the tradition of Chestnut Lodge, where he worked for a long time, Otto Will does not make use of drugs. The Austen Riggs Center is a relatively small institution that has the advantage of being situated in a small town, Stockbridge, and this facilitates communication between patients and townspeople. People from outside can take part in the theatre group activities, for example. If, by chance, a resident of the Austen Riggs Center wanders out into the street stark naked, neither the inhabitants of the town nor the police would pay much attention. The institution, which at present takes young patients, has planned a well-thought-out system of distribution of organization and management tasks where the responsibility of the medical staff is acknowledged—contrary to the case in the antipsychiatric communities (where the caring staff wants to make no distinction between themselves and their patients)—and where the idea of the patients' own responsibility is not rejected.

The research work described by Grinspoon, Ewalt, and Shader contrasts with the preceding texts in that it concludes with the denial of the role of psychotherapy, since only drug medication has brought about an improvement in chronic schizophrenics. The very careful experimental work (control group, objective evaluation of outcome, etc.) nevertheless raises a whole series of questions in the reader's mind. What patients were they dealing with? Patients selected at random; the text omits to mention that they were selected at random from among a group of chronic psychotics considered capable of benefiting from psychotherapeutic treatment, whereas all the texts in this volume which report favorable results from psychotherapeutic treatment emphasize the necessity of pointing this out. Furthermore, many of the psychoanalysts who accept the advantages of drug treatment at certain stages in the course of the illness would refuse to work with a double-blind scheme. Finally, two years is a reasonable length of time for research, taking into account the financial problems, personal input, the necessity of publishing, etc., but it is extremely brief if one considers the fact that it deals with chronic patients. This work contributes to demonstrating the beneficial action of drugs on nonselected patients, rather than justifying any definite conclusions as to what psychotherapy can or cannot do.

Diego Napolitani gives the history of three therapeutic communities in Milan, not from the point of view of their original modalities of functioning, but based on an analogy, which some will find debatable, between a social group and a living individual. The word organism is used to refer to both, but can one justifiably talk about "personation" according to Racamier's concept? A social group, even if it has the status of a "moral person," is nevertheless fundamentally different from a living individual: it has no biologically rooted character and no development arising from the pressures brought to bear on the group by the individuals belonging to it and their problems. It is also subject to the constraints of social structures whose mode of transmission is fundamentally different from that of biological structures. With an engaging, if not altogether persuasive, enthusiasm, Napolitani attempts to use simultaneously Racamier's concept of the personation of the psychotic[3] and Bion's concepts concerning the functioning of small groups.[4]

The La Velotte Home, whose principles of functioning and mode of organization are clearly outlined by Racamier and Carretier, is a recently created establishment. However, Racamier has had long experience in the treatment of psychotics and has worked in particular in Prémontré in France and at Rives de Prangins in Switzerland. Against a very widespread trend, his position is characterized by the rejection of what could be called paninterpretation," or, in other words, wielding interpretation in every circumstance of institutional life. Interpretation should be reserved for the analytical setting, which is the only context where it can be borne and understood. What he does emphasize, as Rosenfeld, Segal, and Kestemberg do in Part I, is the psychotic's need for *care*. In Racamier's view, care is to the psychotic what holding is to the infant for Winnicott.

After this mature, sober, and carefully considered text, the fruit of long experience, we come to a paper presented by a youthful team in Laval which is trying to adapt to a new mode of functioning. They show the internal problems this causes to each of the team's members, the difficulties arising between them and the research of the psychoanalyst, Pierre Doucet, which oscillates between care and the analytic position in the strict sense.

It must be said that what Doucet attempted to do by trial and error, very few teams or institutions in the world are capable of carrying out in satisfactory circumstances, where the psychoanalyst makes himself heard so as to transform the institution with its power to confine patients, which psychiatrists today, as well as antipsychiatrists, are firmly determined to fight against. With regard to psychoanalytical work within an institution. Jean Kestenberg proposes a few guidelines; Hector Warnes gives some reflections on psychosis and community institutions, and Philippe Koechlin outlines the difficulty of ordering the life of the institution. Elsewhere he readily adopted the image of a nautilus to represent the institution: the nautilus is a creature which develops as it winds around itself; it secretes a hard shell and increases in size without changing shape. The nautilus was a great source of interest to paleontologists some 30 years ago, for it was considered the only animal to have undergone no change or mutation since the primary era. It had one other characteristic: it was delicious to eat!

C. C.

NOTES

1. Freud, S. (1895), A reply to criticisms of my paper on anxiety neurosis. *Standard Edition,* 3:135. London: Hogarth Press, 1962.

2. Chiland, C. and Roubertoux, P. (1975–1976), Freud et l'hérédité, *Bull. Psychologie,* 19(4–7):337–343.

3. Racamier, P. C. (1963), Le Moi, le soi, la personne et la psychose (Essai sur la personnation). *L'Evolution Psychiatrique,* 28(4):525–553.

4. Bion, W. R. (1961), *Experiences in Groups.* London: Tavistock.

Chapter 1

THERAPEUTIC EXPERIENCES WITH PSYCHOTIC CHILDREN

**R. Diatkine, M.D., J. L. Lang, M.D.
S. Lebovici, M.D., and R. Misès, M.D.
An outline by Roger Misès[5]**

The following remarks are based on three long-term treatment experiences[5] which were carried out under varying conditions and involving children representing different distributions among the various types of childhood psychoses.

Despite the dissimilar conditions between the three experiences, certain essential common points emerge. The first of these concerns the specific characteristics of psychosis, which we see as a morbid organism whose superficial aspects are less determinant than the underlying psychopathological mechanisms; these have to be viewed within a dynamic and structural perspective, with the psychoanalytical dimension in the foreground.

The complexity of the factors involved seems obvious, and although practice leads us to stress relational disturbances, this should not detract from the importance of neurobiological factors. Psychosis is unquestionably structured within a complex process which excludes any reductive approach, whether organogenetic or psychogenetic.[1]

To this complexity of the reference model there has to correspond a multidimensional therapy capable of bringing into play all the means necessary *at the appropriate evolutive moments*. This therapy necessarily includes the family milieu, inasmuch as it is in that setting, more than any other, that the child has to be seen in a broader pathological structure.

This kind of understanding recognizes the existence of shifts from one syndrome aspect to another, and also acknowledges the possibliity of structural mutations, wherein lies the justification of long-term treatment of childhood psychoses.

Here we should remove a source of misunderstanding as to the delimitation of the boundaries of these psychoses. The notion of incurability traditionally attached to this diagnosis remains so deeply rooted that cases which show a favorable evolution are often suspected of belonging to marginal forms. The children referred to here unquestionably fell within the framework of the psychoses, just as experiments abroad—such as Bettelheim's—also relate to confirmed forms. These children are the same as those followed individually from about 1940 to 1950 by Louise Despert, Leo Kanner, and Lauretta Bender, and of whom we know 90 percent had unfavorable developments, with a high rate of evolution towards dementia. More recent statistics published over the last 5 or 10 years are equally gloomy, although some do bring in the idea of a preponderant influence of therapy. From the methodological point of view, it must be said immediately that statistics may be the worst possible approach to the problem since they do not reflect the great amount of information drawn from these longitudinal observations, and take no account, for example, of the obstacles to the integration of subjects in the process of favorable development. Besides, what does the statisticians' usual criterion of social integration mean? Would it not be more appropriate to take a critical look at the factors which regularly oppose attempts at reintegration?

Our experience leads us to extend the elements of the problem and to reject various criteria put forward as unfavorable prognostic elements—those attached to the absence of speech in a five-year-old autistic child, for example. Experience has shown us that autistic children who do not speak at that age can nonetheless have a favorable evolution if sufficient measures are brought into action; in Bettelheim's experience this has been demonstrated in five cases out of eight. Furthermore, profound changes can be observed in such children even without their attaining the use of speech. It is therefore difficult to accept as prognostic elements, in the customary medical sense of the term, factors such as the greater severity of primary psychoses as compared to the secondary psychoses, or the existence of a fixed deficit, an instrumental disturbance in an older child. Each of these elements is really only one of the factors of a problem which has to be seen from a wider viewpoint, so as to give priority to the measures appropriate to each case. Only when these measures have been applied for a sufficient length of time can there be any discussion of the evolutive criteria—not with a view to setting arbitrary limits but in order to reformulate the modalities of the treatment. It then becomes apparent that far from being dependent on some mysterious evolutive genius attached to psychosis, the results are closely related to the precocity of diagnosis and the quality of the measures used. It should be made clear that these measures do not concern solely the development of specific methods, but must also be brought to bear upon the rearrangement of the structures the child normally lives in. In the extreme, this can mean quasi-preventive intervention at a point where the child is already in the throes of severe developmental disharmony but without the specific distortions already being fixed irremediably. We have all met with a few cases where spectacular evolutive improvements have been brought about by early detection and intervention while keeping the child in his natural milieu. Here the concern for efficiency and the handling of the dynamic parameter prevail over any search for a precise diagnostic label.

The experiences of each of our teams concur in underlining the diversity of evolutive modalities and the direct influence working hypotheses and means used have on results.

To give a broad outline I shall summarize a number of different possibilities:[3]

1. Forms of a schizophrenic type which retain the dimension of a process beyond adolescence are those least frequently encountered. They are nevertheless not as exceptional as thought earlier.

2. More frequently found are the stabilized forms equivalent to states after a pathological process fixed in a general picture expressing a severe pathological personality. In these split, scar-type organizations there is alternate predominance of massive inhibitions and partial aptitudes which accentuate the disharmonic aspect of the personality. Here we find ourselves within the framework of psychic imbalance, psychotic character structures, and severe character neuroses—labels which are inadequate to express the individuality of each case and the factors favorable or otherwise to individual adjustment.

Child psychiatrists come across these personalities under two circumstances: firstly, as I have just mentioned, in the course of longitudinal studies, but also in the parental configurations around psychotic children.

After this brief outline I should like to dwell at greater

length upon development of the deficit type which represents a central problem, as regards both the evolution of psychoses at an early age and the understanding of deficit organizations in the widest sense of the term (debility, retardation, dementia).[4]

On the clinical plane one constantly wonders as to the significance of the efficiency defect found in the majority of childhood psychoses. It has to be seen what share of this overall deficiency can be attributed, respectively, to relational disturbances, instrumental disorders, and the incidence of phenomena of a psychotic order on the emergence and development of cognitive structures. The traditional notion of pseudodementia is often contradicted by experience showing how the modes of functioning of a durable intellectual deficiency are fixed through structural mutations, which perfectly justifies the notion of a process of "debilitation." We thus come sharply to the question of the nature of the mechanisms at work in these deficit evolutions. It goes without saying that we can get no further toward a solution of the problem without holding up to critical scrutiny the traditional organic concepts of debility or mental retardation, and I remind you that in this connection Lang[2] examined in Montreal the differential traits permitting an outline of the opposition between psychotic and deficit structure. Now as it happens, the study of certain psychoses and various severe evolutive disharmonies provides a particularly good approach by a kind of lateral pathway to this deficiency nucleus, which on the contrary is extremely opaque when these investigations are confined to the most typical forms of mental retardation.

In other words, our longitudinal studies enable us on one hand to answer the question raised by the deficit structure of various psychoses and on the other, they lead to a truly psychopathological approach to deficit organizations.

There is not enough space here for me to give even a brief analysis of the results of our investigations, and I shall simply mention a few essential elements. Firstly, it seems clear that is is impossible at present to separate "mechanisms" in the most restrictive sense of the term; their particular aspects in mental functioning and the relational network have to be pointed out, but without arbitrarily isolating them, for the field which has to be studied as a whole covers the entire set of coordinates involved in the building up and organization of psychic life. What we perceive most clearly is how, when confronted with the threat of psychic "annihilation," mechanisms are brought into action whose effect is to maintain object cathexis, but at the cost of a major obliteration of the modalities which normally ensure the elaboration of the primal symbolism, the availability of the instinctual energetics, and the narcissistic cathexis in the free working of mental functioning.

Thus deficit structuring maintains an organization of an adaptative type, but it results in direct injury to the process of symbolization and to the working through of the instinct for knowledge.

It seems impossible to dissociate this from other mechanisms which act through prohibitions, defective processes of sublimation and faulty cathexes or, simpler, in an area which could be qualified as neurotic. We know that the development of childhood psychoses often takes place around these nuclei of neuroticization which provide us with a foothold and which are used in the psychoanalytical therapies. When the course takes the direction of deficit structuring the obstacles at this level to the wish for knowledge and to the pleasure drawn from mental functioning contribute to the long-lasting restriction of efficiency. In a way, the healing of the neurotic nuclei is combined with the lack of working over of the primal conflicts and the abrasion of the instinctual background.

As you see, stabilization in an intellectual deficit leads to an organization which roughly allows hierarchical functioning, especially through secondary processes. In actual fact, the analysis of these deficit structures reveals how far removed they are from the normal working of cognitive structures, which goes on in a moving network allowing an infinite number of arrangements and potentialities. At the level of the secondary processes in deficit organizations instead of this moving pattern we find networks strictly determined by a consolidation mechanism.

This consolidation plays a role both in the isolation of the associative pattern from each other and the severance of the ego from its instinctual sources to the benefit of an "adaptation" whose pathological character escapes no one. Once set in that direction, functioning always tends more towards fixation and extension of the most impeding mechanisms. In fact, these organizations all work toward reducing the individual to silence, hence the obvious load of the repetition compulsion which blocks the symbolic outcome and perpetuates the iterations of this rigidified functioning.

On the practical plane, this mode of understanding makes it possible to grasp how and by what paths purely adjustment-oriented therapies inevitably work towards the most impeding solution.

It must be said that by and through his psychosis the child persistently formulates fundamental questions; because of his deficit structure he tends irremediably to occupy the confined place the family and society assign to the mentally defective.

NOTES

1. Duche, D.-J. (1969), La conception organogénétique des psychoses infantiles. In: *Problems of Psychosis,* eds. P. Doucet and C. Laurin. Amsterdam: Excerpta Medica Foundation, pp. 169–179.

2. Lang, J.L. (1969), Le problème nosologique des relations entre structure psychotique et structure déficitaire (psychoses à expression déficitaire et "arriération psychose"). In: *Problems of Psychosis,* eds. P. Doucet and C. Laurin. Amsterdam: Excerpta Medica Foundation, pp. 97–115.

3. Lebovici, S. (1969), L'enfant psychotique devenue adulte. In: *Problems of Psychosis,* eds. P. Doucet and C. Laurin. Amsterdam: Excerpta Medica Foundation, pp. 140–153.

4. Misès, R., Perron-Borelli, M., & Bréon, S. (1971), Essai d'approche psychopathologique de la déficience intellectuelle: les déficits dysharmoniques. *Psychiat. enfant*, 14(2):341–464.

5. The teams from the 13th District M.H.A., Paris (Diatkine and Lebovici), Jouy-en-Josas (Lang), and the Fondation Vallée (Misès).

Ronald B. Feldman, M.D.

In addition to my work as a child psychiatrist and psychoanalyst, I have been involved for the past 5 years in treating psychotic children with behavior therapy. I have been asked to contribute to this Symposium from the latter frame of reference.

It was not until 1961 that the first systematic attempts were made to apply principles of operant conditioning to the treatment of psychotic children. Ferstner and DeMyer[1] demonstrated that the performances of autistic children could be brought under stimulus control by various schedules of reinforcement. Later, Lovaas and his group[3] at the Neuropsychiatric Institute in Los Angeles devised techniques for modifying deviant behavior of schizophrenic children. He was particularly successful in diminishing self-destructive and repetitive behaviors, and in devising methods for increasing the children's attentiveness to their social environment. Subsequently, behavior modification programs have become widely used throughout North America.

Behavior therapists emphasize that whether or not one accepts the theoretical foundations for their methods, their attempts to quantify behavior allows for a more objective evaluation of the efficacy of treatment than the traditional therapies. As noted in the previous paper, there are many clinical manifestations which are subsumed under the term "childhood psychosis." Rimland,[6] in a recent study, found that a child who had been diagnosed as autistic by one therapist, had only one chance in four of being similarly diagnosed by another. Behavior therapists do not consider differential diagnosis to be an important factor in the consideration of treatment design. Rather, they have focused upon, firstly, the objectively measurable behavior of their subjects, and secondly, assessments of the environmental variables which influence the frequency of occurrence of specific behaviors.

From our own five-year experience at the Jewish General Hospital in Montreal, and from descriptions by various authors, one can now draw the following conclusions about the current status of behavior therapy with psychotic children:

1. Due to the relatively short time that behavior therapy has been used as a treatment method for these children, it is not yet possible to make any definitive statements about the long-term consequences of behavior therapy upon the course of childhood psychosis.

2. With few exceptions, children with very poor prognoses were referred for behavior therapy. Almost all were very severely disturbed, and there was a preponderance of mute children. Their poor prognoses tended to make them available to the behavior therapist, usually after many other treatment methods had failed.

3. Even with the above population, behavior therapy is clearly and demonstrably an effective means of: (a) eliminating self-aggressive and potentially very destructive behaviors, such as head-banging, self-mutilation, etc. The usefulness in these areas has been so clearly demonstrated that it might now be hard to justify the employment of other methods; and (b) increasing appropriate social interactions. It has been found that as one reinforces and increases the frequency of appropriate behavior, then inappropriate behavior, such as stereotypies, twirling, rocking, etc., tend to disappear spontaneously. It is possible to diminish fairly quickly the isolation of the autistic child. It has been repeatedly demonstrated that one can increase the amount of eye contact, imitative behavior, and social interaction.

4. The techniques of behavior modification lend themselves admirably to use by nonmedical workers. Nurses and students can be taught to employ behavior therapy. It is particularly important that parents can also be engaged as therapists for their own children. This entails not only a saving in the use of professional staff, but more importantly, the parents gain a sense of usefulness and renewed interest in their child after years of despair, perplexity, and hopelessness.

5. The contribution which behavior therapy can make to language training is still not fully known. I have not seen any descriptions of treatment programs wherein previously *mute* children have gained normal or near-normal language. However, many significant and useful gains have been made. For example, mute children have learned vocabularies of 100–200 words, and simple sentences and phrases. More importantly, they have been taught to apply their limited vocabularies appropriately in social interactions. It is probable that they do not have the perceptual or central integrative capacity to learn language.

6. There have been several descriptions of remarkable, almost miraculous, improvement in some children.[2,5,7] At the beginning of treatment in all of these cases, the children had some language, usually echolalic, or they were initially responsive to social reinforcement. One could say that these are children who had major problems in the *application* of speech, and that the language which was present was not used for purposes of communication.

One of the criticisms which has often been leveled at behavior therapy is that it is a dehumanizing and mechanistic treatment. However, I have repeatedly seen marked changes in the affective tone and in the amount and intensity of the human involvements which these children have made once they have been taught to begin to relate. They commonly begin to show feelings of pleasure, joy, and happiness. They become less mechanical in their behavior, laugh, show increased self-assertion, and increased interest in people, pets, their own mirror image, and in other children.

I would like to suggest that behavior therapy helps the psychotic child to differentiate internal and external perceptions, self from external object. Also, by reestablishing his social contact, it may help to prevent late intellectual deterioration.

In normal development, the infant, as described by Mahler,[4] comes to "learn from experience that, whereas physiological tensions originated from within [his] own body, the 'confidently expected' relief from instinctual tension, i.e., [the] gratification of needs, came from somewhere outside of the body." The autistic child, whether as a result of failure of development or as a consequence of regression, does not seem to have this awareness.

The skilled behavior therapist, as an initial step in treatment, will give primary reinforcement, i.e., biological need satisfaction, only when the child *attends* to him. For example, in order to receive food, the autistic child must learn to look at the face of the therapist—the face, the mouth, the eyes—and not just at the part object, the hand or the spoon, which delivers the food. That is, the child is compelled to begin, or to begin again, to become aware of the separate and external existence of the mothering person.

He resists this awareness by attempting to withdraw into his autistic shell, his stereotypies, his autoeroticisms, or his world of inanimate objects. This resistance must be overcome, and I would suggest that it is overcome, not so much by coercion, but by the reliability and predictability of the therapist, who thus helps to establish the "confident expectation" and sense of basic trust in the child.

Commonly, the next stage in behavior therapy entails the shaping of *imitative* behavior. The child is taught to imitate the therapist; firstly, gross body movements, secondly, ranges of facial movements and expression, and lastly, vocal and verbal expression. This requires that the child become aware of an increasingly complex range of characteristics of the adult therapist. The ability of the child to imitate provides objective evidence that he has at least attended to, perceived, and remembered the external object.

I have often noted that the relationship between behavior therapist and child quickly transcends that of biological need satisfactions. It is as if, after a period of time, the biological rewards assume diminished importance and are replaced by social rewards, words of praise, a touch, or a smile. The child comes to clearly recognize and to prefer his therapist over substitutes. After periods of separation, the child is more likely than previously to insist upon tangible biological rewards. It is particularly following separations, when one observes regressions, that one becomes most aware of the extent of the relationship which had developed between the child and his therapist.

Summary

I would suggest that the full potential of behavior modification techniques have not been realized because of the selection and referral process, whereby only the most hopeless cases have been referred for behavior therapy. Fortunately, this is now changing. My own experiences lead me to believe that the young psychotic child with some language development is readily helped by operant techniques, and that these techniques can at times rapidly make the child amenable to the usual social influences of school, peers, and family. It may be possible, in some cases of early childhood psychosis, to reverse the psychotic process, and to forestall further intellectual deterioration through the early use of behavior therapies. These techniques do not merely teach rote skills, but further the development of object relationships which permit the child to explore and to learn from his human environment. I think that there is a clearer place for the traditional psychotherapies once the child has been taught these essential language and social skills.

NOTES

1. Ferstner, C. B. & Demyer, M. K. (1961), The development of performances in autistic children in an automatically controlled environment. *J. Chronic Dis.,* 13:312–345.

2. Gardner, J. E., Pearson, D. T., Bercovici, A. N., & Bricker, D. E. (1968), Measurement, evaluation, and modification of selected social interactions between a schizophrenic child, his parents, and his therapist. *J. Consult. Clin. Psychol.,* 32:537–542.

3. Lovaas, O. I., Frietas, L., Nelson, K., & Whalen, C. (1967), The establishment of imitation and its use for the development of complex behavior in schizophrenic children. *Behavior Res. Therapy,* 5:171–181.

4. Mahler, M. S. (1965), On early infantile psychosis: the symbiotic and autistic syndromes. *J. Amer. Acad. Child Psychiat.,* 4:554–568.

5. Marshall, N. R. & Hegrenes, J. R. (1970), Programmed communication therapy for autistic mentally retarded children. *J. Speech Hear. Disord.,* 35:70–83.

6. Rimland, B. (1971), The differentiation of childhood psychosis: an analysis of checklists for 2,218 psychotic children. *J. Autism Child. Schizo.,* 1:161–174.

7.   Sulzbacher, S. I. & Costello, J. M. (1970), A behavioral strategy for language training of a child with autistic behaviors. *J. Speech Hear. Disord.*, 35:256–276.

Chapter 2

BEHAVIOR THERAPY WITH CHRONIC SCHIZOPHRENIC PATIENTS

Teodoro Ayllon, Ph.D.

"The times they are a changin," the song goes, but the concept of treatment in the mental hospital has remained virtually unchanged through the last 20 years. The notable exception is the introduction of psychopharmaceuticals around 1956, which has had a dramatic effect upon the population of mental institutions. According to U.S.P.H.S. figures, the number of resident patients in state mental hospitals was reduced from 550,000 in 1956 to 400,000 in 1968. This means that in a period of 12 years, approximately 12,000 patients left the hospital every year. What can be loosely termed as the "therapies" (psychotherapy, group therapy, milieu therapy, occupational therapy, etc.) have been practiced to some extent for over 30 years. Psychopharmaceuticals have been very helpful to the therapist in that they have reduced the numbers of patients to be treated and have made those in hospitals more amenable to treatment. That these therapies are still highly valuable there is no doubt, but generally speaking, they are conducted only by highly trained and costly personnel, such as psychologists, psychiatrists, and social workers. Although occasionally we now hear about nurses conducting the same efforts, this is often done as a last recourse and almost apologetically. However, because of budgetary crises, many state hospitals are virtually functioning with a skeleton crew of mental health professionals, and the end is not in sight. It is clear that unless there is an immediate reappraisal of the objectives of the state mental hospital there will be virtually no one but attendants to care for the patients.

One might ask, what is a hospital superintendent to do? The answer, it seems to me, is for him to learn about new developments in behavior modification. The development of procedures of behavior modification has relied upon the work of those who practically live with the patients, the attendants, and nurses. These are the key personnel, essentially the therapists of tomorrow, the only persons who make the difference in the life of the patient while he remains in the mental hospital. It was with the assistance of attendants and nurses that my colleagues and I conducted a series of experiments to determine the relative effectiveness of behavioral procedures in a mental hospital setting.[2-9] I would like first to describe to you some of the highlights of this research, and then discuss the implications of these findings for the operation of the hospital of tomorrow.

Initially, we were concerned with patients' symptoms because they were specific, observable, and therefore measurable. One interesting example of a peculiar symptom was that of a female patient who had displayed obsessive-compulsive behavior for nine years. She was regarded as hopeless since she had gone through individual therapy, group therapy, and all other available treatments without any apparent benefit. As you know, these therapies are based largely on the ability of the patient to communicate verbally. This particular patient, however, refused to talk, and therefore she was regarded as unsuitable for further psychotherapy. It was then that we attempted to design a behavioral treatment which would not be limited by the ability of the patient to speak with anyone.[2]

The most prominent feature of the patient's illness was hoarding towels. She collected towels daily from the 40 patients on the ward and kept them in her small room. The staff went daily to the patient and asked very politely for the towels that belonged to the rest of the patients. But she simply refused to give up her towels. Obviously, this represented a logistical problem to the ward staff. How were they going to give baths to 40 patients when one patient kept 30 towels for herself? And so there was some need for more drastic measures, like somebody going to her room and taking all the towels away from her. Right? This is a very common approach which is often the only thing that can be done when dealing with the real practical problems on the ward. The usual kind of interpretation attached to such symptoms is that they reflect a deep need for love. Hoarding towels is thus regarded as just a symptom of this need. This analysis may be very useful as a way of conceptualizing a problem, but it certainly was not very helpful to the attendants or the nurses since they still had to figure out what to do about the towels.

First, we attempted quantification of the symptom, that is, hoarding towels. We began by weighing them, but counting was found easier. This approach illustrates the importance of directly measuring the behavior or behaviors that are to be treated. Measuring the symptom minimized guessing and provided a sensitive check on the effectiveness of the treatment procedures. Indeed, the first procedure was to discontinue the old method of telling the patient not to collect towels or taking them away from her. Instead, attendants were instructed to give towels to the patient. Now, without going into the fine points about data that are available on the use of satiation as a way to reduce behavior, suffice it to say that we were interested in extending this finding to an applied therapeutic situation. This procedure required that the attendants give the patient an average of seven towels a day. At first the patient was very happy to receive the towels and for the first time in 12 years she coherently indicated her pleasure and welcomed the attendants with words like, "Oh, you found my towels, that's wonderful, thank you, nurse, thank you." Although the patient was delighted with this new state of affairs, the staff was getting impatient about finding a solution to the problem of hoarding the towels. So after a few days a decision was made to go for broke and the average number of towels given daily was increased to 60. She seemed rather puzzled at the new change as reflected in such comments as, "It takes me all day to put my things away now, you know . . . I don't think I need so many towels, maybe I have enough now." She continued keeping the towels neatly in her room, however, on her bed, her bureau, and on her chair. But the towels kept on coming, since we wanted the patient to decide to get rid of them, not just to complain about them. Verbal behavior is not enough, we wanted action. That was the idea behind giving the patient more and more towels.

At this point, I think that the efforts of keeping about seven towels in order were a little too much for her. Handling 700 towels became a fulltime job. The patient began complaining that she could not stay up the whole night folding towels and placing them on the dresser and the bureau and so on. Of course the attendant, very understandingly, answered, "Well, you know you do the best you can and we'll just try to give you what you need." The important thing to remember at this point is that the patient was not being coerced either to keep or give up the towels. But the patient became less efficient in arranging the towels and was even irritated by their presence, as was evidenced by her throwing a couple of towels at the nurse after four weeks of treatment. She then found out that nobody picked the towels up and nobody brought them in again, so she tried a few more towels and put them outside her room, and again they did not come back. It took only a few days for her to dispose of towels literally by the hundreds until she was left with only one towel. So there is a moral to this story: "Happiness is having your own towel."

One of the most conspicuous aspects of mental illness is the rather bizarre content of conversation displayed by a mentally ill person. In an effort to explore the influence of social interaction on the frequency of bizarre talk, we selected a patient whose verbal behavior was sufficiently stereotyped as to permit standard recording by the nurses.[7] The patient basically had two classes of verbal behavior: one dealt with Queen Elizabeth and other members of the British Royal family, and the other class excluded any such references. These two gross categories were first identified and then taught to nurses, who in turn recorded the patient's conversation in terms of these two categories. Each nurse had to meet a quota of contacts with the patient daily. This enabled us to ensure a constant number of opportunities for the patient to react verbally to the nurse. What, of course, could not be kept constant was the frequency of patient-nurse contacts when these were initiated by the patient and not by the nurse. Prior to this attempt at quantifying the content of her conversation, she had been reported to make utterances solely concerned with the Royal house and her part in it. In practice, we found that the probability of one content over another being produced in her conversation with nurses was 50:50. With this bit of information, we wondered what would happen if nurses listened to and appeared concerned each time the patient touched upon her rather colorful topic but appeared disinterested and busy whenever she omitted any references to the Royal family? The findings were rather thought provoking. It turned out that the reassurance and attention given to the patient when she displayed psychotic verbal content increased the frequency of such content to twice its original level. At this point a procedure suggested itself: we wondered what would happen if the reassurance were to be discontinued when she engaged in her bizarre talk. Therefore, all psychotic content was selectively ignored and any instances of "healthy" talk were followed by smiles and concern from nurses. (Until this point, we could not predict what actually might happen by so doing.) The results were startling. We found that when the nurses ignored the bizarre talk it quickly decreased. On the other hand, the "healthy" talk went up from 50 to 80 percent of her verbal output when the nurses' attention followed it and stabilized at a level over 30 percent of its original level.

Often the nurses' social attention seems to be necessary for the physical survival of the patient. This was the case with one patient who continuously had been fed by the nurses in various manners. She had been spoon-fed, tube-fed, and on extreme occasions, fed intravenously. Her refusal to eat unassisted, it had been assumed, was an integral part of her psychosis. This "treatment" had been going on for 14 years. Then we withdrew the nurses' assistance entirely and within 4 days the patient, by then ravenous, ran to the dining room and proceeded to eat on her own.[1]

These and other behavioral applications[6] seemed to suggest that the major source of reinforcement for many of the behaviors displayed on the ward was traceable to the particular feedback given to the patient by those working there. The notion that consequences attendant to behavior played a major role in the probability of occurrence of that behavior was, of course, not new. What seemed new was that the social reaction of nurses to patients appeared to have a specific influence on the maintenance of many ward behavior problems.[7]

Now it should be made clear that to generalize our findings to other behaviors in the mental hospital we needed to demonstrate that attention and concern shown by nurses to patients is always a reinforcing event. In practice, we found that many patients reacted to the attention of the nurses as they would to an aversive event, and at best some reacted with total indifference. Nor was this experience confined to the use of the nurses' attention as a reinforcer. In a series of attempts to isolate some reinforcer of wide applicability, we used a variety of consumable items such as peanuts, cigarettes, chocolate, cookies, ice cream, and so on. The outcome of such attempts was rather discouraging; each and sometimes several items were effective as reinforcers, but typically they required a preselection of the individuals who seemed to be particularly affected by such events. Lindsley,[10] in his pioneering work with psychotic patients, had also found many of these potential reinforcers to be just that—potential. This represented a severe limitation in working with the chronic schizophrenic patient, in view of our objective which was to isolate or develop a reinforcer of wide applicability.

Nor was the selection of reinforcer the only problem. Indeed, the selection of behavior represented as much of a problem. Up to this point, we had dealt with most behaviors primarily because of the ease in measuring them. Repeated attempts at objectively measuring behavior in a free field environment involved serious methodological problems. About this time, I went to Anna State Hospital to work with Nathan Azrin. There we spent some time devising time-sample behavioral recording and analyzing the data so derived, until it became painfully clear that time-sample measures were simply impractical with respect to most types of behavior applications. The harder we worked to devise standardized behavioral measures, the more aware we became of the indiscriminate character of our behavioral recording. We were measuring all types of behaviors without distinguishing their functional characteristics in the environment. Gradually, we found ourselves thinking in terms of behaviors which were functional in the ward environment. Parallel with this development, we came to realize that it was not sufficient to identify behaviors that were functional, they should also have relevance to other environments. For some patients this meant that they should learn behaviors which were functional to life in the hospital, while for others it meant that the behaviors should have relevance to living outside the hospital.

But what are the functional behaviors typically observed in mental hospitals? Except for behaviors such as eating, dressing, and other self-care activities, patients have little opportunity to engage in a functional relationship with the environment in which they live. As we started thinking about the possible useful behaviors that patients might engage in, we realized that we simply did not know what the dimensions of "useful behavior" were. In an effort to get an idea of such dimensions, we wondered what would happen if we evaluated the performance of the attendants in those terms. Would that give us a better idea of what the dimensions of useful behaviors were? We observed that the employees worked on jobs such as serving meals, washing dishes, cleaning, mopping, and general housekeeping duties. In addition, they picked up the dirty linen, counted the pieces, wrote the number on the appropriate slip, and then took the bundle of clothes to a collection place for pick-up service by the laundry people. The attendants also made beds, gave baths, conducted patients outside the ward, ran errands, and various other duties which occupied most of their 8 hours of shift work. Since they were necessary for the functioning of the ward, these were useful behaviors. But the problem in defining similar behaviors for the patient still existed. We knew what the attendant's functional behavior was, but we did not know what this meant in terms of the patients. Or did we? In effect, after thinking it over, we wondered if much of the work of the attendants could be regarded as the target behavior for patients to learn. An additional requirement for selecting a behavior was that it should lead to an enduring change in the environment when it occurred. A specific example of such behavior would be washing dishes immediately following a meal. The physical change in the environment that results from this behavior is the cleanliness of the dishes. Other examples that leave an enduring change in the environment are mopping the floors and serving meals, or doing clerical work such as typing, filing, etc. Each of these behaviors fulfills, as well, the initial requirement that a response be useful and necessary. At least we had the target behavior which also had relevance to the functioning of the patient either in the hospital or in the community. To the extent that such performances, as the ones described above, have components that touch upon other work activities outside the hospital, we regarded them as particularly helpful to work with. Still, the one problem not dealt with was how to accomplish the measurement of the behavior. It is obviously impossible to observe each patient every moment of the day and night in order to record when and whether the patient was mopping the floors, setting the table, or folding the laundry. By arranging the environment so that the response selected could only take place at a designated time and place, we finally made contact with the underlying features of previous measurement.

Thus, for example, the mop was available only at a specified time of the day and for a specific duration. This same requirement was imposed on other behaviors. In this manner, the attendants could now easily identify the behavior since it was usually restricted to a time and place.

Now that we had an identifiable, functional behavior which could be easily recorded by the attendants, we returned to our original problem, which was to find some type of reinforcing stimulus of general applicability. This objective seemed rather futile in view of the fact that the hallmark of chronic schizophrenic patients is the apparent absence of effective reinforcers for them. To avoid a priori definitions about what might constitute an effective reinforcer for this type of patient, we decided to rely on direct observation of their own behavior. Close scrutiny of these patients indicated that they showed a wide range of behaviors, but more significant was the frequency with which they did some things over others. For example, some continuously asked to leave the ward; others chose to remain isolated in their rooms and rarely participated in any ward activity. Still others attended social functions every time they were offered. For example, some had a 100 percent church attendance, and others had a similarly high record of attendance at movies. A few consistently requested to speak to the doctor, social worker, or psychologist. Premack[11] has expressed a general principle that of any two behaviors the one that has a high probability of occurrence can be used to reinforce the one with low probability. Following this principle, we proposed to interest the patient in engaging in low-probability or "useful" behaviors at a scheduled time. In this manner the patient's high-probability behavior would operate as a reinforcer to increase the frequency of behaviors rarely displayed. We were, in fact, defining work, leisure, and comforts in the context of the patient's environment.

The following illustration may help to clarify the application of the Premack principle. A patient who had a perfect attendance at church was informed that the pass to allow her to go to church was available for making her bed. Since making her bed was a low-probability behavior, we wanted to strengthen it by making the access to church follow it. The patient, with a little grumbling made her bed, requested her pass, and went to church. The problem encountered, however, was that it was often impractical to offer the reinforcer without causing numerous interruptions of the patient's ongoing behavior. It was the impracticality of such a procedure that finally led us to use a conditioned reinforcer to bridge the delay between the occurrence of the response and the availability of the reinforcing stimulus. We used specially made tokens that were not obtainable outside the ward environment. The tokens could later be exchanged for the reinforcing stimulus selected by the patient. When the appropriate behavior was displayed, the attendant reinforced the patient with tokens. A methodological advantage provided by the use of tokens was that they minimized the subjective aspects of the patient-attendant interaction at the time of reinforcement delivery. In addition, the token allowed the development of a standardized procedure for the delivery of the reinforcement and its exchange.

To determine the effectiveness of these behavioral procedures in maintaining the desired behaviors, we undertook a series of experiments. The experimental design consisted of carefully measuring the desired behaviors for a period of time during which they were followed by reinforcement. The next stage of the design required that the reinforcement procedure be discontinued in some manner. The third stage of the experimental design required that the reinforcement procedure be reinstated. Careful measurements of the behavior through these three periods made it possible to evaluate the role of the reinforcement procedure in maintaining the desired behaviors.

One of the first experiments was designed to answer the following question: What determines the choice or selection of jobs? Intangible factors associated with job satisfaction were often offered as explanations for the patients' specific job selection. We did find that after familiarizing themselves with several jobs, the patients tended to prefer some over others. We wondered what would happen if token reinforcement were made available only for those jobs least preferred by the patient. Would the patients continue working at their preferred jobs because of the intrinsic factors involved in the jobs themselves? Would they perhaps quit working altogether as a natural reaction against someone manipulating their environment? The results showed neither of these outcomes. The patients continued working, but the job they selected was the one which was least preferred, but for which tokens were available. The previously preferred jobs which paid no tokens were not selected. When token reinforcement was reinstated for the preferred jobs, the patients resumed full-time work on them. The jobs selected for study in this experiment were full-time jobs which resembled those performed by normal individuals in the hospital. This made it possible to evaluate the strength of uncontrolled subjective likes and dislikes in selecting a job versus the reinforcement procedure.

These results indicated that the patients would shift their selection of jobs depending on which job resulted in token reinforcement. The question to be asked next was: Was work per se reinforcing enough to be continued without any payoff? We knew that one job was preferred over another because of the payment but we did not know just how reinforcing the job, in and of itself, might be.

Because the attendants paid the patients for working, the patient-attendant interaction was an additional factor which had to be considered in a design that would test the reinforcing properties of work. If we had simply quit paying tokens at the end of the job, we would have automatically terminated this relationship and could not have determined whether the tokens or the interaction were responsible for the changes in work patterns. Our solution was to design an experiment in which the patient-attendant interaction continued.

This time, however, the attendants, instead of waiting for the completion of the desired performance to reinforce the patient, anticipated the patient, and gave each her usual number of tokens at the beginning of the day before her job was to be performed. The results showed that the performance of the full-time jobs by the patients decreased to zero level when the token reinforcement was given independent of the performance. On the very first day when the reinforcement procedure was reinstated, so that the patient was given the tokens following the completion of the job, there was an immediate return to the high level of performance.

At this point, we wondered if these results were perhaps an artifact of the type of patients involved in full-time work. The question was, what would happen if the same procedure were to be used with more seriously disturbed patients, that is, with those who worked as little as 15 minutes and perhaps only as long as 3 hours? This time we included all 44 patients on the ward. Although the jobs varied in complexity from sweeping the floors to running an automatic dishwasher and operating a movie projector, the results were similar to those obtained with the full-time jobs. When the token reinforcement was delivered independent of the performance, the number of hours at work decreased to a near zero level. When the token reinforcement was reinstated for completion of the desired performance, the number of hours at work returned to its original level.

We then decided to see if we could simulate quantitatively the effects of the major characteristics of the typical ward environment, one in which token reinforcement was absent and where the privileges and other desirable items were available freely and generally independent of the patient's performance. Would the high level of performance still be maintained? The results obtained when the token reinforcement was discontinued indicate that the freely available privileges do not help to maintain the high level of performance. Quite the contrary, during this period patients, in general, "lost interest" in their work, that is, they worked fewer hours. In fact, their work decreased to less than one-fourth of its original level. These results offer a very good estimate of the probable level of performance in a typical ward: the patient's level of productivity, in a sense, is underestimated and he is likely to be working at one-fourth of his potential capacity.

Since, up to this point, one feature of the experimental manipulations was the all-or-none use of the reinforcement procedure, we asked ourselves what might the effect be of relative amounts of reinforcement on the desired behaviors? To study this situation, we designed an experiment where the patient was given experience with two different jobs. The completion of each job was rewarded by two different amounts of reinforcement, one larger than the other. Given that both resulted in tokens, which job would the patient select? As it turned out, the patients selected the job which resulted in the larger amount of reinforcement. When the magnitude of pay-off was reversed so that the job which initially paid least came to pay the most, then the patients switched to that job. These results indicated then that the presence or absence of reinforcement was not the only determinant of the high level of performance, but that the relative amount available for the job was also important.

In summary, the reinforcement program was effective in maintaining the performance because tokens were given for the desired performances. When the tokens were no longer given, then those performances decreased. When the token delivery was changed from one job to another, the performance of the job for which tokens were not available decreased immediately and to a near zero level. The mere act of giving tokens did not maintain the high level of performance as is seen in the experiment where tokens were given before the completion of the job. The payment had to be contingent upon job completion. These results demonstrate that the reinforcement procedure used was so effective that the influence of other factors was relatively mimimal when reinforcement was absent. Furthermore, these results indicate that this motivational system would be extremely potent for a wide range of psychiatric problems. First of all, the population of patients included mental retardates, schizophrenics, paranoids, organic psychotics, manic depressives, and so on. Such a wide range of diagnostic classifications might have revealed some differential effect on the type of psychiatric diagnosis. Yet, the results show that patients from all of these classifications had a higher level of performance under the reinforcement procedure. While the number of years of hospitalization ranged from one to 37 years, this factor did not affect the patient's performance either. Neither age, which ranged from 24 to 74, nor level of education, seemed to be a significant factor, for the reinforcement program was effective with young and old, and for patients whose education ranged from primary school to college.

What can a program like this mean for the hospital of tomorrow? This program was designed to facilitate the patient's rehabilitation by making him a responsible, functioning human being. Because it has been found to be effective in maintaining both short and simple performances and long complex ones, this program could be employed to enable patients to become responsible for the functioning of their hospital environment. Instead of allowing the patient to regress, become dependent, or worse, to vegetate eventually, this procedure could maintain the patient operating at maximal level as he would have to upon return to the outside world. The hospital, then, would not be a place in which one would be encouraged to escape, a place in which all comforts would be automatically available. In a motivating therapeutic environment, such as I am suggesting, the patients themselves would cook, serve meals, and do all housekeeping chores. They could also go beyond these simple tasks to the servicing of other needs of the institution such as painting walls, repairing furniture, doing the hospital laundry, and sealing the storm windows.

Eventually, the hospital could establish vocational training in such areas as mechanics, machine operating, cosmetology, and food preparation. Courses could also be offered at high school and college levels so that patients might, if they chose, obtain an academic education. This training could then assist the patient in making the necessary adjustment to the outside world. The motivational level in occupational behaviors would be maintained by the opportunities for reinforcement, which include such social activities as dances, movies, church, picnics, and shopping trips, or other environmental conditions like a private bedroom or a certain bedspread. Similarly, psychotherapy, either private or group, could be made available contingent upon some appropriate and useful behavior. Thus, the choice of patients for therapy would not be the exclusive prerogative of the administration or of the psychiatrists as it is at present. These procedures would make psychotherapy available to all for the small price of behaving as responsible adults. There would never have to be any "giving up" on patients.

A fresh approach to mental hospitals is long overdue. These institutions, by their very nature, possess powerful sources of reinforcement which can be harnessed for the motivation of the patients within their walls. It is here where the behavioral methodology can help in conceptualizing not only the relevance of the goals of the hospital but also the relative effectiveness of methods used to generate and maintain behavior in this environment. Indeed, hospitals need no longer be anachronistic human warehouses, but centers for reeducation and rehabilitation. The major objective of the hospital of tomorrow should be to generate in the patients a desire to rejoin the human family by way of acquiring skills with which to maintain themselves after their release.

NOTES

1. Ayllon, T. (1960), Paper presented at the meeting of the American Psychological Association, Chicago, September 1960.

2. Ayllon, T. (1963), Intensive treatment of psychotic behavior by stimulus satiation and food reinforcement. *Behavior Res. Therapy,* 1:53–61.

3. Ayllon, T. & Azrin, N. H. (1965), The measurement and reinforcement of behavior of psychotics. *J. Exp. Analysis Behavior,* 8:357–383.

4. Ayllon, T. & Azrin, N. H. (1968), Reinforcer sampling: a technique for increasing the behavior of mental patients. *J. Appl. Behavior Analysis,* 1:13–20.

5. Ayllon, T. & Azrin, N. H. (1968), The token economy: A motivational system for therapy and rehabilitation. New York: Appleton-Century-Crofts.

6. Ayllon, T. & Haughton, E. (1962), Control of the behavior of schizophrenic patients by food. *J. Exp. Analysis Behavior,* 5:343–352.

7. Ayllon, T. & Haughton, E. (1964), Modification of symptomatic verbal behavior of mental patients. *Behavior Res. Therapy,* 2:87–97.

8. Ayllon, T., Haughton, E. & Hughes, H. (1965), Interpretation of symptoms: fact or fiction? *Behavior Res. Therapy,* 2:1–7.

9. Ayllon, T. & Michael, J. (1959), The psychiatric nurse as a behavioral engineer. *J. Exp. Analysis Behavior,* 2:323–334.

10. Lindsley, O. R. (1956), Operant conditioning methods applied to research in chronic schizophrenia. *Psychiat. Res. Reports,* 5:118–139.

11. Premack, D. (1959), Toward empirical behavior laws: I. Positive reinforcement. *Psychol. Rev.,* 66:219–233.

Gilbert F. Lelord, M.D., Ph.D.

Dr. Ayllon's interesting work provides a definite contribution to psychiatric semiology and therapy. The author shows that careful clinical observation indicates the existence of laws in humans which become apparent in animals during what we call "operant" conditioning,[7] and that the application of these laws to certain patients brings about behavioral modifications which result in an improvement of their mental state.

It is also instructive to follow through the entire process of this work, for the difficulties outlined here by a clinical specialist in conditioning are very similar to those encountered in the laboratory.

It would be overambitious to try to exhaust here the comments or criticism, whether clinical or philosophical, provoked by a report of this kind. We shall keep to three psychophysiological aspects relating to reinforcement selection, the necessity of measuring reinforcement and behavior, and the possibility of using relatively unspecific therapeutic agents.

As far as humans are concerned, the selection of an unconditioned or absolute stimulus, which we still call reinforcement, is a delicate matter. Experience has shown that cigarettes, sweets, or ice cream are fairly ineffective.

The author, therefore, had to look for sources of reinforcement ranging from movies to walks and sessions of psychotherapy, and eventually narrowing down to the phylogenesis of economic exchange with the gradual replacement of barter by the symbolic reward of token reinforcement.

In our laboratory we use three types of reinforcement:

1. In the experiments with sensory conditioning, we use light.[1] Man, the successor of anthropoids accustomed to catching sight of fruit among the leaves, is, in fact, a "visual" animal for whom light holds an attraction as powerful as olfactory or gustatory stimuli do for dogs.[8]

2. In instrumental conditioning,[2,9] the reinforcement is success. The subject has to guess when an object is within his reach; movement is then reinforced by success. This success does not necessarily imply any social reinforcement, although in our experiments it is nonetheless associated with the doctor's approval, as Dr. Ayllon stresses.[3]

3. Finally, apart from any question of success, reinforcement in therapeutic conditioning can consist of play. In one of the methods we use, this play is inspired by the way an actor behaves on the stage, and is a powerful reinforcer for schizophrenics in particular.[4]

A second constant source of preoccupation apparent throughout Dr. Ayllon's work is that of scientific observation; in other words, the measurement of reinforcement and behavior. The token reinforcement system demonstrates his rigorous method, as does the selection of specifically defined behaviors restricted to designated times and places.

With today's measuring techniques, accuracy can be obtained without any harmful effect. We shall give just one example, which relates to electrophysiological conditioning.[5]

You will recall that in Pavlov's experiment the response under study is salivation elicited by food. After the food stimulus is coupled with sound, eventually the sound alone produces the salivation, i.e., the sound becomes an alimentary stimulus.

In this study,[5] carried out on children, the response examined consists of variations of potential produced by light stimulus on the occipital area. When sound is coupled with the light stimulus, it, in turn, produces a given response in the occipital area, so that the sound becomes— so to speak—a light stimulus.

In normal children this conditioning is demonstrated by the appearance of occipital changes brought about by auditory stimulation (see Fig. 2.1).

The brief high-wave occipital response to the conditioned sound does not appear in psychotic children; in their case a retarded slow wave develops after the sound during coupled stimuli. This slow wave appears on all the derivations (see Fig. 2.2).

This phenomenon is similar to the slow waves observed in newly born infants during conditioning where sound and strong light are associated (see Fig. 2.3). It is modified by neuroleptics (see Fig. 2.4) in disturbed children.

Finally, Dr. Ayllon stresses the nonspecific nature of certain reinforcements in his experiments. He feels that the interest the staff show in a patient is a factor which is generally underestimated. He is convinced that the thirst for attention and interest in humans just as much as in dogs,

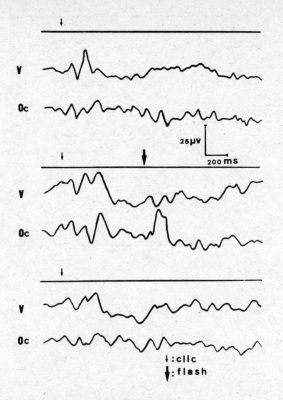

Each line represents the average response to 20 stimuli. The negative deflections go upward.

Top line: vertex; lower line: occipital.

Top graph: sound alone (habituation).

Centre graph: sound-light coupling.

Bottom graph: sound alone (extinction).

Comparison of occipital reactions to sound alone (top) and conditioned sound (centre) shows the appearance after sound (small arrow) of a brief high-wave response somewhat similar to the variation of potential produced by light stimulus (heavy arrow).

Fig. 2.1. Normal child

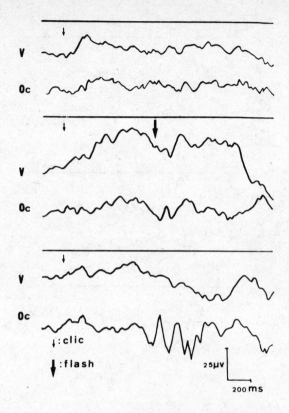

(Same symbols as in Fig. 2.1.)

Comparison of occipital reactions to sound alone (top) and to conditioned sound (centre) shows that the brief high-wave response after the sound does not appear with conditioning. On the other hand, during the coupled sound-light phase a retarded slow wave appears, after the sound, on the vertex and the occipital region. It remains partially present after conditioning (bottom graph).

The very retarded occipital accident which occurs at this point without light stimulus will not be discussed here.

Fig. 2.2.   Psychotic child

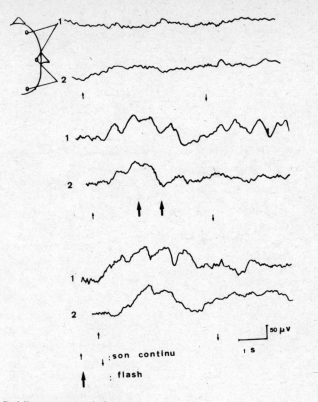

Each line represents a single response, since no averaging technique is used here.

Top line: Fronto-temporal R.

Lower line: Temporo-occipital R.

Top graph: sound alone (habituation).

Centre graph: sound-light coupling.

Bottom graph: sound alone (extinction).

During the coupled sound-light phase a retarded slow wave appears on the vertex and the occipital region and remains present after conditioning (bottom).

Fig. 2.3. Newly born infant

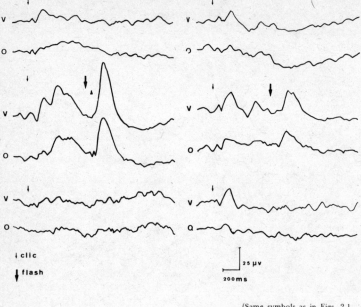

(Same symbols as in Figs. 2.1 and 2.2.)

Without treatment, sound light coupling produces a retarded slow wave visible on the derivations (centre left). This slow wave is virtually eliminated by administration of a neurolepic (pipotiazine), while there appears a precocious brief high-wave response (centre right) to sound.

Fig. 2.4. Young schizophrenic

is almost as great as the thirst caused by dehydration. Consequently, psychotherapy, like Jourdain's prose, is carried out here by people who are not psychotherapists but who possess an intuitive knowledge of this psychophysiological fact.

We have all noted the beneficial effect of Mongolian children on some psychotic children. A recent work[6] shows how a monkey which had been brought up beside a "mother" made of metal and had become autistic, gradually returned to normal behavior through the energetic psychotherapeutic effect of a younger monkey.

Dr. Ayllon's report gives us an example of an attempt to remove the psychiatrist from the miracle worker. His work demonstrates that even with very limited means it is possible to contribute to the clinical and even the therapeutic aspects of psychiatry on the basis of data taken from physiology.

NOTES

1. Gault-Mareul, Catherine (1971), Le Préconditionnement du mouvement chez l'enfant. Doctoral thesis (medicine), University of Tours.

2. Henin-Ribeyrolles, Danielle (1970), Le Préconditionnement. Doctoral thesis (medicine), University of Tours.

3. Lelord, G. F., Laffont, F., Anglade, P., & Wingerter, J. (1971), Etude comparée du conditionnement des activités évoquées par couplage du son et de la lumière chez les enfants normaux et psychotiques. 5th World Congr. Psychiatry, Mexico City, 1971.

4. Lelord, G., Martin, H., Etienne, e., Renaud, P., & Noreau, C. (1971), Introduction à une méthode de reconditionnement en psychiatrie: la rééducation de la personne. 1st Europ. Congr. Behavior Therapy, Munich, July 1971.

5. Lelord, G. F. (1972), Conditionnement électrophysiologique et psychiatrie. In: Activités évoquées et leur conditionnement chez l'homme normal et en pathologie mentale, eds. A. Fessard and G. Lelord. Colloque Inserm, Tours, pp. 25–293.

6. Suomi, S., Harlow, H., & Mc Kinney, W. (1971), Primate research. *The Sciences*, 11:8–14.

7. It should be remembered that in the case of the classic (Type I) reflex, if an animal shows an unconditioned response to a given stimulus (food), an initially ineffective stimulus (sound) immediately prior to it eventually acquires, after a sufficient number of reinforcements, the ability to produce the same response (salivation).

    The instrumental reflex (Konorski's Type II) differs from the latter in that it introduces movement into the conditioned stimulus. In this type of conditioning the reinforcement is preceded by a motor response. Such is the case when a dog puts out a paw to "obtain" food.

8. The electroencephalogram clearly shows that visual curiosity produces reactions in humans as intense as do the major feeding, defensive, and sexual instincts in animals.

9. In Prof. Konorski's laboratory, some researchers condition dogs by using caresses as reinforcers.

Chapter 3

SOME THOUGHTS ON ANTIPSYCHIATRY

André Green, M.D.

ANTIPSYCHIATRY: A DISCUSSION OF THE WORK OF THE ENGLISH SCHOOL

The Scope of the Discussion

It is impossible to cover all the concepts of antipsychiatry within the space available here. I say *all* the concepts, because I feel that it is more accurate to speak in terms of a multiplicity of meanings involved in antipsychiatry, depending on the geographical context within which the movement develops, in relation to ideological and cultural concerns and in relation to existing psychiatric practices. I shall confine my discussion to the work of the London school—represented essentially by Laing, Cooper, and others—where the movement originated.

The variety of forms which antipsychiatry has taken according to its geographical situation can be attributed to the fact that it is a mixture of theories derived from several

different contexts. It comprises, for example, phenomeno-
logically and existentially inspired philosophy, with major
reference to the concepts of Sartre, together with the theory of communication borrowed from the Palo Alto school
of Bateson; elements of Marxist theory relating to social
alienation and applied to the study of institutional relationships; elements taken from Freudian psychoanalysis, inspired by the psychoanalytical training of certain
antipsychiatrists, and so forth . . . No doubt a number of
other parameters could be discerned, but those mentioned
are definitely the main ones. My discussion will be confined
in particular to the *concept of psychosis* as it emerges from the
English studies, and I confine myself to the general outlines, as study of detail frequently leads to the discovery of
contradictory standpoints.

Anti-What?

Antipsychiatry is very much a present-day manifestation,
resulting from the modification of relationships between
madness and social environment. Nowadays madness is a
public phenomenon in which everyone is involved. This
situation arises, firstly, because the tightness of the normal
pathological barrier has proved precarious; secondly, because advances in the field of psychiatry have led to an
alteration of "inside-outside" relationships (mental hospitals versus social environment) together with greater communication between the two sectors; and finally, because
the crisis of civilization sweeping the Western World could
not exclude the notions of mental health, psychic normality, and adaptation to the environment from the questioning of values in general.

I shall not make any unqualified or irrevocable condemnation of these studies—in fact, I must admit that they
make extremely interesting reading. I would even go so far
as to say that some of them show great richness and

strength, and that I only wish that more psychiatric publications were of the same quality. I might also add that the works of the antipsychiatrists are those of excellent . . . psychiatrists. However, because of the mixture on which it is based, antipsychiatry is battling on all fronts at once, and it is difficult not to agree in certain areas. Antipsychiatry condemns not only organicistic, mechanistic psychiatry and the archaic asylum-type mental institution, but also psychoanalysis, and extends its condemnation to the family, present-day society, etc., so that one way or another almost anyone can be said to be an antipsychiatrist to some extent. If being an antipsychiatrist means to denounce a situation in which the psychiatrist is deaf to the patient's discourse and where his sole response consists of a leucotomy, shock treatment, or higher doses of neuroleptics to tighten the chemical straitjacket another notch and reduce the patient to no more than a robot, then of course, I myself can be numbered among the antipsychiatrists. But if it means adopting the theoretical standpoints of these authors concerning the genesis of psychosis and the appropriate response to it, then I cannot be considered an antipsychiatrist, since I am convinced that theirs are mistaken concepts.

The Denials and Contradictions of Antipsychiatry

Antipsychiatric proceedings are based upon a certain number of denials which are difficult to accept. The first of these seems to concern the *biological substrate of psychosis.* I am by no means of the opinion that all schizophrenic psychoses stem from biological factors, but conversely, it seems impossible to affirm with any certainty that no schizophrenic psychosis contains such elements. Studies on heredity and biological disturbances lead us to feel that although no precisely defined mechanism has been demonstrated, it is nonetheless difficult to deny outright the existence of these factors. What has to be done is to define the type of biological causality at work, not simply to conclude that it does not exist. Obviously, reference to biological factors does not imply that we are necessarily obliged to consider a psychosis along the lines of a medical model of a somatic illness —the model itself has already been modified in the light of psychosomatic concepts. It is easy enough for me to say this, since I myself once criticized the organogenetic concepts of schizophrenia. Freud himself referred to the "wall of biology" in connection with psychosis. It is far more a question of consideration of the levels of organization of psychotic disturbance than of a univocal etiological option. It would certainly be more agreeable not to have to take organic factors into account, but a scientific attitude consists not of imagining things as one would like them to be, but of seeing them as they are. Of course, this in no way implies taking refuge behind such organicity, either in order to do nothing at all or to give none but biological responses to psychosis. The facts oblige us to recognize that the vast majority of psychotics receive biological treatment, even in the most antipsychiatric of institutions. Such treatment would have no justification whatsoever if psychosis were solely the product of disturbed social relations. We must repeat, however, that we do not believe that all psychosis necessarily stems from organic causes, or that these are always of a primary type and not a secondary manifestation, although even in the latter case we would still have to take the transition to another register into account.

The antimedical concept of psychosis is closely linked to the *antinosographic attitude*, since this is supposed to belong to the same line of thought. This is, to my mind, a manifest error. The concept of a nosography of psychosis does not in the least infer reference to the medical model of an illness. A psychoanalytical nosography can demonstrate its usefulness, not for labeling patients, reifying or depersonalizing them, or burdening them with a more or less disastrous prognosis, but in enabling us to circum-scribe the structures involved, to study their internal coher-ence and reciprocal relationships, and to understand the spontaneous or therapeutic evolution of the cases we deal with. The authors under discussion are enmeshed in a con-tradictory situation where their theoretical positions and their own texts do not correspond. For example, Laing, in *The Divided Self,* compares the false self of the hysteric with that of the schizoid, making distinctions which are, in fact, extremely interesting. In *Psychiatry and Anti-psychiatry* Cooper states that schizophrenia does not exist, and that the patients he intends to discuss are those *to whom other psychiatrists have accorded the label schizophrenic.* But when he comes to the question of results, he points out that a third of his patients were not diagnosed as schizophrenics at all, and that these were simple cases of "adolescent emotional disturbance." It is one thing to ride a battle horse into purely theoretical combat, but quite another to put it to use in a concrete situation. How could it be otherwise? How-ever debatable the concept of schizophrenia may be, how can one evaluate the results of a therapeutic experience without indicating, for example, whether one includes or excludes cases which come under the heading of "acute schizophrenia," whose prognosis is quite different from the durable personality organizations to which the notion of schizophrenia is confined in France?

Laing does not deny outright the existence of schizo-phrenia, stating in the preface to *Sanity, Madness and the Family* that it can be "an assumption, a theory, a hypothesis, but not a *fact,*" although he does *in reality* deny its existence to the extent that he refuses to attribute to it any specific structures.

The Concept of Psychosis

On reading antipsychiatric literature I was especially struck by the fact that whenever Laing or Cooper mentioned patients and their family environment they seemed familiar to me. I had the feeling that I knew them or that I could have known them. But when the authors came to their interpretation of a psychosis or of its symptoms I found it far less easy to agree with their interpretation of the particular case in question, and when the interpretation reached the level of generality, going beyond the particular psychosis to broach the subject of psychosis in general, I was by then in total disagreement.

Several distinctions have to be made at this point, for it is easy to reach erroneous conclusions if one is familiar with only a few specific works of the English school of antipsychiatry. *The Divided Self,* which I personally consider a fine book, interprets in phenomenological and existential terms processes whose organization is intrapsychic, even though they are the result of an interpsychic process: the false self (closely akin to the concept of Winnicott), the study of defense mechanisms against engulfment, implosion (explosive intrusion), petrification or depersonalization, which can remain within the framework of clinical psychoanalysis. Laing prefers reference to phenomenological and existential terminology and interpretation (ontological insecurity), but it would be no exaggeration to say that without psychoanalysis none of the mechanisms he describes would make sense.

Self and Others and *Sanity, Madness and the Family* represent an important step forward. Criticism of psychoanalysis is a major element of the discussion—which is really a refutation—of the concept of the unconscious fantasy, while there is complete adherence to the theories of communication of the Palo Alto group (Bateson, Jackson, Weakland, Haley, and Watzlawick). In this new perspective, unconscious intrapsychic organization is nonexistent, and the entire clinical picture is interpreted in terms of communication disturbances, with psychosis stemming exclusively from *interpersonal* processes deriving from the "family nexus." I must confess that I fail to understand why "nexus" is preferred to "complexus." Perhaps it is felt that the idea of a confused tangle, a deadlock, or a Gordian knot is better expressed by this word. But then, the reason that Laing finds this in the knot is that he banishes it from the complex. Whatever the case may be, psychosis becomes here the effect of inflicted, suffered violence—an external pathology—arising from communicative distortions of contradictory messages. The subject's own violence, his unconscious conflicts experienced as internal contradictions, the drives tearing him between love and destruction, his pre-oedipal and oedipal desires, his narcissistic and objectal organization all vanish from the scene and give way to a logico-symbolic concept which takes no account of the specificity of the disturbance of the symbolic function in its articulation with primary processes.

Far be it from me to deny the role of the family milieu of schizophrenics. I have worked enough on the subject to recognize its importance and to discern the *real and serious disturbances* revealed by its observation. But when such disturbances are considered solely within the framework of communicative exchanges, even if the role of nonverbal or infraverbal messages are taken into account, one falls into all the traps of oversimplifying abstraction. And when this theory of the "double-bind"—whose justifiability I do not contest, by the way—is formulated in phenomenological and existential terms, one stumbles into what I should be tempted to call "the illusion of the univocal relationship." Just as certain linguists hope to eliminate all ambiguity or all possible polysemy from speech by producing a transparent language, so Laing and Cooper hope to obtain communication with no trace of ambiguity. The phenomenological concept of authenticity comes to their aid: as long as family relationships are sincere, everything will turn out alright!

Within the context of this point of view, interpretation of the symptom is often surprisingly naive. If a patient's delusion brings forth the statement that the family or neighbors are talking about her, it is because they really *are* doing so; if she says that she is being influenced, then people really *are* trying to influence her. If a patient complains that he has a pestilential odor, it is because his parents have always treated him as though he were not there, and that in this way his presence is made impossible to ignore, etc. ... Psychic organization—splitting, introjection, projection, projective identification, the collapse of narcissistic defenses and ego boundaries, the role of homosexuality in delusion, the struggle to counter the destructive activity of bad objects—all these are totally absent from a concept characterized by its commonplace realism. If, as Freud maintains, reality is repressed in the psychotic state, it is precisely because it contains something unacceptable. What really matters, however, is the effect of this *repression of reality* upon psychic organization, and it is pure naïveté to imagine that the consequences can be removed simply by means of frank and sincere communication among members of the family.

Is the schizophrenic whose sickness is the family itself, of whom he is the victim, the scapegoat, the branch which shoulders the entire burden of sickness in order that the tree might live? These are not necessarily erroneous notions, but they are simply unilateral. Through the family of the schizophrenic, it is by extension the family in general whose destructive action is condemned. Strange iconoclasts, who themselves pay homage to the family: Cooper's *Psychiatry and Anti-psychiatry* is dedicated to the memory of his father, and Laing dedicates *The Divided Self* to his father and mother.

Laing prefers to entrench himself among the mirrors of family alienation, with reflecting games of the kind anyone can play ad infinitum. For example, the identity of an individual; the identity which others attribute to him; the identities which he attributes to them; the identity or identities he thinks they attribute to him; what he thinks they think that he thinks, etc. . . . . Cooper breaks out of the circle and goes a step further: in his view, schizophrenia is a microsocial crisis reflecting macrosocial alienation, with obvious political implications. A classless society, the family without parents, would be free from madness. The relationship between psychology and politics seems to me far too serious a subject to be dealt with so summarily by facile recourse to the illusion of a futuristic golden age.

At this point the question arises as to who is, in fact, mad. Both Laing and Cooper produce the same answer: we are—the nonschizophrenics, doctors, psychiatrists, all imprisoned within our false self.

I should like to show how Laing's and Cooper's theoretical options—their phenomenological and existential references, their theory of communication, or their concept of social alienation—have managed to draw them away from their patients rather than to enable them to approach them more closely or to consider them as people rather than objects. It is obvious that their patients constantly confront them with situations which express sexuality, prohibited desire, aggressivity, destruction, the death instinct, and particularly the aspiration to nothingness, lived through the transference relationship. Although perfectly well aware of the presence of these elements, they deliberately ignore them, and reject them out of hand. Antipsychiatry has become the preamble to antipsychoanalysis. Laing and Cooper favor an existential encounter purified of all manifestation of instincts, an abstract, logic-symbolic type of communication. It is perfectly true that dynamic— or at least, so-called "dynamic"—studies on psychosis have so far shown a serious gap concerning psychotic thought processes (a gap which is now being filled in, thanks to the work of W. Bion), but there is no justification whatsoever for concluding, as some already have done, that these processes are simply learned from the parents or transmitted by the social context according to criteria of time and place. In the view of the English antipsychiatrists, and doubtless of others too, psychotics are the embodied expressions of the intrapsychic organization of the outside world of the family and society.

According to this view, when psychosis is eventually considered within the perspective of an internal crisis, it will not be seen as the result of a painful collapse, but as an experience of truth, the accession to a higher state of humanity, or, to put it bluntly, a mystical adventure in which the psychiatrist becomes the Zen master—Laing makes explicit reference to this. But there is something more serious yet, for Laing, particularly, but Cooper also, gives in to a dangerous propensity for *fascination with the aesthetic seductiveness of madness.* Freud himself was led to compare the symptomatology of a neurosis to an epic poem, but that did not make him yield to any temptation to try his hand at poetry. The nexus of the psychotic takes on the character of a poetic theme and the patient himself becomes the poem of the psychiatrist. We have always been aware that psychotics often know a good deal more than we psychiatrists do about psychosis and the inner life, but Laing and Cooper want them to strike in us the same holy fear as gurus, and let them continue their voyage of *metanoia* unhindered. It is much easier to let people set sail for a dangerous continent when one has a return ticket. To consider the psychotic as the poet of our universe is no doubt one way of rendering homage to him. I am less convinced that it is a way of helping him.

In my own experience, I must admit that one thing which seems to constitute a formidable obstacle to the cure of psychosis is the fact that for a single poet I have met a hundred other people suffering from what I shall call "psychological poverty."

The Reasons for the Chronicity of Psychoses

If, finally, we look for the reasons underlying the chronicity of psychoses, a number of answers come to light. Possible factors include the existence of an unknown biological process, the severity of the psychotic disturbance (characterized by the intensity of the repetition compulsion and the obvious role of the destructive instinct and the death wish), and probably an unfavorable family milieu or the intolerance of the social environment. Let us include another factor, namely, the inadequacy or the complicity of our therapeutic methods and institutions—and here I am referring to the most up-to-date of them just as much as to the most archaic—but there is in addition another factor, which I rarely hear mentioned and which seems to me to be of the utmost importance: *psychological poverty.* The poverty of working through (which has nothing to do with debility or intellectual deficiency) constitutes a serious handicap to our psychotherapeutic efforts and forces us to adopt very limited modes of assistance, with only partial effects. This distinction between psychotic process and psychological poverty may appear somewhat arbitrary, since psychological poverty may be interpreted as an old psychotic scar. However, I am convinced that these are two distinct realities. It is impossible to enter into a long discussion on the subject in this short address, but what I should like to emphasize here, although I disagree with the antipsychiatrists' view of the matter, is the importance of the role of social structures upon this state of psychological poverty. For it can well be asked whether the absence of psychic development—which is quite a different thing from the degree of personal education or professional qualifications —is not the result of an absence of cultural development.

Industrial societies have reached a high level of development of material standards of living in strong contrast with the curiously low degree of development of standards of cultural life. We may have here a parallel to the relatively satisfactory response to problems of physical health as compared with the notorious lack of attention to mental health, which could explain in some measure the emergence of antipsychiatry.

Conclusion

The problems seem to be the same as those raised in Montreal. They could not, of course, have changed a great deal in such a short span of time. One notable change, however, is that psychiatry is now openly in a state of crisis. Nonetheless, the fact of crisis point having been reached as the result of sudden awareness of the situation, does not mean that interrogation has been followed by answers, and the same questions still remain open. It is not simply a matter of proceeding by a process of elimination in regard to etiopathogenic concepts, and hence also in regard to therapeutic methods, but rather of making an effort to articulate the various levels of operation of psychotic mechanisms in order to obtain a more exhaustive understanding of them and, if possible, to find more effective means for their treatment—psychiatrically or antipsychiatrically.

Philippe Paumelle, M.D.

THE SIGNIFICANCE OF PSYCHIATRIC INSTITUTIONS FOR PSYCHOTICS

In this paper, which is an introduction relating to what antipsychiatry puts before us with its way of seeing things and with its radical rejection of institutions, I want to point out that antipsychiatry is doing us the favor of continuing the long chain of resistance to oppression and violence in psychiatry and it is important to start by showing how antipsychiatry is renewing or continuing a long tradition. In fact right from the very start of psychiatry there have been attacks made from the inside upon psychiatric institutions, by both the psychiatrists themselves and the patients, and I think this is something that should not be forgotten. The dialectics of violence, fear, and repression are at the root of psychiatry, and I cannot help but quote here one of Pinel's male nurse attendants who accompanied him on his first rounds. Pinel, questioning him in front of the chained patients, asked him "What do you do when they get too excited?" "I take their chains off" replied Pussin. "What happens then?"—"Well, they're quiet when I do that," came the attendant's answer. So you see that opposition to structures from within began right from the start, in front of the first psychiatrist and by the first attendant. At a more medical level, Pinel himself questioned the value of bleeding—and taking 2 liters of blood, at that—to calm agitated patients on their arrival at the Hôtel-Dieu in Paris. There have always been parallel manifestations like the antipsychiatrists denouncing abusive nosographical tendencies among psychiatrists.

I should like to remind you here, to quote just one French author, of Esquirol's extraordinary article on frenzy in the *Treatise on Mental Disorders,* where his closeness to the patient led him to the following conclusion: manic rage has nothing to do with nosography, it is simply the "anger of delusion." At another level, sharing the experience of the insane by means of the "trip," through hashish and oneirism, has been a constant factor throughout the history of psychiatry. Here too, antipsychiatry in particular is reminiscent of Moreau de Tours and also of Freud, for whom delusion signifies the recreation of the world after a catastrophic experience of the end of the world and the end of one's self.

Let me finish this review of certain antipsychiatric standpoints and the overall history of psychiatry, by mentioning the renewed phenomenon of actually listening to patients in the world of psychiatry and the world in general. I think it was in 1907, that a patient made himself heard by American psychiatrists. This was a patient by the name of Beers, at the time of the first Mental Health Association in the United States and of the creation of the first psychiatric social service. In 1962—and here I must refer to the history of psychiatry in Quebec—a psychiatrist prefaced his treatment of M. Paget, a patient in the 6000-bed Saint-Jean-de-

Dieu Hospital, with the words "The insane are crying out for help!" The insane calling for help were heard well before antipsychiatry came along.

But what does antipsychiatry do, apart from continuing this tradition? What accounts for its impact? What makes it something new in the order of opposition to psychiatric structures and institutions?

I shall stress three points:

1. The antipsychiatrists feel they have to go beyond condemnation of the violence *in* psychiatry I have just mentioned, to denounce the basic violence *of* psychiatry. I think that in the discussion following it is the question of "violence in" or "violence of," that is, the "fundamental violence of the psychiatric position" that should be the subject of debate.

2. Although schizophrenia, as Green says, is viewed from a poetic standpoint, it is also seen as a normal process of recovery which, we are told, diagnosis and treatment prevent from reaching completion.

3. Finally, the third point of departure between antipsychiatry and the most lively psychiatric positions, such as that of Daumezon inventing "institutional psychotherapy," could be summarized as follows: against the idea of attempting to cure patients in asylums, and since they themselves have no solution to curing the patients, they oppose the notion of a general revolution as the only means of doing away with the alienating institutions; it is society which is crazy, not the insane . . .

With the psychiatric discourse as a starting point, many observations have been made by nonpsychiatrists. A sociologist, Robert Castel, wrote in his recent article *L'institution psychiatrique en question,* that "The sociologist does not attempt to occupy the only ground from which he can really stand up to question the social fact of the existence of psychiatry as a power system. . . . This failure on the part of sociologists takes two forms under which can be perceived *the same inflation of medical ideology.*" He goes on to define these two forms as: "Firstly, to espouse the problems of psychiatry and psychoanalysis, perceiving and taking literally their hopes and ambitions; secondly, the attitude of the antipsychiatrist sociologists, which is to reverse the problems completely in an abstract way by expounding arguments which although verbally contentious in fact do no more than *apply to the social field the very medical model they are supposed to be taking issue with.* There is no such thing as a madman, it's society that is crazy." The sociologist, like we psychiatrists, finds himself trapped and torn between two positions: either having too great a faith in our therapeutic ability or "verbally" challenging the medical model while reviving it in a different form as a partisan of world-wide revolution.

With regard to what danger threatens us, is psychiatry simply a certain kind of power system of which there are other examples? I myself would answer "no" to this question. What hangs over us is the inevitable danger involved in power, which is that of omnipotence, of excessive power. Thus just as I suggested that we discuss "violence in" and "violence of" separately, I also propose that we make a distinction between "power" and "omnipotence." I do not think that the sociologist can understand the tremendous depth to which the patient invites us to demonstrate our omnipotence. We know by experience what the sociologist cannot possibly understand—since he has not been through it himself—the fact that those who treat the insane actually share and repeat the psychotic experience in its megalomanic or manichean aspects, and that living with him in daily contact, finally forget the patient as a suffering being.

Now for a second proposition and question: if this means a psychiatric "revolution," and taking into account the risk of the experience of omnipotence, as I think it does, then should it not begin with an internal revolution of the caring staff's[1] attitude towards psychotics, which our analytical experience in particular could make it possible for us to do or provide us with a model for it? It seems to me that such an internal revolution could be articulated around certain themes, certain points of impact.

Indeed, I do not believe that our encounter with the psychotic should be any kind of merger, but rather that in this revolution we have to stress the *value of the difference*, and that there is no meeting point possible unless there is prior recognition of the differences between the parties involved—here, the caring staff and the patient. We feel that the psychotic does not possess *the* truth (Laing), but that he possesses his *own* truth, and that on our side and with him we have *ours*. This idea of difference is the source of inspiration for the multidisciplinary team, which is only the concrete expression of difference, where people who retain their identity and their specific function are not drawn into a kind of risk of mutual destruction or narcissistic confrontation. I must tell you that in connection with the psychiatrist's internal revolution, for several years now psychiatrists—those working in mental hospitals just as much as analysts—have been using words which touch upon this internal revolution. To quote but a few: "backs to the wall," "bare-handed," "without a safety net," "face to face," "to be capable of receiving with no possibility of failure," as Balint would say. Hanna Segal spoke of "receiving," "understanding," "containing," but never allowing our personality to appear as a wall or a screen sending the patient's projections bouncing right back to him.

In short, I join others in proposing that we discuss the caring staff's depth, elasticity, durability, and indestructibility. This internal evolution or revolution leads us to feel that it could produce a stand antagonistic to the omnipotent position, but that at the same time it demands power.

At the risk of scandalizing you, I must say I feel that today, if we are to get away from *the dialectics of real powerlessness towards fantasy omnipotence,* then we absolutely have to *assert our claim for certain powers, and in particular powers over the institutions which govern both ourselves and our patients.* In this internal revolution proposed to them, it is up to the caring staff to invent, create, manage, and dominate, in short, to assume a legitimate power over the institutions they want to be considered responsible for. Secondly, they have to recognize, as does Racamier, who in my view expresses it most effectively, that within this framework we have only one leading, essential, and initiating institution, which is the team—the only institution without walls. It also has to be recognized that once one accepts inwardly the idea of teamwork, one encounters a number of difficulties which are, as you know, a constant trial. For any given patient we have to coordinate several different proceedings involving the analyst and the catchment-area team, and the catchment-area and the institutional team; we must be capable of dealing first of all among ourselves with the inevitable conflicts which the patient himself continually stirs up and sets in motion. In fact, it is up to us to make a reality— perhaps for the first time—of what Esquirol said about the mental hospital, namely, that it is the psychiatrist's finest instrument. It is curious to note that, although the instrument is normally in the hand of the worker, in the traditional structures the psychiatrist is the only worker to use an instrument within which he is himself enclosed. To have power over the institutions means hammering out an instrument of which we demand the creation, management, and direction. Let caring staff thus find themselves in possession of a constantly creative power over the institution, let them in this way be obliged to assume for the psychotic a triangular situation between the patient and society, adopting a mediating function to buffer the tremendous ambivalence of both the one and the other. Finally, the question is this: *Is there no straight and narrow path, that of the psychiatrist between the patient and a world to which he also belongs, between the two terms of a manichaeism that paradoxically throws out both the patient and his doctor?*

NOTES

1. See editor's note, Part II, Chapter 9 (Racamier)

THE EXPERIENCE AT CHESTNUT LODGE ON LONG-TERM TREATMENT OF PSYCHOTIC STATES, WITH PARTICULAR REFERENCE TO INEXACT INTERPRETATIONS

Ping-Nie Pao, M.D.

Chestnut Lodge celebrated its 60th anniversary in 1970. As early as 35 years ago, under the leadership of Dr. Dexter M. Bullard, Sr., Chestnut Lodge began devoting its effort to the intensive psychotherapy of psychotic states. This effort was greatly enhanced when Dr. Freida Fromm-Reichmann joined the staff in 1936, and when Dr. Harry Stack Sullivan agreed to participate at Chestnut Lodge staff meetings and exchange his views with the staff in the early 1940s. In subsequent years, many of the staff members of Chestnut Lodge—from the period of Drs. R. Cohen, M. Cohen, Stanton, Will, Searles, Jackson, Burnham, Gibson, Schulz, and Stierlin, to the present group of John Fort, John Cameron, Edward Podvoll, and myself to name only a few—have continued the therapeutic and research interests of the pioneer group. Some of the studies for which we are best known are those which elucidate internalized early object relations as they appear in the patient's behavior in the therapeutic situation, the rich source of determinants to the analyst responses, and many other psychodynamic is-sues which arise in the treatment of schizophrenic, manic-depressive, and severe borderline states.

To speak of the "Chestnut Lodge experience on long-term treatment of psychotic states" would require a sum-mary of all that was published by these and other authors in the past 35 years; this seems an overwhelming task for a 30-minute paper. During this allotted time, I have there-fore selected to speak about inexact interpretations. I choose this topic for presentation, anticipating that this congress, like many others, will have a sufficient number of papers dealing with clinical matters in broad general terms. In order to offer a change in pace, I shall give case illustra-tions.

In the following, I shall not discuss blatantly inexact interpretations which lead to a disastrous therapeutic out-come. Rather, I shall speak of those inexact interpretations which are relatively undramatic in terms of their magnitude and of their consequences. Yet, they are an inevitable com-ponent of all long-term intensive psychotherapy and espe-cially so in the treatment of psychotic states. While cure marked by some dramatic major event does occasionally occur, the progress of lengthy therapeutic work lies essen-tially in the bulk of experience shared by the patient and his doctor. A particularly significant aspect of their shared ex-perience is the occurrence, recognition, and correction of relatively insignificant inexact interpretations. I believe that Winnicott[16] was addressing the same point when he said, "What is it that may be enough for one of our patients to get well? In the end the patient uses the analyst's fail-ures, often quite small ones, perhaps maneuvered by the patient . . . the operative factor is that the patient now hates the analyst for the failure that originally came as an envi-ronmental factor, outside the infant's area of omnipotent control, but that is now staged in the transference." [P. 258] This then is my main point: emotional growth of the patient is facilitated through the recognition, and rectification of inexact interpretations.

New Developments at Chestnut Lodge

Before presenting clinical examples, I shall present some background information. At Chestnut Lodge we have noticed in the last 12–15 years, a change in our patient population. Because of a greater acceptance of intensive psychotherapy as the major approach to psychotic states, patients now enter our hospital before their illnesses have become entrenched. Formerly, a typical, newly admitted patient, who would be in his thirties, was hospitalized elsewhere for six to nine years and had been given several courses of ECT, often combined with ICT. While the patient might have initially sought psychiatric help, he would be so distrustful by the time he arrived at the Lodge that he would fight bitterly against every attempt on the analyst's part to establish a working alliance. Today, the average patient is in his early or middle twenties and has been hospitalized elsewhere for two to five years, where various combinations of psychotropic drugs were tried with limited or no success. Few of the recent patients have been given ECT and/or ICT; and if such were the case, no more than one course. Upon arrival at the Lodge, most of them could make good use of intensive exploratory psychotherapy after a much briefer period of preparatory work.

The changes in the patient population required a shift in our approach. Since the beginning of our treatment of severely disturbed patients, we have recognized the importance of the continuity of the analyst-patient relationship and the need to separate therapeutic and administrative care.[1,13] Until about 12–13 years ago, we did not give equal importance to the continuity of administrative care. We no longer segregate the more regressed patients and move them after they improve. Instead, we initiated a policy of having a patient remain on one ward throughout his stay and of having the same administrator and social service workers assist his family. On the ward level, we began a study of group process. Our nursing staff to patient ratio has always been high (2.3 to 1). In the last five years we trained our nursing staff to make more sophisticated behavioral observations. We have made it a regular part of the treatment program for the nurses to consult with an administrator and on his advice to offer selected observations to the patients at the ward meeting of patients, nursing staff, social worker, and administrative physician.

However, the kernel of our therapeutic endeavor remains intensive, individual psychotherapy. All Chestnut Lodge patients are seen for 50-minute sessions four to seven times weekly. Our primary purpose has always been to understand the psychodynamics of the patient's pathology, and to use our increased knowledge to improve the psychotherapeutic process. It is out of these considerations that the issue of inexact interpretation became crystallized.

DEFINITION OF INEXACT INTERPRETATION

Interpretation has long been considered the *basic* tool of psychoanalysis and psychoanalytically oriented psychotherapy. Broadly speaking, interpretation is understood as the procedure by which the analyst tells his patient something that the patient should know or experience at a given time but does not. First the analyst must assign meaning and causality to a psychological phenomenon of which the patient was oblivious and then he must communicate his conclusion to the patient.[18] For the interpretation to be useful, it must be accurate in content and appropriately timed.

The most comprehensive treatment of inexact interpretations is that of Glover.[4] He carefully distinguishes inexact interpretation from incomplete interpretation. In his view, a preliminary statement that would lead to a full interpretation is an incomplete interpretation; an incomplete interpretation becomes an inexact one if the full interpretation is permanently neglected. Glover's stress is on content when he speaks of inexact interpretation; timing is dealt with less directly. He sees that inexact interpretation can, at times, even be "curative" in terms of symptoms, as the patient seizes upon the inexact interpretation and converts it into an ego-syntonic displacement substitute. He observes that "a glaringly inaccurate interpretation is probably without effect unless backed by strong transference authority, but slightly inexact interpretation may increase our difficulties." [P. 356] The patient may enter a period of resistance or even break off treatment.

Fenichel's stress[2] is on the timing of interpretation. He says "since interpretation means helping something unconscious to become conscious by naming it at the moment it is striving to break through, effective interpretations can be given only at one specific point, namely, where the patient's immediate interest is momentarily centered." [P. 25] He further stresses that there may be negative effects from incorrect timing of an interpretation. "A much too early interpretation will not be grasped by the patient at all. But there is also a time when the ego, as yet unable to accept an interpretation, nevertheless understands enough to take it as a danger signal and to increase the defending resistances." [P. 502]

In this paper, I shall speak of inexact interpretations as inaccuracies both in content and in timing. While I agree with Glover and Fenichel that inexact interpretations can have untoward effects on the therapeutic or working alliance, if they are dealt with properly they can be the source of much therapeutic gain. In any case they are unavoidable *especially* in long-term treatment of severely disturbed patients. In the following, I shall illustrate with clinical material the kind of errors commonly seen in an ongoing treatment. After considering the factors that might determine the occurrence of inexact interpretations, I shall describe measures we have taken at the Lodge to minimize and repair their untoward effects.

CLINICAL MATERIAL

During the summer before college, Cynthia became overactive, defied parental restraints, and began to experiment with whatever she believed to be thrilling and unfamiliar. Because of her bizarre patterns of behavior and thought, she was taken to psychiatrists, was heavily drugged, and repeatedly hospitalized. Two years later, following an attempt of suicide, she was regarded as a candidate for long-term intensive psychotherapy and was admitted to Chestnut Lodge. At the Lodge, at times, she acted like an average teenager; at other times, her behavior was childish, primitive, and bizarre. On the surface, her thinking seemed intact; on closer scrutiny, it was apparent she assigned autistic meaning to things and words and was at times unable to differentiate her ideas and feelings from those of others. Following her admission, Dr. X. began to work with her. In her therapy hours her moods would change with little warning. For several months, she protested to Dr. X. that she felt all right and needed no treatment. She acknowledged that there had been an abrupt change in her but was not curious about its cause. While she insisted that she had had a great deal of fun in the last two years and that she should be released from the hospital and allowed to continue her life, she was making practical arrangements to remain at the hospital. It was in this setting that the sessions described occurred.

Monday, Cynthia started by speaking of herself as

needing no therapy. She went on to talk about her parents. Both of them were never at home. Cynthia and her younger sister were always left with different babysitters. In talking about this, Cynthia was relatively emotionless. Tuesday, Cynthia reported the following dream: a lot of kids were playing together in the upper loft of a barn. Her mother was looking on from the side. Everyone was gay. Then, her mother disappeared. Cynthia did not know what to do (the other children were then in the background). She was anxious and woke up. After reporting the dream, Cynthia went on to describe examples of her good times with other children during various periods of her life. Obviously, Cynthia was using fun with other children to deny her distressful feelings because of the uninvolvement and disappearance of her mother. But Dr. X did not detect her use of denial to defend herself from a sense of abandonment, and therefore made no pertinent comment. Wednesday, Cynthia reported a telephone conversation she had with her mother in the previous night. She expressed annoyance at her mother, who had suggested that she remain in the hospital despite her complaining that she was not happy and wanted to come home. After a short pause following her critical comments about her mother, Cynthia told Dr. X. that she had stayed up until 3:00 A.M. the previous night to write to her college, requesting readmission. Thereupon, Dr. X. asked Cynthia if her desire to leave the hospital and therefore the treatment could in any way be related to discussing her critical feelings toward her mother. To this suggestion, Cynthia neither agreed nor disagreed, and the hour ended. Dr. X. suddenly felt very dissatisfied with the development of the therapeutic situation. On reviewing the sessions, he realized that he had made mistakes.

On Thursday when Cynthia reported a phone call to her referring physician in which she tried to convince him that she would work better with him now if he agreed to take her out of the hospital, Dr. X. intervened and got

Cynthia to talk about Tuesday's dream. They clarified how she felt lost when her mother left her and how she tried to use activity to overcome her feeling of being lost. As she went on to talk about her feelings of being left in a hospital, thousands of miles away from home, she became more serious in thought and mood. That evening she told the nurses she had had a good hour.

The kind of error made by Dr. X. is interesting. It was not made because he lacked a general understanding of the case, but it was due to his inability to get hold of the full meaning of Cynthia's mental production at that given moment. It occurred at a point when new unconscious conflictual material was rising to the surface. On Monday she spoke of her parents being busy and leaving her with sitters, and followed on Tuesday by reporting a dream which further characterized her mother as one who merely looks on and then disappears. This degree of focus on her mother's inattention stirred up unbearable emotions. Instead of allowing herself to have the affective experience of "I feel lonely and abandoned because my mother was busy, didn't do enough for me, and disappeared from me," she forced herself to feel "It doesn't really matter for I can have a good time with my playmates anyway." In that split second when she unconsciously effected the defensive reversal of her ideation and affect, she succeeded in getting Dr. X. to unconsciously join her in the denial of her painful childhood experiences. Denial alone is usually not long successful in warding off painful affects. Cynthia, therefore, also adopted affect reversal during the Tuesday hour, and after the hour made further attempts to avoid her painful emotions by agitating for her mother to take her out of the hospital, writing to the college to ask for readmission, etc.

Anyone who undertakes the treatment of a patient as sick as Cynthia will attest that he has made similar mistakes. After all, the patient is always in conflict. As much as the patient wants to gain deeper awareness, he is equally dedicated to defend himself against the attendant painful emotions. His verbal production is always a compromise. The more he is inclined to reveal himself, the clearer will his verbal production be; and vice versa. The same influences may affect the analyst since the psychic structures of analysand and analyst are two open systems. It is conceivable at a time when a patient makes a sudden shift in mood that the analyst's thought process may easily become disrupted by his effort to follow the patient. The analyst is then temporarily inaccessible to the associative material prior to the disruptive denial. Under this circumstance, an inexact interpretation is particularly likely to occur.

Since Dr. X. had been working with Cynthia for less than five months, it might be questioned whether he knew her well enough to detect her sudden defensive reversal of affect. We shall, therefore, illustrate with another example in which the patient, Frances, had responded extremely well to treatment in the course of over four years. There was every reason to believe that the analyst, again Dr. X., knew her quite well.

Eight years ago, Frances dropped out of college during her sophomore year. She was deeply preoccupied, seclusive, and "eccentric." After being hospitalized, she received psychotherapy, to which she responded well. She reentered college while continuing psychotherapy in the office setting. Soon, however, everything was too much for her and she was readmitted to a hospital. After two years of unsuccessful treatment, she was transferred to Chestnut Lodge. By now, she was mute most of the time, did not eat well, and neglected her personal hygiene. Wherever she went, she left a trail of urine or menstrual blood. At one point, she ate her excreta. While her progress in her work with Dr. X. was slow and sometimes disheartening, she did respond steadily. Some four years later, she was once again an attractive young lady. Although still shy and withdrawn, she was no longer overtly psychotic.

In the fifth year of her treatment at the Lodge the following occurred: Monday, Frances was extremely feminine looking and had on a beautiful dress. Dr. X. praised her and her clothes. She was pleased. Tuesday, she began her hour by reporting calmly (her recent demeanor was quite different from her shouting and berating of Dr. X. several months before) that she had phoned her parents the previous night and had asked them for money. For reasons unclear to him, Dr. X. found himself saying to Frances that since she would now be going to concerts, museums, and doing other things, she should have more allowance and that it was right for her to ask for the money. Instantly Frances started a barrage, calling Dr. X. all sorts of names. As in her past barrages, she could not be interrupted. Dr. X. waited and she persisted until the hour was up.

As Dr. X. put it, "I couldn't do much thinking while she was berating me, not that I was angry with her, but I was bewildered. Not until after she left did it occur to me that my praise of her dress and my comment on her deserving more of an allowance reflected my desire for her to expand her activities. Crowded with my own feelings and expectations of her, I made a comment that inadvertently stirred up her conflict over her greedy designs on her parents. Her berating me was a return to her craziness in order to defend against her guilt-ridden urges, which she felt I was encouraging rather than exploring." Thus, on finding Frances in a working mood on Tuesday, Dr. X. brought up for discussion her behavior in yesterday's hour. She told Dr. X. that she felt he had been expecting too much from her. Dr. X. agreed and apologized. Thereupon, they could proceed to explore the meanings of her distress.

In the two clinical illustrations we have given, inexact interpretations were made. In these instances neither the magnitude nor the consequences of the errors was deleterious to the overall outcome of the therapy. In fact, both errors were inducive to a better therapeutic atmosphere, for (1) through the errors the analyst learned more about specific areas of his patient's problems and could later help her to see them, and (2) through the recognition and correction of the errors, the analyst set an example showing that not only is erring not so terrible but also that an error can be repaired; because of the patients' narcissistic problems, they were accustomed to feel extreme discomfort when making an error.

CONDITIONS CONDUCIVE TO INEXACT INTERPRETATION

Inexact interpretations are likely to occur in the following circumstances:

An Insufficient Rapport. Freud[3] advised that only when there is an "effective transference," a rapport, can an interpretation be given. We can say positively that this is not a factor in Frances' case. But is it the cause with Cynthia, who had been working with Dr. X. for only about four months? We are inclined to think not. It is true that the analyst often finds it difficult to establish a relation with his schizophrenic or borderline patient. There is, however, ample reason to believe from the material Cynthia brought to the hours that she and Dr. X. had achieved a therapeutic alliance based on trust.

A Failure in Mutual Comprehension. To have good rapport with someone is not the same as to know him. In the therapeutic arrangement, to know the patient would mean to know what is his major conflict, what makes him anxious, how to reduce his anxiety, what defense he uses under which circumstance, etc. In this respect, Dr. X. knew Frances well in their close relationship of over four years' duration. Thus, Dr. X. would know how to respond when Frances berated him, and he succeeded in helping her not to experience undue or prolonged anxiety. Dr. X.'s knowledge about Cynthia was more limited. This may account for the omission of an exact interpretation in response to her dream, and to his slowness to understand the meaning of her acting out. Consequently, he became like the mother in her dream—an unhelpful onlooker. Having become an unwilling participant in the enactment of her conflict, he could not help her to avoid a period of anxiety and acting out.

Just as the analyst studies his patient, the patient will study the analyst. It seems likely that because of four years' close relationship with Dr. X., Frances did not find it necessary to get unduly upset by the mistake he made. Cynthia and Dr. X. had had much shorter contact. Because Cynthia was less able to size up Dr. X., she may have reacted more intensely and was not as able to bring her reaction directly into the therapeutic work with Dr. X.

Some people have expressed a belief that certain therapists are more fit to treat schizophrenics than others. In the course of years, we have noticed that staff doctors work at the Lodge for an average of five to seven years. During their tenure, each of them demonstrated competence and success in treating schizophrenic and severe borderline patients even though their personalities are quite different. We would say that certain doctors are at certain times more or less tolerant of specific defenses and symptoms of their patients. It is rare that a doctor can deal only with a patient like Cynthia who tends toward constant activity, or with a patient like Frances who allows the doctor time to figure things out; he is usually equipped to treat both. In fact, he is apt to enjoy the encounter with a variety of problems.

Unresolved Countertransference Problems.   In his comprehensive review of countertransference, Kernberg[7] has indicated that in the treatment of psychotic states it is best to conceive of countertransference in terms of the total emotional response of the analyst to the patient. He contrasts this "totalistic" view with the "classic" view that countertrans-ference refers specifically to the neurotic conflicts of the analyst. Kernberg's broader usage therefore encompasses both the negative and positive effects of countertransfer-ence.

Since primary conflicts of psychotic patients center around aggression and annihilation, the overt or covert daily barrage to which they subject their analyst puts to a severe test the extent to which he has resolved his primitive rage reactions. One therapist tended to behave in an ex-tremely passive and masochistic manner whenever a male paranoid patient began verbally attacking him. This ana-lyst's normal capacity for active interventions was under-mined by the acute onset of anxiety associated with his own primitive rage fantasies.

Fear of personal attack by an assaultive schizophrenic patient may lead to timidity or intemperate haste in inter-pretation. Fear of suicide in a severely depressed patient may lead to overtimidity in interpretation. A clinging manic patient may be irritating. The analyst simply cannot follow the rapid change of topics and is made to feel useless. A borderline's swift mood change is upsetting because it tends to make the analyst experience a paralyzed degree of inner disequilibrium.

Problems Arising Outside the Specific Patient-Doctor Pair.   Jacobson,[6] Tietze,[15] Hill,[5a] Lidz,[10] and also others have characterized the sickness in the family members of the psychotic pa-tients. Symbiotic units formed by the patient with one of his family members is common. Thus, if the patient becomes responsive to the treatment, his symbiotic partner in the family may become exasperated and will make an attempt to interfere with the treatment. Especially with less experi-enced therapists this is likely to threaten the analyst and increase his tendency to make errors.[19]

PERIOD IN WHICH THE ERROR IS CORRECTED

I have stressed that, especially in the long-term treatment of psychotic patients, inexact interpretations are inevitable and that when corrected, they can lead to an improved working alliance and a better outcome of the treatment. However, the longer the interval between commission and correction, the less likely will the outcome be favorable. Sometime ago, I was working with a postpsychotic patient on his tendency to say "no" to everything. I had been exasperated for some time because he would disagree with anything I said. One day, he asked me if I cared enough for him to want him to get well. I rapidly evaluated this question and then told him words to the effect that in the frame of mind he was in, probably he wished me to say no. Immediately I considered adding my own positive wish for his recovery but I also felt as negativistic as he was feeling. So I said nothing. If I had, I could also have told him the negativistic feelings I had just experienced. Probably I could then have gone on to study his negativistic attitude, but I did not. The next day, he went on his usual business and I "forgot" all about my error. A month later, I went away on a vacation. In my absence, he saw one of my colleagues as an interim therapist and told him that he was hurt that I did not care if he got well or not. Upon my return, I learned about his hurt feelings and discussed it with him. By then, I could state the true nature of my concern for him as well as my understanding of how my error had occurred. But we could not go beyond that. The negativistic feelings were no longer fresh. What had been a live issue then seemed now to be out of place.

Another disadvantage of lengthy intervals before an error is corrected is the chance for additional errors. Dr. X.'s tardiness in correcting his first error with Cynthia led him to commit another error in his initial work with her acting out. The sense of accumulating errors can put a strain on the therapeutic alliance and on the levels of problem solving available to both therapist and patient. (Lichtenberg and Slap.[9])

PRECAUTIONARY MEASURES AGAINST INEXACT INTERPRETATION

Recently Greenson[5] wrote about "management of errors in technique," where, by using his own dissatisfaction following an hour as an index, he reflects over the hour and then corrects the error with the patient when they meet again. In principle this is what Dr. X. did with both of his patients. This capacity for self-reflection may be acquired through personal analysis. We make a mandatory requirement that the doctors who work at the Lodge must be analyzed. Also, groups of four or five doctors meet regularly twice a week to discuss their patients and their feelings about them. We find small group discussion reduces some problems of inexact interpretation. For instance, one doctor who was partially disabled, but struggled to come to work, was helped by the colleagues in his small group to see that he repeatedly failed to notice patients' dependent pleas. After that, he was able to connect his own fight against dependency with his therapeutic blind spot. In addition to the small group, we encourage "case supervision" or "talking to someone regularly about a specific case." In order to work with severely sick patients, it is extremely important to have someone "to talk to." Listening to a catatonic patient who makes disconnected, cryptic statements day after day, it is extremely helpful to have someone to sort out one's formulations of the patient's problem. Facing a paranoid who projects all his hatred on the doctor, it is useful to have someone help trace the introjective-projective process that is going on in the hour. Confronting the borderline who constantly uses special devices to distract the doctor at the emergence of new unconscious fantasies, it is important to have someone help us to stay on the track. After feeling sucked dry by an extremely depressed, severely narcissistic patient's lament of being unloved and unfed, one needs someone to help to restore his evaluation of himself as a person capable of giving. Of course, all these measures do not obviate inexact interpretations; they aim only to minimize their occurrence. It is hoped that they help to spot those that do occur, so that a therapeutic correction and working through may be made in time.

CONCLUSION

In reporting the Chestnut Lodge experience with long-term treatment of psychotic states, I have tried to focus on a limited issue: the causes, effects, and correction of inexact interpretations. We feel these interpretive errors are inevitable. While we try to minimize their frequency, we aim particularly at their prompt recognition and correction. I have mainly stressed the factors that play a part in their causation to indicate the therapeutic gain that is achieved by actively working with the dynamic issues that are involved in each instance of an inexact interpretation.

NOTES

1. Bullard, D. M. (1940), The organization of psychoanalytic procedure in the hospital. *J. Nerv. Ment. Dis.*, 91:697–703.

2. Fenichel, O. (1945), *The Psychoanalytic Theory of Neurosis*. New York: Norton

3. Freud, S. (1913), On beginning the treatment. *Standard Edition*, 12:121–144. London: Hogarth Press, 1958.

4. Glover, E. (1931), The therapeutic effect of inexact interpretation: A contribution to the theory of suggestion. In: *The Technique of Psychoanalysis*. New York: International Universities Press, pp. 353–366.

5. Greenson, R. (1971), Management of errors in techniques. Paper read at the Washington Psychoanalytic Institute, April 1971.

5a. Hill, L. B. (1955), *Psychotherapeutic Intervention in Schizophrenia*. Chicago: University of Chicago Press.

6. Jacobson, E. (1956), Manic-depressive partners. In: *Neurotic Interaction in Marriage,* ed. V. W. Eisenstein. New York: Basic Books, pp. 125–134.

7. Kernberg, O. (1965), Notes on countertransference. *J. Amer. Psychoanal. Assoc.*, 13:38–56.

8.   Klein, M. (1932), *The Psychoanalysis of Children*. London: Hogarth Press, pp. 58–59.

9.   Lichtenberg, J. & Slap, J. (1971), On the mechanisms of defense. Paper to be read at the American Psychoanalytic Association meeting, December, 1971.

10. Lidz, T. et al., (1957), The intrafamilial environment of the schizophrenic patient: The father. *Psychiat.,* 20:329–342.

11. Loewald, H. W. (1970), Psychoanalytic theory and the psychoanalytic process. *The Psychoanalytic Study of the Child,* 25: New York: International Universities Press, pp. 45–68.

12. Loewenstein, R. M. (1957), Some thoughts on interpretation in the theory and practice of psychoanalysis. *The Psychoanalytic Study of the Child,* 12:127–150. New York: International Universities Press.

13. Morse, R. T. & Noble, D. (1942), Joint endeavors of the administrative physician and psychotherapist. *Psychiat. Quart.,* 16:1–8.

14. Olinick, S. L. (1954), Some considerations of the use of questioning as a psychoanalytic technique. *J. Amer. Psychoanal. Assoc.,* 2:57–66.

15. Tietze, T. (1949), A study of mothers of schizophrenic patients. *Psychiat.,* 12:55–65.

16. Winnicott, D. W. (1965), *Maturational Process and the Facilitating Environment.* London: Hogarth Press, p. 258.

17. I am indebted to the whole medical and paramedical staff at Chestnut Lodge and its medical Director, Dexter M. Bullard, Jr. I am especially grateful to Dr. Joseph D. Lichtenberg, my friend and colleague of many years, for his detailed critiques and helpful suggestions.

18. Of course, prior to interpretation, initial steps such as confrontation and clarification are employed. Questioning is one form of preparatory step toward interpretation.[14] While interpreting, tact and the choice of wording are important.[12] These will not be detailed here.

19. In recent years, more extensive work with the family by our social workers has eliminated many patient-family collaborated actions against the therapeutic alliance. In the case of Cynthia, that her family did not respond to her plea to take her out of the hospital as they did before is one evidence of achievement in working with the family.

CLINICAL OBSERVATIONS REGARDING THE DIAGNOSIS, PROGNOSIS AND INTENSIVE TREATMENT OF CHRONIC SCHIZOPHRENIC PATIENTS

Otto F. Kernberg, M.D.

INTRODUCTION

The C. F. Menninger Memorial Hospital is dedicated mainly to the long-term, intensive, psychoanalytically oriented treatment of severely regressed patients. Approximately one-third of the 150 inpatients, and approximately the same proportion of our 50 to 80 day-hospital patients, suffer from chronic schizophrenic reactions.

The typical schizophrenic patient has usually undergone different treatments over varying periods of time before coming to our hospital, such as treatment with ataractic drugs of varying duration and pharmacological sophistication; intensive psychotherapy as an outpatient; and some psychotherapeutic approach in inpatient settings. He reaches our hospital as a "last resort" after the gradual deterioration or acute breakdown of a therapeutic program. The contribution of a pathological family structure in bringing about the breakdown of treatment programs with such patients is well-known, and our patients are no exception in this regard. In other words, our schizophrenic patient population reflects predominantly those chronically developing schizophrenic conditions that have not responded to the usual approach of pharmacological treatment, outpatient psychotherapy, and weeks to several months of hospital milieu treatment.

I would like to present some clinical observations regarding the diagnostic process in the case of these patients, their prognosis for improvement with the treatment approaches available in our hospital, and some considerations about these treatment approaches. These observations reflect a developing consensus among the staff of our hospital. We are at present at an early stage of a more systematic evaluation of these observations within specific research designs, and of an experimental treatment approach within a specialized unit of the hospital.

DIFFERENTIAL DIAGNOSIS WITH BORDERLINE CONDITIONS

We often face the task, in the early stages of the evaluation of our patients, of making a careful differential diagnosis between borderline conditions and schizophrenia.[14] The importance of such a differential diagnosis derives from the differences in the prognosis and treatment of the two conditions. We have become more optimistic about the prognosis of borderline patients in a specially designed treatment program that combines intensive, psychoanalytically oriented psychotherapy with a highly structured hospital milieu program. In contrast, the prognosis for chronic schizophrenic patients is, of course, always serious.

The two major considerations in differentiating schizophrenia from borderline conditions are the issues of reality testing and transference psychosis. When a patient comes to the hospital with a typical history of chronic manifestations of formal thought disorder, hallucinations and delusions, bizarre behavior and affect, and disintegration of the connection between thought content, affect, and behavior, the diagnosis is usually that of a schizophrenic reaction. However, many borderline patients who present severe, chronic disturbances in their interpersonal relationships and a chaotic social life, and who have undergone psychoanalysis or intensive psychoanalytic psychotherapy on an outpatient basis, may have developed transitory psychotic reactions which raise the question of schizophrenia. Also, both borderline and schizophrenic patients who have received intensive drug treatment over a long period of time, or have socially stabilized in the form of chronic withdrawal from interpersonal interactions (while still functioning relatively appropriately in some isolated, mechanical work situation) require this differential diagnosis.

Reality Testing

While both borderline and psychotic patients present a predominance of pathological, internalized object relations and primitive defensive operations (which distinguish these two categories of patients from less disturbed neurotic and characterological conditions), the functions of these primitive defensive operations in borderline conditions are different from those in schizophrenia.[19] In patients with borderline personality organization, such primitive operations (particularly splitting, projective identification, primitive idealization, omnipotence, denial, and devaluation) protect the patients from intensive ambivalence and a feared contamination and deterioration of all love relationships by hatred. In contrast, in schizophrenic patients, these defensive operations, and particularly the pathological development of splitting mechanisms (leading to generalized fragmentation of their intrapsychic experiences and interpersonal relations)[1] protect the patients from total loss of ego boundaries and dreaded fusion experiences with others reflecting their lack of differentiation of self and object images.

Clinically, the implications of these formulations are that while interpretation of the predominant primitive defensive operations in borderline patients tends to strengthen ego functioning and to increase reality testing, the same approach to psychotic patients may bring about further regression, uncovering the underlying lack of differentiation between self and nonself. While interpretation of these primitive defensive operations may increase the psychotic regression in schizophrenic patients, this does not imply that a psychoanalytic or expressive approach should not be attempted. The regressive effect of interpretation of primitive defenses in the transference is only a short-term one; in the long run, intensive psychoanalytic psychotherapy with psychotic patients may develop their capacity to differentiate self from non-self, and strengthen their ego boundaries.

The temporary increase in disorganization that occurs in schizophrenic patients when primitive defensive operations are interpreted in the transference enables the clinician to differentiate these cases from borderline conditions, whose immediate functioning, particularly their reality testing, tends to improve when primitive defensive operations are interpreted in the transference. In practice, this approach means that the diagnostic interviews with patients who require the differential diagnosis of borderline conditions versus a schizophrenic reaction, may be structured in such a way that this testing of their defensive operations can be carried out.

It is, of course, useful to explore first whether, in the diagnostic interviews, there is any formal thought disorder, hallucinations and/or delusions, which, if present, would confirm that the patient is psychotic. If the interviews reveal no formal thought disorder, no clear-cut hallucinations or delusions, I would then focus upon the more subtle aspects of the patient's thinking, affect, and behavior which would indicate some inappropriate or bizarre quality within the context of the interpersonal situation of the interviews. Confronting the patient with such subtly inappropriate or bizarre aspects of his behavior, affect, or thought content is usually anxiety-provoking for him. However, when done tactfully and respectfully, and with an effort to clarify the confusing, disruptive, or distorting influence of this aspect of his behavior upon the relationship with the interviewer in the "here-and-now," this confrontation may provide an opportunity for meaningful support of the patient.

The interviewer, following such an approach, actually carries out a boundary function between the patient's intra-psychic life which the interviewer tries to reach empath-ically, and the external reality represented by the social relationship between the patient and the therapist. This approach is in contrast to (1) the classical, descriptive search for isolated symptoms in an effort to establish the diagnosis of schizophrenia; and (2) the psychoanalytic effort to empathize with the intrapsychic experience of the patient regardless of whether the patient can maintain real-ity testing of this experience.

For example, if the patient presents a strange lack of affect in the face of an emotionally meaningful subject mat-ter, this discrepancy may be pointed out to the patient and its implications explored. A borderline patient will be able to recognize this discrepancy, while identifying with the reality implications of the interviewer's question, and will become more realistic in this regard. The schizophrenic patient, in contrast, confronted with the same discrepancy, may be unable to grasp the therapist's point, or may inter-pret it as an attack, or react by further increasing the dis-crepancy between affect and thought content. In other words, reality testing increases in borderline patients with such an approach, and decreases in schizophrenic patients.

This same approach may be applied in focusing upon an inappropriate gesturing (a behavior manifestation which may reflect a psychogenic tic or a stereotype), or upon any specific content which appears to be in serious contrast with other related thought contents, affects, or behavior. Often, multiple discrepancies among affect, thought content, and behavior are present, and the total emotional situation of the interpersonal relationship between patient and therapist will determine which of these elements represent the highest priorities for investigation in terms of their urgency or their predominance in distorting the "here-and-now" relationship.

If this confronting approach geared to diagnosing the presence of reality testing indicates that it is, indeed, maintained in all areas, a second line of exploration would be to focus directly upon primitive defensive operations, and their interpretation in the transference. For example, if the patient seems highly concerned about philosophical or political matters on the one hand, and completely unconcerned about a serious immediate problem in his daily life on the other, the denial (the dissociation of concern from his immediate life situation) may be interpreted; or, if the patient indicates massive projection of aggression plus tendencies to exert sadistic control of the interviewer, a tentative interpretation of projective identification in the transference may be formulated. Again, borderline patients usually react to such interpretations with an improvement in reality testing and in their general ego functioning in the hour; schizophrenic patients tend to regress, and to experience such interpretation as frightening intrusions which threaten or blur their self-boundaries.

The interviewer often senses intuitively that such regression may occur as a response to his interpretive efforts; thus it needs to be stressed that this approach is indicated only for diagnostic purposes. If excessive anxiety is aroused in the patient with such an approach, the psychotherapist, after reaching his diagnostic conclusion, should decrease the patient's anxiety by clarifying the relationship between the psychotic distortions and the therapist's interventions. The psychotherapist acting as a diagnostician has to balance the need to remain objective enough to arrive at a diagnosis, with the need to remain sufficiently empathic with the patient to protect him from excessive anxiety.

In summary, using the total interpersonal relationship in order to explore discrepancies among thought content, affect, and behavior leads to clarifying the presence or absence of reality testing. Also, the interpretation of primitive defensive operations, particularly as they enter the transference situation, further intensifies the exploration of the presence or absence of reality testing.

Loss of reality testing in any one area indicates psychotic functioning. It should be stressed that this conceptualization of reality testing is a restricted, delimited one, referring exclusively to the presence or absence of the patient's capacity to identify himself fully with the external reality represented by the patient-therapist relationship. This formulation implies that there is no continuum, no gradual shift from presence to absence of reality testing, and that there are qualitative as well as quantitative differences between the structural organization of borderline and psychotic conditions. As mentioned before, this essential qualitative difference derives from the particular vicissitudes of self and object images in borderline and psychotic conditions, and the related capacity to differentiate self from nonself, which, in turn, determines the capacity to differentiate perception from fantasies, and intrapsychic perceptions from those of external origin and the capacity to empathize with social criteria of reality.

Transference Psychosis

Borderline patients may, however, lose reality testing transitorily under the influence of severe emotional turmoil, alcohol, drugs, and especially in the context of a transference psychosis. This leads to the criteria by which transference psychosis, particularly in borderline patients who undergo regression under psychotherapeutic treatment, and the psychotic transferences of schizophrenic patients may be differentiated from each other. I have examined this issue in earlier papers,[15,19] and will merely summarize here the diagnostic implications of these conclusions.

The similarities of transference psychosis in borderline conditions and the psychotic transferences of schizophrenic patients are: (1) Both present a loss of reality testing in the transference situation, and the development of delusional thought involving the therapist (hallucinatory or pseudohallucinatory experiences may develop in the treatment hours); (2) In both, primitive object relationships representing fantastic part-objects and fragmented self-images predominate in the transference; and (3) In both, there is an activation of primitive, overwhelming affection reactions in the transference, and a loss of sense of having a separate identity from the therapist.

The following are the differences between the transference psychosis of borderline patients and the psychotic transferences of psychotic, particularly schizophrenic patients who undergo intensive psychotherapy: In borderline patients, the loss of reality testing does not seriously affect the patient's functioning outside the treatment setting; these patients may develop delusional ideas and psychotic behavior within the treatment hours over a period of days and months, without showing these manifestations outside the hours. Also, their transference psychosis responds dramatically to the structuring of the total treatment situation outside the hours and to specific modifications of technique, such as clarification of the reality in the "here and now" combined with systematic interpretation of primitive defenses in the hours.

In contrast, the psychotic transferences of schizophrenic patients reflect their general loss of reality testing, and the psychotic thinking, behavior, and affect expression in their life outside the treatment hours. The initial detachment of the schizophrenic patient (described in the "out-of-contact" type of schizophrenic transference by Searles[30] is usually reflected in psychotic behavior in the hours which is not markedly different from his psychotic behavior outside the treatment hours. However, at more advanced states of development of his psychotic transference, the schizophrenic patient develops fusion experiences with the therapist by virtue of which the patient feels a common identity with his therapist. In contrast to borderline patients, this loss of identity in the transference is not due to rapid oscillation of projection of self and object images (so that object relationships consist of rapidly alternating, reciprocal role enactment on the part of patient and therapist), but is a consequence of refusion of self and object images so that separateness between self and nonself no longer obtains, i.e., regression to a more primitive stage of symbiotic self-object fusion.

Borderline patients, even in the course of a transference psychosis, do experience a boundary of a sort between themselves and the therapist. It is as if the patient maintained a sense of being different from the therapist at all times, but concurrently he and the therapist were interchanging aspects of their personalities. In contrast, psychotic patients experience themselves as one with the therapist; however, the nature of this oneness changes from frightening, dangerous experiences of raw aggression and confused engulfment to that of exalted, mystical experiences of oneness, goodness, and love.

In summary, the underlying mechanisms determining loss of ego boundaries, loss of reality testing, and delusion formation are different in the psychotic transferences of borderline and schizophrenic patients, thus contributing to the differential diagnosis between these conditions.

PROGNOSTIC CONSIDERATIONS

The Capacity for Establishing Significant, Deepening Object Relationships in the Hospital Setting

Our experience has been very much in line with what Freeman, Cameron, and McGhie[9] have pointed out, namely: "Apart from time, the only index that might differentiate between the benign and the malignant case is the patient's capacity to relate as revealed in a psychotherapeutic relationship. The slightest ability to react in an organized and specific way to the impact of the therapist may be of greater prognostic significance than defects in visual perception or loss of self-object discrimination. . . . What must be determined is whether or not the patient retains, even in the smallest degree, the capacity for relations with an individual outside himself. This capacity may appear only transiently and be impaired by difficulties in self-discrimination. Nevertheless, its very presence is indicative of a potential for transference." [P. 110] We have found that chronically regressed schizophrenic patients, who are able to establish a significant, deepening interpersonal relationship within the hospital setting, have a definitely better prognosis than those who do not. This overall conclusion derives from several criteria reflecting the patient's overall adaptation to the hospital.

Mutual Withdrawal of Staff and Patients Despite Adequate Treatment

If the overall milieu program and those who carry it out are adequate and yet no differentiated interpersonal relationships develop within a reasonable period of time, the prognosis is poor. "Adequacy" refers both to the program itself, and to the skill of those who implement it. The overall milieu program needs to be individualized for each patient so that an array of nonthreatening social situations are available, within which the patient may select one or several members of the staff or other patients to establish differential relationships with. Under these circumstances, some schizophrenic patients are, indeed, able to modify the available social structure into a net of differentiated relationships which eventually can be understood as a reenactment of the patient's internal world of object relations and interpreted to him as such. These schizophrenic patients have a better prognosis than others who present a gradual, undramatic but relentless withdrawal from all social interactions in the hospital and, even more important, induce a generalized, reciprocal withdrawal on the part of staff around them. We have come to consider such long-term social withdrawal from the patient by the hospital staff as an ominous prognostic sign.

The question may be raised as to what extent this social withdrawal reaction on the part of staff reflects their "inadequacy" in that it corresponds to shared countertransference acting out, induced by the patient's psychopathology, which, if diagnosed and worked through in time, could be better used for diagnostic and therapeutic purposes. However, given the overall interest and dedication of a well-trained and well-supervised treatment team with generally high morale, it may be that there are certain limits beyond which the mutual withdrawal process is hard to prevent or reverse.

The Persistent and Repetitive Need of the Patient to Destroy Those Who Help Him

In an earlier paper,[21] I referred to the particularly ominous prognostic implication of a certain regressed level of psychopathology (including both some borderline and some schizophrenic patients) in which the negative therapeutic reaction becomes very predominant. These patients typically present a combination of severe pregenital aggression, some degree of blurring of self-nonself boundaries, a chronic use of self-destruction as a weapon to preserve a magical omnipotence, and the unrelenting need to defeat all who threaten the status quo, particularly by stirring up the patient's intolerable envy and need of love.[6,29]

A Deepening Relationship With the Psychotherapist

Perhaps the most important prognostic indicator is the capacity of the patients to develop a deepening object relationship with the psychotherapist. This process may take from months to years, and is under the influence not only of the patient's personality and psychopathology but also the personality, the skill, and the personal investment of the psychotherapist in the treatment.[33]

The Combined Impact of the Patient's Family and the Social Life in the Hospital on the Psychotherapeutic Process

It is a well-known observation that the families of schizophrenic patients tend to exert pressures on the treatment situation which reflect their unconscious efforts to maintain the status quo and to avoid the patients' freeing themselves from the family structure. We have observed in many cases how the family, in unconscious collusion with its most destructive members, interferes with the treatment program in spite of conscious wishes that the patient be helped, and how, particularly when the patient is improving, efforts on the part of the family to sabotage the treatment may increase. We have also observed the opposite situation, how supportive tendencies within a certain family constellation can be of crucial help in preserving a therapeutic program and helping the patient to improve. Preliminary observations by Green[11] indicate that in the first few months of treatment, particularly, and then again after a two to three year treatment period, pressures of the family tend to increase, and the degree to which they can be resolved may have an important overall prognostic implication. In this regard, we have found that when all these family pressures and influences are brought into the treatment situation and related to the patient's primitive distortion of his experience in the hospital, the negative effects of family pressures can be reduced, and their positive influences increased. The extent to which complications arising from the family can be monitored, diagnosed, and worked through in time is an important prognostic indicator.

A similar situation develops regarding the influence of the total hospital social field on the treatment situation. Often the diagnosis of the social field surrounding a schizophrenic patient in the hospital can be arrived at more easily than in the case of borderline conditions because the higher-level, relatively less fragmented splitting operations of borderline patients are typically reflected in their perception of some staff members as "all good" and others as "all bad." Thus the total transference situation as reenacted within the hospital milieu can only be diagnosed by an interpretive integration of all the contradictory relationships of the borderline patient with others. In contrast, in severely regressed schizophrenic patients, more primitive, pathological types of splitting,[1] leading to serious fragmentation of all experiences tend to blur any sophisticated distinction between different members of the staff, particularly in the early stages of treatment. The disturbing "uncanny" effect of these splitting mechanisms on the staff often leads to the latter's withdrawal and avoidance of the patient.

The relationships of regressed schizophrenic patients with most staff members and other patients are quite repetitive in their chaotic quality; and the complex splitting of the staff into opposite groups, the subtle manipulation of staff members and patients against each other so characteristic of borderline patients is less of a problem with schizophrenic patients. Paradoxically, the more regressed the patient, the more similar are the experiences that different staff members and other patients have in their interactions with him.

As the schizophrenic patient establishes over a period of time the individually differentiated relationships with others that have such great prognostic implications, he begins to be seen in very different ways by various members of the treatment team. It is at this point that the varying countertransference reactions and relationship patterns of the patient with staff members need to be observed, diagnosed, and integrated into the psychotherapeutic relationship. Open communication between the psychotherapist and all other members of the treatment team permits an overall integrated view of the patient which can be included in the work of the psychotherapeutic relationship, and has a prognostically helpful implication. The opposite is true when psychotherapy is isolated from the rest of the patient's experiences in the hospital, or when the psychotherapist becomes engaged in a power struggle with the hospital team managing the patient's daily life in the hospital.

For example, a senior, prestigious, and potentially powerful psychotherapist may influence the total treatment program to such an extent that the patient becomes able to act out his primitive wishes for omnipotence and control over his hospital setting (as that setting represents his world of internalized infantile objects) through influencing his psychotherapist. Some psychotherapists may achieve spurious and temporary improvements in a severely regressed patient by unwittingly joining him in such acting out of primitive omnipotence. A similar situation may occur when a patient, unconsciously provoking his family to control the treatment situation, thus is able to act out his self-destructive unconscious omnipotence; and the psycho-therapy is terminated by the family's intervention before the psychotherapist has been able to interpret or even fully grasp this development. At times, the patient may induce the hospital team to react with unconscious hostility toward the psychotherapist, consequently sabotaging and termi-nating the psychotherapeutic relationship.

These prognostic considerations have several thera-peutic implications: first, the psychotherapist and the hos-pital managing team, through its team leader, need to communicate with each other while remaining autono-mous, so that unconcious fights for power can be diag-nosed and resolved in time. For reasons which, because of lack of time, cannot be stated here, this requires a func-tional, nonauthoritarian hospital administration.[18] Second, the psychotherapist must see as one of his crucial tasks that of carrying out a boundary function between the intrapsy-chic life of the patient and the external reality represented by the total treatment setting within the hospital and by the patient's family. The psychotherapist needs to bring this reality into his work with the severely regressed schizophre-nic patient; this reality inevitably affects the patient, and if it is not brought into focus in the hours by the psychothera-pist, the disorted, threatening aspects of the patient's social reality can only militate against the treatment.

SOME CONSIDERATIONS REGARDING THE THERAPEUTIC PROGRAM

Our Basic Treatment Approach

The total treatment approach to chronic schizophrenic pa-tients who require long-term hospitalization has been changing in our hospital. We do not have, at this point, full agreement on the part of our staff on what one might consider an ideal combination of therapeutic modalities. However, a consensus is developing regarding the following points: (1) We have been convinced for some time that for chronic schizophrenic patients who have failed to improve with previous treatment efforts (outpatient psychotherapy, ataractic drugs, short-term hospital milieu treatment, social rehabilitation, or a combination of several or all of these modalities) intensive, psychoanalytically oriented psychotherapy with a concomitant, specially structured hospital milieu treatment is the treatment of choice. This conviction is becoming more rather than less firm as we see more patients who have experienced these various other modalities in other settings without responding favorably to them. (2) Ataractic drugs do have a place within this treatment approach, especially under the circumstances described below.

The Place of Psychopharmacological Treatment

If a full-fledged, pharmacologically sound treatment with ataractic drugs has not been carried out in the past, it should be tried concomitantly with intensive psychotherapy. Sporadic, irregular administration of ataractic drugs for acute panic situations or treatment crises can defeat their overall, long-term pharmacological effectiveness and should be avoided. Also, from a psychotherapeutic viewpoint it seems preferable to provide the patient with medication on a steady level. This makes it possible for the therapist and the hospital team to analyze the fluctuations in the level of anxiety in terms of the total psychotherapeutic and social interactions of the patient. Use of multiple ataractics, with frequent changes in dosage, complicates such an analysis if it does not indeed make it impossible. An individually determined, optimal level and combination of ataractic drugs should be reached which decreases sufficiently the patient's anxiety and increases sufficiently the perceptive thresholds without such an overall reduction in the patient's alertness and communicative capacity as to interfere with the psychotherapeutic relationship.

Some psychotherapists working with schizophrenic patients (e.g., Will[37] consider all treatments with ataractic drugs as interfering with the subtle aspects of the psychotherapeutic interaction with schizophrenic patients; however, in our experience, ataractic treatments conducted within the guidelines sketched above have significantly improved some patients' capacity to develop a psychotherapeutic relationship. Ewalt's finding[7] that "A" type therapists (therapists with presumably optimal personality characteristics for treating schizophrenic patients) have a higher level of effectiveness than "B" type therapists (therapists with presumably less than optimal personality characteristics for this purpose) in patients receiving ataractic drugs, but not in patients receiving placebo, supports the hypothesis that ataractic drugs may improve the patient's psychological functioning to a point where his ego may make better use of the psychotherapeutic examination of his intrapsychic and interpersonal fields. Whenever ataractic drugs are part of the treatment situation, the psychological implications of their use need to be interpreted as part of the psychotherapeutic relationship. Again, in this regard, the psychotherapist has to carry out the boundary function between the patient's intrapsychic life and the hospital managing team, particularly the hospital physician who administers the medication.

The rationale for this overall approach which combines intensive psychotherapy and drugs derives from the findings of May[26] and the Massachusetts Mental Health Study.[7] In addition, we have been impressed by recent research on the psychological functioning of schizophrenic patients, indicating defects in their perception, cognitive structures, affect experience, and control, and in their external and internal perceptive thresholds. It seems to me that it would be naïve to interpret complex clinical findings in schizophrenia directly in the light of these psychological and psychophysiological defects. The intrapsychic world of the schizophrenic patient needs to be understood in terms of his pathological intrapsychic structures (particulary his internal world of object relationships). The problem is how underlying defective psychophysiological and psychological structures influence the consolidation of a pathological world of internalized object-relationships.[20] However, the before-mentioned defects may also interfere seriously with the immediate functioning of the patient in the interpersonal realm and their correction may improve the patient's chances to work psychotherapeutically and change his intrapsychic as well as his interpersonal life.

From a clinical viewpoint, there seems to be good evidence that phenothiazines reduce the level of anxiety and increase affective thresholds; they may also indirectly normalize perception by decreasing information input. In any case, the effect of phenothiazines would be a direct reinforcement of some structures of the ego involved in perceptual, cognitive, and affective control, which, in turn, may permit the patient better to evaluate the interaction between his internal and interpersonal worlds, particularly the psychotherapeutic relationships. This treatment approach is in contrast to many psychoanalytically oriented clinicians' suspicions about drugs reflected in an inadequate or inappropriate use of them. It is also in contrast to a mechanistic treatment approach which loads the patient with medication in order to eradicate target symptoms, and which conceives as the main goal of treatment the patient's release from the hospital rather than to develop a long-range treatment strategy which will gradually expand his autonomous functioning and social rehabilitation.[17]

Psychotherapeutic Theory and Technique

Although the psychotherapeutic approaches at the C.F. Menninger Memorial Hospital and at the Menninger Clinic at large are basically characterized by a psychoanalytic, ego-psychological orientation (Boyer and Giovacchini,[2] Brody and Redlich,[3] Freeman, Cameron, and McGhie,[8] Wexler,[34] we have been impressed more recently by the psychoanalytic approaches developed in the United States by the Sullivanian oriented school (Cameron,[5] Fromm-Reichmann,[10] Lidz and Lidz,[22] Searles,[31] Will[35,36]) and by the British object-relations school of Fairbairn and Melanie Klein (Bion,[1] Guntrip,[12] Heimann,[13] Little,[23,24] and Rosenfeld[27,28]). Although combinations of theoretical and technical elements derived from these approaches vary in the case of practically every individual psychotherapist within our setting, a general consensus appears to be developing regarding the following points:

The primitive ("psychotic") mechanisms described by the British school have been very helpful in understanding and interpreting the primitive transferences of psychotic patients. However, the rather forceful, and at times almost overpowering aspects of early and "deep" interpretations, particularly as described by Kleinian authors, may create the danger of omnipotent control exerted by the psychotherapist over the patient, thus feeding into this particular mechanism characteristics of borderline and psychotic psychopathology. Also, the relative neglect on the part of some Kleinian authors—at least as revealed in their written communications—of the external reality of the patient seems to militate against the need for the psychotherapist to carry out a boundary function between the patient's intrapsychic life and the psychosocial reality impinging on the treatment from the family and the total hospital milieu. In addition, it is questionable to what extent severely regressed schizophrenic patients do have the capacity to respond to the kind of verbalization implied in this technical approach, and to what extent their reactions to complex verbal interpretations may actually correspond to other, nonverbal cues in the therapeutic relationship (Freeman,

Cameron, and McGhie,[8] Searles,[31] Zetzel).[38] Finally, neglecting to consider the structural differences between varying types of psychopathology seems an important limitation within the Kleinian approach.[16]

The ego psychological approach within our setting focuses predominantly on the patient's ego functions and structures—including his internalized object relations, and on the reality elements of the total social system within which the treatment is carried out.[18] In agreement with many Sullivanian oriented and other authors who have carried out intensive, psychoanalytically oriented treatment of schizophrenic patients, we have found that in addition to a general theoretical and technical background in psychoanaysis, treatment of these patients requires a capacity, on the therapist's part, to deal with the powerful countertransference reactions triggered by the patient's fusion experiences in the transference. The therapist must be able to tolerate uncertainty, lack of contact, and confusion for a long time before the schizophrenic patient is able fully to establish an object relationship with him. The building-up of a gradual tolerance on the patient's part of the therapeutic relationship as he loses his fear over the destructive nature of his primitive rage contributes to a gradual delimitation of boundaries in his interaction with the therapist, and to an eventual phase of integration in the patient in which he can coordinate contradictory aspects of himself, and differentiate himself fully from the therapist.

I have mentioned before the importance of the therapist's carrying out a boundary function between the intrapsychic life of the patient on the one hand, and the external reality impinging on the total psychotherapeutic situation on the other. This approach is in contrast to the temptation of magical or messianic isolation of the psychotherapeutic relationship from the rest of the patient's environment. This approach also implies a gradually developing, cautious interpretation of the transference in the "here and now" only, in contrast to a forceful, intrusive introduction of interpretations which may act in magical (in contrast to communicatively meaningful) ways.

Hospital Milieu Treatment and the Relationship Between the Hospital Managing Team and the Psychotherapist

The hospital milieu program for chronic schizophrenic patients requires a quite different structure from that optimally geared to the treatment of borderline conditions and severe types of character pathology. Although it is possible (particularly when there are sufficient staff resources available) to provide such differentiated hospital milieu programs simultaneously within the same hospital section or area, it may be that specialized sections for chronic schizophrenic patients may make their treatment both easier to implement and more effective.

The degree to which severely regressed schizophrenic patients tolerate interactions with their human and inanimate environment varies greatly. We try to provide opportunities for schizophrenic patients to relate themselves in a regular, routine way to staff members and other patients around activities in such a way as to promote greater socialization while providing an "escape hatch" for withdrawal into the impersonal aspects of the task and away from its interpersonal implications when the latter become too threatening or too close. For example, work in the garden or a regular walk with a group of not more than five to seven patients, or a mechanical activity in a workshop under the supervision of a skilled activities therapist provides such possibilities.

Severely regressed schizophrenic patients may experience intensive group situations, particularly within large groups, as very threatening, and may not be able to participate in the therapeutic community structures that are part of the overall milieu treatment program for most of our patients. On the other hand, the tolerance of patient groups of "deviants" or "outsiders" may be therapeutic to the group as well as to the schizophrenic patients themselves. A combination of open communication within the group, clarification of the "here-and-now" situation within the group, including the role and effects of the schizophrenic patient's interactions within the group, and tolerance of varying degrees of "nonparticipation" on the part of individual patients are some of the potentially helpful aspects of a group-centered hospital milieu program. We do not see, however, group processes of this kind as an ideal or necessary treatment ingredient for all regressed schizophrenic patients.

We are also in agreement with the findings of Burnham, Gladstone, and Gibson[4] that a structuring of the hospital experience for the patient in the form of clearly delimited, repetitive time and space experiences is an important aspect of the daily program for schizophrenic patients. An orderly scheduling of daily activities with sufficient opportunities for privacy as well as for work and social interactions needs to be established both for the individual patient and the unit on which he lives. This is difficult to achieve in a unit which combines borderline patients with regressed schizophrenic patients.

The hospital management team, consisting of all those staff members who have a direct function regarding the individual patient or who are leaders of groups in which the patient takes part, needs to be coordinated by a team leader who carries out the total boundary function of relating the intrapsychic world of the patient to the total interpersonal field around him, including the hospital treatment team. This team leader must have fully delegated authority from the hospital administration for major decision making regarding the patient's daily life in the hospital. He must delegate, in turn, such authority to different members of the treatment team according to functional needs of the patient's hospital milieu program. The total team concerned with an individual patient's program thus constitutes a functional group, with shifting task leadership with a clear-cut, openly communicated delegation of authority.

For example, an aide taking a patient on a town trip must have sufficient authority for making numerous decisions regarding concrete issues which may come up on such a trip; the art therapist working with the patient, or the nurse in charge of a group on the unit of which the patient is a part must have authority commensurate with their task, and be able to relate openly and freely with other members of the team, including the team leader. This treatment structure is in contrast to an authoritarian, hierarchically organized team with fixed (in contrast to functionally shifting) authority and leadership.

The team leader (usually the hospital physician acting as "administrator") also needs to carry out a boundary function with the patient's psychotherapist. As mentioned before, we have found it extremely important for the team leader and the psychotherapist to have complete autonomy, while still openly communicating with each other, and they should not be in a hierarchically or politically determined relation of dominance and subordination to each other.

The main function of the psychotherapist is to explore systematically the patient's intrapsychic world, and the reactivation in the "here-and-now" of his pathological internalized object relations as they are experienced by the patient in the transference. The main functions of the hospital team leader are to explore systematically with the patient his total social interactions in the hospital, including their appropriate and inappropriate implications and the patient's difficulty in coping with his tasks; and to monitor, and temporarily take over, those ego functions which are inadequate or inappropriate in the patient's dealings with his environment. Within this treatment arrangement, the hospital team leader carries out a tripartite boundary function: between the intrapsychic life of the patient and the treatment team, between the treatment team and the psychotherapist, and between the treatment team and hospital administration at large. In addition, the hospital team leader also carries out a boundary function between the total treatment structure (including the hospital milieu treatment and the psychotherapy) on the one hand, and the patient's family and the social reality external to the hospital on the other.

It is impossible, within the limits of this brief overview, to examine the reasons for and the advantages of this proposed hospital milieu treatment system. Since I have examined the underlying philosophy of this approach elsewhere,[18] I will only mention here that such a treatment structure is ideally geared to avoid the damaging influences of covert conflicts within the hospital administrative structure on the treatment of individual patients,[32] and the negative effects of the patient's intrapsychic conflicts on the social structure of the hospital.[25] The proposed treatment structure should also permit an optimal, open examination of the total social field surrounding the patient's treatment and of the mutual effects of the patient's intrapsychic life and this social field. All this information, given to the psychotherapist, may then be incorporated into the psychotherapy as well as utilized by the hospital managing team.

The described hospital milieu treatment structure implies a dual therapeutic arrangement—the psychotherapist and the hospital management team. While some members of our staff think that for some chronic schizophrenic patients there are advantages in a different therapeutic structure within which the psychotherapist and the hospital administrator roles are combined in one person, most prefer the dual system. We plan to experiment with varying combinations of one or two psychotherapist-hospital administrator systems, but, for the average chronic schizophrenic patient, the advantages of the dual system outlined seem to predominate over the disadvantages.

Some of the advantages of the dual system are: (1) a protection of the psychotherapeutic relationship from overwhelming outside influences; (2) a maximal position of technical neutrality on the part of the psychotherapist; and (3) an optimal, flexible hospital team leadership which can carry out the numerous boundary functions mentioned before. The main disadvantage of this dual system lies in the potentially confusing effects of these various members of the staff on the severely regressed schizophrenic patient. The main advantage of the combination of psychotherapist and hospital team leader in one person is to reduce significantly the confusing aspect of the dual system. However, the disadvantage of this "one-person" model is the enormously increased danger for omnipotent control of the treatment program on the part of the psychotherapist, and of acting out of countertransference reactions to the patient's primitive needs for omnipotent control. At times, the dual system may be introduced in an advanced stage of the treatment, when the schizophrenic patient is better able to distinguish the dual role.

Perhaps the main problem for the psychotherapist treating chronic schizophrenic patients is carrying out the various boundary functions mentioned in this overview. There is a strange attraction in the bizarre and yet so meaningful intrapsychic life of schizophrenic patients, and the temptation for the psychotherapist to neglect the patient's external reality may be as strong as the temptation to reject a schizophrenic patient's inner experience as "crazy" or "meaningless" out of fear of confrontation with what lies, more or less deeply buried, in all of us.

NOTES

1. Bion, W. (1967), *Second Thoughts; Selected Papers on Psychoanalysis.* London: Heinemann.

2. Boyer, L. B. & Giovacchini, P. L. (1967), *Psychoanalytic Treatment of Characterological and Schizophrenic Disorders.* New York: Science House.

3. Brody, E. B. & Redlich, F. C. (1952), *Psychotherapy with Schizophrenics.* New York: International Universities Press.

4. Burnham, D. L., Gladstone, A. I., & Gibson, R. W. (1969), *Schizophrenia and the Need-Fear Dilemma.* New York: International Universities Press.

5. Cameron, J. L. (1966), The Psycho-analytic Treatment of Psychoses. In: *Studies on Psychosis,* eds. T. Freeman, J. Cameron, and A. McGhie. New York: International Universities Press, pp. 197–229.

6. Cooperman, M. (1970), *Defeating processes in psychotherapy.* Reported in Transactions of the Topeka Psychoanalytic Society, *Bull. Menninger Clinic,* 34(3):36–38.

7. Ewalt, J. (1970), Psychotherapy of Schizophrenia. Presented at the Conference on Schizophrenia, Washington, D.C. (unpublished).

8. Freeman, T., Cameron, J. L., & McGhie, A. (1958), *Chronic Schizophrenia*. New York: International Universities Press.

9. Freeman, T., Cameron, J. L., & McGhie, A. (1966), *Studies on Psychosis; Descriptive, Psycho-analytic and Psychological Aspects*. New York: International Universities Press.

10. Fromm-Reichmann, F. (1959), *Psychoanalysis and Psychotherapy, Selected Papers*. Chicago: University of Chicago Press.

11. Green, P. (1971), Personal Communication.

12. Guntrip, H. (1968), *Schizoid Phenomena, Object Relations and the Self*. New York: International Universities Press.

13. Heimann, P. (1955), A Combination of defense mechanisms in paranoid states. *New Directions in Psycho-Analysis*. London: Tavistock, pp. 240–265.

14. Kernberg, O. (1967), Borderline personality organization. *J. Amer. Psychoanal. Assoc.*, 15:641–685.

15. Kernberg, O. (1968), The treatment of patients with borderline personality organization. *Int. J. Psycho-Analysis*, 49:600–619.

16. Kernberg, O. (1969), A Contribution to the ego-psychological critique of the Kleinian school. *Int. J. Psycho-Analysis*, 50:317–333.

17. Kernberg, O. (1970), Discussion of the Paper "Psychotherapy of Schizophrenia," by Jack R. Ewalt, M.D. (unpublished).

18. Kernberg, O. (1971), Psychoanalytic Object Relations Theory, Group Processes and Administration (Toward an Integrative Theory of Hospital Treatment). Presented (in an abbreviated version) at the Annual Meeting of the Central Neuropsychiatric Hospital Association, Chicago, March 1971 (unpublished).

19. Kernberg, O. (1971), Diagnostic and Therapeutic Implications of Ego Weakness. Franz Alexander Memorial Lecture, Los Angeles, March 1971 (unpublished).

20. Kernberg, O. (1971), Early ego integration and object relations. Presented at the New York Academy of Sciences Conference, May, 1971. To be published in *Ann. N.Y. Acad. Sci.*

21. Kernberg, O. (1971), Prognostic considerations regarding borderline personality organization. *J. Amer. Psychoanal. Assoc.*, 19:595–635.

22. Lidz, R. W. & Lidz, T. (1952), *Psychotherapy with Schizophrenics*. New York: International Universities Press.

23. Little, M. (1958), On delusional transference (transference psychosis). *Int. J. Psycho-Analysis,* 39:134–138.

24. Little, M. (1960), On basic unity. *Int. J. Psycho-Analysis,* 41:377–384, 637.

25. Main, T. F. (1957), The ailment. *Brit. J. Med. Psychol.,* 30:129–145.

26. May, P. (1968), *Treatment of Schizophrenia.* New York: Science House.

27. Rosenfeld, H. A. (1964), *Object relations of the acute schizophrenic patient in the transference situation.* Psychiatric Research Reports No. 19. Washington, D.C.: American Psychiatric Association, pp. 59–68.

28. Rosenfeld, H. A. (1965), *Psychotic States, A Psychoanalytical Approach.* New York: International Universities Press.

29. Rosenfeld, H. A. (1970), Negative therapeutic reaction. Reported in Transactions of the Topeka Psychoanalytic Society. *Bull. Menninger Clinic,* 34:189–192.

30. Searles, H. F. (1964), Transference psychosis in the psychotherapy of schizophrenia. In: *Collected Papers on Schizophrenia and Related Subjects.* New York: International Universities Press, pp. 654–716.

31. Searles, H. F. (1965), *Collected Papers on Schizophrenia and Related Subjects.* New York: International Universities Press.

32. Stanton, A. A. & Schwartz, M. S. (1954), *The Mental Hospital.* New York: Basic Books.

33. Ticho, E. (1969), The effects of the psychoanalyst's personality on the treatment. Presented at the American Psychoanalytic Association, December, 1969. To be published in *Psychoanalytic Forum.*

34. Wexler, M. (1952), The structural problem in schizophrenia: the role of the internal object. In: *Psychotherapy with Schizophrenics,* New York: International Universities Press, pp. 179–201.

35. Will, O. (1961), Psychotherapy in reference to the schizophrenic reaction. In: *Contemporary Psychotherapies,* ed. Morris I. Stein. New York: The Free Press, pp. 128–156.

36. Will, O. (1967), Schizophrenia: psychological treatment. In: *Comprehensive Textbook of Psychiatry,* ed. A. M. Freedman and H. I. Kaplan. Baltimore: William and Wilkins, pp. 649–661.

37.   Will, O. (1970), Personal Communication.

38.   Zetzel, E. R. (1964), Discussion of the paper by Herbert Rosen-feld, "Object Relations of the Acute Schizophrenic Patient in the Transference Situation." In: *Recent Research on Schizophrenia*, eds. Philip Solomon and Bernard C. Glueck. Psychiatric Research Report No. 19. Washington, D.C.: American Psychiatric Association, pp. 75–79.

Chapter 6

PSYCHIATRY AT THE AUSTEN RIGGS CENTER

Otto Allen Will, Jr., M.D.

INTRODUCTION

Psychiatric concepts and institutional programs do not exist apart from society, but are, to a large extent, a reflection of cultural ideologies and social practices—these not being of necessity synonymous with each other. In describing the functioning of a psychiatric institution, it is advisable to say something about the society to which it belongs, the individual and group needs which it is designed to meet, and the conception of man and his disorders to which the patients and members of the staff subscribe.

We live in a time of open questioning, and of great and rapid change—both actual and potential. There are many vital issues that cannot be denied or put aside with impunity for future consideration; they are for the present, and for some now may be too late. Among these concerns are the increase in world population; the tremendous facilitation of communication in both amount and form, with the attendant need to control and evaluate input in terms of human welfare; the often abrupt and startling confrontation of individual, cultural, and social differences; the demand for a reduction of educational, economic, and social disadvantages as these are recognized and means for dealing with them are made available; the challenge to a society's seemingly fundamental systems of value—as evidenced in religion, family structure, and sexual standards; the mechanization and urbanization of society with the threat of "dehumanization," even as physical well-being is improved; the threat of war; and the recognition that natural resources are limited, and that man must soberly—and painfully—take a hand in designing his future, if there is to be a future for him.

The concept of man, developed somewhat in harmony with 19th century physics, has been modified during the past 50 years. Man may be seen as a participant in multiple, serial, and concomitant social fields—being molded by these and, in varying degrees, molding them in turn. Studies of the organization of the family, the hospital ward, the total institution, the local community, and the larger society as well as the psychotherapeutic encounter, have emphasized the interrelatedness of the multiple factors involved in the formation and expression of human behavior.

The following comment by Sullivan is relevant at this juncture: "Psychiatry . . . is the study of processes that involve or go on between people. The field of psychiatry is the field of interpersonal relations, under any and all circumstances in which these relations exist. . . . The science of psychiatry has been nurtured by work with the mentally ailing, has grown in the milieu of hospital and clinic, but is no more a science of mental illness than geography is a science of Western Europe. . . . The science that has grown from preoccupation with these mentally disordered ways of living has naturally to become a science of living under the conditions which prevail in the given social order."

Psychiatric disorders themselves may be thought of as destructive, inadequate, inappropriate, unduly complicated, or overly simplified forms of human behavior, exhibited in interpersonal situations, and arising from experiences in a variety of previous interpersonal fields. Although we do not disregard man's genetic-biological foundation, we consider the behavior that we call "sick" as having been developed largely in response to social, cultural, and existential necessities, as learned, and as having purposes and goals. Among these last are the maintenance of required human relationships, the continuation of life itself, the reduction of anxiety to tolerable levels, and the provision for meaningful communication without destructive self-revelation. To meet such requirements in the face of a threatening environment the behavior often becomes so complex and devious—or so stereotyped and simplified —that its primary-goal directedness is lost, communication becomes increasingly defective, relationships are attenuated or give way to fantasy, anxiety increases, and despair and panic supervene. The resulting deviant behavior may be looked upon as evidence of devil possession, personal wickedness, malingering, genetic defect, disease of the body in the classical medical sense, disorder of a vaguely defined "mind," and so on. The history of psychiatry lives in the present as well as in the past, each concept has its adherents, and treatment procedures are as varied as theories of etiology. Without attempting to define causation in precise terms, we consider psychiatric disorders as ways of human living, multiply determined, modifiable for better or worse, and in varying degrees, through interpersonal social experience.

It is useful to remind ourselves that major concepts of personality have been based largely on the idea that there is a dependable stability in man's relationship with his past, the traditions of his culture, his values, and his institutions. We often speak in terms of a norm and deviations from it. At present the norm itself undergoes change so rapidly that it cannot be encompassed adequately in a stable framework of self and society, but is in need of constant evaluation and definition. On this subject Lifton[1] comments as follows: "It is quite possible that even the image of personal identity, insofar as it suggests inner stability and sameness, is derived from a vision of a traditional culture in which man's relationships to his institutions and symbols are still relatively intact—which is hardly the case today."

HISTORY OF THE AUSTEN RIGGS CENTER

The Center is a small, non-profit, open, psychotherapeutic institution located in Stockbridge, a village in the Berkshire mountains of southwestern Massachusetts. The Austen Riggs Foundation was established in 1919 by Dr. Austen Fox Riggs "for the study and treatment of the psychoneuroses." It was designed to be more like a school than a hospital or sanitarium in the ordinary sense. Emphasis was placed on a "team" approach, and patients who could not cooperate with staff members in carrying out a strict and carefully regulated program of reeducation in an open setting were not accepted. Each hour of the day was scheduled, a temporary separation from previous stress was provided, emphasis was placed on making use of the patient's abilities and strengths, and support was found in the benign authoritarian and charismatic qualities of Dr. Riggs and other members of the staff. During this earlier period (to about 1945) the median age of patients was 40 years, and 75 percent were discharged within six weeks. A common diagnosis in those days was a form of depression. The program of reeducation did not favor strong emotional expression, but stressed control and conformity to accepted upper-middle class conventions.

The "typical" patient (if there was one) of those times was a man in his mid-forties, married, successful in his profession, accepted in his home community—and yet anxious, uncertain, and discouraged despite his accomplishments. He was usually a member of the "establishment" as then defined, and the medical staff, if not actually also members, could at least identify with it. Patients most likely to benefit from the program believed in it and cooperated and, after a few weeks returned to their families and employment.

Dr. Riggs died in 1940, and after a transitional period of seven years, Dr. Robert Knight, from the Menninger Clinic, became Medical Director, a post which he held until his death in 1966. During this 19-year period changes occurred in American psychiatry and in the institution. The concepts of psychoanalysis had found support in this country, and Dr. Knight, an analyst, brought a psychoanalytically oriented form of psychotherapy to the Center. Systematic studies of the family and of the hospital milieu were by this time well advanced; it was increasingly evident that the total hospital environment was influential in the treatment program. The median age of patients declined, and with this younger group the conflicts of what we now call the "generation gap" were more evident. As the struggle of the young with adult authority, cultural standards, and social structure was more evident and acute, attention necessarily turned to the development of institutional controls. There was no resort to locked doors, other forms of physical restraint, convulsive therapy, heavy drug dosage, and so on. Patients were carefully selected in terms of their seeming suitability for the program, and those who were unable to adjust to it after a 30-day trial period were sent elsewhere. Intensive studies were made of the social system of the Center in an effort to define its therapeutic and antitherapeutic aspects. Emphasis was placed on the patient's responsibility to himself, his peers, and others within and outside of the institution; he was encouraged and helped to make use of his "ego strengths," and not to give in to a state of regression.

It should be noted that during this period—1947 throughout 1971—the society was not static. The economic depression of the 1930s brought with it suffering, disillusionment, and and major social changes. Following the depths of depression came the Second World War, the United Nations, the Korean War, and the formation of national blocs confronting each other with the realities and mythologies of the Cold War. There was the nuclear bomb and the threat—never readily grasped—of a final holocaust. Genocide was no longer a concept, but an event of the present. The racial struggle was intensified in the United States and elsewhere, and the discrepancies between what was professed and what was practiced were more evident. A president and his brother were assassinated, as was the foremost leader of the blacks. The country was caught up in an Asian land war that seemed to many people to be futile, meaningless, and destructive to all concerned. As technology was advanced and men walked on the moon, for many the human spirit seemed to be increasingly impoverished. The communications explosion brought an immediacy to starvation, violence, and war, as well as to beauty, creativity, and a plethora of trivia. Change was evident, but certainty and security were declining, and the future on earth was uncertain if not dismal. Refuge was no longer readily available in family, religion, or other hitherto dependable verities. These are some of the influential factors in the lives of our patients today. Words and phrases common now in the therapist's office are "despair," "emptiness," "the meaninglessness of life," "the failure of belief," "estrangement," "lack of commitment and goals," and "the absence of intimacy."

THE PRESENT

In 1967, the median age of patients at the Center was 26 years; it is now 21, starting at 17 years. People for whom this program is not suitable include the following: those unable to care for their ordinary, everyday needs; the persistently and violently assaultive; those chronically addicted to alcohol and other drugs; the mentally defective; and persons unable to assume a minimum of responsibility for living within a group and abiding by its regulations.

With few exceptions, the applicant to the Center has had previous psychiatric treatment. He may have been in one or more hospitals, has usually been exposed to some form of individual or group psychotherapy, and has taken some form of ataractic drug in an effort to limit deviant behavior. His intelligence is above average, and he may have been an excellent student in high school or college before his difficulties became clinically evident. Although in some instances severe behavioral problems were noted in childhood, these appear more commonly in adolescence as the young person finds himself unable to meet the demands of that age, such as the patterning of sexual behavior, separation from the home, selection of a career, clarification of systems of value, and a dependable sense of of identity, and so on. He may seek to reinforce a failing self-esteem by resorting to drugs—marijuana, amphetamines, LSD—and their use may at times accentuate or precipitate an acute psychotic episode.

The prospective patient is likely to be hostile to anything psychiatric, and opposed to what he considers to be the "establishment." He has little trust in anyone—including himself—and he does not take kindly to advice, reassurance, or anything that appears to him to be coercive or restrictive. At the same time he is afraid of his own unrestricted impulses, and hopes to discover some sort of acceptable protection from a destructive exposure of them.

While he proclaims his independence and his need for no one, he is obviously bound to the pathology of his family. The greater number of these patients are diagnosed as borderline, schizoid, character disorders, severely neurotic, schizophrenic, and so on. They all have had difficulty in "growing up"; they have "dropped out" from home, school, job, and society in general, and their existence is marginal. They need help and they resist what is offered.

The Institution

The Center is a psychotherapeutic institution, which means that the essential ingredient of the work is the use of the human relationship. Drugs are used at times to reduce destructive degrees of anxiety, but there is no resort to such treatment as insulin coma, electroshock, and so on. The human transaction—in a one-to-one relationship and in larger groups—is the unifying concept of the organization, the basis of therapy, the subject of study and education, and the source of research.

As the institution is open, admission is voluntary, and except for social restraints, patients come and go as they please. Forty-one patients live in a large building known as The Inn. Each patient has his own room, although there are times when two patients may wish to share a room. Another group of eight to ten patients live in The Elms, an old house on the hospital grounds which is run on the model of a "halfway house," the patients there receiving no direct nursing care and being largely on their own.

Prior to admission a careful evaluation is made of an applicant's suitability for the program. The Director of Admissions reviews relevant psychiatric records and interviews the prospective patient and members of his family. Once accepted, every effort is made to continue therapy despite increases of anxiety and behavioral disturbances that may occur during its course. Because of the emphasis on the study of the vicissitudes of the therapeutic relationships, the majority of patients remain in treatment for at least a year.

THE TREATMENT DESIGN

Each patient is seen in individual psychotherapy for four or more sessions (hours) each week. These meetings are designed to observe and study the development and course of an interpersonal relationship in an effort to comprehend and modify those difficulties in living that necessitated treatment.

In conjunction with individual therapy, patients are expected to participate in the general group program. The new patient is introduced to this program by a committee of patient sponsors who show him around and make him familiar with the way the place is run. He discovers that even with help the transition period is not easy. He must adjust to a variety of groups, including the one-to-one relationship with his therapist. He is assigned to one of four districts in The Inn, meeting weekly with this group of ten patients and representatives of the nursing staff to discuss and devise ways of dealing with the problems of community living. Much of the administrative function of the patient community is carried on by a Community Committee of elected patients and staff consultants. Social and work activities are dealt with by an Activities Planning Group composed of patients and a staff advisor. Instead of the conventional occupational therapy program, there is the shop where patients can work with skilled craftsmen and artists. An excellent theater group is part of this program, and casting is open to townspeople and staff members as well as patients.

That is the general outline of a social system that defies

adequate description—by me, at least—in this short time. It may be helpful to outline briefly what happens to a patient in this system.

THE PATIENT

Mary was 18 years of age and a senior in high school when she was observed to be increasingly withdrawn and depressed, and began to fail in her studies. She was referred to a psychotherapist with whom she was in treatment for one year. Her withdrawn behavior increased despite the use of medication, she made an attempt at suicide with barbiturates, and she was hospitalized for a few days in an institution near her home. A month later she was admitted to the Center, the dosage of phenothiazines that she was taking being reduced and removed over a period of six weeks. The first two months were uneventful and she seemed to get along well with her therapist. In the third month she became more disturbed, broke a window, cut her arms with a razor blade, insisted that the program and the therapist were of no use to her, and said that she wanted to leave the place and might kill herself. Special nursing care was given and she was referred to the Community Council where the social impact of her behavior was discussed with her. The point was made that what she did affected others as well as herself, and that she was responsible for the welfare of others as they were responsible for her. The therapist met with the consultants in psychotherapy, the nursing staff, and other colleagues in daily all-staff meetings. At the same time that an attempt was made to explore analytically the dynamics of the behavior, its social implications and consequences were studied and reflected to the patient. At the height of disturbance the Clinical Evaluation Committee (composed of the therapist, consultant, Clinical Director, Medical Director, Director of the Inn

Program, and nursing representative) met to evaluate the suitability of the treatment program for this patient. Sometimes transfer of a patient to another hospital is recommended, but Mary stayed with us.

The question of interest is this: How do you carry on intensive, analytically oriented psychotherapy with borderline and psychotic people—most of them poorly motivated, discouraged, and hostile to the "establishment"—in an open setting and without restraints beyond those afforded by the growing attachment to the therapist, the group, and the therapeutic enterprise itself? To put the matter simply, you do it by continuous involvement with all members of the group. That involvement is marked by anxiety, disagreements, open expression of emotion (often unpleasant), and the recurrent feeling that no one has any idea what this is all about. One participates more in the problems of growth and change than in a clearly defined program of treatment, and one may discover with his patients that change, allegedly desired and sought, is feared and resisted by all concerned—including members of the patients' families with whom much therapeutic and educational work must be done.

EDUCATION

The psychotherapeutic process is a special instance of an interpersonal relationship, and in this sense would seem to be well suited for intervention in disorders that are themselves derived largely from human involvements. As used here, the term "psychotherapy" includes the following concepts: (1) that past experience is a major factor in determining current behavior—the genetic approach; (2) that variants of past experience are continued into the present —a fragmentary and distorted repetition of what has been; (3) that what one does is influenced by what has been, by what is, and by what is anticipated of the future; (4) that the therapist (or other person involved, e.g., a nurse) will be the target of motivations developed in earlier relationships (transference)—in other words, the present is seen in varying degrees in terms of the past; (5) that motivation toward a goal is never absent, albeit often obscure, hidden, and difficult to comprehend; and (6) that regardless of how deeply seated behavioral patterns may be, relearning can occur at any age.

The therapist's task is marked by frustration, by the arousal of a wide range of emotion, and by loneliness. His needs for affection, companionship, understanding, and reassurance cannot be met in any major sense in the relationship with his patient; they must be resolved elsewhere, or their lack of resolution accepted.

There is a training program at the Center for third and fourth-year residents in psychiatry and postdoctoral fellows in psychology. In this program are included the following: (1) personal analysis, required of all therapists and provided for some nurses; (2) weekly supervision of individual cases; (3) biweekly staff conferences at which clinical work is presented and discussed; (4) two to three weekly seminars on theory and technique; (5) weekly clinical seminars; (6) training in the principles of group dynamics; (7) monthly seminars presented by visiting speakers; (8) supervised consultations with patients' families; and (9) experience in the Berkshire Mental Health Center, long associated with the institution. Inservice education is provided for nurses, aides, and the staff of The Elms (halfway house).

Conclusion

Few patients can be cared for in a program such as that outlined here. Treatment is expensive, usually prolonged, and we do not have at this time a follow-up study to demonstrate our degree of effectiveness. We work with the idea that the human relationship is vital to human growth and existence; we attempt to study how it is used for good or bad in this setting.

It may seem that this work has little relevance to the many and great needs of people in these hurried and troubled times. To this concern I reply that I do not think that we are engaged simply in the treatment of schizophrenia or mental disease. In our view, these disorders are paradigms of human living, revealing in stark and disturbing clarity many of the ways of life that we impose on ourselves, destructive though they may be. In this institution we deal with problems related to the fear of attachment, the dread of separation, the uncertainty of identity, aggression, major dissociation of sentiments (ideas and affects), the blind and often hurtful devotion to self-created symbols, poorly developed and unrecognized needs, distortions of the body image, and so on. In the small laboratory of the psychotherapeutic center there is the opportunity to look closely at phenomena related to all human living as I know it.

Again, I refer to remarks by Sullivan:[4] "I plead the urgent necessity for much broader investigation as to adolescence and as to schizophrenia. . . . I am convinced that in the schizophrenic processes and in the preliminaries of schizophrenic illness—so common among adolescents who are having trouble in their social adjustments—can be seen, in almost laboratory simplicity, glimpses which will combine as a mosaic that explains many more than half of the adult personalities that one encounters."

NOTES

1. Lifton, R. J. (1971), Protean Man. *Arch. Gen. Psychiat.*, 24:298–304.

2. Sullivan, H. S. (1953), *Conceptions of Modern Psychiatry.* New York: Norton, p. 10.

3. Sullivan, H. S. (1953), In: *The Interpersonal Theory of Psychiatry.* eds. Helen S. Perry and Mary L. Gawel. New York: Norton, p. 367.

4. Sullivan, H. S. (1962), *Schizophrenia as a Human Process,* New York: Norton, pp. 201–202.

Chapter 7

THE THERAPEUTIC TRIAL CARRIED OUT AT THE MASSACHUSETTS MENTAL HEALTH CENTER WITH CHRONIC SCHIZOPHRENIC PATIENTS

**Lester Grinspoon, M.D.,
Jack R. Ewalt, M.D., and
Richard I. Shader, M.D.**

An intensive study of chronic schizophrenic patients was conducted at the Massachusetts Mental Health Center over the course of four and one-half years. This study included investigations in the areas of psychopharmacology, psychotherapy, psychoendocrinology, psychophysiology, and biochemistry. The present report focuses on the relationships between long-term pharmacotherapy with phenothiazines and long-term intensive psychotherapy conducted by experienced psychotherapists. Investigations previous to ours have concentrated either on pharmacotherapy alone or on psychotherapy of relatively short duration, i.e., under six months.

In a search of the literature, we were unable to find any reports of controlled investigations which compared long-term individual psychotherapy with phenothiazines and

long-term individual psychotherapy without phenothiazines. Furthermore, we could find no studies which compared long-term psychotherapy alone with long-term
phenothiazine therapy alone. We did find that there is
considerable agreement that phenothiazines are of use
in reducing manifest psychopathology in chronic schizophrenics.[5,6,13] Moreover, phenothiazine therapy does appear to facilitate group therapy[3,9] and milieu therapy.[2,10]
Long-term studies by Greenblatt et al.[12] clearly demonstrate the value of chemotherapy in the treatment of
chronic schizophrenia when used in conjunction with an
"active milieu."

However, short-term studies and those with acute
schizophrenia patients yielded conflicting results.[11,18,23]
For example, Savage and Day[20] concluded that reserpine
interfered with psychotherapy because patients avoided
painful issues. Hoch[14] suggested that drugs are "ego supportive" while Ostow[19] claimed that they decrease the
amount of libido available to the ego. Other researchers
have applied some rather unflattering terms to drug use,
such as "chemical strait jackets"[22] and "brainwashing."[17]

However, Zetzel[24] concluded that phenothiazines reduce "projection and delusion formation, without, at the
same time, reducing the patient's ability to communicate
and to think." In doing so they "may enable the growth of
a therapeutic relationship which could not otherwise be
possible." Allen[7] reported that phenothiazines "alleviated
delusional and hallucinatory trends and facilitated communication and psychotherapy." In addition, Bordeleau and
Gratton[4] have suggested that phenothiazines facilitate verbalization in intensive psychotherapy with withdrawn, autistic patients

A report by May and Tuma[15] deserves particular emphasis because it makes comparisons among psychotherapy alone, drugs alone, and psychotherapy in combination
with drugs. Although it does not deal with chronic schizo-

phrenic patients, it challenges or raises questions about the opinions presented above. In studying "first admission schizophrenic patients in the middle section of the prognostic range," the authors found that patients receiving drugs alone ranked higher on posttreatment health status than did patients receiving psychotherapy plus drugs or psychotherapy alone. However, there were no statistically significant differences among these three groups. Patients receiving drugs plus psychotherapy or drugs alone did significantly better than patients receiving "control" treatment, or, in other words, the hospital's basic level of ward care. Interestingly there was no significant difference between this control treatment group and the psychotherapy alone group. Because this study did not employ a placebo control group, it is difficult to assess the role of drugs properly. However, these data do suggest that, while psychotherapy alone did not significantly enhance patients' chances for improvement, drugs alone were able to produce significant improvement in these patients.

It therefore seemed important to us to apply careful observational techniques to the question of the relative value in chronic schizophrenia of phenothiazine therapy in conjunction with individual psychotherapy and an active therapeutic milieu, as compared to a combination of the latter two without concomitant phenothiazine therapy.

METHOD

All of the patients in the present study were between the ages of 18 and 35, unmarried, hospitalized as schizophrenic for three or more years, and free of organic disease. Two successive groups of ten such patients were randomly chosen and transferred to a small, specially built research ward (the Clinical Research Center) at the Massachusetts Mental Health Center. Each group was studied for somewhat more than two years. Upon transfer to the Clinical Research Center or shortly thereafter, patients began to receive identical capsules which contained an inert placebo. At this juncture the collection of data began, and it was decided to organize it according to two-week periods. Beginning in the 13th week of the study, five patients were chosen from the first group of ten (Group I) to receive thioridazine; the remaining five continued to receive a placebo.

Dosages of thioridazine were gradually increased over a three-week transitional period. Thereafter, the ward administrator, who was unaware of the design of the drug study, was instructed to manipulate drug doses at his discretion within a certain prescribed range of dose units. The range for thioridazine was between 300 and 1000 mg per day. In the 83rd week, the contents of the capsules for the patients receiving the active drug were changed from thioridazine to placebo, and after a period of three months thioridazine treatment was resumed and maintained until the end of the study. Selection and transferral of the second group of ten patients (Group II) was accomplished in an identical manner, and except for a few minor modifications, the overall design was similar with regard to both psychotherapy and drugs.

All patients on thioridazine were to receive that drug for 60 weeks prior to a three-month drug withdrawal. However, one patient in Group II, who had been receiving thioridazine when he arrived at the Clinical Research Center and was subsequently assigned to the placebo group, developed a severe hypertension which appeared to be related to drug deprivation. Subsequently he was reassigned to thioridazine and continued to receive this drug for the duration of the study. At about the same time, another patient developed severe dystonia and was changed to placebo.

Since each change was made early in the study, the patients were considered to belong to the reassigned treatment group; only data generated after these reassignments were employed in the data analysis. And finally, one other Group-II patient was so destructive and potentially homicidal that it became necessary to give him large amounts of supplementary chlorpromazine in addition to his placebo capsules. Since his status as a placebo patient was thereby questionable, data gathered on him were not included in the analyses.[26]

In regard to the other two primary treatment modalities—psychotherapy and milieu therapy—all patients in both groups were treated equally. With regard to milieu therapy, a nursing staff of 25 people, an occupational therapist, and a social worker involved the patients in an intensive program for the entire two-year period. Included were diverse activities, ranging from therapeutic community meetings and other group or individual ward functions to frequent beach outings, museum visits, sports events, and the like.

In addition, each of the patients began intensive individual psychotherapy about one week after commencement of an active drug regime, and all were seen at least twice a week over the remainder of each two-year period. The therapists were senior staff psychiatrists, all of whom were either psychoanalysts or psychoanalytically oriented, and all of whom were considerably experienced in the psychotherapy of schizophrenia.

As part of the ongoing longitudinal research program, many different types of observations were made regularly during the study. However, in this report we shall restrict the focus to changes in manifest psychopathology and adjustment to the ward environment, as measured by a modified form of the Behavioral Disturbance Index,[7] and by the Hospital Adjustment Scale (HAS).[16] Briefly, the Behavioral Disturbance Index (BDI) is a 54-item scale which reflects the degree to which a patient's behavior, thinking processes, and affect are disturbed. This index, developed originally by Framo and Alderstein as a device for coding nursing notes, was modified and adapted on the Clinical Research Center ward for use as a rating scale to assess the behavioral disturbance level of schizophrenic patients as viewed by the nursing staff. Throughout the course of his stay on the ward, every patient was rated regularly on this scale by the nursing personnel. Except for periods when reliability studies were being made, each patient was rated a minimum of four and a maximum of ten times per week. The Hospital Adjustment Scale is a 90-item scale designed to measure a patient's capacity to adapt to his environment. It is not meant to provide a measure of degree of pathology. As the authors[16] state: " 'Hospital Adjustment' should not be equated with degree of pathology or with severity and extent of symptomatology . . . (the scale) does *not* furnish a summary of the patient's pathology. It indicates rather the extent to which he is incapacitated in the context of the hospital environment as a function of his illness." Every two weeks the scale was filled out on each patient by two trained ward personnel, one from the day shift and one from the evening shift; the ratings were done independently. In the present paper scores for both these scales are given as two-week means. A third source of data of interest for the purposes of this presentation is the diaries which were kept daily by each of the patients and the nursing notes written by the ward staff.

RESULTS AND DATA ANALYSIS

Since the main interest of this presentation is to illustrate the results through case presentations, I shall merely summarize the results of the data analysis by saying that these data from both Group I and Group II were treated statistically by a two-way analysis of variance, and that this analysis demonstrated as highly significant, on both the Behavioral

Disturbance Index and the Hospital Adjustment Scale, the greater efficacy of the combination of phenothiazines and psychotherapy as compared to placebo and psychotherapy.

Case Examples

Only four of our cases will be discussed in this paper. BDI and HAS scores for the first of these patients, a Group-I patient who remained on placebo during the two years of study, are presented in Fig. 7.1. This patient's course is remarkable for its steadiness. While there is some fluctuation in both the BDI and HAS scores, for the most part the observations indicate a fair degree of constancy from one study period to the next.

These data suggest not only that the patient did not change much over the course of these two years, but also that he did not react in any observable fashion (i.e., as measured by these scales) to what one would assume to be important events in his life. A more microscopic look at the BDI scores for the days immediately preceding and following the occurrence of each important event reveals no increase in disturbed behavior as a result of that event. In fact, in some cases one finds a slight drop in the BDI score on the days following a "trauma," such as the departure of the ward doctor or the death of President Kennedy.

Psychotherapy with an analytically oriented psychotherapist began for this patient in the 17th week of his clinical course. Initially, he was seen three times a week, but after ten months the frequency of meetings was reduced to twice a week. Of course it is not possible to know how the patient would have progressed without psychotherapy, but it is clear from the data presented here that the therapy did not result in any significant improvement. An analysis of mean BDI scores during the therapist's single prolonged absence, and for the four weeks preceding and following this absence, shows no significant change in the patient's condition. In fact, in spite of the frequency and duration of

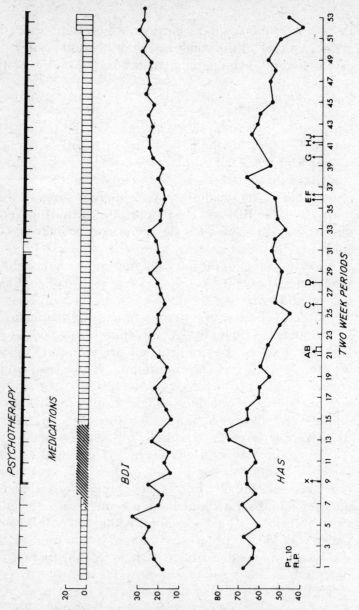

Fig. 7.1.   BDI and HAS scores for a patient who remained
on placebo for the two years of study

therapy, we have reason to question through our examination of the patient's diary and the nursing notes, the importance of this relationship to the patient.

The second patient to be discussed here also belonged to the group whose drug capsules always contained a placebo. Steady progressive deterioration marked this patient's course. This gradual decline is recorded in both the BDI and HAS scores, as presented in Fig. 7.2. Regarding psychotherapy, a review of all sources of data fails to establish that it was a distinctly meaningful experience for the patient, or for that matter, that there ever developed any kind of therapeutic relationship. After a year of intensive treatment, analysis of BDI scores before, during, and after his therapist's three-week vacation failed to show that the patient was any more or less disturbed during the therapist's absence. It can also be inferred from the daily BDI scores, as well as from more impressionistic data such as ward observations, diaries, and nursing notes, that the patient did not take note of or become involved in important events. The diary entries were always brief and uncommunicative, containing garbled, misspelled words and neologisms which are undecipherable. For the final four months of his clinical course, the patient made no diary entries at all; he spent these times scrawling on the entry sheets and was often noted to be hallucinating angrily.

These data demonstrate that the patient was consistently uninvolved with events and experiences which might have been expected to stir him emotionally, and that he rarely emerged from a private world of delusions and magical systems. In summary, all evidence indicates that this patient not only showed no improvement during his two-year stay, but clearly that he left the Center exhibiting more florid symptoms than he had upon arrival.

In Fig. 7.3, the same types of data are presented for one of the five Group-I patients who began to receive thioridazine in the 13th week. Shortly after withdrawal of the

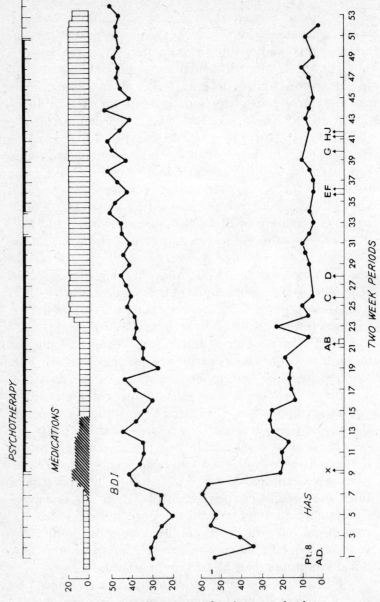

Fig. 7.2.   BDI and HAS scores of patients on placebo

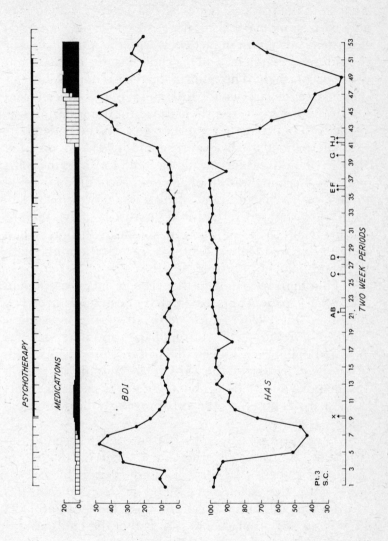

**Fig. 7.3. BDI and HAS scores of a patient receiving
thioridazine in the thirteenth week**

chlorpromazine which he had been receiving until his transfer to the research center, his BDI level began to rise, and correspondingly his HAS scores fell. These trends were reversed almost immediately with the introduction of thioridazine treatment, and his clinical status began to improve accordingly. The on-drug plateau is remarkably stable, despite the fact that the drug dosage was reduced from 500 to 300 mg, apparently because the thioridazine was thought to be having a soporific effect on the patient.

The patient's BDI level rose and his HAS scores fell rapidly when the thioridazine was withdrawn in the 83rd week. So alarming was the change in his condition that the dosage of his "medication" (which was now actually lactose) was increased several-fold: first to 12 units, then to 14, and finally to the allowable maximum of 20 units. When thioridazine was again substituted for placebo in the 95th week, the patient improved rapidly.

Although, according to the types of data presented in Fig. 7.3, the patient appeared to have been undisturbed by important life events which occurred during his clinical course, information culled from diaries and nursing notes revealed that he was indeed touched by some events, such as on the departure of the ward doctor and the absence of his therapist on vacation. This sensitivity to external events is in sharp contrast to the two previously presented patients.

The fourth patient to be presented also received thioridazine. However, his drug course differed from that of the other patient's because in Study Period 22 he was thought to have developed a blood dyscrasia, and for this reason all medication was discontinued. In Study Period 23 he was started on placebo again, and at the end of Study Period 24, when it was clear that there was no danger of agranulocytosis, the active drug regime was resumed. Also of importance is the fact that in Study Period 30 his therapist accepted a position in another state and the patient was assigned a new doctor.

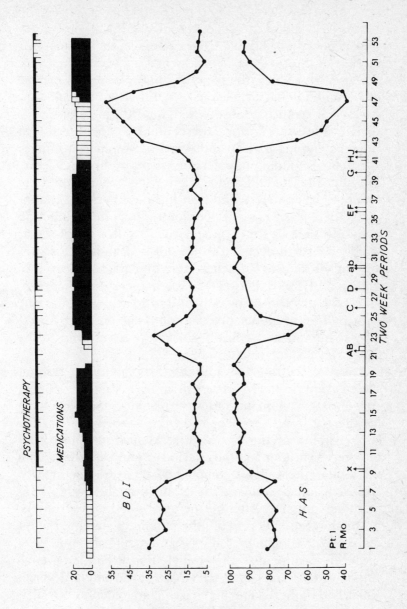

Fig. 7.4.   BDI and HAS scores of a patient
on and off thioridazine

As revealed in the data presented in Fig. 7.4, this patient's course was strikingly dependent on the presence or absence of thioridazine. When he first arrived at the Clinical Research Center, the patient manifested highly bizarre and agitated behavior, characterized by frequent auditory and visual hallucinations. When thioridazine was introduced in the Study Period 7, his condition improved almost immediately; his BDI score began to plummet and there was a corresponding upward movement in the HAS score. The scales leveled off and remained fairly stable until the patient's drugs were withdrawn in Study Period 22, after which there was a sudden deterioration. Upon resumption of thioridazine treatment, the patient's status improved as rapidly as it had declined with both BDI and HAS scores leveling off and again achieving a remarkable degree of stability. In Study Period 42, when the research design called for placebo being substituted for thioridazine, the same pattern of sudden deterioration was repeated. Reversal was immediate when thioridazine was restored to the patient's capsules.

While receiving thioridazine, this patient was responsive to events in his environment and was able to comment appropriately on them. This was true of incidents involving his therapist and the people on the ward as well as the larger drama of the Kennedy assassination. During his therapist's vacation in Study Periods 27 and 28, the patient was a bit depressed. He complained about not feeling well and occasionally remarked that he thought parts of his body were missing. After his therapist's departure from the hospital in Study Period 30, the patient commented in his diary, "I have feelings of nobody wants me around." Thioridazine treatment seemed to help him attend to his environment, to "tune out" selectively those internal voices which had bothered him in the past, and to maintain a fairly clear sense of identity. This impression is verified by a comparison of the patient's diaries during a two-week segment of his drug regime and a two-week period of placebo treatment. On placebo, the patient had rather vague ideas of reference and usually called himself "we" rather than "I." He was preoccupied with events and people of his past, and often concluded his diaries with long lists of names— some real people, others imaginary. The structure and organization of his thoughts were fairly loose, and his ideas frequently degenerated into sexual fantasy and obscenity. It appeared that the patient was dwelling in reveries, and that his identity was a confusion of past and imagined selves. He talked at length about Negro boxers with whom he identified, and he remembered scenes out of his boyhood.

In sharp contrast to this material was the style and content of the diaries written while the patient was receiving thioridazine. Instead of confused sentences and lists, he focused on the present and its attendant problems. He wrote that he was on a diet, that he was worried about his health and about being a Negro. He also noted that he was resentful of his father "who never treats me right," and of his mother "who never says anything to me." In addition he indicated his faith in the staff of the research center whom he trusted to help him.

DISCUSSION

It was our objective in this study to determine whether any enduring salutary changes in chronic schizophrenic patients can be induced through the use of long-term individual psychotherapy and what has been called "active milieu therapy." We were further interested in the question of whether concomitant pharmacotherapy catalyzes the patient's capacity to achieve fundamental emotional growth in therapy. It was felt that in order to approach any definitive statement about the efficacy of individual psychotherapy in the treatment of chronic schizophrenic patients, a minimum of 20 months of intensive psychotherapy would be necessary. The fact that psychiatric residents generally work with hospitalized chronic schizophrenic patients for a maximum of two years was considered further justification for choosing a study period of this duration.

There are those who would argue that even nearly two years of psychotherapy with exceptionally well-qualified therapists is not enough time in which to draw any meaningful conclusions about its usefulness as a therapeutic tool with this kind of patient—that it takes five or even ten years of psychotherapy with such sick patients to accomplish anything substantial, let alone to effect a cure. If this were the case, then intensive psychotherapy as a treatment for chronic schizophrenic patients would have merely heuristic worth, since it would be available for only an infinitesimally small number of patients, and would therefore have no public health value.

On the other hand, if after almost two years of intensive psychotherapy it appears that little or no fundamental change has occurred in the patients (and in fact there was in most instances very little to suggest that any substantial working alliance had even been established), then by extrapolation one might certainly question whether any number of years of individual psychotherapy would effect a fundamental alteration of the patient's ego in the direction of greater health. Our observations on the patients in this study do not allow for more encouraging conclusions.

The patients who received psychotherapy and a placebo appeared not to change over the course of the two years. On the other hand, the patients who received psychotherapy and the phenothiazine did exhibit some change, as evidenced by quantitative changes in their BDI and HAS levels and, in a less precise manner, in the nursing notes and diary entries—particularly with regard to their responses to important events occurring during the study.

Presumably, without phenothiazine treatment this group would have been as changeless as the placebo group. However, it is impossible to determine how the absence of psychotherapy might have affected their degree of improvement. The only observation that can be made with certainty is that changes in patients receiving thioridazine were more closely related to on/off drug conditions than to any other variable. This finding is borne out by the data cited above, and also by the fact that during drug withdrawal periods these patients moved toward the general manifest psychopathological level of the placebo group.

The question has been raised whether phenothiazine treatment is an asset or a liability to psychotherapy. If, as we have suggested, psychotherapy itself cannot produce fundamental changes in patients, then such a question is meaningless. However, while the BDI and other behavioral indices generally indicate minimal response to the therapist's presence or absence, there are some hints in diary and nursing note material that those patients receiving phenothiazine had the capacity to exhibit some sensitivity in responding to losses.

In other words, there is just a suggestion that for five of the patients on phenothiazine (as opposed to only one of the placebo patients) the therapist may have had some importance. This, of course, would signal the first step in the development of a working alliance. Moreover, these active drug patients, in contrast to the placebo group, were quite frank in their expression of pleasure or distress rather than masking or avoiding feelings. Their day-to-day variability in response to the environment is what sets these drug patients apart from even the "best behaved" of the placebo group patients. There is no evidence, conversely, that drug treatment retarded any progress the patients might otherwise have made in psychotherapy.

Within 10 to 12 weeks after the onset of thioridazine treatment, most of the active drug patients reached a drug plateau: that is, their BDI and HAS scores leveled off and remained remarkably stable despite changes in medication dosages or critical events on the ward. In fact, once the majority had reached this plateau, there was much less week-to-week fluctuation in the scores of the drug patients (as long as they remained on drugs) than there was in the placebo patients' scores during the same period. This steadiness indicates that in general, once a drug plateau level has been attained, a patient's behavior will not change, no matter how much of the drug is given or for how long.

There is no question that the patients on phenothiazines changed dramatically in relation to the on-off drug condition. However, it should be emphasized that the observed changes did not suggest that the patients were any less schizophrenic, but for the most part merely meant that the group exhibited less florid symptomatology. For example, one patient still heard voices while receiving thioridazine, but he no longer shouted at them or did cartwheels in response to their commands. In consequence, he appeared to be more "normal," and people were able to relate to him in a more reasonable fashion. In fact, in this patient's case the drug plateau was such that he could go out and work for short periods of time while he was on the drug. Had the drugs been a bit more effective, they might have reduced his bizarre behavior to a point below the critical threshold, making it possible for his family and the community to accept him again.

The drug enables some patients to function independently of the hospital, while for others bizarre behavior is not sufficiently reduced and they must remain hospitalized. A third group of patients improved enough while on drugs to function part-time on their own. Nevertheless, all of these patients are still schizophrenic, and there is no evidence that any enduring and fundamental change has been achieved by medication. This appears to be the case a year and a half after the onset of drug treatment, just as it had been at the very beginning.

SUMMARY

Psychotherapy alone (even with experienced psychotherapists) does little or nothing for chronic schizophrenic patients in two years' time. Psychotherapy for a much longer period is rarely feasible, because of the expense and time involved. Its effectiveness therefore becomes a largely academic question.

Phenothiazine therapy in conjunction with psychotherapy seems to be effective in reducing florid symptomatology and also perhaps in making the patient more "accessible," more receptive to communication with therapists and others. Our findings do not bear out the claim of some psychotherapists that pharmacotherapy can only interfere with progress in psychotherapy.

There are certain limits, however, to the efficacy of pharmacotherapy. Response to drugs varies from patient to patient, and even those who improve most dramatically are still basically schizophrenic.

There is ample evidence (BDI, HAS, nursing notes, and diaries) to show that the combination of drugs and psychotherapy had beneficial effects on these patients, and that the drug variable played by far the most important role in producing changes in the patients' statuses. It remains impossible to make any statement regarding the therapeutic effect of drugs without concomitant psychotherapy, since both drug and placebo patients received psychotherapy during most of their stay.

The data in this study all point to the fact that phenothiazine treatment is perhaps one of the most useful tools now available for the management of chronic schizophrenic patients.

NOTES

1. Allen, V. S. (1959), Trifluoperazine in the treatment of drug-resistant schizophrenics. *J. Clin. Exp. Psychopathol.*, 20:247–250.

2. Barrett, W. W., Ellsworth, R. B., Clark, L. D., & Ennis, J. (1957), Study of the differential behavioral effects of reserpine, chlorpromazine, and a combination of these drugs in chronic schizophrenics. *Dis. Nerv. Syst.*, 18:209–215.

3. Bindelglas, P. M., & Gosline, E. (1957), Differential reactions of patients receiving group psychotherapy with concomitant drug and somatic therapies. *Int. J. Group Psychother.*, 7:275–280.

4. Bordeleau, J. M. & Gratton, L. (1958), Etude d'un nouveau neuroleptique: le trifluoropérazine; rapport préliminaire. *Un. Méd. Canada*, 87:1552–1557.

5. Casey, J. F., Bennett, I. F., Lindley, C. J., Hollister, L. E., Gordon, M. H., & Springer, N. N. (1960), Drug therapy in schizophrenia: a controlled study of the relative effectiveness of chlorpromazine, promazine, phenobarbital, and placebo. *Arch. Gen. Psychiat.*, 2:210–220.

6. Casey, J. F., Lasky, J. J., Klett, C. J., & Hollister, L. E. (1960), Treatment of schizophrenic reactions with phenothiazine derivatives: a comparative study of chlorpromazine, triflupromazine,

mepazine, prochlorperazine, perphenazine, and phenobarbital. *Amer. J. Psychiat.*, 117:97–105.

7. Cohler, J., Grinspoon, L., & Fleiss, J. (1965), An extreme situation on a chronic schizophrenic treatment ward. *Psychiatry: J. Study Interpersonal Process.*, 28:4, November.

8. Cohler, J., Grinspoon, L., Shader, R., & Chatterjee, S. (1966), Behavioral correlates of the guessing game. *Arch. Gen. Psychiat.*, 15:279–287.

9. Cowden, R. C., Zax, M., Hague, J. R., & Finney, R. C. (1956), Chlorpromazine: alone and as an adjunct to group psychotherapy in the treatment of psychiatric patients. *Amer. J. Psychiat.*, 112:898–902.

10. Evangelakis, M. G. (1961), De-institutionalization of patients (The triad of trifluoperazine—group psychotherapy—adjunctive therapy). *Dis. Nerv. Syst.*, 22:26–32.

11. Gibbs, J. J., Wilkens, B., & Lauterbach, C. G. (1967), A Controlled Clinical Psychiatric Study of Chlorpromazine. *J. Clin. Exp. Psychopathol.*, 18:269–283.

12. Greenblatt, M., Solomon, M., Evans, A., & Brooks, G. (1965), *Drug and Social Therapy in Chronic Schizophrenia.* Springfield, Ill.: Charles C. Thomas, p. 324.

13. Grinspoon, L., Shader, R., Cohler, J., & Chatterjee, S. (1964), Side effects and double blind studies I. A clinical comparison between thioridazine hydrochloride and a combination of phenobarbital and atrophine sulfate. *J. Psychiat. Res.*, 2:247–256.

14. Hoch, P. H. (1959), *Drugs and psychotherapy. Amer. J. Psychiat.*, 116:305–308.

15. May, P. R. A., and Tuma, A. H. (1965), Treatment of schizophrenia. *Brit. J. Psychiat.*, 3:503–510.

16. McReynolds, P. & Ferguson, J. (1966), *Clinical Manual for the Hospital Adjustment Scale.* Palo Alto: Consulting Psychologists Press.

17. Meerloo, J. A. M. (1955), Medication into submission: The danger of therapeutic coercion. *J. Nerv. Ment. Dis.*, 122:353–360.

18. Newbold, H. L. & Steed, W. D. (1956), The use of chlorpromazine in psychotherapy. *J. Nerv. Ment. Dis.*, 123:270–274.

19. Ostow, M. (1962), *Drugs in Psycho-analysis and Psychotherapy.* New York: Basic Books.

20. Savage, C. & Day, J. (1958), Effects of a tranquilizer (reserpine) on psychodynamic and social processes. *Arch. Neurol. Psychiat.*, 79:590–596.

21. Shader, R., Cohler, J., Elashoff, R., & Grinspoon, L. (1964), Phenobarbital and atrophine in combination, an active control substance for phenothiazine research. *J. Psychiat. Res.*, 2:169–183.

22. Szasz, T. (1957), Some observations on the use of tranquilizing drugs. *Arch. Neurol. Psychiat.*, 77:86–92.

23. Wirt, R. D. & Simon, W. (1953), *Differential Treatment and Prognosis in Schizophrenia.* Springfield, Ill.: Charles C. Thomas.

24. Zetzel, E. R. (1966), Discussion, Drugs and Psychotherapy. In: *Psychiatric Drugs,* ed. P. Solomon. New York: Grune & Stratton, pp. 75–85.

25. From the 13th through the 29th week the patients on placebo in Group I received an active placebo consisting of phenobarbital and atropine sulfate as part of a separate study that involved an attempt to mimic the side effects of thioridazine in order to insure double blindness in the experimental design.[8,21]

26. None of the other placebo patients received supplementary phenothiazines.

Chapter 8

A SERIES OF THERAPEUTIC COMMUNITIES: THE PROCESS OF PERSONATION OF COMMUNITY INSTITUTIONS

Diego Napolitani, M.D.

As the history of the movement of community psychiatry shows, therapeutic communities grew out of the conjunction of the long-standing *social demand* for psychological and psychiatric aid, for psychotic patients in particular, and the new *technical possibilities,* arising from the development of psychoanalysis in its application to the treatment of psychotics in groups and institutions generally.[6]

It can therefore be said that the therapeutic community started as an institution set between the social need and the technical capacity of a specific social milieu with its history, laws, and basic cultural mechanisms.

This triangular perspective is no more that—a reproduction at a social level—of the original situation formed around the mother-child relationship, which is determined by the linkage between the mother's capacities and the child's needs within a given family setting.

Analysis of the mother-child pair indicates that this dynamic relationship is organized on the basis of two totally interlinked components. I refer explicitly to the narcissistic and symbiotic component of the pair which means that it can be defined as a fusional, unitary reality within which exchanges of nonobjectal (or preobjectal) "parts" take place; the other component relates to the triangular objectal perspective of the family "institution" by means of which the partners of the pair, which was originally symbiotic, are in turn hurled into the stream of objectal exchanges within the family as a whole. It is, in fact, in the family agora that objects become defined in their total dimension, and in this agora that the subjective time and space of the symbiotic couple are confronted with the times and spaces held in common by the "others," and again in the agora that the law of objectal exchanges holds sway and ensures the personal identity of each member of a specified family collective entity.

The entire history of the family can be defined by the conflictual confrontation between narcissistic and objectal tendencies to the extent that tendencies to narcissistic pairing are prevented from biologically overstepping the original symbiotic situation. All the members of a family invariably lean towards retrieval of this "lost treasure" and the fantasy family constantly recurs in each one as a violent elimination of the "third party" and restoration of the all-powerful dyad.

Thus the family code is set up as a collective defensive structure to parry the threat of the invasion of narcissistic fantasies into the collective reality.

The authority of this code, which is generally personified in the paternal "image," stands as the bulwark of individual identities against the depersonalizing fusion upheld by the narcissistic and symbiotic agencies usually condensed around maternal images.

In this framework the process of personation,[6] which supports the formation of the child's individual self, is interlocked with the process of formation of the collective self of the family. In fact, the family group is personalized either in relation to its own particular way of organizing its defense structures, or according to their articulation in establishing the roles assigned to each member of the family and the cultural mechanisms within which the roles have their point of reference.

Analysis of therapeutic communities enables us to retrace in the genesis and evolution of their structure, in the composition of their present triangular perspective (roles and cultural mechanisms) in relation to the emergence of narcissistic and symbiotic collusions, a process of personation in many ways analogous to that which occurs in families.

At present, in a time when psychiatric institutions are going through a crisis regarding traditional mechanisms of social exclusion, symptomatic repression, and segregation so typical of mental asylums,[3] we are seeing the establishment of mental institutions of a new kind, namely therapeutic communities, which also help to resist manic-type temptations towards negation, institutionalized in their turn by the antipsychiatry movement. These new therapeutic communities are characteristically collective structures in a constant state of evolution, for the simple reason that they take firmly in hand the dialectic conflict between the tendencies relating to the fantasy family and the needs specific to the family as it really is.

The therapeutic potential of these institutions in themselves, quite apart from the specialized psychotherapy, is mainly due to the fact that they facilitate the maturation of the individual self of each patient by means of his deep participation in the process of personation of the institution as a whole.

Basic Assumptions as Expressive Modalities of Institutional Narcissism and Their Elaboration in Three Therapeutic Communities

Here I find I have to make a choice, within the community structures in which I have participated, among the various aspects or points in their development which could be useful in a comparison of the processes of personation in each community. The most interesting period for this purpose is undoubtedly the initial stages of the life of the institution, for I feel that by analogy with what happens in the history of a family the therapeutic communities, as parafamily institutions, each present, as I have just mentioned, a kind of family history of its own. In other words, each one has a personation process particular to it, strictly conditioned by the way in which the original narcissistic and symbiotic component is developed within each one. This narcissistic component is basically what Bion notes and stresses in therapeutic groups when he defines a particular fantasy activity in terms of a basic assumption.[1]

I have been lucky enough to witness the fact that the birth of a therapeutic community is invariably accompanied by dynamic group phenomena relating to one or the other of the basic assumptions indicated by Bion. I also think I can safely suggest that the choice of one or the other of these assumptions is related to very precise historical, sociological, and "personalogical" conditioning. It should be pointed out that the basic assumptions do not appear explicitly as such (in this connection, Freud's remark[2] on the extreme difficulty of recognizing and analyzing certain particular narcissistic personality structures remains totally valid); hence it sometimes happens that we can work for months or even years engulfed in a narcissistic dimension while all the time convinced of being in a realistic dimension. Therefore I feel that the contribution of some reflections on this fundamental question will not be lacking in interest and usefulness for all those who deal with institutional psychiatric activities.

THE MENTAL HEALTH CENTER COMMUNITY

In 1960 I was working as an assistant at the Mental Health Center in Milan, and it was here that with a small group of colleagues (doctors, social workers, and nurses) I founded a therapeutic community of the day-hospital type for about 20 psychotic patients.

This community was situated in the same building as the headquarters of the Board of the Mental Health Service, where other outpatient diagnostic and therapeutic activities were also carried on. Relations between the staff working with the therapeutic community and those working for the service gradually deteriorated, until the therapeutic community finally became increasingly the object of suspicion, declared hostility, and even boycott.

From the moment a selected group organized as a sub-group in relation to the service staff as a whole and manifested its intention of creating a new kind of institution inspired—on the ideological level—by a polemical attitude towards the official psychiatric culture, I think that the implicit premises were already laid for this subgroup to be mobilized by the fight-flight basic assumption.

This type of narcissistic assumption was made even easier for the group because of the fact that its leader was involved in a direct power struggle with his director. In other words, I myself was exposed to the temptation—an easy one at that—to use the real project of the therapeutic community and the emotional reinforcement of my colleagues as a weapon in a narcissistic-type personal conflict with my superior.

The community group was extremely closeknit and involved in this conflict. I was seen as the flag bearer of the group's ideas whereas that which was "bad" was blamed on the outside and cathected upon people who, in fact, lent themselves to this projection—and all the more so because they may have been moved by a deep feeling of envy toward the community's sophisticated undertakings. The community patients themselves were, in turn, involved in these conflictural tensions. The frequently acute and dramatic aggravation of their symptoms (which can be compared with what Stanton and Schwartz[8] have shown with regard to the institutional iatrogenic syndrome) inevitably accentuated the hostile reactions from outside. These reactions, in turn, stirred up new tensions of the fight-flight type within the community group, with the result that the real work done was gradually eroded and the aggravation of the patients' symptoms was consequently stabilized.

It was at this point that I decided to abandon the field of imaginary battle, symbolizing in this way a suicide as an act of violent accusation against the hostile institutional structures.

I think, then, that the conclusion of this initial community experience with a suicide was rooted in the increasingly paranoid attitude of the community group with regard to the enemy on the outside, and that this attitude was linked to the group's inability to establish properly its basic assumptions. Or simply, that the emergence of basic assumptions in an institutional group is not in itself a pathological occurrence which necessarily has to put the group in jeopardy. On the contrary, it should be considered as an inevitable component of the group's psychic life, just like that observed with narcissistic components present or reemerging at given points in the process of individual personation.

I would go further and say that the emergence of these narcissistic components can be the expression of a moment of crisis in the objectal relations of the subject (collective or individual) at a given point. Therefore it constitutes the premises for the development of new objectal relations; this development can usually be seen as long as go functions are sufficiently intact, that is, not fragmented in paranoid productions. At the Mental Health Center community, the major basic assumption was not contained inside the community group, but on the contrary, was elaborated in a paranoid fashion and became irretrievable within the group.

THE OMEGA THERAPEUTIC COMMUNITY

The Omega Therapeutic Community sprang up from the ruins of the previous community experience. We were convinced that what had been impossible to do within the framework of a public administration would be feasible in the private sector, in view of the greater freedom one could expect there. In actual fact, as we have just shown, this conviction was based on paranoid premises although at the same time in touch with realistic elements. However, the paranoid components undoubtedly had quite a profound effect on the culture of the new community, as I shall try to show to you.

The creation of a free community, in other words, independent of any other administrative structure, was a project inspired by a process of idealization of the prior failure. Hence the incapacity shown in managing the relations between dependence and the paranoid elaboration of the fight-flight basic assumption which resulted from it was transformed into a value in itself. It was I myself who narcissistically encouraged and fed this elaboration; furthermore, it fell on very fertile ground with the colleagues I had rallied around this new undertaking. The more I linked the development of the privateness of the project to the necessity of getting away from the "bad" outside, the more I intensified a splitting between the latter and the "good" inside, represented by me, of course, as the natural leader of the new group. In order to fulfill this ideal role, I brought into play manic-type defensive resources which, in turn, helped along the process of idealization of my person within the group.

All these facts facilitated the emergence of a dependent basic assumption in the working group, which fell into a position of deep passivity vis-à-vis its leader. Any undertaking which meant operating more independently or with a greater degree of responsibility in relation to the staff and the patients themselves presented a special difficulty when it came to actually carrying it out. Staff supervision meetings eventually came to bear a close resemblance to psychotherapy sessions, with each member pouring forth his own needs, rather than a period of joint reflection upon the object of our group work.

We have already pointed out the fact that in the fight-flight group which characterized the first Mental Health Service community experience, relations with patients were set on the paranoid plane with regard to the outside enemy, and on the obsessional plane as far as activities within the community were concerned. The opposite was the case with the dependent group of the first two years of the Omega community, where relations with patients were connected with a multiplicity of dual relationships. Community meetings, and all other collective undertakings with realistic aims had either minimal attendance or were carried out with inadequate emotional participation, while the greatest possible amount of time was devoted to increasing the number of individual relationships.

The dependent group's fantasy of a symbiotic and narcissistic relation was always reflected in the community life and tended to take concrete form in a web of dual relationships which, in many respects, claimed kinship with the phenomenology of "madness à deux."

Setting this state of things straight was a very long and

difficult process, and it is impossible to summarize here the major stages which paved the way to change. Let me just say that the most important instruments the community group used were the staff's systematic analyses of their own institutional narcissism, and falling back on a strict set of norms which provided each one with an institutional compass point to fend against the danger of coming to grief on the rocks of dyadic relationships.

In recent years, various basic assumptions followed one after the other, including the pairing group, but they have turned out to be far less effective on a realistic level. That is to say, they have a far less disturbing effect on the working group which, on the other hand, is better able to make use of the experience of its own basic assumptions in understanding and controlling the complicated institutional reality.

THE VILLA SERENA SOCIOTHERAPY CENTER

In 1967, three years after my resignation from the Milan Departmental Administration and two years after the creation of the Omega community, I was invited by the Psychiatric Assistance Deputy in Milan to rejoin the administration and continue my community experiment. I accepted the proposal and at my request a new medical service called the "Centro di Socioterapia 'Villa Serena'" was organized, independent of the mental hospitals and even of the Mental Health Center.

The mere statement of these objective facts may suffice to indicate the significance at fantasy level that this new undertaking must have had for myself and for my new colleagues.

Villa Serena was rather like the place of a marriage ceremony; after so many vicissitudes of fighting and fleeing, promises and betrayals, I renewed contacts with the administration with the mutual intention of producing a Messiah-like child; to be precise, of creating a new structure capable of promoting, in "messianic" terms, a change in the psychiatric tradition in our region. That was the fantasy underlying the culture of Villa Serena's initial stages, just as the Omega community had been stamped by a fantasy of idealized dependence.

The working group which went into action at Villa Serena was very soon blessed with the basic assumption of pairing since it had already internalized the prior pairing of myself, the bearer of an idea, and the administration, bearer of a realistic structure. The fact of being at the same time both technicians (promoters of a very special psychiatric ideology) and employees of the administration (autonomously responsible for administrative management and regulations) enabled the members of the group to internalize the pairing fantasy first shared between myself and the administration and then adopted by everyone. Working together at the beginning took on deep libidinal significance for the group. Its union was seen as the fusion into a single body, pregnant with a new "thing" of great importance which should have been born under the sign of change. Psychoanalytical language, at last predominant within a public institution, had acquired the prophetic force of a kind of Archangel Gabriel. Everything had to bow before the force of persuasion of this language, witness, and annunciator of the new coming.

However, as Bion shows in his description of the pairing group, any hopes of staying that way had to be protected by the materialization of the hoped-for advent; this meant that change, of which the group was the fertile womb, would be the most formidable danger if it were to come about. The diversifying identity of each operator's role could be assumed only as a condition of the state of pairing, but had to be rejected as soon as there was any possibility of its jeopardizing this same pairing group by taking on a truly diversifying significance for the working group. Time, an entity denied by any narcissistic group, whatever its particular basic assumption, was in theory neutralized although always spoken of as "future."

This set of conditions produced a characteristic phenomenology in the general organization of the community —a phenomenology which the brilliant intuition of one of my colleagues summarized by the Italian word "pantanalisi" (pan-analysis). This neologism denoted firstly the magical divinatory nature of the psychoanalytical language which aimed at replacing concrete sociotherapeutic action and intervention, and hence the entire (pan) area designated for the exchange of realistic expression. Furthermore, the expression "pantanalisi" is also derived from the combination of the word "analysis" with the Italian word "pantano," which means a "stagnant marsh." One can see in this allusion the sign of stagnant water, which evokes a state of immobility where the personal characteristics of everyone the marsh engulfs are corrupted, in the physical sense of death and corruption.

When we tried to establish contacts with the staff of other psychiatric institutions in the region by organizing study seminars at regular intervals, our attempt was met by the other institutional groups with such an icy attitude and such a low degree of participation that we were deeply disturbed about it. We were convinced we had something to contribute to the wealth of others from our own resources and found ourselves faced in answer with a declaration that no use could be made of our experience! Even this situation was stigmatized by a remark which was later to contribute to the awareness of our basic assumption: "You are just a tiny island of aristocrats" (as you know, the sophisticated working unit of the pairing group is precisely what constitutes the aristocracy in Bion's thinking).

The realistic changes which occurred during the initial states of Villa Serena are apparent in that there was acceptance within the community culture of a precise function of a particular working group. The emergence of an institutional superior had a deeply disturbing effect on the pairing group within which, by its very nature, the chief must be contained, with no dialectical or conflictual distinction between him and the group itself. Bion states, in fact, that the real head of a pairing group is simply the messianic idea, the ideology of salvation, the aspiration itself, and not a concrete presence whose very concreteness would contradict the sense of the "hoped-for advent" which is the basis for the group's cohesion. This initial change, which was made possible by the analysis of these phenomena within and outside of the groups I have just mentioned, in its turn brought about the necessity for the narcissistic nuclei present in the group itself to create new outlets for expression. This resulted in a whole series of frequent and rapid changes of basic assumptions. But the group's level of narcissism was on the whole kept within limits compatible with good institutional work. (There were, "of course" critical moments every time a new procedure was introduced, as though the pairing group's previous experience had left its mark on the character of the institution).

CONCLUSION

Hampered by the limits of time allowed for this chapter, which I rather fear I have already overstepped, I can see that it might be difficult for the reader to grasp entirely the import of our experiences. I set out to put forward the hypothesis that the birth and development (the personation) of community institutions, inasmuch as they are parafamily institutions, are characterized by the conflictual confrontation between narcissistic tendencies, with their dual structure, and objectal tendencies with a triangular structure.

With a view to documenting my hypothesis which, as far as the identification of the narcissistic components of the group is concerned, tallies with Bion's discoveries on basic assumptions, I have given the clinical histories of three therapeutic communities. However, as usually happens in the presentation of clinical cases, these histories have neglected most of the objective data in order to emphasize solely those few aspects considered the most important for the theoretical dissertation I wanted to put to you.

Apart from a certain number of objective facts, it might be said that insufficient light has been thrown upon the aspect which constitutes the basis and justification for this entire discourse. I mean the therapeutic significance to patients of this complex process of personation proper to any community institution.

Indeed, I do think that the idea of regression for the benefit of the ego (proposed by Kris in his explanation of the necessity for a kind of controlled connivance on the part of the analyst in the patient's psychotic or neurotic process) is given documented confirmation in the organization and development of the therapeutic communities. Here the nursing staff's regression takes place through the emergence within the group of basic assumptions, that is, through the staff's participation in the metachronic dimension in which psychotics live. The aim of this metachronic dimension, whose concept is developed in greater detail in one of my recent publications on *Il sociale nella psicoanalisi e la psicoanalisi del sociale,*[4] is to create strong bonds between the staff and the patients, to eliminate the differences, expel the notion of time, to consider the principle of change as no more than a messianic vocation, marking time in the realm of the imaginary, misreading symbolism with its own institutional syntax.

Segregationist psychiatry (asylums) and biological psychiatry (mental hospitals), with their bureaucratic administrative structures and their pseudoscientific objectivity, constitute a solid and rigid defense against the danger of psychotic "contagions," against any danger of metachronic fusion between staff and patients. One might say that as a system of defense, traditional psychiatry is inspired by obsessional components and splitting. Nevertheless, it does not condition encounters between individuals, with all their diversity, but instead maintains a distinct separation between individuals who are deeply equalized by similar introjective and projective identification mechanisms, even though these are inverted and reciprocal.

One inevitable reaction to this fundamentally psychotic psychiatric model is—starting with Laing—antipsychiatry, the antiasylum response, with its idealization of institutional metachrony and the equalization between the nursing staff and patients within a fantasy body resting on basic assumptions with continual displacement on both sides. On the other hand, we can state that the task of community psychiatry is to take in hand the metachronic components in the overall psychic reality of a collective unit in order to make them recognizable for what they are. It is precisely in this process leading to collective awareness that the group's ego matrix with its own technological, administrative, and political capacities can be seen.[5]

Here we can come to the conclusion that it really is through the gradual recognition of the diversity of individuals, against the background of metachronic assumptions that each one's experience can be historicized and it becomes possible to confront individual diachronics with each other (process of maturation of the individual self) in the synchronic dimension, that is, in the present triangular perspective of which the institution in itself can do no more than offer its guarantee and testimony.

NOTES

1. Bion, W. R. (1966), Dinamiche di gruppo: una revisione in *Vie Nuove della Psicoanalisi,* M. Lane: Il Saggiatore.

2. Freud, S. (1914), On narcissism: an introduction. *Standard Edition,* 14:73–102. London: Hogarth Press, 1957.

3. Napolitani, D. (1970), Significati e prospettive della socioterapia nella crisi della falsa coscienza psichiatrica, a paper presented at the 1st Symposium on *Community Psychiatry and Sociotherapy* held in Milan 1970 and to be published in *Minerva Psichiatrica e Psicologica*

4. Napolitani, D. (1971), Il sociale nella psicoanalisi e la psicoanalisi del sociale, in *Psicoanalisi e istituzioni psichiatriche,* Fienze: G. Barbera.

5. A detailed hypothesis on the emergence of the ego in a therapeutic group is given in Napolitani, D., La conduzione di un gruppo di lavoro psichiatrico. Riflessioni sui rapporto tra l'Individuale e il sociale nelle istituzioni. Paper presented at the *1st Symposium on Community Psychiatry and Sociotherapy,* Milan, 1970, to be published in *Minerva Psichiatrica e Psicologica.*

6. An original contribution and complete bibliography on the sub-

ject can be found in Racamier, P. C. (1970), *Le psychanalyste sans divan*. Paris: Payot.

7.   I use this term in the same sense as P. C. Racamier (1963), Le moi, le soi, la personne et la psychose (an essay on personation), *Evolution Psychiatrique,* 28:525–553. The expression is taken up and elaborated upon in a psychosociological dimension by Hochmann, J. (1971), *Pour une psychiatrie communautaire,* Ed. du Seuil, Paris.

8.   Stanton, A. & Schwarz, M. (1954), *The Mental Hospital,* New York: Basic Books, Inc.

9.   The term used in the French text is a neologism—"personnation"—expressing the idea of becoming a person; this was introduced in 1963 by Racamier (see references). After some reflection we felt it preferable to translate this simply by the English neologism "personation" (Editor's note).

Chapter 9

A THERAPEUTIC HOME: REMARKS ON THE METHOD OF TREATMENT IN LONG-TERM EVOLUTIONS[12]

**Paul-Claude Racamier, M.D., and
Léopold Carretier, M.D.**

BASIC VIEWS

Introduction

History, psychiatric experience, psychoanalytical knowledge, and culture all underlie the great efforts being made
today in the treatment of long-term psychotic patients. Institutional methods for these patients are still being sought,
and this search requires theoretical and practical reflection
on a number of different concrete experiences.[6] We have,
therefore, chosen in this chapter to deal with and draw your
particular attention to the following points:

1. The organization of a care home for the treatment of a small number of long-term patients;
2. the method of care,[13] in its dynamic and economic aspects; and
3. the evolution of the patients' disorders in response to treatment.

The patients who are entrusted to us and who trust us are all relatively young and are cases with a psychotic structure, although, given our present limitations, the disorders they present do not necessitate immediate or long hospitalization. Their parents are directly associated with the therapeutic undertaking on an individual and a collective level. This treatment organism, which we call a "home," corresponds to a broader definition of a "day hospital." It does not serve a catchment area, but fits into the social fabric of a town.

History

It is sufficient to list the main elements of the history of this organization:

1. It was *created* and did not simply ease into existing structures, like a hermit crab.
2. Its creation resulted from an *encounter* between the aspirations of some patients, some parents, and some doctors and caring staff.
3. From the very beginning this creation has included both expectation and improvisation, and although for the most part the expected element has been predominant, the unexpected has, it seems, never been lacking.
4. The organization *established its structures* and methods of functioning in the course of its own development, which has not yet come to an end; its structure appeared as it developed, rather like a nautilus; however, throughout its development, this organization has never changed either its principle or its direction.

With this kind of evolution, we can justifiably hope that our organization has avoided setting up anachronistic structures and contradictory regulations such as are so often seen in older institutions founded by anonymous interests rather than on the basis of the will of the individual and concrete requests determined by explicit principles.

Obviously, every treating organism goes through critical stages, and those which function in closest alignment with their patients' psychic reality are the most flexible and the most fragile. The one we are describing is about four years old; as far as an institution is concerned, it has passed the period of infancy, but is still in its first youth.

Basic Conceptions and Principles

Even if it does no more than deal with things of most pressing urgency, and all the more so when it launches into long-term care, a therapeutic organization has a certain number of basic conceptions and principles, whether these are explicit or otherwise. What can I say about ours, in as brief a way as possible?

Our understanding of psychotic processes is rooted in a *psychoanalytical* model, balanced by both the practice of classic psychoanalysis and psychiatric practice of various kinds. I shall not elaborate upon this theory here, but it runs like a thread throughout our experience and our reflections.[1,4–6,9]

In particular, we know that psychotic processes correspond to internal psychic organizations of great variety where economy is a factor of major importance, and where not only psychic mechanisms but also psychic structures are involved. We know that conflicts, fantasy activity and even ego activity, are inadequately internalized, and particularly in the schizophrenic orbit, where what we call the "projective identification mechanisms" produce a true outpouring of psychic contents and functions, which puts the patient completely at the mercy of those objects he uses as containers. Psychotic "regressions" must not be confused with neurotic regressions as they are reactivated and used by the psychoanalytic process; the dynamic severing of relations between the primary and secondary processes of mental functioning severely deprives the ego; the needs of omnipotence are dominant in contrast with the fragility of the energies at the disposal of the ego; an object relation is psychotic when it is preobjectal and symbiotic, either on the economic level (in the depressive sphere) or on the economic and structural level (in the paranoid sphere). In short, we know that psychotics of all kinds are engaged in a struggle to the last breath between the desire to be and the defense against being what they are or being anything at all by personal right; and finally, that the psychoses are a threat not so much to pleasure as to survival and that, this being so, nobody clings to his defenses more than the psychotic whom they cost more dearly than anyone else.

Our work is therefore based on a few simple postulates which would be easy to demonstrate:

1. *Narcissistic* factors are of the greatest importance to patients and to their parents, and hence to caring staff and therapists; we are dealing with people fighting desperately and at great cost to defend a narcissism in ruins, and our first task is to repair bankrupt economies without destroying our own economy in the process.[7,9,10]

2. Institutional care inevitably presents a *conflictual* character, due to the fact that patients reject and evacuate their interior conflictuality, so that the institution has to take it over to some extent before they can reinternalize it.[8,11]

3. The caring staff, the parents, and the patients themselves have a *potential for development* which can be realized, provided it is given sufficient credit and is put in a situation favorable to its emergence.[10]

4. The *model of relations* and functioning set up in the institution by the leaders is most likely to permeate gradually the institutional network as a whole.[7]

5. A number of different people confronted jointly with common problems have a good chance of producing reactions which are *complementary* through their diversity.

Organization and Techniques

So there are our possibilities, which have to be organized in order to materialize. We therefore believe in the virtue of *organized situations,* provided that they give the freest rein possible to potential for reconstruction and that they always leave an opening for the unexpected, for invention, unforeseen initiative, and pure luck.[11]

Because we insist on the specificity of techniques (and also different cases and functions), we feel it essential to give extremely careful consideration to the prescription of treatments, particularly the psychotherapies, as well as to distinguish the various levels of action which although interdependent are quite different. Therefore we do not talk in terms of institutional or family psychotherapy, or of intake, but of *care,* and attribute to this notion a wider significance than we have indicated elsewhere.[5,8,9]

Finally, let me point out that although a small-scale organization may have certain disadvantages, its great advantage is at least that the overall picture of its functional aspects can be observed fairly accurately.

PATIENTS AND THE HOME

The Cases

The field of operation we have chosen is that of a care group organized along the lines of a therapeutic community. The group is mixed and open and is a small one, never going beyond ten patients at a time so far. The home started on a smaller scale three and a half years ago, and we feel that it could expand without any change in style or direction to take about 20 patients. Our observation relates to about 24 cases or so in all; as you see, it is somewhat limited in numbers.

This treatment community, which has two part-time doctors and a full-time nursing staff of three, functions on a very flexible basis as a house, a home, or a day, night, or full-time hospital, and accepts only selected voluntary patients. These are either psychotics in the full sense of the word (there are an average of four confirmed schizophrenics out of every ten cases), or prepsychotics subject to psychotic episodes, or else marginal cases who are psychotic in structure but not in their manifest symptomatology. All of them are young, between 18 and 32 years of age. Acute psychoses are not and cannot be accepted, which means that there are no emergency admissions and if hospitalization becomes necessary at some stage along the line this is done outside the home. We have been able to take severe schizophrenics, on the other hand.

Three-quarters of the patients have a more or less lengthy, complicated, reiterative, and unfortunate hospital history, and all of them had previously undergone one or more unsuccessful therapeutic attempts.

In spite of being very different from each other, our patients had the following aspects in common:

1. *failure* of the psychotic type, multiple failure, deep and polymorphous;
2. *defective individuation,* either at the economic level in the depressive register, or on the double economic and topographical level in the paranoid register.

Our patients are young, all of them were affected before, and sometimes just before, they finished their training and were able to take a job. Hence all of them are heavily dependent on their parents; their dependence is financial (since they themselves do not have the means to pay for the treatment and the Social Service is not in the picture at that stage), and this material dependence is interwoven with psychological dependence. As these are psychotic structures requiring institutional support, we see that the parental figures are badly internalized, that individual limits are porous and that the respective conflicts of the subjects and their parents interpenetrate, flow into each other, and are sometimes blended together by the complex interplay of all kinds of projective identifications.

The Association

As we had wanted, the organization is managed by a non-profit-making association that operates under the terms of well-known legislation which in France goes back to 1901, and the patients' parents essentially and necessarily belong to this association. The respective roles of parents, statutory members of the association and the elected members of its committee; that of the doctors, appointed by the association to advise and to supervise the medical and psychological management of the home; and that of the nursing staff, who work as a team in close collaboration with the medical personnel; all of these respective roles are quite clearly articulated, defined, and based on practical reality. The patients themselves have no clearly defined role, and we consider it preferable for them not to be burdened with artificial roles to play. They are, however, consistently requested to participate in all decisions which concern them and those which concern the therapéutic community. This participation is carried out in the association's meetings which the patients attend as nonvoting participants, and most especially at the full meetings of the caring community, which are held twice a week. Thus the organization is conceived in such a way that *power is held by no one person, but each one concerned has some effective power.* At the same time, we wanted to make sure that no real problem would be excluded from consideration at some point or another in the network of all the interrelationships established among the various people concerned.

Thus financial matters are quite open and concealed from no one; as often as possible they are used for treatment purposes, and have even been used for research.

The Home

The care home is situated in an ordinary house in the outskirts of a provincial town of moderate importance, but which does have socioeconomic and university facilities. It has three rooms which can take five beds, and on the average four patients out of ten sleep on the premises, although nurses are present at night only on exceptional occasions. Thus the majority of patients live outside the home, where they stay for an initial phase and to which they can sometimes return for a short period at a time.

As you see, the emphasis is on the team rather than the equipment; this means that the caring personnel's field of action extends far beyond the home itself. To this double inside-outside polarity is added the flexibility of the intake, since a patient's contacts with the team and the group can cover anything from two hours a week to twelve hours a day according to his needs.

On the other hand, because of the fact that the organization's definition is in psychological and not in geographical terms, patients are admitted upon request and after selection. The request and the selection are two-fold, involving both the patient and the parents. Two operational concepts are hence explicit: that of the care *contract* (which is a contract of mutual cooperation among three parties, i.e., patient, family, and team), and that of the *limits* of the care possibilities of the home which can admit or retain no patient in an acute state or against his will.

ORGANIZATION AND METHODS

Organization

As we have already shown, the functional organization has adopted a network type of structure, polarized by the medical staff in the position of leaders.

There are two doctors with conceptions, experiences, views, and reactions which they share in common (and who meet regularly to compare their viewpoints), and a nursing staff of three, very carefully selected for their personal and professional qualities and given a wide scope for initiative, responsibility, and expression (and remunerated at the highest level of their profession). These five people, who together form a real team, play distinct and complementary roles within the treatment group, in which the patients are active participants, and in the association constituted by the parents, whose president is a long-standing stable and well-informed member.

Methods of treatment are coherent with this type of organization.

Meetings

According to the method we use, the treatment of each of our patients is tailored to each individual, but the care—or admitting into care—invariably goes through a collective melting pot. If it is true that the care is above all conditioned by the organization and the style of relations between caring staff and patients among each other; if it is true that these relations have their regular privileged moments at meetings, which constitute the organizing moments of the life of the institution and the treatments carried out there; if community therapy is something more than a pious hope, a fashion, or an empty ideology, in short, if it is a *method,* then this method is best defined by the system and technique of these meetings.

Our method has already been described elsewhere.[7] It comprises: (1) *community meetings*—patients, caring and medical staff, and occasional visitors (parents or members of the psychiatric profession); (2) *team meetings,* for medical and caring staff; (3) *team* sessions, involving the medical-caring staff and one patient at a time, sometimes with his family; and (4) there are assemblies where everyone is present, especially the parents. These various meetings are different from each other but are complementary and together they form a whole unit made up of well-knit parts.

Within this system of exchanges the community meetings hold a central position; the problems posed by the existence of each one and by the coexistence of all flow into these meetings as though they were filter beds; they are directly linked with the daily life of the group and the patients. (This direct connection, which distinguishes these meetings from real sessions of group psychotherapy, requires from the caring team a firm adherence to its working principles and very careful attention, to their application, otherwise these meetings run the risk of degenerating either into "ersatz" psychotherapy sessions or into hollow fellowship meetings.)

Therefore these are meetings for information, confrontation, discussion, mixing, and decision making. They are held regularly (at least once a week) and with rules of operation which form a framework for the spontaneity manifested on these occasions; more often than not one of the patients acts as chairman which is not a fixed office.

Two principles are put into effect:

1. The starting point is always present and concrete facts, going through the affects involved in order to reach, if necessary, a practical decision;

2. We always start with the person of each patient concerned, via the opinions expressed by other participants, in order to reach a clearer definition of the patient's own intentions and possibilities.

Although expression of affects is encouraged, this is not in order to lead on to fantasies, but rather to focus or strengthen the sense of reality of oneself and others. Although other voices are encouraged to make themselves heard, this is not to blend the group into a merged identity, but to reinforce the individuation of each one by means of a multiple effect of focusing *refraction.*

Similar principles direct the team sessions, which are prepared and decided upon by the preceding meetings, should the patient's difficulty require a more personal, intensive, and concentrated intervention by the caring team. (These offshoots of the collective melting pot are therefore not regular events.)

Finally, the team meetings, which are a feature of most institutions, are brief when they are a matter of summarizing things in between the collective meetings, and longer when they involve commenting simultaneously upon these meetings, the patients' dynamic evolution, and the functioning of the institution in general and the caring team in particular.

An Example

We will give just one illustration of the community group's work in order to clarify its mechanisms. At the end of each month we make a joint evaluation. This refers to the care required during the previous month (care required is not necessarily care given if, for example, the patient withdraws from the direct attention of the group and the caring team, even though he may need it). Therefore the *care required corresponds to the part of his own existence which the patient does not deal with himself.* In order to simplify this evaluation, reference markers or categories have been established, indicated by the letters A, B, C, D, running by degrees from the most intensive care to the lightest; patients very quickly become familiar with these evaluation markers. First of all the patient's own view is asked for, followed by that of the other participants. In some cases the patient sees himself objectively and his view, which is relevant and accurate, is adopted with no difficulty. In other cases the patient over- or underevaluates his accomplishment and his opinion then gives rise to a lively discussion which can provide him with a many-faceted mirror, and from which a decision finally emerges.

(These animated discussions are led at a brisk pace so as to avoid eroticization of the interest it arouses. As it happens, the group or the team does not seem to fall in to any temptation to use these discussions as a means of punishment or gratification or of imposing any standards. We have also added here a monthly assessment of the overall functioning of the institution.)

Now these assessments, whose maturing function is apparent, have a *practical theme.* The association deliberately decided that it was fair to divide general expenses on a pro-rata basis, it was also fair that medical and caring expenses should be carefully balanced individually; in other words, the care of a patient who is about to leave the home and is hardly any burden on it, costs in fact far less than that of a patient who still leans on the institution with all the weight of the needs he cannot cope with himself. The assessments made within the group are then used as a basis for the accounting calculations of the distribution of medical and care expenses. In this way parents are always kept informed of the expenses they are paying for.

Hence the necessity for sharing financial contributions, which was adapted to the real care situation, produced a mechanism which is itself used for treatment purposes and which, in addition, provides us with a convenient and sufficiently objective means of assessing patients' evolution. This evaluation is in turn used for research purposes, because the successive results enable us to establish graphs of evolution in which our own wishes and impatience are reflected to the minimum extent possible. (This example is chosen because it demonstrates the interlinking of a number of different views in a working method which integrates instead of juxtaposing them. It seems to us, indeed, that a satisfactory and lively institutional organization has to make an effort to *establish and maintain dynamic links between a variety of different people and outlooks*).

The Institutional Atmosphere

In contrast to the psychotherapies, in the institutional field exchanges with patients always have to take place on a neutral ground, and it is up to the caring staff to select or accept this meeting ground. This can be the group, under the conditions described above, or the caring staff alone or within a normal activity, such as mealtimes, leisure, sports, research, visits, shopping, medication, work, and so on. (This role appears imperative if we are to avoid finding the caring staff unwittingly involved in unexpected and inextricable psychotherapeutic situations).

However, the description of a method is not complete without mention of the atmosphere around it (taken in the sense of emotional and relational atmosphere. We prefer this rather vague term to other words used indiscriminately under the influence of badly assimilated theoretical notions. If would be easy to prove that any method whatsoever can perfectly well be invalidated by an atmosphere which works against it instead of supporting it).

Our method is only conceivable in an atmosphere of warmth. Establishing and maintaining this warm atmosphere is therefore our fundamental objective, provided that it is not brought about at the cost of a collective and correlative position of effusion inside and persecution outside. (It is in fact by means of a confusing identification of all the members with each other against an "outside" world imagined and deliberately seen as bad, that institutional groups frequently try to acquire their own cohesion and combat psychotic anxiety and destructiveness. Nothing better illustrates this tendency and shows the deadlock to which it leads than the theses of antipsychiatry).

The cohesion of the care group is based on the joint pursuit of common aims, which are the treatments and improved well-being of the patients, and on the collective observance of the rules of functioning which are all explicit and easy to explain. The atmosphere of warmth by no means excludes the circulation of aggressive currents within the group, but on the contrary, makes it easier. If, as sometimes happens, it is possible for a doctor, a member of the caring staff, or a patient to make an open attack on one patient or another's manifestly self-deteriorating attitude, it is inconceivable in any but this kind of deep-running and warm receptive ground. (As we know, the more one is accepted, the easier it is to question a subject's internal attitudes; we also know that we can venture a great deal with patients as long as we have liking and consideration for them; finally, psychotics have to be stirred up at exactly the right moment to get them to move.)

It should, nonetheless, be made quite clear that we by no means engage in systematic activism and that, on the contrary, patients, those close to them, and the caring staff themselves often initiate or give rise to movements or functions which we have, no doubt, made possible, and might comment on, but definitely do not control.[11] We shall see exactly when are the times for action and when noninterference is necessary.

EVOLUTIONS

Guidelines

Any treatment, particularly when dealing with long-term evolutions, is a kind of game. The development and outcome of the game largely depends on the opening moves, after which there are low-key phases and accentuated points, periods of calm and crises. The final crisis, if all goes well, comes when the patient breaks away from the institution, which he is going to do without from then onward.

If it is true to say that any psychotic patient, either in fact or structurally, sees and conceives of himself as an organic enclave, always real and wounded, within an overwhelming parental image, then the therapeutic evolution is designed less to "cure" the patient of his symptoms or even of his badly internalized conflicts than to enable him to regain possession of what belongs to him. The double process of repairing the economic and even structural deficit, and making possible the initiation of new and more autonomous modes of existence and functioning is translated in relation to the institutional body in terms of a process of integration and liberation which often overlap and which are never brought about without hardship and effort.

First of all, we shall point out what brings the various and widely different cases together.

The Starting of Care

Obviously the fact that a patient needs care, or even the care that a given organization is specifically in a position to provide, is not enough for the therapeutic process to be automatically set in motion. To be more precise, in our practice it is necessary but not sufficient for a patient to suffer to start treatment. We consider the therapeutic commitment itself as a dynamic process with a decisive influence at a later stage. This process is centered around the patient's admission, but is also prior and subsequent to it; the patient is almost invariably seen several times before he is admitted, and his definite admission or otherwise is decided upon after a trial period. This means that sometimes a year goes by between the first meeting with the patient and his eventual admission.

On the transaction level the commitment is in the form of a verbal contract of cooperation which takes into account from the outset both the limitations and the resources of the three contracting parties, namely, the patient, his family, and the home. (The home also has its limitations, which it makes no attempt to hide. Our observation, as well as personal experience, leads us to have little faith in long-term care whose initiation has been given little attention or has been too easy; we are also convinced that in the largest of the organizations of community-based psychiatry each one of the different institutions has to be capable of determining and imposing the scope and style best suited to it.)

On the dynamic level, this initial phase consists of noting, clarifying or bringing out the motivations for treatment on the part of the patient, his family, and the team itself, which is responsible for the final choice.

For example, there was a young girl who had been recommended to us and whom we saw while she was hospitalized and under neuroleptics after her third suicide attempt, which had been as sudden and as apparently motiveless as the other two. Several attempts at treatment had come to nothing, and the pathological process seemed doomed to repetition. The father was insistent in his request, but the patient herself remained passive, despondent, and resigned, made no request at all and did not quite get through to us. We told her that she did not convince us that we could do anything for her, or even that she had any desire for help; our response brought to light the fact that the patient had undergone hospitalization on various occasions but had never once asked for it, and we understood that in fact she had never been able to bear wanting anything at all. A few weeks later she sent us a very clear written request for admission; we saw her again and although under just as much medication as ever, this time she had a real and controlled presence for us; in other words, she had become convincing. We were then able to accept her for admission. Obviously, though, during this preliminary phase, starting with a carefully controlled amount of frustration, we set a dynamic process in motion.

Crises in Evolution, Crises in Care

It goes without saying that once a patient is admitted, he is taken over completely, although this does not imply that we indulge him. His relations with the home, his family, the world around him, are all the subject of an unbroken series of redefinitions through situations and relationships experienced in reality. On the whole, the evolution of our cases shows progressive low-key phases which are more often than not slow-moving and during which the most difficult problem for us and the most important one for the patients is to maintain our watchful alertness, interest, presence, and even confidence, although without imposing them in any way. This evolution does however also go through crises, which we feel to be inevitable and even fruitful, considering them as evolutionary crises which our patients had previously never been able to overcome. These crises are deep, dramatic and short-lived processes of expression and resolution of conflicts which are both internal and external, caused by the failure of the former defensive organization, involving some disorganization and definite anxiety and, if the crisis comes to a head, resulting in the installation of a new psychic functioning, better integrated and more autonomous internally as well as on the level of social and family transactions (the process of crisis, which is one of transformation and evolution, affects the functioning of the subject's personality, just as it affects the reciprocal relationships between the patient, his family, and the institution). The crisis is not only a conflictual outbreak but also a transformation of identity, and its emergence can only come about as a result of a previous forward-going evolution; this does not stop it from being accompanied by a resurgence of anxiety and disturbance. The worst, which must not be minimized, precedes and can conceal the best, which must not be ignored either; it is as though the subject takes a step backwards to get a better jump forward; with great distress he calls in question his defenses, his identifications, his mode of cathexis of himself and others. The caring staff is repelled, attacked, and rejected, while all the progress made seems to be demolished. Another possibility, which is not surprising, is that the parents on their part also act the crisis out, and sometimes they are the ones who show the warning signs.

Now if the crisis does not occur prematurely, if it is correctly handled, the patient emerges with greater strength and moves on to more autonomous positions which we then make every effort to consolidate. Every successful evolutionary crisis has an organizing quality. Itself the result of a less noticeable process leading up to it, it sets in motion a new process, which once gained is never lost. The patient's relations with the institution are redefined as though a layer of skin had been shed. (On several occasions, and even often enough for us to perceive a tendency inherent in the patients' unconscious needs, this "shedding" process which begins to germinate in our midst and matures in our care, breaks through amd materializes through the patient's voluntary withdrawal to a distance, or a brief period of hospitalization necessitated by his state at the time. Precisely because we do not have our own hospitalization facilities, any decisions of this kind, you may be sure, are very carefully weighed. This process reminds one of the ritual among so-called "primitive" societies whereby people move away from the tribe for a time to return with a new status.)

If the care is evaluated from a quantitative standpoint during the course of the crisis, it first of all follows an oscillating curve, then a tremendous increase followed by a stable decrease which translates directly the highest degree of psychic autonomy the patient finally attains. During the progressive phases, the main task falls to the caring staff, while the doctors' work consists of watching over the general orientation and holding the therapeutic course, but through the crisis phase the entire team is completely mobilized and the medical staff takes control. The most difficult challenge for the team here, and the most important one for the patient, is to recognize and support the process which sets in even before it becomes apparent.

Patients, their families, and sometimes even the caring staff dread these evolutionary crises and therefore try to stifle them. At the opposite end of the scale some therapists and staff members find them somehow satisfying and fabricate crises which are really their own and not the patient's. Finally, if the crisis is ignored, wrongly approached, misunderstood and erratically followed through, instead of terminating in progress, it will end with a breakdown in therapy, a defensive induration, retrograde stagnation, or repetitive pathological outbursts.

Phase and Crisis of Adaptation and Integration

These evolutive phases of long-term treatments remain to be settled. Following admission the patient goes through a fairly satisfactory phase; he feels relieved, welcome, he relaxes, and in short seems a lot better.

This improvement must not be underestimated, but it

does not last for long. The first crisis makes its appearance between the second and fourth month, and this is a crisis of integration. If the patient feels accepted by the caring group, has enjoyed some degree of narcissistic repair, and has begun to like the men and women who are taking care of him, he is again engulfed by anxiety. While he wants to become enclosed within the institution, he is afraid of becoming engulfed in it and resists drowning; the parents, no less than the patient, are afraid of losing him because he has come to love others. At the same time that the patient's symptoms reappear, he deploys his defensive strategy and injects it into the group. No doubt, he also feels the need to try the institution out, test its reactions, its power, and its limitations. We have had a few runaways and some suicide attempts during this period of upheaval, and one of our patients, on the decision of his parents, stopped treatment at that point. In the cases with a fortunate outcome, the crisis leads through to a more trusting mutual alliance between the patient (his parents), and the institution, a more accurate awareness of personal difficulties and a more solidly based therapeutic motivation. The subject has really entered the group, and his treatment has really started. During this time the parents have been getting to know the life in the home and are settling into the association; in favorable cases, after the initial relief, they have already overcome the frustration of feeling dispossessed by their sick offspring and understood that the treatment consists of a *collective* process, or even work.

Phase and Crisis of Separation

The second crisis area is entered with the process of the patient's leaving the home for the outside world, at which point there is a violent confrontation between his need to belong and his desire for autonomy; in other words, when he has one foot inside the institution and the other outside.

The patient's ambivalence is intensified and he clings to the home while at the same time rejecting it, imposes himself while trying to get himself thrown out, advances and reverses, improves and deteriorates. We have observed during this phase outbreaks of delusion or depression which have sometimes made temporary hospitalization necessary, and some patients have run back to their families who overprotect and reject them at the same time.

The stakes in this struggle are settling into independence and taking up regular work. Once the crisis is overcome the patient gains a greater degree of autonomy and stability, and becomes more active and less ambivalent and dependent. Parents are not always able to accept this change without difficulty and we have occasionally seen mothers suffer from depression at this stage.

In the less straightforward cases the crisis recurs again before coming to a head; or else it is finally resolved by a break from the home whose motivation is difficult to ascribe to either the parents or the patient himself. However, this separation is not necessarily a final one, and we have to bear in mind the possibility of having the patient return after a month or a year to get to the end of a path which he has to some extent kept on traveling along during his absence.

Terminal Phase and Crisis

Patients usually show a definite improvement following a well-prepared and well-managed crisis. However, as you know, he may have made interior progress while acquiring a new set of symptoms. The most common evolution is of the neurotic type, but in our view a character evolution of a slightly *perverse* type is no less frequent with schizophrenics (pessimism or inexperience might lead one to fear that after so much trouble all the patient has done is to go from Scylla to Charybdis. Special attention must be paid at this stage to parents, who are all too likely to feel that the game is lost.)

However, we know that with psychotics it is at the point when all seems to be lost that things are really getting started. The temporary character organization indicates the reestablishment of lasting cathexes and the uneasy reintegration of the pleasure principle in mental functioning.

The terminal phase of treatment covers three stages: preliminaries, elaboration, and consolidation. At a more advanced point in the evolution the main characteristics of the separation phase are reproduced. There is also often a crisis in this stage.

In long-term treatments, this terminal phase of the care is a specific dynamic process which is an integral part of the care itself, just as much as its initiation and development are; while it results from a therapeutic process, it is in turn a therapeutic process itself. This process of termination, or of "disenclaving" therefore starts before the patient is cured. Its aim, then, is not mental recovery—if we can really say what that means—but psychic autonomy.

We find two forms of termination, progressive and disruptive:

1. In its *progressive* form, the winding-up process occurs gradually in easy stages, with the three phases outlined above dovetailing so that the development is easy to anticipate and follow, and the caring team is able to detect the third phase, even though the patient often keeps some contacts at a distance.

2. In its *disruptive* form, termination is somewhat abrupt, the point of entry less easy to anticipate, its course more critical and its outcome less predictable; the first two stages are close together and the consolidation phase takes place out of sight. This really is a decisive crisis of autonomy. As it has already been shown,[2] many psychotics can only attain autonomy, after a certain amount of progress,

through a complete break whose internal movement is not altogether devoid of some projective leftovers.

The caring team is less able to cope with the disruptive form of termination than with its progressive form. The mourning is increased by narcissistic frustration. The parents are not unaffected by similar feelings either, although less clearly so; patients' fears are not solely a matter of unconscious fantasy. Here more than anywhere you see the importance of the deep reactions of the caring team whose economy of satisfaction must not rely too heavily on observed results. Our experiences and observations have convinced us that if the institutional team is ill-disposed and badly prepared for the termination of a patient's long-term care, the process is not only difficult, but becomes impossible, and this impossibility is seen in terms of sterile ruptures, unsuccessful departures, repeated returns, or interminable care.

We have often observed that patients get greater benefit out of care once it is over than while it was going on. The essential development is that the patient throws off the weight of the maternally enveloping power attributed to the institution, and this does not necessarily have to happen before our eyes as long as it does happen.

Results

The above attempt at systematization must not lead to the conclusion that patients all evolve at the same rate and in the same manner. In some slow-moving evolutions the variations are only slight, changes hardly noticeable, and the crises, which are very gentle, are more easily discernible a posteriori. The more stormy type of patient, on the other hand, goes through tremendous ups and downs, sudden jolts and sharp oscillations for a long time. Any nosological attribution is made all the more difficult by the fact that the same patient can quite easily slip from one type of evolution to the other. In any case, as far as those providing the care are concerned, we have to be ready for monotony one minute and the unexpected the next.

With regard to results, if we can talk of such for so small a number of cases (20), we have observed the following:

1. Three cases (15 percent) did not get beyond the initial phase;
2. Four treatments (20 percent) were stopped at the separation stage and resulted in one unfavorable outcome, one indifferent, one fairly satisfactory, and one quite good;
3. Four cases (20 percent) are still current and showing progress;
4. Four cases (20 percent) have successfully completed the separation phase;
5. Five cases (25 percent) have left the home entirely under satisfactory circumstances.

Of the patients who passed through the adaptation phase successfully and really followed treatment, two-thirds have today acquired advanced or total psychic and social autonomy.

FINAL REMARKS

Psychotherapies

Warm and consistent attention; reverberating reactions; meaningful acts; carefully dosed frustrations; open praise of anything which indicates the beginning of new functions and more mature positions in patients; these are the conditions essential for the subject to be able to regain or take in hand his personal psychic functioning and his own person. Interpretations are the exclusive concern of the field of psychotherapy.

Experience has shown us that psychotherapy is rarely necessary for psychotics from the outset, and that its opportuneness becomes apparent quite naturally in the course of care when the patient's psychic organization shows a space for a psychotherapeutic relationship, in other words, when the patient begins to have an existence and fantasies of his own.[2,11] This moment usually arrives during the course of one of the crises described above. In our present practice, psychotherapy begins and ends later than the treatment.

The complex dynamic relations between psychotherapy and the care have already been dealt with in other works[3,8] and we will not go into this here.

Families

With regard to the parents, apart from very specific individual cases, we avoid following a certain fashion and do not involve them in either acknowledged or undercover psychotherapeutic processes.

On the other hand, their responsible joint participation in the overall therapeutic undertaking through the association; their contacts with the patient via the mediation of the medical and caring staff, the team, and the group; their identification with the caring staff (which is done more readily than with the medical staff); the method of functioning with which they are associated; the information they are given; and finally, the effects of the group situation; all of these processes, which are sometimes controlled but more often spontaneous, very often help them to overcome their narcissistic demands and injuries and move into new positions without the necessity for risky and expensive psychotherapy. The most positive process we have observed and encouraged in families is the discovery of the *fathers*. [10]

The Dynamic Strategy of Relationships in Care

We still have to indicate how we, the staff, stand in the match which is played throughout a long-term cure in several episodes and on different levels.

It was shown that care seems to be sometimes in the hands of the group supported by the team, sometimes the caring staff backed by the medical staff, sometimes the doctors followed by the caring staff and the group. You saw that the intervention of the team can be massive and at close quarters or discreet to the point of apparent nonexistence. We have to accept that part of the game is played outside of our field of action; we are convinced that the caring organization has to be important to the patient simply because it exists.

This means that the relationship between the team and the patient is not easy to define. Do we go *ahead* of the patient and precede him mentally in his internal proceedings, we who unlike him are capable of imagining a future for him (not a clearly delineated future we impose upon him, but the *possibility* of a future)? Or do we walk *behind* the patient to follow and inform him, and let him get on with it by himself, encouraging every step he takes?

To precede or to follow? We cannot and must not choose between the two. They are always associated, even when one or the other is predominant. Looking at these evolutions from a distance, we see that we go ahead of the patients before we follow on, and that we follow them more and more discreetly until the moment of separation.

NOTES

REFERENCES

1. Diatkine, R. (1970), L'apport de la théorie psychanalytique à la compréhension des maladies mentales et éventuellement, à l'organisation d'institutions destinées à les traiter. In: *Le Psychanalyste sans Divan,* ed. P.-C. Racamier. Paris: Payot, pp. 15–42.

2. Kestemberg, E. (1958), Quelques considérations à propos de la fin du traitement des malades de structure psychotique. *Rev. fr. psychanal.,* 22(3):297–342.

3. Kestenberg, J. (1971), Propos sur le rôle d'un psychanalyste dans une institution psychiatrique (psychiatres et psychotiques aujourd'hui). *L'évolution psychiatrique,* 36(3):528–543.

4. Lebovici, S. (1970), Le Psychanalyste et la psychiatrie d'aujourd'hui. In: *Le Psychanalyste sans Divan,* pp. 43–53.

5. Racamier, P.-C. (1967), Le psychanalyste et l'institution. *L'evolution psychiatrique,* 1969, 34(3):525–558.

6. Racamier, P.-C. (1970), Présence de la psychanalyse dans les organismes psychiatriques. *Le Psychanalyste sans Divan,* Paris: Payot, pp. 54–74.

7. Racamier et al. (1970), *Le Psychanalyste sans Divan,* Paris: Payot, 424 pp. (cf. in particular: L'expérience institutionnelle, 3è partie).

8. Racamier, P.-C. (1970). Le soin institutionnel des psychotiques: nature et fonction. *L'information psychiatrique,* 46(8):745–761.

9. Racamier, P.-C. (1969), Perspectives actuelles sur les applications psychothérapiques et institutionnelles de la Psychanalyse au traitement restructurant des psychotiques. In: *Problématique de la Psychose,* ed. Laurin Doucet, II, 1971, pp. 387–399.

10. Racamier, P.-C. & Carretier, L. (1971), Les familles de psychotiques dans l'expérience institutionelle psychothérapique. *L'information psychiatrique,* 47(9):771–823.

11. Racamier, P.-C. (1971), Psychoses de toujours et psychiatres de maintenant (psychiatres et psychotiques aujourd'hui). *L'évolution psychiatrique,* 36(3):544–564.

12. Contribution by the Foyer thérapeutique "La Velotte" in Besançon, France, where P.-C. Racamier and L. Carretier are Head Physician and Joint Head Physician, respectively.

13. The concept of "soin," which is translated as "care," is particularly important to Racamier, and is therefore rendered as such in the translation each time the word appears in the French text. Similarly, the term "soignants," which refers to nursing and nonmedical staff, is translated by "caring staff," which suggests the specific role of actually taking care of the patient as opposed to providing psychotherapy proper or other therapeutic techniques. *(Editor's note.)*

Chapter 10

TEAM TREATMENT OF A PSYCHOTIC PATIENT[1]

Arthur Amyot, M.D., Pierre Doucet, M.D., Denise L'Ecuyer, I.L.P., and co-workers[2]

THE EXPERIENCE OF THE MEMBERS OF A CATCHMENT AREA TEAM WITH REGARD TO THE PRESENCE OF THE ANALYST IN THE CASE OF TREATMENT OF A PSYCHOTIC PATIENT[3]

The possibility of a catchment area team working together with an analyst in the treatment of a psychotic looked like an extremely interesting experiment which we endorsed very quickly.

We use the word "experiment" because at the Institute Albert-Prévost we have no analysts working with the catchment area teams or in close collaboration with any of them.

It is important to state that the Laval team was one selected by the analyst and Dr. Paumelle. There are several catchment area teams (for adults and children) at the Institute Prévost, and among them a number of possible candidates to carry out this experiment which everyone considered a very valuable one. We do not know why the

Laval team was selected, but the feeling among them was one of tremendous pride at being the chosen team.

The operation started off in the following way: the catchment area team proposed to the analyst (Dr. Doucet) the case histories of seven male and female patients among whom he was to select the patient he would accept for treatment. It should be noted that all the cases presented to the analyst were psychotic patients already known to the team and with whom the team's attempts at therapy had been unsuccessful.

The experiment was of such great interest to the Laval team, which had just been split up into two separate teams, that they rushed to submit their cases to the analyst. Which patient, male or female, would the analyst choose? The choice finally settled on a young girl patient (the analyst's choice) who had been followed for three years by one of the two Laval teams, and was now to become the responsibility of the other team.

The compromise, which was to develop into a deadlock a few months later, was for Aline (the patient) to be followed at the same time by members of each of the two teams, thus forming, what was in effect, a new team.

The patient's psychologist-therapist, who was leaving Quebec, was to be replaced by the analyst (Dr. Doucet), while the team doctor became her medical "administrator." The nurse and doctor of the original Laval team volunteered to see the family regularly. There was a state of ambiguity in the Laval teams right from the outset, and the experiment of an analyst's work within a single catchment area team was therefore distorted.

The Initial Stage of the Experiment

This encounter, the pairing of a catchment area team and an analyst was launched under the watchful eye of Dr. Paumelle. His presence among us was felt as a mediating element in case of differing viewpoints or conflict between the parties involved, or else at times as a catalyzing factor between these two parties.

With Aline as the analyst's choice, it seems important to give you a brief outline concerning this 22-year-old patient who was brought to the team through the mediation of her father in 1969. Her first period of hospitalization lasted four months, during which time she ran away from the Institute on several occasions. The team had very little cooperation from the family, for the father was himself disturbed—though unaware to all—a paranoiac. Once outside the Institute Aline refused to be followed up by the catchment area team and also refused to take any medication. We lost contact with Aline and her family; a so-called "hypnologist" got in the way of the new triangular relationship between Aline, her family, and the catchment area team. A few months later, in January of 1969, Aline's father once again asked for help from us and we had to hospitalize the young girl for a period of three months. The many differences Aline caused between the catchment area team caring staff and the intra-hospital team on the one hand, and the family on the other, finally brought about her total rejection by the hospital, and she was blacklisted by the Institute's Intensive Care Unit.

We shall not go into detail on the ins and outs of the patient's experience or the charades she conducted with the Institute nurses and the catchment area teams, as well as her own family, but simply emphasize the fact that this was a very difficult patient to treat; instead we shall bring out certain aspects of a negative countertransference.

In the midst of this context of therapy failure and the catchment area team's feeling of inability to get the patient out of her deadlock, the analyst appears on the scene.

The Team's Expectations of the Analyst

Rightly or wrongly, the analyst remained a somewhat mysterious character who was felt to have some kind of great power, derived from his use of the words, speech, and voice, for patients to reveal their innermost feelings and the hidden motives underlying their behavior.

How was the analyst going to behave and how far was he going to get involved in the case of Aline, who tended to put her conflicts into action, with run-away escapades and acting out?

Familiar as we are with the image of the analyst working with neurotics in his private consulting rooms, we were curious, perplexed, and attentive to see how the analyst worked without the couch, how he would function when faced with a psychotic. At last his secret, his magic, and even his difficulties were going to be revealed. Proposing Aline to the analyst was one way of testing him, of making his task more difficult, in other words a means of reminding him of the opacity of psychosis. But it was perhaps more than anything else giving him a patient who would force his hand and oblige him to work with us. It was rather as though the team had said to itself: "the analyst will not be able to do without us, he will not be able to shut himself up with Aline in his consulting room and work in camera, because the patient will certainly bring him right back to us by her way of acting." By introducing Aline to the analyst, the team was making sure that he would not ease them out of the picture.

On one hand, if Aline showed no improvement, we would be able to deflate the analyst; the difficulties encountered by him would make us less uncompromising with regard to our own limitations. If the analyst's therapy were to meet with failure, our state of confusion would be increased and we would have to ask ourselves if we should abandon ship in the face of psychosis.

On the other hand, if Aline showed marked progress, our admiration for the analyst could be maintained. The myth surrounding him might well be perpetuated, but at the same time we would find an invaluable ally in the battle against psychosis.

Materialization of the Experiment: the Course of the Experience

The initial phase got off to a very positive and almost gratifying start. The analyst got involved with the patient and let her know how he felt about her attitudes and statements. He moved out of the neutral position and intervened directly on different levels; for example, reading with Aline certain extracts from books which had attracted her attention, or buying her books which might interest her, or perhaps making coffee with her during the interviews, and so on. . . .

We had the impression that the analyst wanted to be accepted by the members of the team and that he was trying to present us with an image different from the one with which we were familiar.

Gradually, the members of the team began to feel that the analyst was somehow trying too hard, and that he was determined to be the "good guy." He gave us a distinct impression that we had to maintain our contact with Aline at all costs, the object and cause of so many differences.

We got the feeling that, confronted with the treatment of a psychotic, the psychoanalyst was groping for his therapeutic identity—with all due allowance for his traditional role oriented more toward the neurotic.

Referring to Recamier, the analyst told us that he wanted to step into the background for a while to let the team get a better control over the patient. We discerned his doubts as to the relevance of his therapeutic presence and saw even more clearly his difficulty in working as part of a team.

The problem of the specificity of each person's role became so acute, that eventually no one was sure of the roles played by everyone. There was a certain amount of overlapping for some time. The "day-off" doctor, as Aline called him, obtained interview material very similar to that brought by the analyst when we met. On his side, the analyst claimed that there was very little for him to add if the treating doctor, whose responsibility was supposed to be administrative, gave his summary of the material provided by Aline. The team often felt that the analyst's interventions were trespassing on the function or the role which should be carried out by the nurse of the treating doctor. These impressions, this interpretation on the part of team members reflect to a large extent two opposite wishes: firstly, to see the analyst become increasingly involved (with Aline, a psychotic) and secondly, to see him step beyond his traditional role. Paradoxically, any intervention set in what we might call a "nontraditional framework" produced negative reactions and criticism from the members of the team. Some members reacted by saying that "He's doing my job," or else "I don't know what I'm here for, I've got nothing new to contribute, the analyst has said all I had to say," and so forth. ... Could these remarks justify our thinking that the team's hopes and expectations, often contradictory with regard to the presence of the analyst, were merely the reflection of our profound ambivalence?

Although this ambivalence towards the analyst was quite definite at times, we can safely say that at other times our feelings were not influenced by it. On several occasions there was complete unanimity as to the disappointment of the team's expectations. One of the team's disappointments concerning the analyst lay in the fact that he simply

gave us a description of what Aline did and said. We found
that he went no further than appearances or the manifest
content of Aline's narratives. A particular clarification specific to the analyst, in the sense of an in-depth explanation,
a dynamic explanation of the latent material was not forthcoming, and this gave rise to a certain amount of frustration.

Finally, another disappointment with regard to the analyst was when he did give us an explanation at the point
where he feared he was loosing contact with Aline, and that
there might even be a break! We saw that on several occasions the analyst undertook interventions which were debatable as to their form, such as buying books for Aline,
going to fetch her at a restaurant after she had run away,
etc. . . . We were in deep disagreement not so much on the
many different types of intervention he considered necessary to make, but much more on the fact that they were
simply devices to keep a hold on Aline. Several times we
had the impression that the idea was not so much whether
such and such an intervention would have a greater therapeutic value for the patient as whether with such and such
a maneuver "*I* shan't lose the patient, *I* shall keep hold of
her, *I* shall avoid a break." Or perhaps even "*I* shall do
better than the others."

We developed from a team who felt itself powerless,
and left all the therapeutic effectiveness to the analyst, into
a team which gradually regained an awareness of its own
worth and was able to distinguish the weaknesses, the fail-
ings, and the deficiencies of the object of this ideal.

After a mutual exchange of feelings set between the
two "all-or-nothing" poles, we found ourselves inclined to
think that we should continue to work together and try to
avoid excluding each other, as Aline tried and still tries to
make us do.

Conclusion

Taking into account the very particular context of the experiment, the ambiguity of the teams involved, the reciprocal search for definition of the respective functions of team and analyst, we remain firmly convinced of the importance of the analyst's presence in a catchment area team. The specialized angles he can elucidate in the understanding and treatment of the psychotic seem to us necessary, and even indispensable at certain points. Even though such elucidation was not forthcoming during this particular experiment, this does not invalidate the possibility of the analyst's presence in the team being more positive and clearly defined as a really effective element, and not as a simple matter of circumstance, i.e., for a single well-identified case. His commitment and involvement would be exactly the same as that of the other members of the team, and in this way he would shed the marginal status which has too often and for too long been attributed to the analyst. Is it not time for him "to be integrated completely into the life of the team and for the team to work in complement to the analyst?"

NOTES

1. This chapter constitutes an introduction to a film made by the authors.

2. A. Amyot, psychiatrist, is the head of the Laval Community Psychiatry Service, and D. L'Ecuyer the team's psychiatric nurse. P. Doucet is the patient's psychoanalyst. The other colleagues are Maurice Leduc, M.D., Jean-Jacques Lussier, L.Ps. and Gérard Duceppe, t.s.p.

3. Written by A. Amyot, D. L'Ecuyer, and Co.

A Psychoanalyst's Countertransference Reactions To A Psychotic[1]

In their vocabulary of psychoanalysis Laplanche and Pontalis give the following definition of countertransference: "The sum of the analyst's unconscious reactions to the analysand as an individual, and more specifically to the latter's transference." In the experiment, that is the subject of this report, we have the presence of an analyst within a team of professional mental health specialists engaged in the long-term treatment of a psychotic. I propose to examine, using a wider application of the original definition, my reactions to the team and its members, and go on to show how these factors influenced my countertransference in the strict sense of the word. It is a well-known fact that the treatment of a psychotic is a severe trial for the analyst's countertransference, but I think that the trial is even more difficult when a team has to work with the psychoanalyst in a given case requiring this multidisciplinary treatment.

The Treatment

I propose to follow the course of my own countertransference over a period of a year. My feelings towards the team, which consisted of two ward nurses, a medical administrator, and a doctor and a nurse dealing with family therapy, were positive at the outset. These were all people I knew and with whom I worked at the Albert Prévost Institute. All of them were younger than myself and seemed to have the qualities I appreciate in younger people, i.e., well trained, sensitive, sociable, and enthusiastic. Naturally, I was aware of my position in relation to them as an older man with greater experience in many fields. This position of older brother is, in fact, the reality of my family situation and has always served me well, although this does not apply, of course, to my younger brothers and sisters. Another person was involved in this experiment who should be mentioned: Philippe Paumelle. To me he was and still remains an accepted father figure. Apart from some normal discussions concerning my education as a psychoanalyst of psychotics, I considered him as an interesting father. With his experience greater than mine, he could help me by listening to my difficulties and giving me diplomatically offered advice.

The honeymoon was soon over. There followed a long period of more than six months which can only be described as follows: almost continual alternation of periods when I felt that the team was helping me and times when I had the impression that the team was doing me more harm than good and was causing me a certain amount of annoyance. It is true that the patient contributed a great deal to this process through the very nature of her pathology, for she provoked friction and created interchangeable good and bad objects within our team. However, in order to back up my statements, let me give you some examples of the helpfulness and the obstacles I was aware of.

During the first year the patient presented the psychoanalyst with a somewhat negative transference, which obviously concealed a positive transference she felt to be dangerous. The team helped to improve the transference by praising my work in front of everyone. In addition, I was given a great amount of information on matters as varied as the patient's depressive, and even suicidal ideas, hospital activities, the course of the family therapy and data on the family in general, the methods of approach used with the patient (mediating objects), which I accepted and used liberally myself in initiating and improving my relations with Aline. I, who had always believed that I could and should manage alone, found this an extremely gratifying experience.

As for the obstacles: The sessions were to take place three times a week for a variable length of time, but as long as was possible for the two of us. There was no couch, for this was not acceptable to the patient, and the sessions were therefore held face to face at the hospital during the day. I am giving these details because they are important in the context of the difficult periods. Other members of the team were able and eager to do the same with Aline as I did; these were not the nurses, but the two doctors, who were students of psychoanalysis to boot. They frequently devoted as much time to the patient as I did, in order not only to deal with the sociobiological aspect of her treatment but also to collect psychotherapeutic material similar to that which I had obtained. Hence, elements such as feelings of hostility, particularly toward objects around the patient both in the hospital and in her family, the occasional ghost of a positive transference, the study of delusion, ego functions, all of which I perhaps studied in greater depth than the others, nonetheless often seemed to be the center of their preoccupations in sessions which, when all was said and done, bore considerable resemblance to my own. At this point I lost my superior role and on several occasions, under all kinds of pretexts, I explained that I wanted to drop out from the experiment, since the team was capable of taking complete charge of my patient on its own. I think that these times have come to an end now, or at least I see and feel about them differently, even if the situation reappears from time to time. It seems to me that at this stage of the long-term treatment I accept as necessary and even useful that matters should stand where they are. There is no doubt whatsoever, though, that I dream of the day when the patient moves away from the team for all practical purposes, is able to function outside, and can be given more orthodox psychoanalytical treatment. Then she will be able to come to my consulting room several times a week, lie on the couch and hand over her psychotic fantasies to me. I shall give skillful interpretations of this material and bring her through to recovery or at least to acceptable social functioning excluding any possibility of further psychotic crisis and falling into the hands of the team again.

Conclusion

Finally, I should like to give some details as to the influence of these countertransference reactions on my countertransference vis-à-vis the patient. At the beginning, my countertransference was very positive, but in the second period, where help and hindrance alternated, there was a change in the situation which can be summarized as follows: While countertransference to the team was positive and the team, as I saw it, was helping me, my countertransference to the patient was also positive and I was able to help Aline. On the other hand, however, when my reaction to the team was negative, my countertransference to the patient became negative, and we became bored and irritated with each other. I think that to do valid work with a patient like Aline, at least at the time when we took her for treatment, it is essential for the psychoanalyst to be supported by a multidisciplinary team. Even so, there are innumerable difficulties involved which cannot be solved without frequent meetings between all the treating personnel where, besides discussing the patient's evolution, a great deal of attention would be given to discussion of the feelings of each of the participants in order to facilitate a positive collective countertransference indispensable to the success of the undertaking. These meetings benefit greatly, especially at the beginning, from the presence of a multivalent expert in this kind of work, which our group was lucky enough to have in the participation of Philippe Paumelle.

NOTES

1.   Written by P. Doucet.

Chapter 11

INSTITUTION AND PSYCHOANALYSIS

Jean Kestenberg, M.D.

Let us accept that the various psychoanalytical concepts relating to the therapeutic handling of psychoses can be condensed into the well-known formula: to repair, to restore, and to initiate, i.e., to repair a deficit, to restore a process which has been blocked or inhibited in the course of the development of the personality, and to initiate a new process on the basis of this restoration. Then we can perhaps reach a clearer understanding and closer definition of the limits, differences, and complementarity of psychiatric and psychoanalytic intake, respectively.

Repairing a deficit is primarily the concern of the institution, the psychiatrist, and the caring team, and comes under the heading of psychiatric intake. The psychiatrist's position is dictated by the idea he forms of the current state of the patient's ego within the psychosis. The understanding of the psychotic regression determines the therapeutic conception and its handling; the intake must therefore emphasize tolerance of instinctual discharge and also stress the importance of its control. It has to be supported by certain rules which constitute a kind of charter governing the functioning of the institution, and which are clear and valid for everyone; the work has to be based on the understanding of the specificity of the functioning of the ego.

A psychiatrist following a patient must not only provide the latter with support from the institution, but must also have face to face talks with him at more or less regular intervals. The psychiatrist has to be able to become the superego, the parental, father or mother imago, according to the various points in the course of the psychotic process. This is not a matter of falling back upon a continually interpretative function, but of being able to provide the patient with a form of support which is essential to him at any given time. A psychiatrist who has been analyzed will probably carry out these functions more skilfully, with fewer apparent manifestations of countertransference than would a psychiatrist with no psychoanalytical training, although this is by no means always necessarily the case.

We feel that it is nonsensical to try at all costs to center an institution on psychoanalytical psychotherapy by handing over a few patients to a few psychotherapists if this aspect of psychiatric work, as we understand it, is neglected.

However, psychoanalytical intake should also be part of an institution's normal functioning for certain patients judged to be able to benefit from it, although it should nevertheless be borne in mind that this involves very lengthy treatments which are expensive, difficult, and often disappointing.

Initiation of a new process requires the cooperation of an experienced psychoanalyst with the support of the institution (relapses and need of mothering are frequent), but whose possibility of maintaining the specificity of his action and his theoretical field are unequivocally guaranteed.

Without psychiatric intake psychoanalytical intake is often useless. We have come across numerous instances of this in the exercise of psychoanalytical psychotherapy.

As far as the institution is concerned, we make no clearly defined distinction between the nurse, the social worker, the resident, and the treating psychiatrist, and consider them as a single unit which we call the "caring team." Here we are in no way trying to minimize the hierarchical element, which, in our view, is necessary for an institution to function, but I feel that in the care of a patient each one has his or her share of the responsibilities and their own individual task to carry out. To me there is no factor of hierarchical value between the work of the various people involved; they complement each other, and without this complementarity the cure of the psychotic is extremely problematical, if not impossible. The diversity of functions implies a diversity of approaches and actions which must be able to harmonize together in rearranging the psychotic's psychic organization, and this is where we feel that analytical theory and the analyst's inclusion in the functioning of the institution should be particularly fruitful. What he has to stress above all is precisely this coordination of the contribution of each person in his own capacity toward the reorganization of the psychotic's ego. He must thus enable each one to understand exactly what his or her function and way of functioning mean to the psychotic's reorganization on a new basis: the therapeutic objective of the team as a whole.

Of course, bringing a psychoanalyst into an institution by no means implies that this institution is "going psychoanalytical." Sometimes it is just the opposite. A very careful distinction should be made between the fact that an institution comprises a large number of pyschoanalysts, or even that all the doctors working there are psychoanalysts, and the fact of its being a psychoanalytical institution whose action is wholly directed towards psychoanalytical, interpretative handling.

Psychoanalytical doctrine should make it possible, in an institution ideally constituted by analysts, to make subtle differentiations in the various modes of intake and action necessary for a group of inhabitants in a catchment area—since we are dealing with area psychiatry—without continually falling back on interpretation and analysis, for the latter can only be usefully practiced within the clearly defined framework of psychoanalytical psychotherapy or psychoanalysis, which is reserved for the personal dialogue where a truly transferential experience can be achieved and handled. The presence of managing or part-time psychoanalysts in an institution should ensure the understanding of the patients' psychic organization and therefore permit the appropriate selection of the various types of action to be carried out in the institution. These types of action, once again, must not be confined to interpretation, for this limitation carries with it a constant danger of uncontrolled or abusive analysis, and psychotization.

Paradoxically, some institutions run by analysts and completely "psychoanalyzed" have ended up with a situation where overall psychotization has taken the place of the rigid defense against psychosis, but without this giving any access—with an evolutional potential—to the psychotics' specific ego organization to which the institutions' staff and organization have to respond.

There seems to have been some confusion between the transparent reading of the content of the patients' unconscious expressed in primary processes and the latent content of the manifest expression through conflicts, which means that the door is shut to the elaboration of the primary processes by secondary structuring processes.

If interpretative action has to be confined to precise and strictly observed limits in an institution whose therapists are all analysts, this should a fortiori be so in a place where analysts and nonanalysts, analyzed and nonanalyzed people (whether psychiatrists or other members of the caring team) have to work together, often under the difficult circumstances we know are inherent in a situation of this kind. The indiscriminate and inappropriate use of interpretative activity not only dilutes the effect of this action, renders it inadequate or even produces results opposite to those aimed at, but also inevitably encourages an increasingly dense hostility which can only damage the atmosphere of work in common and is at the same time a real betrayal of the analytic perspective.

In this way so-called "psychoanalytical institutions" can, in fact, become antipsychoanalytical, even though they consider themselves psychoanalytical by definition. The very action of the analyst, this clinical understanding of each case, should be a far more eloquent translation of the psychoanalytical thought than any interpretations that might arise.

I should point out here that in my view the psychoanalyst who works in an institution without being really involved in it, working there only on an irregular part-time basis and who is shut in his office, makes no fruitful contribution to the institution, or, I am sure, to his own knowledge.

Let us take the example of a psychoanalyst who works in an institution but does not have a hand in running it. What would I consider his function to be? First of all, I feel that it is not to psychoanalyze the staff or to train analysts there (when this kind of training is possible it takes place outside the institution and on the analyst's couch through a personal analysis), but that his function resides more than anything else in a teaching activity. I do not mean the teaching of psychoanalytical theory, for this would be of little value to the caring staff and other members of the team, and would also present the danger of facilitating psychoanalytical acting out or "wild" psychoanalysis. This teaching must above all be clinical, and must be addressed to the team in order to give it an understanding of what psychosis is to the psychoanalyst.

This may not be to the liking of some people who feel that the staff's contact with psychotics teaches them a great deal more than all the lessons and textbooks in the world, but experience has shown that this is not always the case. The staff members are given a theoretical psychiatric training whose value must not be underestimated, but it nonetheless seems that today the analytical theoretical concept and understanding of psychosis should be included in the institution, not with a view of turning the staff into analysts, but in order to put them right at the heart of the personality organization of psychotics, so that each individual is able to grasp the limitations as well as the importance and wealth of possibilities of his own particular function.

This should lead to an understanding of the role of the institution in this psychic organization, how it can be internalized—either as a superego or in the form of mothering which allows for regression, for example—and therefore of the psychotherapeutic value of the aggregate of the institutional gestures in their integration within the psychic organization of psychotics.

One possible form a psychoanalyst's teaching could take in an institution would be seminars for supervising psychotherapies in the strict sense, about which much has already been said; these would take place not only in the presence of the other psychotherapists but also with the participation of the team and even those who are not part of the team directly involved in the care of the patients in question, but belong to other teams. This way of presenting a psychotherapy is very helpful in understanding the modalities of interaction between the institution and the course of the psychotherapy, the integration of the experience of the former into the process of the latter, and also of the necessity of the institution. This is valid not only for us psychoanalysts but also for the caring staff themselves, who might sometimes be led to ask the naïve question: if all the patients were in psychotherapy, what need would there be for the institution or ourselves even, and should not the institution then be done away with? It may be a "naïve" question, but certain people have posed it with some success, as we know. Now in this type of work, as has already been said, the necessity of the institution has been demonstrated not only as constituting a superego, but also as a place for regression and mothering which is limited in time and space. I cannot emphasize too strongly the importance of this limitation in time and space, for despite the favorable evolution of thought over the past several years and the infiltration of psychoanalytical thinking into psychiatric institutions, the institution nonetheless tends to be seen as being in itself the objective of the therapeutic work carried out there. This can be manifested in various ways, but I found it essentially in its subtle incorporation into the caring staff's cathexis of patients. Such and such a "cathected" patient very easily becomes "so and so's patient," his or her own personal concern. Here the staff member takes possession of the patient to whom he has given a great deal, and through this very appropriation there is a "depersonification" of this same patient. Instead of an individual who has come into the institution, he becomes an object of satisfaction, disappointment, or exchange, used to contribute to the staff members' own satisfactory interior functioning and also to the good internal functioning of the institution, which thus becomes an end in itself. The patient's own individuality, his person, his discharge from the institution, are all lost from sight and relegated to a far distant horizon whose existence is vaguely registered but not really believed in. The more the staff identifies with the institution (although this is in some respects a very positive thing), the greater the danger of their trying to merge the

patient into an alloy with the institution. This may be satisfying in some ways, but it is prejudicial to the patient's own
person.

In my view the psychoanalyst's teaching should bring
out when and to what extent regression is necessary, how
and within what limits the patient should be an object of
cathexis—this cathexis must be of a kind which makes it
possible to accept the patient's desires for autonomy and
also to avoid taking these as so many more or less aggressive frustrations. I know we are touching here upon the
staff's personal organizations; we lay no claim to being able
in this way to change their unconscious fantasy life, but we
can help to make them face the patients' desires and the
value of these at given points in the course of their stay in
the institution. So we feel that with this kind of teaching we
can contribute to a new understanding of what psychotherapy and psychotic organization are, and substitute this
understanding for the previous "compromises" with
psychotics.

Hector Warnes, M.D.

REFLECTIONS ON PSYCHOSIS AND COMMUNITY INSTITUTIONS

I propose to put forward some reflections on psychosis and community institutions.

In line with Osmond, several hypotheses can be formulated as to the origin and perpetuation of insanity:

1. a medical model based on definition and diagnosis;
2. a moral model based on the concepts of responsibility, deviation and sin;
3. a psychodynamic model based on the theory of defense and regressive or progressive continuity between the neuroses and the psychoses;
4. a model of family interaction based on studies on distorted communication within the family which gives rise to illness in one of its members;
5. a model of conspiracy or plot in which a number

of individuals agree, even though it may be unconsciously, to exile or to scotomize someone in a total institution;

6. a social model which examines factors of isolation, anomia, stress, competition of different kinds, and cultural conflicts common to everyone, which indicate social dysfunction; and

7. a psychedelic model in which insanity is taken in its positive aspect of rupture, liberation, and boundary breaking, as a journey into the unknown and the possibility of renewal.

To deal first with the relationship between psychosis and the community institution, are the origin, the frequency, or the form of mental disorders influenced by any given society? What desires will be modified by this society, and which of them will remain unchanged? And finally, which of them will be resorbed by the social structures obtaining?

The psychiatrist attempts to discover the deficiencies in the social, psychological, or biological order whose removal would enable his patient to recover a lost plenitude. There is general agreement that in the world of alienation people are reduced to the level of objects, and that the human person is no more than a word leading to the psychological annihilation of the individual. The alienated conscious lives in a depleted universe, in an inhuman world where the quantitative aspect of existence overweighs its qualitative aspect to the detriment of the latter. Aspirations are dictated by greed and competition. People lose contact with their bodies and their own fate, the universe filled with things becomes a hostile, alien, and crushing world. According to Searles, behind the uncertainty as to their sexual role many psychotics hide doubts as to whether they are human beings or objects. The individual feels torn by conflicts between tendencies toward accumulation, the

objectification of existence and inclinations toward plea-
sure-seeking.

Social repression (the institutions used for domination
and social oppression) in Marcuse's sense of the term, gives
rise to alienation and a false consciousness of the world and
throws the relationship between man and his environment
out of gear.

In a given society, does the lack of sharing, compulsive
work, the accumulation of wealth, and the principle of non-
pleasure lead to an alienated and alienating life? Are the
onset, the evolution and repetition of paranoid reactions in
any way modified by such conditions? Does the world of
tools affect relationships between people? What are the
social situations and conditions favorable to the externalization and affirmation of positive factors, of personaliza-
tion and mental health? Can defenses be manipulated by
modifying social structures? I have the impression that the
schizophrenic has more difficulty in adjusting to a society
of abundance with a wide range of choice and alternatives
where the individual has to make his own decisions in order
to escape the ambiguity of the equivocal and the vague.

Schipper and Colageros talk of the swing in "ego"
defense in our society, where the predominant defense has
become a regression displayed by the phenomena of por-
nography, unisexuality, homosexuality, hippy-type behavior, and the increase of crime. It is highly likely that in a
society where regressive phenomena are institutionalized
and ritualized, they play a part in maintaining an equilibrium through phenomena of collective catharsis.

To be brief, let me quote Dr. Henri Ey: "Either the
concept of alienation (*Entfremdung*), borrowed from Karl
Marx and handled so complacently by philosophers and
sociologists, has as its objective the subjection of man by
capitalist society, and by virtue of its very generality reduces mental alienation (illness) to no more than a purely
social condition, psychiatry to a political ideology, and the

psychiatrist to a police function; or else, following the Hegelian standpoint (in fact taken up by Freud), alienation is a moment, a phase in the dialectical movement whereby man through the progress of his consciousness overcomes himself (*Aufhebung*) and becomes what he wants to be, and mental alienation (mental illness proper) is a pathological form of the ontogenesis of the person, psychiatry is the pathology of freedom, and the psychiatrist is a doctor whose aim is to free the mental patient of his suffering."

Society provides us with the vital space to develop our potential in, a space which can be experienced quite differently in Asia or in Europe. With this outlook, one wonders which is the space and setting most favorable to the schizophrenic's adjustment.

Philippe Koechlin

My paper may appear somewhat succinct and give the impression of too broad a demonstration guilty of overgeneralization concerning all psychotics and all institutions; but the space at my disposal is too short to allow for any elaboration on the subject. Its aim is to warn against excessive schematization of the roles handed out to members of a caring team, and against the possible tendency to give a particular person the responsibility of a role to play in the treatment of a patient and not that of a personalized relationship.

In his paper, "Psychoanalysis and Hospital Organisation"[1] D. Geahchan noted, in 1966, that in the institutional environment of the Hôpital Charcot, the analyst was able to act as an analyst integrated into the team even if he was not recognized in his capacity as analyst by the patient and even though, worse still, the analyst was sometimes seen as the distributor of the biological treatment and the nonanalyst psychiatrist as the psychotherapist.

So for the psychotic there is some confusion of the established roles. He will go to see the nurse when he needs some professional advice, the work therapist when he feels rejected by his family, the psychiatrist when he needs physical care, and so forth. We thus find ourselves in the midst of confusion, created by the psychotic who mixes up the various roles.

Society itself has managed to give each of us our role and prepare us for it, often through long years of study: the analyst deals with the unconscious, the psychiatrist with the biological field and the understanding of the psychopathological mechanisms, the nurse with day-to-day existence, the social worker with professional and family relationships, etc. This all seems clear, simple, established, reassuring us of our own capacities, or rather, of our own identity. But in actual practice we find ourselves dealing with a psychotic who confuses all our established roles and sets himself with admittedly unconscious spite to put each of us at a disadvantage in a field which may or may not be our own specialty, but which in any case puts our own identity in question. We simply have to be aware that it is not merely a matter of identity as character parts, but—and this is where the difficulty lies—of our identity as a person linked to the psychotic by ties completely different from that which forms a bond of reciprocity between one who gives orders and one who obeys, one who authorizes or gives permission and one who acts, or one who gives and the other who receives. Let it suffice to bear in mind that the request of the psychotic is simple only in appearance. Any number of requests can be concealed behind the patient's stereotyped demand to leave the open hospital, such as: show me you love me enough to refuse to be separated from me; show me your love is strong enough to fill my life outside of the structures in which you live or which you run; I can't accept your love and have to get away from it. . . . These are only a few propositions given as examples, and in each case the word love could just as well be replaced by the word hate. Nonetheless, they do get right to the heart of the problem of psychosis, i.e. a relationship is set up between the psychotic and his circle which goes well beyond the simple functional plane and holds an individual up to question at a more archaic, more vital level. If we compare neurotic and psychotic transference, we see that in the latter unconscious wishes are actualized on the objects contained within the therapeutic framework in a more intense and more immediate, as well as a more fickle way, but it can paradoxically be more constant, for this same cathexis can also remain unchanged as far as these same objects are concerned, sometimes after years of absence.

The preceding remarks on psychosis do not have the merit of being original, but before going on to the constitution of a caring team and what we call the "articulation of its members," I should like to bring these few points to mind again: the psychotic immediately and massively cathects the objects in his surroundings, according to his own unconscious wishes and regardless of the role attributed to each individual by the institution or his professional training, or even his usual field of action. Cathexis of the analyst is not necessarily particularly special; on the contrary, the affects most susceptible to mobilization in a therapeutic direction are often, in fact, turned toward some relatively uninfluential member of the team.[2] Some of these cathexes cannot be transposed from one subject to another, and the person who is their object has to be able to play his role even though he may not be a psychoanalyst—an extremely difficult role and one which is often unbearable, for it challenges the existence of the patient as well as that of the more or less improvised therapist.

Doucet, a psychoanalyst, told us that he had no hesitations about helping Aline to wash her clothes; on the other hand, it can also happen that nurses and even "servants" assume in the patient's unconscious a function which could almost be qualified as an analytical ear. Yet, I know perfectly well that Doucet and Amyot's team spent many hours in discussion trying to define the role of each individual and to coordinate them.

As we see, a certain theoretical approach on the one hand and clinical experience on the other, both seem to indicate that each one should be able to do anything and everything if this appears to be of use to the patient, whatever their professional capacities and qualification might be. As the omniscience of all psychiatric technicians is a totally utopian idea, we therefore find ourselves in a state of complete confusion, and one might wonder how anyone can get their bearings in a team where the psychoanalyst is also the nurse, psychologist, and social worker, and vice versa. And in this case how will the patient, for whom it is so absolutely vital to adjust himself, manage to get his bearings if we ourselves have difficulty in doing so? In fact, experience has shown just that—that the psychotic can sometimes find his own place far better than we can; for if we lose our way here, it is because we have difficulty in getting away from our sociocultural system of references whereas in his relationship with us the psychotic involves us as individuals. Whenever he can, he communicates not with people in character parts, but with individuals who, of course, have a parental value for him. When his condition improves he will be quite capable of classifying one person as the psychotherapist, the other as the psychologist, and someone else as the nurse, but this will indicate his ability to go beyond the purely interpersonal relationship; this often comes about with the establishment of obsessional defences which are of such well-known importance in the process of improvement in schizophrenia.

Who has not been beguiled by the thesis so cleverly presented by Racamier, where he defines two levels of action in the treatment of the psychotic:

1. The level of care carried out "at the level of processes which are conscious and preconscious" and which takes the form of compensating the ego, encouraging it, and guaranteeing its integrity; and

2. The level of psychotherapy proper, which is concerned with the unconscious process.

Of course, Racamier recognizes that the "care" is as much the concern of the psychoanalyst as that of the other mental health technicians, but the reverse is not similarly explicit. The conclusion could therefore be drawn that in Racamier's view there exists a dual privileged therapeutic relationship between the psychoanalyst and the patient, that can only develop favorably if the patient's ego is protected, supported, incited, and even put in question by the rest of the team; interdependence, the organic link between the members of a team, is built and structured in this way.

However satisfying this schema may be from the purely intellectual standpoint, in the light of all we know about psychosis its application requires that the patient should be capable of falling in with it and immediately setting up the appropriate relationship with each member of the team according to their particular specialty. This may be feasible for a psychotic who is still sufficiently adjusted to social life. However, clinical experience seems to indicate that the dual privileged relationship, when it does exist, does not necessarily start with the analyst but with the psychotic himself, and that it is not always with the analyst that the patient chooses to establish this relationship. Now the person who is thus cathected must be able to intervene, otherwise the advance is brought to a halt. The question arises as to whether, when the patient seems to accept the system proposed, he does not in fact see it as one which is imposed by us and seizes hold of it to work it into a new system of defense which, since it is experienced as imposed by the therapeutic set-up, is received and incorporated so strongly ("violently," Basaglia would say) that it is impossible to overcome it in a dynamic psychotherapeutic relationship.

Thus after trying to make a critical analysis of the concepts upheld by Racamier—an analysis which may be somewhat tendentious but which is based on our own experience —we find ourselves back where we started. In a psychiatric team the psychotic's cathexes will arise at different points, but each time it is with considerable and devouring intensity and apparently at random as to the person involved. Once again, everyone in the team should be completely versatile.

Obviously none of our theoretical or academic knowledge puts us in a position to respond to this demand on our own, for the register which encompasses the psychotic's problem is that of death, i.e., the relationship of fusion, of destruction. If alone in this, each one will react, depending on his personality or knowledge, by setting himself at a suitable distance or else with a certain fascination with madness or death. I tend to feel that, apart from a few exceptional individuals, no interlocutor of a psychotic is capable of responding on his own if he is, or becomes, aware of the entirety of the affects mobilized in his direction by the psychotic he is dealing with. It is quite striking to see the spectacular results obtained with schizophrenics by a good many "sorcerer's apprentices" (in whose ranks we used to be ourselves), young doctors or staff from every quarter who in all innocence were able to respond to the demand of the deeply entrenched schizophrenic. However, after the initial spectacular progress, everything ground to a halt when, once they were enclosed in the dual relationship, it became apparent that in reality the patient could not become the therapist and the therapist could not become the patient.

Matters developed in quite a different way when, instead of this dual situation continuing, other members of a team were able to intervene, at the same level of action.

This seems to have been the only way to break the vicious circle the dual, fusional relationship is dangerously likely to set up. I agree with Racamier that to the psychotic the level of action he defines as "Institutional care" is of capital importance to the extent that it is concerned with the ego, which has to be cared for at the same time as all the rest, but I should like to ask him if he knows of any way to silence the psychotic's unconscious with regard to those caring for him and to prevent the latter from responding to it?

He will certainly reply that these responses are not interpretations and that the nursing staff should be put on their guard against any tendency they may have to try playing the sorcerer's apprentice and making interpretations. My rejoinder would be that I am as much against this extremely dangerous mania for interpretation as he is, and that the role of the psychoanalyst, of which we have lost sight in the course of this exposition, will come back into its own at the point when he can give his technical directions by examining with the other members of the team the evolution of their relationship with the patient. Nevertheless, he will not have the entire monopoly of interpretation. Indeed, many of the staff's responses will inevitably have an interpretative value to the patient. For taking the preceding observations into account, these responses to the expression of the psychotic's unconscious can well possess two of the main qualities of interpretation, (1) they are set within the framework of transference; and (2) their aim is to make new associations possible. This means that they are genuine when they fulfil this function and inaccurate when they act as an obstacle to this process.

Like it or not, no staff member can help overstepping the bounds of purely institutional care, and his interventions can have extremely important repercussions at the level of the patient's unconscious, both positively and negatively. No amount of warning will prevent verbal or nonverbal interventions from having some interpretative connotation. It seems to me that for the analyst to fail to recognize this institutional reality is tantamount to depriving himself of a mainspring of his action, for, again, depending on his personality and knowledge, any nurse can play the role of therapist as well as a nursing role. He can also, despite—or because of—some would-be analytic knowledge, cause disaster; nonetheless, as Dr. Ping-Nie Pao has shown, on condition one knows how to handle it, an inaccurate interpretation often marks a further stage in the process of individuation of the psychotic.

In conclusion, I should like to bring to mind again the following points:

1. The intensity of the affects mobilized by psychosis absolutely requires that the treatment be carried out not by the psychotherapist alone, but by a team.

2. The role the psychotic makes us play in the course of his treatment is often not that which our professional qualifications were designed for.

3. It is impossible to establish a priori a set program for treatment of the psychotic assigning to a given member of the team the responsibility for a closely defined individual function.

4. The internal links within the team and its size should be such that, as far as his personal relationship with the psychotic is concerned, each member can take into consideration what is happening with the rest of the team and turn to good account any mistakes which may occur.

5. Like everyone else, I found completely incoherent the way Dr. Segal's patient was treated when he was simultaneously going through psychodrama, psychoanalysis, and yet other different types of psychotherapy. This shows an even more serious confusion than the fact of my centering this presentation on the patient rather than on the established role of the multidisciplinary team may have led you to think I was advocating.

Nonetheless, my last word on the subject will be to tell you that I am convinced it is possible to give effective long-term treatment to the psychotic by respecting the role confusion imposed by the patient, on condition that the team is one whose coherence lies in its being centered on the patient.

NOTES

1. Psychanalyse et Organisation Hospitalière. *L'Information Psychiatrique,* 1968, 44/1.

2. The psychotic's affects are often actualized upon someone with little training and little accustomed to word manipulation. This is all the more likely since the means of communication with him will be nonverbal and therefore better adapted to his archaic possibilities for relating to others.

Part III

EPIDEMIOLOGICAL AND TRANSCULTURAL STUDIES

INTRODUCTION

Although epidemiological studies are of unquestionable importance, they are difficult to carry out. Research workers must be used, for a single person can hardly be expected to cope with the administrative problems of a catchment area team and responsibility for the diagnosis and treatment of patients from this area and at the same time deal with the study of the general population, with all the necessary transcultural comparisons this entails. More often than not, we do not have these researchers at our disposal, and when we do get one, other difficulties arise. The clinical practitioner is entirely committed to his very subtle work which is based to a great extent on his personal insight; it is difficult for him to accept the necessity of working with precise definitions, objective criteria which though broad can reflect intrapersonal fidelity and interpersonal concordance. How does one go about making psychiatric investigations acceptable to people in a random sample taken from the general population? And so forth . . .

The 13th District Mental Health Association in Paris presents a sample of its attempts to record its therapeutic action in order to permit a valid discussion of the results on a statistical rather than a personal level, in an objective, not subjective fashion, and also to be able to determine the Association's policy with regard to its therapeutic work. It was possible to make some comparisons with patients hospitalized in the French public services, and we are shown how the length of hospitalization can be reduced through day-institution facilities that allow the patient to maintain his family and social life.

Hélènc Chaigneau's team worked in a totally different way, leaving aside epidemiological records and statistics and concentrating on the memories a caring team retains of patients. Can the psychotic, who lives in a state of internal discontinuity, reconstruct his unity and retrieve his feeling of continuity if the caring team's own composition and cathexes are such that its experience with the psychotic is one of discontinuity?

Pierre Vincent contributes the example of an effort, made in the context of Quebec's "quiet revolution," to fight chronic impairment and pry loose from the hospital patients who have become too well adapted to asylum life despite the limitations and even the mutilations it imposes. A home maintenance firm was set up to provide employment for patients, who then left the hospital. A few brief vignettes illustrate the results obtained.

Whether in France or in Africa, we see that whatever the different conceptions of madness may be, therapeutic possibilities depend on the support the patient can count on in his community, starting with his family. Henri Collomb also points out the danger of a situation of no return for the patient who is abandoned by traditional African medicine and turns to the white man with his drugs and his hospital.

H. B. M. Murphy indicates the part played by social

integration and the value systems of different societies or social groups in the chronic impairment of schizophrenics. The treatment of patients must take account of the conception of sickness and also the philosophy of life held by the patient and his family and circle of friends.

The study carried out by Christian Müller at the Lausanne Hôpital de Céry, in the Swiss canton of Vaud, leads to the conclusion that schizophrenic symptoms have a general tendency to improve with old age.

C. C.

STUDY OF THE PSYCHOTICS TREATED AT THE 13th DISTRICT MENTAL HEALTH CENTER (PARIS) DURING THE YEAR 1965

Claude Balier, M.D., Sylvie Faure-Dayant, M.D., Anne-Maire Bodenheimer, M.D., Eva Weil, M.A., and Philippe Meyer, M.A.[1]

To set about the study of the course of long-term treatment of psychotics, our first idea was to examine all the patients who had been under treatment for more than five years. With this approach, however, we would have lost sight of one essential aspect of the problem, a negative one, which was the study of the group of psychotics who ceased attendance at the Center. Our observations would thereby have lost their epidemiological value since they then related only to limited material selected on the basis of fidelity. We were lucky enough to have something which is unique in France —a population in the 13th District perfectly valid from the statistical angle since it was geographically defined—and decided to make use of this advantage and pick out an unselectively chosen sample from this population. So we decided to deal with a group comprising all the patients who were admitted for the first time in a given year. We chose 1965 because it is distant enough to enable us to go back over a sufficiently long period of six years but also recent enough for most institutions to have opened up their doors on one hand, and on the other hand for the group of patients remaining not to be too limited. It should be noted that the average stay at the Center is three years.

This group of psychotics will be taken firstly as a whole unit, and secondly in comparison with the group of discharged patients and that of patients still under treatment. This way, we shall try to identify the characteristics of prolonged treatment. In 1965 the Center admitted 98 patients diagnosed as psychotic according to INSERM[2] definitions. This group represented one fifth of the total number of patients (492) admitted that year, who were used as a reference population for the data studied. There is no catchment area in France similar to ours in its recruitment and which could have been used as an element of comparison.

GENERAL INFORMATION

The following data are taken from admission cards systematically filled out by the team at the beginning of treatment immediately after their examination of the patient.

In 1965, 98 psychotics were admitted which means that the first admission rate for psychosis at the Center was 98 per 160,000 inhabitants, or approximately six per ten thousand inhabitants. This is nearly twice the rate of first-time hospitalizations for psychosis in mental hospitals throughout France, which is of the order of three per ten thousand. Since half of our psychotics had only outpatient treatment, we can say that the number of patients treated with hospitalization or a stay in an institution corresponded to the rate of three per ten thousand for the whole of France. We had just as many severe cases as anywhere else,

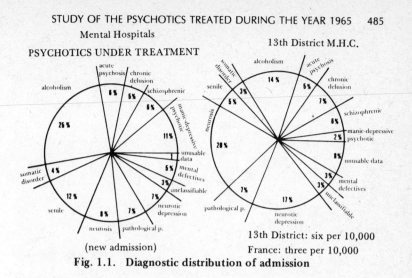

Mental Hospitals
PSYCHOTICS UNDER TREATMENT

13th District M.H.C.

13th District: six per 10,000
France: three per 10,000

(new admission)

Fig. 1.1. Diagnostic distribution of admission

but the treatment is different, more varied, and of shorter duration, and we complete it with outpatient treatment which reduces or obviates the necessity for hospitalization.

The ratio of men to women in our group was 40 to 60, whereas the ratio in the overall population in 1965 was 45 to 55.

Age distribution was roughly comparable between our group and the mental hospitals, with the exception of psychotics under 25 years of age, of whom there were fewer (no doubt they remained under the care of the Children's Center).

The *diagnostic distribution of admissions* is fairly similar to that of the mental hospitals, with the exception of the group of manic-depressive psychoses, which were less frequent in our sample (see Fig. 1.1).

With regard to the *marital status* of our patients, the main point to note is the size of the unmarried group, and men in particular (see Fig. 1.2).

We shall also indicate *professional distribution.* As we do not have the mental hospital figures, we compared our group with figures for the general population of the 13th District in Paris. Here, our group showed a lower rate of

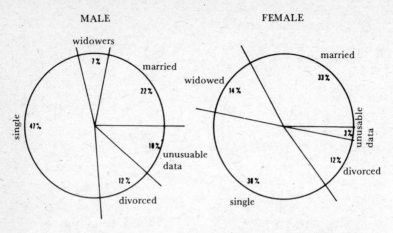

Fig. 1.2.   **Marital status of psychotics admitted to the 13th District M.H.C.**

senior and management executives, for men at least; as far as the nonworking population is concerned, the figures are much higher for our group because those given for the general population include children, who account for 20 percent, not represented in our own distribution. We therefore have 15 percent more inactive people than in the general population.

With regard to the *mode of admission in the 13th District,* this is much the same for psychotics as for other patients; the noticeable feature is the low rate of transfers from other hospitals, or patients sent for treatment by the administrative services. On the other hand, almost 30 percent of patients came of their own accord or on the initiative of their family or friends. What we mean by mode of admission, of course, is the establishment of records at the Center, whatever the means by which treatment is carried out (it need not necessarily be a matter of hospitalization or admission to an institution, but is more often a simple consultation).

The *admission prognosis* is favorable in 33 percent of the cases and unfavorable in 24 percent.

One final element we found important was *previous*

hospitalization at some earlier stage in the patient's history: Thirty-five of our 98 psychotics had never been hospitalized, while 59 had been hospitalized at least once before.

Now we shall take a look at our psychotics as "consumers" of therapy, or the number of days in hospitals (H) or institutions (I) necessary and the number of consultations they had (A). These team consultations grouped together consultations given by the nurse, the social worker, or the doctor (approximately one-third of the total number) as well as those given by the work adviser and the home nurse. We propose to take separately the specific treatments (B), i.e., individual or group psychotherapies and relaxation sessions, as well as supplementary treatment (E) consisting mainly of kinesitherapy and evening classes. Psychotics as a whole spend an average of 42 days in the hospital per year, which is a particularly low figure. There is no equivalent annual average given by mental hospital statistics, but it is worth noting that 35 percent of all patients admitted to these hospitals stay there for more than a year, in comparison with 1 percent of our group. This being said, the mental hospitals have no other alternative but to hospitalize the patient or to leave him in his family. Our low rate of hospitalization is largely due to the fact that we have the possibility of having a good number of our patients taken over by institutions. For this reason we felt it essential to give the exact average total number of days spent in the hospital and in different institutions, in order to be able to add up hospital and institution days and put together patients having had one or the other. To calculate a comprehensible average it seemed necessary to bring in the stabilizing factor of the institutions, which is of the order of 0.50, not including day hospital treatment which has a coefficient of 0.70, and foster families whose coefficient is 0.40. These coefficients give a rough idea of the volume of patients taken under care: hence, two days of institutions in our figures in actual fact represent four workshop days, for example. The annual average of the total of hospital plus institution days for the overall group of psychotics is 59 days per year.

We thought it would be interesting to complete this average with a study of the way the various consumers were distributed: for some 45 percent of all the psychotics, outpatient treatment (A or B) was sufficient, while about 30 percent had to be hospitalized and 25 percent spend some time in institutions. We shall go into detail as to the distribution of consumption in the two separate groups. There appears a difference in consumption according to diagnosis: the level is much higher for schizophrenics, in regard to both institutions and the hospital (70 and 104 days, respectively, on average), and lower in the case of the chronic psychoses (an average of between 40 and 51 days, respectively). The number of consultations and hospital or institution days is affected by many different factors, and is lower, with better results, for married people than for the unmarried; it increases with unfavorable admission prognoses, and finally, shows little variation according to age with psychotics, whereas it rises with age levels in neurotics.

An overall assessment of the therapeutic outcome was entered on a card filled in systematically after the patient's discharge or on a very detailed evaluation sheet if the patient is still here. Twenty-six percent of the cases showed a favorable outcome, 29 percent a fair outcome, with poor results in 11 percent of the group and none in 7 percent, while 1 percent deteriorated, and the other cases were impossible to assess. Apart from the influence of the length of stay, which we shall deal with later, we were able to determine the influence of the age factor. Results were better for psychotics over 45 years of age (the opposite is true in the case of neurotics); they are more satisfactory for married patients than for those who were single or divorced, and varied with diagnosis. More satisfactory results

Table 1.1. Psychotics, therapeutic outcome in relation to previous hospitalization

	Psychotics, not hospitalized	Psychotics, previous hospitalization	Nonpsychotics, not hospitalized	Nonpsychotics, previous hospitalization
Number	35	59	224	104
Outcome				
Good	26%	29%	24%	18%
Fair	31%	25%	22%	29%
Poor	6%	15%	13%	20%
No change	11%	5%	17%	12%
Deteriorated	—	2%	3%	2%
No response	26%	24%	24%	20%

were obtained with acute chronic psychoses, and particularly for schizophrenics, with the least favorable outcome; they were not affected by the occurrence of a period of hospitalization during their stay in the 13th District, in comparison with neurotics for whom hospitalization is often accompanied by bad therapeutic results. Previous hospitalization is not an adverse element in prognosis, but a change in the therapeutic program seems to be a preponderant factor. Any such modification does in fact very frequently appear to go hand in hand with bad therapeutic results, whatever the program may have been (whether or not hospitalization had been considered, for example). The same phenomenon reappears with nonpsychotic patients as well. Finally, we have attempted to summarize the factors which seemed to influence the results of treatment (see Tables 1.1 and 1.2).

Influence of Length of Stay on Treatment Modalities

Now let us look at how the length of stay influences the type of treatment given. Two populations can be considered here; patients discharged and those still under care at the Center.

Table 1.2.   **Distribution of subjects in percentages:**
Therapeutic outcome in relation to execution of the program

Results	Program followed	Program modified	No response
Psychotics			
Good—fair	38%	2%	60%
No change—deteriorated	7%	86%	7%
Neurotics			
Good—fair	56%	15%	29%
No change—deteriorated	9%	39%	52%

1. With regard to the general characteristics of these two populations, there seems to be a certain degree of continuity depending on diagnosis: the acute psychotics leave more quickly, while schizophrenics tend to stay longer.

2. The number of therapeutic interventions and hospital days rises as time goes on. After a fairly high rate during the first year (no doubt due to immediate hospitalization and transfers), they gradually increase and diversify as time goes on. The proportion of nonhospitalized patients decreases from an initial 50 percent to no more than 25 percent after six years, so much does the variety of consumption increase (see Figs. 1.3 and 1.4).

It is worth noting that when patients go to several institutions in the course of their stay, the overall time spent in these institutions is longer; variety is definitely linked with an increase in the length of stay. Patients who used more than one institution were also invariably hospitalized (see table). The number of team interventions is considerably higher when hospitalization or commitment to an institution are inevitable; the team does not reject a patient who turns out to be too difficult, but on the contrary, everyone's efforts are united in dealing with major cases.

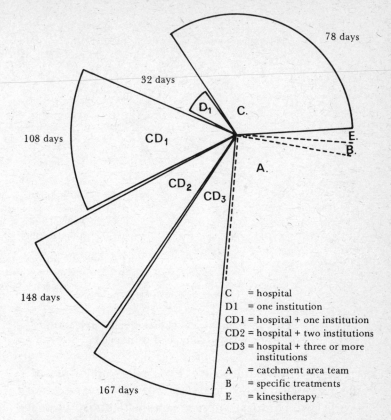

Fig. 1.3. Number of days per year in hospital and institution by psychotics

In contrast with other data which appear to show a regular course according to the length of time spent in the care of the Center, the therapeutic outcome is rather different for patients discharged and those who remain, namely, it is a good deal better for patients still under treatment, since more than 80 percent of psychotics show good and fairly good results. This divergence can perhaps be attributed to the difference in the establishment of the cards, for the evaluation card was filled in, not systematically, but

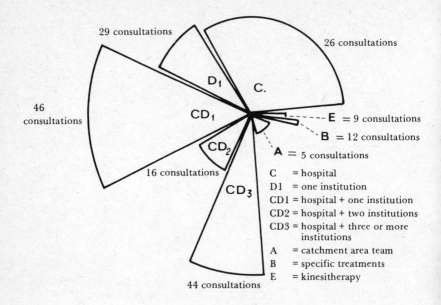

Fig. 1.4. Distribution of consumption by psychotics (in relation to type of treatment)

especially for the purpose of this paper and particularly for the examination of patients still with us at the Center. However, if we compare these results with those obtained in other types of diagnosis for patients still at the Center (neurotics, for example) we see that there is a great difference, that is, only psychotics show such good results. This difference is no doubt explained by the definition of the 13th District and its original project, which was to take psychotics for treatment on a long-term basis and using outpatient techniques to the greatest extent possible. These psychotics would have become chronic in other establishments.

It should therefore be no surprise to find that the teams seem pleased with the results of the treatment of psychotics while apparently less satisfied with the treatment of other patients. These results would appear to indicate that the 13th District has demonstrated the possibility of treating psychotics without lengthy hospitalization, and should now address itself to the problem of neurotics, whose treatment is perhaps not all it could be in a center primarily organized to deal with the treatment of psychotics (possibly due to the overburdensome nature of treatment requiring the attention of three different people?).

Given the fact that the 13th District favored treating patients on a long-term basis, it might be surprising that 60 percent of them should have been discharged in five years, and it therefore seemed useful to examine the circumstances under which these patients left the Center and the effect their leaving had upon the therapeutic outcome. The reason for leaving was noted on the discharge card: 16 percent withdrew from the Center because of relocation, although this is probably lower than the real figure, considering the major upheavals taking place in that district, and it is fairly sure that a certain percentage of withdrawals were due to the relocation without our having been informed of the fact. Thirteen percent of our psychotics were able to be discharged from the Center because of satisfactory improvement; but 40 percent of the patients broke completely with the Center and left or drifted away through consistent absenteeism. These *self-discharges* occurred throughout the whole period, and more or less evenly over the different years. They are accompanied by low incidence of hospitalization and stays in institutions. They are not specific to the psychoses (40 percent of the psychotics as opposed to 37 percent of the total number of patients). They were not invariably accompanied by bad results, although the outcome was naturally always more satisfactory for patients who were discharged because of their improvement. Self-discharges were no more frequent in any one of the various categories of prognosis, but, on the other hand, the prognosis for patients who left because of improvement had usually been a favorable one.

Conclusion

To review the main points of discussion:

1. There was definite success in demonstrating the possibility of uninterrupted treatment of psychotics with a minimum degree of hospitalization, thanks to the existence of a wide range of institutions which are used only with great discretion (fairly frequent but short stays). Remember that 25 percent of the psychotics managed to avoid being hospitalized in six years, and that the averages for hospitalization and stays in institutions are remarkably low, even including those for patients still in the care of the Center, and who, of course, represent the highest figure.

2. With regard to the continuity of treatment, there may be some surprise at the number of patients who left the Center and, in particular, the number of self-discharges. It should be pointed out that the latter do not necessarily represent therapeutic failures and may be for psychotic patients the only way to continue their improvement after a certain length of therapy. Nonetheless, in order to avoid this type of separation, perhaps we should seriously consider the advisability of reducing treatment to some extent so that patients can abandon it without thereby entering into open collision with the team's desire for continuity.

3. Finally, it emerges that although there is no correlation between hospitalization and therapeutic outcome, hospitalization by no means being an adverse factor as far as prognosis is concerned (providing it is calculated for at the outset), there does exist an extremely high correlation between the modification of the therapeutic program and the deterioration of outcome. Results are not affected by the prognosis on admission, and neither is the length of stay. There is therefore no rejection of patients with unfavorable prognoses, either in the actual carrying out of treatment or in the assessment of results.

We should, however, emphasize the fact that this study relates to a group too small for these results to have any formal value, and it should more than anything bring new questions to the fore. The "therapeutic outcome" factor, which is far too subjective and too general a concept, should be gone into in greater depth on the clinical level, which is the aim of the evaluation card tried out for purposes of this paper. From the objective standpoint, however, it is the subject of a sociological survey being carried out at present, which should provide a more subtly shaded background against which to set the notion of improvement.

The results of this study are further illustrated by Figs. 1.5–1.9 and Tables 1.3–1.6.

Table 1.3. Mode of discharge in relation to admission prognosis, percent

	Favorable	Unfavorable	Unspecified	No response
Total	33	24	34	9
Self-discharged	28	22	35	15
Recovered	60	6	27	7

Table 1.5. Days per year spent in hospital or institution by discharged patients

	Self-discharge	Recovery	Remaining
All patients	5	24	63
Psychotics	7	29	100

**Table 1.4.   Factors affecting results of
treatment of psychotics**

Diagnosis	Most satisfactory *Chronic delusion M.D.P. acute psychoses*	Least satisfactory *Schizophrenia*
Marital situation	Marriage	Single or broken marriage
Profession	Executives	None, manual workers, domestic
Age	Over 45	Under 45
Admission prognosis	Good	Poor undetermined
Duration of stay	Long	Short
Discharge	With medical approval	Self-discharge
Therapeutic program	Carried out, whatever the type	Not carried out, whatever the type

**Table 1.6.   Distribution of psychotics according to
duration of stay**

	Manic-depressive	Schizophrenic	Chronic depressive	Acute psychotic
Years				
1	3	3	6	2
2	2	3	5	8
3	3	1	5	2
4	2	4	1	2
5	—	3	2	4
6	1 (10%)	14 (50%)	14 (45%)	8 (30%)
Total	11	28	33	26
Average stay, days				
6-year patients				
Hospital	10	79	12	24
Hospital and institution	32	120	49	70
All patients				
Hospital	28	70	40	26
Hospital and institution	30	104	51	41

Key:

1 — senior industrial executives
2 — management executives
3 — junior executives

4 — salaried employees
5 — manual workers
6 — domestic personnel
7 — others
8 — inactive

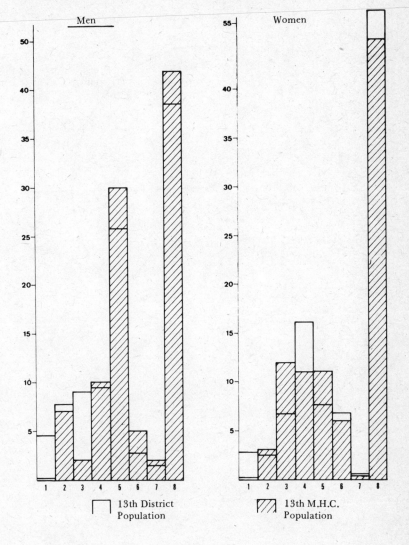

Fig. 1.5. Long-Term Treatment

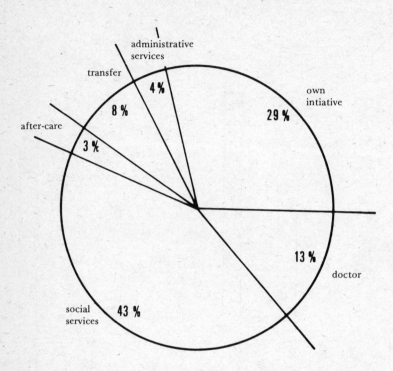

Fig. 1.6. Mode of admission for total 1965 cohort

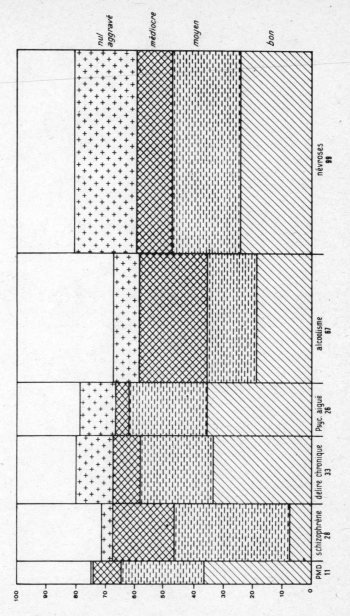

Fig. 1.7.   Therapeutic outcome to relation to diagnosis

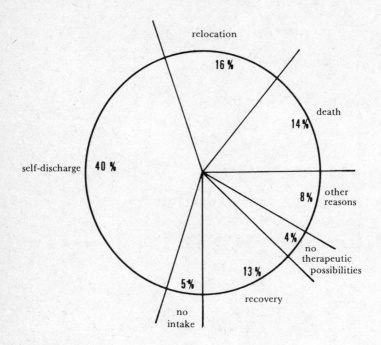

relocation

16 %

death

14 %

self-discharge   40 %

other
reasons

8 %

4 %

no
therapeutic
possibilities

13 %

recovery

5 %

no
intake

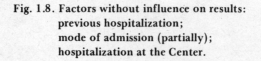

Fig. 1.8. Factors without influence on results:
          previous hospitalization;
          mode of admission (partially);
          hospitalization at the Center.

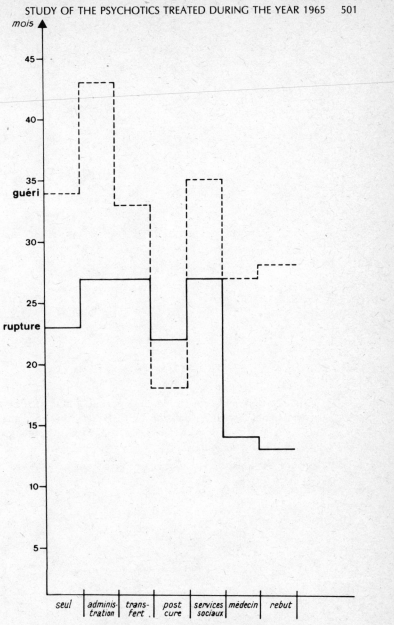

Fig. 1.9   Duration of stay of self-discharged patients in
relation to mode of admission (in months)

NOTES

1. Study carried out by the Research Department of the 13th District Mental Health Association by C. Balier, M.D., S. Faure-Dayant, M.D., A. Bodenheimer, M.D., E. Weil, psychologist, and P. Meyer, sociologist.

2. Institut National de la Santé et de la Recherche Médicale.

Claude Balier

Let me just briefly put forward a few clinical notes, reflections arising from a number of observations on the report given by the 13th District Research Team.

I do not think I am the only one to notice the high number of acute psychotics in comparison with the other categories diagnosed among the patients admitted in 1965, as well as in the group still under treatment after the six-year period (eight acute psychoses out of a total of 35 cases). However, these are quite obviously acute manifestations of disorganization appearing sporadically over long periods during which the psychosis remains dormant, which may be due to the fact that the patient continues to maintain a positive relationship with the 13th District organization, even though this is done at a distance.

This brings us to the fate of patients in their relationship with our therapeutic facilities.

The number of self-discharges on abandonment of treatment is paradoxically high, although this does not necessarily indicate poor therapeutic outcome. This reminds us very much of the process of which Dr. Segal has given such an enlightened description. It is a fact that we sometimes find patients in a painful state of depression just at the point where he is showing an improvement. The ego is too weak to cope with this depression and a relapse ensues shortly afterward; or else the patient avoids his therapist, and we have even seen that this can be taken so far as for the patient to leave the 13th District Center altogether. Perhaps it is just as well that it should be so since he has the freedom to do it; on the other hand he may only end up in another mental hospital.

This brings us to ask ourselves how patients experience the 13th District organization. We have found that either the "13th," in its entirety or one or another of the institutions are experienced as entities in themselves, with which the patient establishes a relationship.

In view of the multiplicity and variety of the institutions (about ten of them) and the youthfulness of the teams, we cannot give any guarantee as to the total mastery of the caring teams' therapeutic capacity.

The institution is sometimes unable to absorb or understand the patient's destructive drives, in which case it obviously represents his outwardly projected "bad object," and the patient starts a career consisting of using the greatest possible number of institutions by which he is invariably rejected. It is hardly surprising, then, that Sylvie Faure-Dayant's paper observes that modification of the therapeutic program, which in fact amounts to the absence of control over the patient's anxiety, is accompanied by unfavorable results.

In other cases, which are fortunately more and more frequent, the institution is able to avoid letting itself be destroyed by the patient's aggressive drives and can react with understanding (not tolerance) rather than rejection. A positive link is established; over the years the psychotic uses the institution of his own free will whenever he feels the need to do so. Treatment becomes progressively less difficult for the staff, and stays are of shorter duration. In cases of this kind the patient comes to the institution not to hide but for help. When he leaves, he does not have the feeling of a final departure, but keeps within himself what he acquired there, which is an impression of strength and serenity.

It would be overambitious to talk of internalization here; we can say, in a more modest vein, that this is a stage in the process of internalization for patients whose narcissistic capacities enable them to escape the permanent battle of megalomaniac omnipotence.

One might wonder about the situation of the catchment area team doctor, whose role it is to ensure the continuity of the treatment during and outside of periods spent in institutions. Paumelle speaks of "inside" and "outside" in relation to the institution. The "outside," of course, has nothing to do with the geographical situation of the catchment area doctor. But by making it easier, through analysis of his relationship with the institution, for the patient to become aware that he possesses within himself what he is looking for in the institution—a force capable of controlling his destructive drives—he is also making it easier for the patient to discover his own psychic reality.

Chapter 2

RECOLLECTIONS OF
A TEAM ABOUT
TWENTY PSYCHOTICS

Hélène Chaigneau, M.D.,
Dimitri Karavokyros, M.D., and
Guy Baillon, M.D.

This paper offers:

1. Reflections on a public-service team's study relating to the hospital and outpatient treatment of a number of psychotics.
2. Reflections on the possibility and necessity of multidisciplinary research work and its disadvantages.
3. A criticism of statistical inferences to the extent of their inadequacy for bringing out, through collective history, the articulated vicissitudes of the life of a psychotic.

The team was initially asked, through its chief physician, to participate in a symposium being organized by the 13th District team, and it was proposed that we should make a comparative study of a group of patients observed in 1962. This study was to provide material for comparison, a parallel undertaking using a common base.

This study, which included a number of different

parameters and was designed to obtain a considerable amount of statistical information, was submitted to our team as a starting element for research. At the same time it was suggested that the study should deal with 20 to 30 cases, and all adult psychotics taken for treatment during the same year, 1962.

The project was carried out, between October 1970 and June 1971, within the framework of activities at the Treatment and Social Readjustment Center of Neuilly-sur-Marne, which is a public psychiatric service for the treatment of male adults. The hospital service was situated in six detached buildings belonging to the Ville-Evrard Mental Hospital, while the nonhospital premises were scattered over the northeast of Paris and the adjacent suburban area. This vast territory covered a large catchment area of over 500,000 inhabitants. The team itself was hospital based, and only a few doctors and social workers also worked at the outpatient department or did home visits. When we tried to set up rules, a social worker pointed out that only very few of the patients to be followed by the outpatient department had been selected. At this level, whatever anyone might say, there are two different fields. The work of the team in question definitely had a hospital-oriented starting point based on its history, and it was decided from the beginning to orient the development of this research to fit in with the methods we wanted to adhere to.

First of all, the multidisciplinary character of the research team was emphasized, given the various professional elements which formed the treating teams. Doctors, nurses, psychologists, social workers, and as well as all the various categories of trainee personnel and medical students—resident and non resident—were all recruited for the task. To make this possible, it was decided that the research would be carried out in such a time and place that it would be integrated into normal work. This led to the choice of Monday mornings, which were devoted to a departmental meeting that had always been multidisciplinary and of high attendance throughout the history of the service.

Each Monday 30 minutes of the departmental meeting an hour and a half long were used to deal with the research. On each occasion the meeting was to study a single case, announced in advance by a group of four people comprised of an assistant doctor, a resident, a social worker, and a nurse.

On one Monday a month a synthesis was made, a kind of pause during which everyone had to give comments arising from the sessions where the cases were dealt with. To ensure the best possible degree of participation from the nonhospital team members, this session was held in one of the offices of the outpatient department at Pré Saint-Gervais.

It was very soon decided not to use this plan which had been proposed to us, and not even to attempt to constitute one at all. A decision emerged to let each participant comment freely on the case under consideration. Each time the record was made available to participants, who treated it from a number of different angles. Some summaries were made and several sessions were tape recorded.

In this way 21 cases were dealt with in 25 to 30 sessions which had very varied attendance of participants between eight and 30, with a normal attendance of about 20.

There was a break of several months between the end of the research in June 1971 and the time when the work was taken up again by the three authors of this paper. It would be useful to bear in mind that during this lapse of time the team was completely reshaped as a consequence of administrative decisions and appointments which had resulted in the departure of the doctors and the team being split up into several different services.

From all these working sessions a certain number of reflections emerged, and we tried to put them together as a contribution to the Symposium on Long-term Treatments of Psychotic States.

First of all the difficulties of working as a team seemed enormous, as it turned out to be impossible to draw any common conclusion from the sum of general comment, and the doctors took over responsibility and credit for the overall results of the team work. With regard to the method itself, which consisted mainly of reviews drawing upon the service's memory as it were, we felt it might be interesting to give some details on the aspect of research which perhaps hardly conforms to statistical custom.

Several notions, which are in fact deeply inherent in any consideration of the treatment of psychotics, should be emphasized or recalled: reflections on the public service, the continuity of treatment, what elements should contribute to establishing a basis for team work, the chronological aspect of evolution with regard to the moments when the patient is accepted for treatment, when relapses occur, and so on.

This will, therefore, be mainly a series of reflections, without figures or elements of objective inquiry other than the initial data setting out the framework of our research.

Through the method chosen to review the case and permit the assessment of the key elements in long-term evolution, it emerged during the course of our work that the presence of the greatest possible number of people who had known the patient was most valuable. The resulting general discussion drew out recollected elements which were then assembled, and the fragmentary memories lodged, as it were, in the various people dealing with the treatment, were gathered from these trustees of scraps of the patient's history, or at least, scraps of his life relating to his transit via the institution. In this way, our method seemed far more relevant to real life than a record study, which can only give a partial view of the biographical segment under consideration.

In this way the recollection and reference to the patient took shape through the network of relations within the service. By both continuity and proximity, by reference to the chief physician, an assistant, a resident, a nurse, or a social worker, we were able to reconstitute what happened at a given moment, between such and such a person and the patient, with the patient remaining the focal point of this network of converging memories.

Information had to be assembled. A priori, as much information had to be gathered as possible, an exhaustive collection, information of every kind. First of all we thought of written information of every type, but also oral information from the service and the outpatient department, and gradually we began to think of all the other people who could provide information, such as the family, neighbors, and finally the patient himself. Ideally, this should supply a vast quantity of data, although in actual fact it was hopelessly incomplete, either because of the poor quality of the notes or because we were unable to contact the people we thought of, and we became aware that the more we gathered the more was lacking.

What was to be done in the face of this difficulty? We could establish a pattern; but patterns seemed to us from the start an open door to arbitrariness. However, this procedure immediately led us to something essential, which was the search for its significance, for we discovered that the choice of elements making up the patterns can and have to be interpreted and this interpretation brought the team itself into direct question. Why did it make this particular choice, why did it function in this way, what is this team, who works in it, since when, why does it change; people come and go—why? What is the team's objective, what is the aim of each of its members? . . . None of these questions could be avoided, and general or abstract answers—in other words, impersonal ones—cannot remove the personal reply of each individual. But if the establishment of a pattern reveals the unconscious of the members of a team, can it have the same effect as far as the psychotic is concerned?

Certainly not, we feel inclined to answer; the psychotic had no hand in setting up the pattern, even if he is trapped within it. However, we have to remember that the psychotic was the cause for the pattern, simply because everything about him says"I am a psychotic." Furthermore, the mere study of the "therapeutic contacts" shown by a pattern (the number of hospitalizations, consultations, treatments, their rhythm, etc.) is significant of *his* psychosis.

Thus we found ourselves involved in a search for meaning, the meaning of psychosis, what it means to the psychotic Mr., Mrs., or Miss. So and So. Of course, we had neither the financial means nor the energy to gather this kind of information. There you have some of the reasons why we were relieved not to be using the pattern.

What really was our working hypothesis? Frankly speaking, research on "the long-term treatments of psychotic states" immediately seemed to us to have financial repercussions. In our view, the heading could have been subtitled: "What does a psychotic cost the country?" We were reticent here. Not that we were by any means indifferent to the penury and poverty of our services and our future catchment areas. It seemed both useful and necessary to take steps to obtain financial support, because nursing staff and premises for treatment were totally indispensable. There was no pretense at disinterest. This was a subject for vehement discussion with public opinion and public authorities. Not here, for among ourselves we can do nothing but observe that poverty and the struggle against it add nothing to our knowledge of the psychotic, but clearly madness cannot be reduced to that; madness is the breaking of relations between the insane and the sane.

Therefore we wanted to keep before us the fundamental question: "What about psychosis?"

Since the desire to obtain money to enable us to work better was no longer a working hypothesis, we asked ourselves: "What exactly are we doing?" One of us, a social worker, came up with a new hypothesis: "In fact, what really interests us and what we really have to say is not so much what we have done as what we remember having done."

Thus recollection entered into the life of the service once a week for eight months, and was sometimes noted down.

But why recollection?

Perhaps because this kind of effort was partly our way of working in the service?

Perhaps because it was the only way to reproduce ourselves and put ourselves back on the stage?

This is, in fact, what we accomplished together by discussing about 20 psychotics; talking of one and then another, we repeated ourselves as we spoke about them—the only way to understand what we were attempting to do when we tried to give a response to the psychotic before us. In this way we discovered how truly empty were some of the records until then considered "complete." This emptiness was glaringly apparent when no one had been marked at all by any encounter with the patient. Some case studies were skipped over for this reason; on the other hand, often, the work became valuable when a team member spoke of such an encounter; from that moment on a history emerged, formed by the encounter between a psychotic with his history and a team from a service with its history. From this starting point words like "continuity," and "availability" came on the scene in their full reality.

This all leads us to the rather obvious statement that there can be no recollection without the existence of a history, although research has shown that the statement is not quite as self-evident as it might appear, and that when we are talking about a psychotic the feeling is precisely that his history is lost and forgotten. It is essential that it should be rediscovered, but by whom is it transmitted? What are the conditions necessary?

Does not a real elaboration occur at this point? Indeed, only this discovery makes it possible to give any real assurance through the understanding which is the true promise of availability. This history can therefore only be discovered if "time" takes a hand, the time covered by the duration of a stay, the time of a relapse, moving time, and only if the history is put into words.

In other words, only if this history is experienced by the speaker and reconstituted by him still alive, interpretable and narrated to others who have not experienced it. All of this is possible only in the context of continuity of a service able to count on the continued presence of certain members of the team—the chief physician, nurses, and others—but to ensure its richness this continuity needs the complementary brief passage of young people in training, residents, nurses, and others, who "break" routines. There seems a curious contrast between this effort to go back to a continuity closely linked to a history and the fact of using to this end memory, whose very function seems to necessitate discontinuity.

The records played an instigating role in all this. Prodding the memory of those who had known the patient, sometimes provoking pure repetition, sometimes also giving rise to a discovery on the part of those who thought they had known all the facts, sometimes this time and place devoted to the effort or recollection actually seemed a possible place and time for elaboration.

But what kind of elaboration? Bringing up to date something implicit in our relations with the psychotic, an interest aroused in each of the psychotics we discussed, an interest which went beyond wondering what had become of this or that psychotic lost from sight, but an interest due to the fact that a number of questions were again brought to the fore, and to which only the psychotic himself could possibly give the answers.

This was also linked to the grief we felt for something experienced with him; it then appeared that this grief was a condition necessary for something new to be able to happen if the patient were ever to come to us again, seeing that we were preparing ourselves so that this new encounter would not be simply the "repetition" of a relationship, but a repetition with something added to it.

Some more explicit remarks about the team itself. A new light was shed on the functioning of team members: we compared the team at the time (1962 or 1964 or. . . .) with the present team. It was the same (no change of management or on the whole in the nursing staff) and yet quite different. Which brings us back to the notion of continuity. It came as a surprise to talk about psychotics with whom we no longer seemed to be in the same relationship of involvement as usual, as though an emotional factor had been eliminated and defused (to be replaced by another, but only related to the fact of talking to the present team).

The functioning of the present team came in to question. Of course the medical psychiatrist still talked about diagnosis and treatment, the nurse of everyday life in the service, the instructor about activity within the hospital, and the social worker about the boss, the family, the return to work. However, at the same time the individuality of the relationship which each one had established became apparent and became very distinct from the hierarchical function of each individual. What, then, is the significance of hierarchy, function, and role for each one and for the psychotic? There ensued a considerable amount of reflection as to the "breaks" between the patient and ourselves, in other words, concerning the interruption of contacts.

Here we will discuss the distance introduced by the psychotic, and how we deal with the distance he sets. It is certain that this again has to do with the continuity of a history. But what becomes of this continuity when the break occurs? There is still the continuity of availability. Here there intervenes a whole range of possible relationships, consisting of subtle shadings which the psychotic uses and manipulates, on condition that he does not feel that his future is already part of some kind of project on our part.

One young patient was hospitalized several times in the service because of psychotic outbursts of the paranoid reaction type. The first of these dated back to 1962. We were able to identify when he had been treated in the service and given relatively little attention in aftercure. An attempt to clarify the discontinuity of this patient's treatment by the notion of a possible choice of service by the patient gave interesting results. Each termination of a treatment series, which were at first occasionally taken for breaking off contact, should be interpreted as the subject's modulation of his distance in relation to the request for treatment. Each one of these instances corresponded to a solution of his difficulties at various levels and also to a choice and a further degree of autonomy. The distance set could be so far removed that the patient no longer came to his consultations. We knew to expect him back with the onset of the next critical period, in the widest sense of the term.

The service was able to accept him when he needed it, and for the first time this happened during a disastrous delusional experience. The ties he seemed to have formed were rooted in the very principle of the public service, where the staff are always available. He was therefore able to return and be taken under the care of the people who had treated him before, at a point where he himself was incapable of speech. It is significant that at the sole request of the family, for reasons of convenience and particularly because of boarding problems, the final hospitalization was terminated by the patient being sent to a private clinic. The patient opened and read the service resident's letter to his colleague at the clinic, which gave a description and diagnosis of the disorders involved. He was not admitted; in fact, he refused to go there and came instead to the catchment area outpatient department where one of us continued the treatment on an outpatient basis.

The notion of continuity of treatment, which is the theoretical and practical basis of catchment area policy in public service psychiatry, must, it seems, leave some indispensable margin for the possible discontinuity of treatment. In fact, the real underlying continuity of the public service is the continuity of the treating team's availability to the patient.

There remains yet another notion to be clarified, which is the fact that continuity of treatment does not mean that arrangements have to be forever the same. This remark has to transcend the obvious point that the asylum is the very archetype of the unchanging arrangement. Beyond all this, there has to be vigilance in the up-to-date organization of psychiatric equipment up to and including the direction of catchment area policy. Here we come back to Bonnafé's remark that the paraphrenic asylum is already being replaced by modern schizophrenia-inducing structures. The dispersion and fragmentation of treatment arrangements constitute a danger which has to be guarded against, most particularly when an organizational outlook, carried along by the current towards technocracy, leads right into the trap of an organization in which permanency of arrangements—and especially if this involves dispersion and fragmentation—replaces the notion of continuity of treatment and availability. A fair amount of justified criticism is already emerging concerning the neo-alienating catchment area, which freezes arrangements into permanent structures under the pretext of ensuring continuity of treatment.

The important thing, then, is that the psychotic can always find us there. In this way he decides how to manage his own distance in relation to all the therapeutic objects, and not only to the doctor. He comes to see the doctor and he himself, after all, sees whether or not he is going to use the therapeutic object constituted by hospitalization, for example.

In this respect, the following hypothesis could be proposed: the mental hospital contains overall more psychic reality than any other place, although in our view this hypothesis has weight only if it involves the notion of the quantity of energy concentrated in this psychic reality.

This can enable psychotics, and schizophrenics in particular, to experience a certain degree of happiness. Here we mean the narcissistic rapture which cannot take place without inevitably provoking the narcissism of others, whether these others are acknowledged psychotics or recognized as nursing staff, and therefore supposed not to be psychotic.

To our mind the upholders of institutional psychotherapy are those who take account of the extraordinary amount of institutional psychic reality. Without considering themselves sheltered from it and permanently outside the circuit it imposes and without, at the other end of the scale, yielding to the psychotic spell they "share" the psychic reality of the schizophrenic trip, eliminating the differences which give the schizophrenic experience its own dynamics. For this "sharing" is an illusion, if not pure fraud. Indeed, what seems to us to belong to the common good of psychic reality is simply the quantity of energy. But with regard to the person of the schizophrenic, what makes him an original individual is the manner of dialectalization of the relationship between psychic reality and actual reality.

Can we clarify some concepts concerning material reality, still within the overall picture of institutional psychotherapy?

Can the reference to material reality be aggregated—

even if more or less artificially—in the same way as psychic reality, and conceived in terms of quantity of energy? We feel that this way of looking at it could summarize quite well the fantasy of those dispensing treatment, that is, the domination of material reality could confer a certain therapeutic mastery.

Here we come to what is introduced under the term of "schizophrenic message," i.e., that whatever the authority and import of the material reality involved, this reality is immediately subjected to fantasy and the fantasy woven into a chain where the treating objects are closely intertwined with the subjects being treated.

A resident with a certain bearing established a house rule and made it respected by a schizophrenic who also had his bearing. The schizophrenic noticed a small label on the resident's car indicating the garage where it had been bought at X . . . He left both the hospital and his apragmatism at the same time, and went to work in X . . . at the garage in question. But through this intermediary he renewed acquaintance in X . . . with some people who had once known his family. He was going back toward his own family, under the impetus set off by a label. This interwoven network gives an idea of what is quite simply the vital importance for a schizophrenic to live literally as he feels best. Under the care of a team, tangled networks of this kind are extremely complicated. Transference relations are set up among the treating subjects, and this transference is nonschizophrenic. Putting into force a well known ruling, a codification of certain acts, the staff-patient pattern can bring out signs which, when referred to a common good, permit a so-called "institutional analysis" which will reappear in other terms, neither spoken nor interpreted, at the level of transference—again nonpsychotic (among treating staff). It seems justifiable to make the supposition that when these transferences are left alone they attempt, through a latent process of recovery and maturation, to replace the infinitely weighty burden of narcissistic imperialism. However, this narcissistic imperialism is not to be eliminated at such little cost, and it would be a good thing to demonstrate this by making it apparent that only the liberation of the energy of the schizophrenic fantasy so as to permit negotiations with material reality—negotiations which take place at the symbolic level (the label)—only this liberation can have any dynamic significance in the schizophrenic originality, which is a life originality; in other words, an originality which could only lead to death if it tried to come about without the multiple mediations traced by the dialectics of fantasy, symbol, and realities.

As for the results of our research, we shall deal with these at length.

The initial result appears to be one of failure with regard to the "accumulated material", which was at first unusable and scanty, and a failure in respect to the starting hypothesis which was that this research was to be carried out and then assembled by the service as a whole.

What were the reasons for this failure? We did not pay the price of research. What happened was that we wanted it to be completely integrated into the work of the service, it was to be carried out with the possibility (above all not the obligation) for everyone to participate. We thought that there would be a sufficiently wide range of motivations for everybody to join in, and wanted there to be no obstacle to participation whatsoever (we wanted everyone to wish to participate). It was rather as though we wanted to try to find here, through a research project handed to us out of the blue by the 13th District, something we had always wanted to discover, a kind of complicity or connivance, the sign of a concordance never brought to light and which Dr. Chaigneau had once called a "common good," something we held in common, durable and solid.

Could this not be the fantasy of a group constituting the fulfilment of the chief physician's own desires?

To go back to the price we did not pay: we did in fact want this research to cost us nothing (in the figurative sense). In this respect, it is quite true that even at the beginning we never talked about money (in the proper sense) for this research, which was financed by no one. A strange return of the repressed, which was already heralded by our reticence towards work on psychosis, whose sole aim would have been to persuade the authorities to allocate more funds for our treatment premises and the team. Paying the price was not only a matter of stating "it is possible," but also of arranging things so that it would be feasible in reality.

We did in fact find ourselves virtually immobilized inasmuch as by organizing this research we tried to pursue different objectives at no extra cost, namely, to make no change in the treatment of patients while interesting those taking care of them.

Perhaps we reached this state of confusion because we had more or less explicitly decided that this research would be integrated into the normal life of the service. What is meant by integrated research?

Let us first take a look at what is meant by integrated teaching. First of all it involves recognition of the necessity for teaching as an aim apart (the teaching of future practitioners is a priori an objective quite distinct from the care of patients). Here two opposite-oriented observations arise: firstly, that the practitioner can only acquire his practice with the patient, and secondly, that it is quite out of the question that the patient should be an object for use in teaching. At the same time, it seems obvious that the teaching effort could contribute a certain amount of enlightenment useful directly to the patient. Afterward, an activity based on a mutually enriching dialectical process between treatment and teaching is set in motion.

To get back to the research in question, we think that as far as the service was concerned, "research," unlike teaching, had not yet acquired autonomy status, or, in other words, was not so far an activity of a necessary kind in the way teaching is. And yet we approached the undertaking as though we were dealing with integrated research —integrated into the life of the service in the same way as Dr. Chaigneau's teaching is with residents preparing examinations, without paying the price, either, even though she has devoted her Thursday afternoons in the service to teaching for the last 20 years. There was no specific time allocated for the research. This is, of course, in line with the normal way the service functions. Decision making in this service was disconcerting at first sight, for problems of treatment and nursing were dealt with at meetings, but no decision was taken on them although the meeting was objectively the reference point for each member of the service. In the end, decisions became blurred, as it were, giving way very subtly to a heightened responsibility for each individual in his own role. This delicately shaded mode of functioning was efficient as far as treatment was concerned but proved quite unsatisfactory when it came to research. This seemed to be a matter to be referred to the hierarchy, to the chief of the service, but to no avail; the hierarchy did not regulate treatment, and it was not about to give orders as to research either. Since this research was not within the usual objectives of the service, this brought us back to the desire of the medical director. What was this desire? She herself supported the research, but could the same be said for the other members of the team? So the research was likely to be only carried out if the other members accepted and shared the desire of the medical director.

Was this not the hierarchy quietly moving in again?

If one wants to avoid the intervention of the medical hicrarchy—or the hierarchy of any group for that matter, medical or otherwise—something else has to intervene, a magnetic pole to direct the group's energy, some joint cathexis, a common good for all.

Failure or loss? Or again "of the effects of a research project on a service".

The loss in question was that of the ties established with these 20 psychotics of whom the majority had been lost to sight or had gone elsewhere for treatment, and it brought up again a whole series of "misunderstandings" which had been buried in people's memories but not resolved. These misunderstandings could at last be talked over again, but to the extent that, since they were things of the past, they took place second to the previously mentioned availability, the availability to any new question raised by the psychotic in his own way. This is what it was in fact, since our cathexes relating to the psychotic were free again. However, this made us insist upon the necessity of carrying out this work on all the psychotics who left the service; this was the price of our availability. Without this loss we can be quite sure that our renewal of contact, if it occurs, will be trapped, as programed, in a deathly repetition.

Research is essential. This necessity was in our view another positive aspect. We feel that any psychiatric care undertaking is jeopardized, unless it is supported by a research undertaking and built on a purpose of training and teaching.

An attempt at isolated treatment is what constitutes the asylum, or else a profit-making enterprise. Treatment and teaching form the outline of a teaching structure, but not necessarily a training structure. The pairing of treatment and research produces a risk of experiment and its abuses.

The three concepts, treatment, teaching, and research, should be firmly linked in integrated activities, and this should apply not only to hospital and university centers, but should also be a requirement for all public psychiatric services.

We are not trying to propose a model for the structure of treatment of psychotics. We are even saying that to talk about a model in this field, whether it is psychiatric or antipsychiatric, is tantamount to closing the question, which is a fundamental one, that of the psychotic. A watchful eye must be kept so that interrogation on psychosis continues to be directed by the relentless challenge of psychosis itself. Those groups or teams who want to face up to it must be able to choose, not the premises or the means, for this is beyond their reach in public service, but the method of functioning best suited to their own particular originality. The support of treatment by research and teaching seems the only possible guarantee of the continued questioning of psychosis.

Finally, we should say that it seems that in speaking of "history," we have touched upon the heart of one of the questions of psychiatry and the study of the psychoses in particular. For the mention of history upsets that very disturbing notion of chronicity, and to talk of distance is to bring up the interrogation inherent in every psychotic. What are we aiming for, what do we expect in the treatment of psychosis, if it is not a mobilization of libidinal cathexes? Those histories we recalled together at the center concerning 20 psychotics seemed to recount just that. Something in the psychotic gave way at this level because of the multiple roles we had more or less consciously attributed to ourselves for him, but especially because of a more or less conscious gratitude on his part, with ruptures between times.

From that point onward, this mobilization of libidinal cathexes interspersed with "ruptures," made possible the inscribing and the writing of a new history. What is left to be done, then? To call into existence structures, a clearly defined but varied caring staff, whose essential quality is not the extent of their resources but their availability.

These structures have to be flexible; flexible does not mean liberal at all costs; flexible means rigid or elastic according to . . . the requirement of the psychotic.

On this basis the psychotic has a choice. He can choose the structure, the people, the object put at his disposal, he knows that he is free to come or not, to come and go away again! . . .

Does it matter what the last word is?

NOTES

1. Work carried out by the Treatment and Social Readjustment Center of Neuilly-sur-Marne.

Chapter 3

CHRONICITY OR THE DIFFICULT MOVE FROM THE ASYLUM INTO SOCIETY[6]

Pierre Vincent, M.D.

The Hospital of St. Michael-the-Archangel, where the patients referred to in this study were hospitalized for long periods of time, has much the same background as most of the major North American mental hospitals. Founded in the mid-19th century with humanitarian aims, it grouped patients together to provide them with a refuge and subsequently expanded steadily to cope with the increasing needs arising within a geographical area twice the size of France. The more the hospital's clinical volume increased, the more it was organized into rigid, compartmented structures similar to those described by Goffman.[1] In 1962, the hospital population reached an all-time high of over 5200 patients. It was at this point that, in the context of Quebec's "quiet revolution," there began a movement for reform of psychiatric services in general. There were the scandals of the huge repressive institutions revealed by a former patient in a best-selling book called *Les fous crient au secours*[2a] (The insane are crying out for help). The establishment of a government Commission of Inquiry was followed by the creation of the Quebec Psychiatric Services under the direction of Dr. Dominique Bédard, Chairman of this Commission, which was to mark the first step in the quiet revolution of Quebec's psychiatric treatment facilities.

To understand the situation of the patients in our group, it seems necessary to describe the development of the sociopolitical situation in Quebec during that period. Until the early 1960s, Quebec society was of a classic, rigidly structured traditional type which had changed little since the 19th century. At that time, it was clearly dominated by a rigid political and religious hierarchy which was represented to the point of caricature in our hospital until the beginning of the 1960s. The administrative management was totally controlled by the religious community which owned the hospital, while the medical board had extremely close ties with the political figures who had been in control of the province for the last 25 years. Protest or challenge was quite out of the question in a country which enjoyed, to quote in the very words of a politician of the day, "the quiet possession of truth." Within such a context the treatment of insanity, which is the contradiction of logical order, could only be associated with repression. The patients lived in a setting designed for a prison, both architecturally and in its staff recruitment. The supervisors in charge of the patients were actually quite openly called "the guards." Biological therapeutic techniques prevailed and any form of psychoanalytical approach was undisguisedly rejected out of hand.

This report constitutes an attempt at retrospective analysis of the experimental reintegration into the community and the work situation of a group of 24 psychotics diagnosed as unquestionably schizophrenic prior to 1963, and who had spent a long time in this traditional psychiatric environment. This experiment was launched at the end of 1967 with the establishment of a home maintenance company of which the majority of the employees had to be former patients of this hospital. The aim of this company was strictly to provide a source of employment where the psychotic would not be subjected to the permanent threat of rejection on account of the mere fact of being or having been psychotic. It therefore had, of itself, no direct therapeutic intention. Diagnostic criteria had no bearing on the selection of employees, and in fact there were among them representatives of the entire diagnostic scale of psychiatric nosology: organic psychoses, schizophrenias, mental retardment with or without psychosis, severe character and behavior disorders, alcoholism, severe neurotic states, and so on. For our study, we selected from this wide range of patients all those diagnosed as schizophrenics who had first been hospitalized before the end of 1963 and who had worked for this company for a trial period of more than one month during 1968 and early 1969. With the exception of two patients, who had left the hospital a few months before, all these patients were hospitalized at the time of their engagement, and were to leave the hospital within a month of this initial recruitment. On discharge, they were paid the average wage paid in the Quebec area for this kind of work (this wage is determined by decree of the Ministry of Labour after negotiation, and is, at the time of writing, $2.04 per hour).

The end of 1963 was chosen as the boundary line in view of the changes which began to occur at this time as a result of the events described above, and in order to be sure of the "chronicity" of the patients' mental state.

Retrospective examination of the records of each of these patients shows that all of them exactly fit the classic picture of the so-called "chronic" patient, that is, a psychiatric syndrome progressing for several years before eventual hospitalization and admission precipitated by exacerbation of symptoms and their repercussions on the family environment. The record of the observations of psychiatrists and nurses on the subsequent development of each of these patients after admission shows the following clinical picture: fairly rapid attenuation of secondary symptoms such as hallucinations, openly expressed delusion which was, superficially at least, repressed by biological methods (neuroleptics, electroshocks and, in some cases, insulin shock treatment). Many patients then withdraw into more or less total apragmatism, or else make a place, a territory, for themselves in the asylum environment. As they seem to have no desire to "get better" quickly and under the pressure of the number of new arrivals, they are then transferred to the "long-term" wards, where the classic asylum structures are more firmly and radically entrenched than ever. The break with society is total and permanent. In patient language, going to stay with the family for a while is referred to as "holidays," and the weekly allowance of $2.00, or cigarettes received, are known as "salaries," and so forth. Each one has to do all he can to be a "good" patient, ready to make himself useful when necessary and to keep himself "busy" in the workshops.

Once we had obtained this summary of the psychiatric history of each of the members of this group, we decided to compare them with another group of chronically hospitalized patients, under various headings unconnected with their illness and which could have had a strong influence on their social reintegration. We felt that it was important for this purpose to take into consideration factors such as age, marital status, previous experience in the employment market, geographical origins (rural or urban), and previous psychiatric experiences. As a comparison group, we chose the entire set of male patients with schizophrenic diagnoses chronically hospitalized since 1962 and who had therefore undergone much the same therapeutic approaches as the patients in our study group. Fifteen of the patients admitted in 1962 were still in the hospital in November 1971, and we were given access to their biographical record cards.

On the whole we found the two groups quite closely comparable, taking the end of 1962 as the reference-point. The average age of the members of our group was 44.3, with 27 and 54 as the two extremes, while that of the control group was 41.5, with 26 and 53 as the lower and upper limits. In our group, 70 percent were unmarried in 1962 and 30 percent separated (legally or otherwise). None of these has gone back to married life since then. All members of the control group were unmarried in 1962. Geographical origins were comparable in the two groups; about 25 percent of each were from the city of Quebec, 25 percent from small provincial towns, and 50 percent from rural areas. The incidence of hospitalization in a psychiatric setting prior to 1962 was similar in the two groups: in our group 75 percent had been hospitalized before 1962 for periods varying between one and 13 years, with an average duration of 4.7 years, while 60 percent of the control group had already spent periods of one to 15 years in psychiatric hospitals, with an average of five years. With regard to levels of education, few patients in either group had gone much further than primary school. Finally, the vast majority of the members of the two groups were of poor socioeconomic origins and their employment experience was, for the most part, limited to agricultural work, lumberjacking, or manual labor. Hence the members of our group do seem to be fairly representative of what are known as "chronic psychotics" in our mental hospitals.

Through this home maintenance company these chronic cases found themselves rushed very quickly from the asylum into the world of work and society. Their psychiatric treatment went through three completely distinct phases. In 1968 and up to September 1969 the hospital's outpatient clinic (which was then a service carved out of the intrahospital set-up and consisted of a staff pared down to an absolute minimum even though they dealt with such enormous needs) took over during periods of crisis, and the patient was seen only on request, in the eventuality of incipient relapse. Between September 1969 and September 1970 a psychiatric team was set up specially for the after-care treatment of the patients working in the company. It comprised a psychiatrist, a sociologist, a social worker, and two social helpers. However, this team concentrated essentially on the new patients recruited by the company and, but for a few exceptions, had practically nothing to do with those in our group. Since September 1970, following an overall review of the 175 former hospital patients then employed by the company, we took on, with a reduced team, an aftercare undertaking providing regular superficial psychotherapeutic support and full-scale intervention in periods of crisis. Be it noted in passing, that during this third phase several of the patients in our group were seen by the outpatient department for the first time in over a year (their drug prescription had been renewed on request, automatically).

We have attempted in this study, as well as in our daily practice, to make an analysis of the evolution of these patients' chronicity. The results described here, with a three-year retrospect for this group, seem, on the whole, to be confirmed by the aftermath of this experiment, which has enabled a considerable number of patients to break out of the vicious circle of institutional chronicity. Perhaps the following four clinical illustrations will give a better idea of the development of these patients.

Case 1

In 1962, N.B. was 17 years old and was brought to us from a small provincial town because of his megalomanic delusions around a religious theme. He declared that at his birth the devil had entered the left side of his body and God the right side, and that his crises were connected with the devil's attempts to get out of his body. At the same time, he presented himself as God's representative, who had to transmit his message to the Ecumenical Council. Within a few months the delusion had been brought under control by neuroleptics; several attempts to return to live with his family had met with failure after a few months. His efforts to work failed time after time, and what was particularly noticeable, apart from psychotic exacerbations, was the establishment of a very strong dependence in relation to the hospital setting. In August 1968, he began employment with the maintenance company and left the hospital. After spending a few months in an aftercare home, he then moved out on his own. He was twice readmitted to hospital for a few months in 1969, but even during his hospitalization he began working again as soon as his mental state allowed. However, his chronic status had become debatable by then. In March 1970 he left the hospital and this time his social reintegration was unequivocal. He married a work colleague in the summer of 1971, and for the last 18 months at least has never fallen back on any psychotic defense mechanism, in spite of the difficulties he encounters in real life. At the very most, he has some minor functional gastric disorders in periods of stress. The heavy neuroleptic drug treatment previously necessary for him has been reduced for more than six months now to a single low dose before retiring. This is the prototype of the chronic patient who has "succeeded."

Case 2

Patient C.D. was 24 years old when first hospitalized at the mental hospital in 1959. From an isolated village on the north coast of the gulf of Saint Lawrence, he had already been treated some years previously at the general hospital in Montreal for "depression." At this point he was committed as a result of his aggressive behavior toward people around him and because of his considerable badly systema-

THE DIFFICULT MOVE FROM THE ASYLUM INTO SOCIETY 533

tized paranoid experience. The aggressive behavior was quickly suppressed by neuroleptics, and a further attempt was made at living with his family at home; the delusions persisted, however, and the patient was readmitted to the hospital with the same clinical picture. In view of the virtual absence of any change in his condition he was transferred a year and a half later to another mental hospital "for chronic cases." He ran away from there in 1965, and returned to the St. Michael-the-Archangel Hospital, giving the pretext that he was given no treatment for the diabetes he thought he had. Apragmatism and discordance dominated the clinical picture at this point. The patient was kept busy doing small jobs in the kitchen. In May 1968, he was sent to a half-way house in the country; there he felt he was being exploited and again returned to the hospital after a few months. In August 1969, while employed on the home maintenance work, he once again left the hospital and went to live in lodgings with a family. This lasted until the summer of 1971, but his adjustment remained marginal and his performance at work was unsatisfactory. He dropped his employment, spent some weeks wandering about aimlessly during the day, and later returned to work in the sheltered workshops at the hospital. This patient broke out of the asylum confinement, but his dependence remained and his readjustment was very marginal. This was a partial failure.

Case 3

Patient J.-M. B. was 14 years old when he was admitted in 1959 on the grounds of bizarre and aggressive behavior, an influence syndrome, and auditory hallucinations. Outside of periods of disturbed agitation he appeared to be in a state of indifference, autistic. All therapeutic approaches had failed. At times, however, he did participate in some maintenance work with teams of patients. In April 1969, we managed to persuade him to accept employment with the home maintenance company, and he left the hospital for an aftercare home. However, his adjustment turned out to be very difficult. The conflicts (of a homosexually based type) reemerged and he was once again hospitalized in the midst of a psychotic attack. This was soon brought under control and he went back to work leaving the hospital for another home. Gradually he acquired an increasing capacity for self-appraisal with regard to his unconscious homosexual drives, and with the help of constant psychotherapeutic support, he has managed to live outside the hospital up to the present time.

Case 4

Patient P.V. was 32 years of age when he was hospitalized in 1949 for delusions of absurd jealousy with acting out upon his wife. For many years he seemed to his family to be in a state of complete incoherence and delusion. He spent whole days writing disconnected letters to important people. He presented deep disturbances of an anatomical order; his wife's brother had stolen his head from him, or his stomach, his organs, his mind, and so on. During the moments when his psychosis had subsided, he got his life in the asylum organized: petty clandestine trade, docility towards the guardians in exchange for certain favors. A trial discharge of a few months in 1965 met with failure. In 1967 he took a small job in the patients' cafeteria, and in June 1969 he was employed by the home maintenance company and settled in a room near the hospital. He renewed contacts to some extent with his children, who came to visit him. His work performance was sometimes very low, but he explained this by saying that what really interested him was getting back to his old job as shipyard plumber working on ship maintenance (which he had dropped in 1948). In November 1971, he handed in his resignation as home maintenance worker, since he had found work at his old job. The patient's psychotic structure, nonetheless, appears to have changed very little, and he easily returns to his paranoia in interviews with him. He has therefore overcome the asylum factor more than anything else.

In a retrospective study of this kind it is particularly risky to attempt to assess the extent of a psychotic's "recovery," change or "psycho-social improvement," for this would, in fact, mean trying to quantify in different time settings a subjective experience hardly possible to objectify. What we can do is to observe the repercussions of the psychotic experience (what we can glimpse of it) upon the psychotic's adjustment to reality, on his life in society, and his relations with people around him, including ourselves. We did attempt to do this, however, using factors including rehospitalization, the use of neuroleptics, the state of financial and psychological dependence or independence, and rating scales such as the American Medical Association's scale for evaluating "permanent" disability due to psychosis[4] and the Jurgen Ruesch scale designed to quantify psychosocial disability.[3]

Rehospitalizations and Abandonments

At the present time only one of the original twenty-four patients in the group is in a psychiatric hospital. This patient had already been hospitalized three times since 1968 for periods of one, two, and four months, and had stopped working altogether in February 1971. Nine other patients were hospitalized once or twice for periods of a few weeks to several months and all, except for two cases now in the protected workshops, have reentered the work situation without further hospitalization. Five other patients dropped out after working for more than a year and are also in the protected workshop; one patient went back to his profession as a plumber after a gap of 20 years.

Evolution of Disability Due to Psychosis

The American Medical Association[4] has suggested a number of criteria for assessing the percentage of disability due to psychosis and sets up four major categories, according to the gravity of the clinical condition. We have tried to compare each patient's degree of disability in 1971 and that of the year preceding his discharge from the hospital. Three patients show exceptional improvement with the more or less total disappearance of all psychotic phenomena. Six other patients show an excellent improvement. Seven patients show a good improvement, seven slight, and only one appears to have remained stationary. The most persistent clinical picture consists mainly of a reduced sense of initiative, a need for superficial support from the group, and limited social life; it appears difficult to distinguish here what is rooted in the psychosis and what is the result of a long period spent in an institution.

Evolution of Psychosocial Disability According to the Ruesch and Brodsky Scales

Ruesch and Brodsky[3] propose four levels of psychosocial disability. On the basis of their scale, three patients can now be considered to be suffering from no disability at all, twelve have gone up two steps, six have gone up one, and three have remained stationary.

Neuroleptic Treatment

The daily quantity of neuroleptics can perhaps also be used as an indication of the clinical evolution of psychotics. We do not have to determine the limits of this procedure, however, because it presupposes the invariably rational use of drugs (which is by no means necessarily always the case).

The drug-use curve can be summarized as follows:

| | | Decrease of | | |
| | | 25% | 50% | 75% |
Increase	No change			
12.5%	41.6%	8.4%	21%	16.5%

Discussion

The favorable clinical evolution of the majority of these patients who had until then been considered "incurable" chronic cases, brings us to reconsider the multiple aspects of chronicity. In 1964, Le Guillant, Bonnafé, and Mignot,[2] as well as a number of authors before them, reviewed the problems posed by chronicity in the context of psychiatric institutions. For several years this has been the first problem encountered in all the attempts to reform psychiatric services in America and in Europe. Solutions proposed have varied from taking up the challenge of ensuring continuity of treatment come what may (the experience of the 13th District in Paris) to the officially proposed suggestion of grouping these chronic cases together in specific institutions along with incurable organic cases (in *Action for Mental Health*[5]), and this in the name of so-called "community-based psychiatry" itself.

Our experience leads us to feel that chronicity is a double-defense mechanism originating in both the psychotic and in society in reaction to psychotic phenomena. Faced with his anxiety the psychotic organizes his survival by cutting himself off from reality and reducing his contacts with others, trying to find a new equilibrium within his disorder to settle himself into as best he can. In dealing with this defensive strategy set up by the patient the therapist has to make use of all the biological, psychotherapeutic, and institutional tools he can get hold of, and which have been discussed in detail by others in this symposium.

If we sometimes come up against insurmountable difficulties, perhaps it is because we try to ignore the defensive role chronicity plays for society. Psychotic behavior is a major source of anxiety to society, which reacts to dam up the evil and to encyst it in the clearly defined social role of the chronic madman, whose ideal place is the mental hospital for an indefinite length of time. Within this institution a neo-society is created where work, in particular (which in normal society is given an important place), is devalued both at the level of tasks allocated and in the remuneration given for them. The experiment described above may have turned out to be positive for the patients mainly because it fought against chronicity, a defensive attitude caused by society. Nevertheless, this struggle was by no means an easy matter, as is borne out by our failures and the reluctance only recently overcome by these patients' employer to give them responsibilities if they demonstrate their ability to shoulder them.

NOTES

1. Goffman, E. (1961), *Asylums.* New York: Anchor Books, Double-day & Co.

2. Le Guillant, L., Bonnafé, L., & Mignot, l. (1964), *Problèmes posés par la chronicité sur le plan des institutions psychiatriques.* Paris: Masson.

2a. Pagé, J.-Ch. (1961), *Les fous crient au secours.* Montréal: Edition du Jour.

3. Ruesch, J. & Brodsky, C. M. (1968), The concept of social duability. *Arch. Gen. Psychiat.,* 19:394.

4. American Medical Association (1966), Guide to the evaluation of mental illness. *JAMA,* 198(12):1291 ff.

5. Joint Commission on Mental Illness and Health (1961), *Action for Mental Health.* New York: Basic Books.

6. Considerations on the evolution of a group of psychotics treated in a traditional mental hospital structure, and their subsequent path when put to the test in a normal work situation.

Chapter 4

PSYCHOSIS IN AN AFRICAN SOCIETY

Henri Collomb, M.D.

It would be a good introduction to define the topic, its terms, and its limits.

Psychosis does not have any single universal meaning; nosographic systems are always difficult to establish outside the boundaries of their origin. Underlying the term "psychosis" there is, of course, schizophrenia, and perhaps also other forms of chronic mental illness; there is also an opposition to everything that is not psychosis.

Since we shall talk about psychosis in an African society, it would perhaps be useful to mention madness and its definition in this society. This will be discussed later, but it can be said that the image of the "madman" is a rather imprecise one. There does exist the word "döf" in the Wolof language. If one askes who is "döf" in the village, everyone will point out the same individual. When one inquires exactly what characterizes this person as "döf," the answer is that "He's the one who goes off naked into the bush." The image is symbolic. Somewhere else we would get the answer concerning a psychotic—psychotic according to our scales of reference—"He is sick, not mad." More often than not, the answer will consist of an etiological statement: "He has been attacked by the spirits or the sorcerers." Each of these responses contain a different truth which defines a type of relationship between the disturbed individual and society. They emphasize the fact that psychosis is a matter involving too great a number of participants for it to be objectified. The definition refers us back, then, to these participants, to what they feel or experience about it.

To take just the medical practitioner or the psychiatrist in a transcultural situation, the psychosis perceived by him can only be that which comes within his personal experience. It corresponds to the extent of his perception of the other culture. In this confrontation—for confrontation and critical examination are inevitable—defenses are organized in the direction of similarity or even identity, or else toward a radical alternative. In both cases the view is distorted. It can always be said that psychosis is defined by a set of symptoms and that these symptoms, which constitute fragments of behavior, can be observed by everyone in exactly the same way and that by using strict methods it is possible to withdraw into objectivity and talk the same scientific language. I think that this would be avoiding a difficulty and reducing psychosis to a model which does not contain it. To give an example, the incidence of schizophrenia in Africa, calculated according to hospital statistics for similar aid facilities, varies between 60 and 6 percent. As many psychiatrists have lamented, every time statistical comparisons are quoted, it is a great pity that there are still no definite biological criteria to indicate schizophrenia.

A second difficulty resides in the expression "African society." I know that being restricted to "an African society" makes it possible to refer to a very limited society. Black Africa is composed of some 300 ethnic groups, be-

tween 10 and 20 in each country, who have until now preserved their cultural purity and a specific social
organization. There are undeniably some elements common to all of these groups; these shared characteristics
have given rise to concepts such as "Africanism" and "ne-
gritude." It is also obvious that there is tremendous diversity. Reference to Africa or Africans in general, the
attribution of specifically African characteristics as opposed
to those of other populations—Western peoples in particular—are generalizations which meet with much resentment.
Side by side there is a claim to an ethnic identity and a
personal identity; this justifiable claim is very apparent
throughout the social classes and in individuals who have
undergone a transcultural process. This is hardly surprising. Researchers in the human sciences, whose desire for
accommodation does not necessarily exclude due consideration for truth, express the same claim.

In order to appreciate the concepts about to be presented, it is therefore important to orient the observer and
his milieu.

My experience of Africa is essentially Senegalese, although frequent trips to the interior of Africa have brought
me into contact with eithnic groups other than those (themselves numerous) in Senegal. I was a general practitioner
in East Africa for a long time before becoming first a neu-
ropsychiatrist and then a psychiatrist. In my case, the experience of colonization and subsequent decolonization was
perhaps attenuated by having spent a long period in a free
African country (Ethiopia). I am giving these details concerning myself as a "witness" because I feel that it is no
easy matter to shed the weight of history and to throw off
the cultural influences one has been subjected to. One's
observation and perception are inevitably influenced by
them to some extent. This is a subject over which there was
a considerable amount of disagreement and opposition,

whether tacit or outspoken, in the group discussions at Fann. Because of these differences, I still carry with me the impression of all those people, psychologists and sociologists, who for varying lengths of time shared this Senegalese experience. Perhaps they will be able to recognize themselves in the following pages.

Is Senegal representative of Africa today? For our purpose, its diversity could be the echo of the innumerable faces of changing Africa. Each one discovers there what he thought he had come to find or what he wanted to find after a traumatic initial contact. It will be a difficult matter to attribute to psychosis its specific dimensions within each ethnic group, each social class. Besides the original diversity, colonization, foreign religions, technical cooperation, and the technical-administrative invasion have all added further differences, to which the observer is more or less sensitive. What does it mean to be interested in traditional Africa? A search for a certain way of existence in the world . . . a lost paradise which is no more than the projection of a personal desire? At the other end of the scale, what does it mean to echo the anguish of an ambiguous adventure which essentially concerns the African threatened with losing his own culture?

We are aware of our own tendency to look for a traditional Africa and pick out the fundamental differences which set it apart from the Western world.

Still with the idea of giving an adequate introduction, I shall now outline a scheme according to logical categories and designed to provide proof and demonstration. I feel less able to do this now than I would have a few years ago. The purpose escapes me a little, or perhaps more and more, I should say. Therefore I shall give you some ideas, not necessarily in any order; perhaps each of you will be able to gather some information from them.

The Space of the Psychotic

The space of the psychotic is in the street, the family, the village, the healer's hut, or the mental hospital. These various spaces do not all have a similar significance; they imply different attitudes and different relationships between the affected person and people around him.

Asylums, cells, huts, and special areas still exist. This is the most common form, an inheritance from colonial hospitalization reflecting Western models still in existence in Europe. The colonial medical practitioner had other things to worry about, such as the major endemic diseases, malnutrition, and climatic sickness. Little heed was paid to psychosis; trypanosomiasis and syphilis were enough to explain dementia. The mentally disturbed were taken directly to the healer or sometimes sent away for ever into the bush.

In response to the request of the public authorities, asylums have been built over the last 20 years. Each institution had to have cells, and the insane were shut away. Premises intended for 30 patients were rapidly filled with 200, for there were no discharges and never could be. The doctor, a general practitioner, made a brief visit once a week to the anonymous crowd of patients huddled together, steadily drawn along by an accelerated regression.

This situation still exists; many African states have only a single psychiatrist, or worse still, none at all. For aesthetic purposes and to spare the eye of the tourist, there are periodic roundups in Dakar of all the vagrant "insane," tramps, beggars, and lepers. These are always taken to the same place, which was intended for 100 mental patients. The result is easy to imagine. The medical practitioner, completely unable to cope, goes into a state of depression.

This image of Western psychiatry has contributed to the establishment or reinforcement of a very enduring picture, that is, the madman is irrevocably eliminated from society and from the community of the living when he is put into the mental hospital.

In big towns the street is preferred to the hospital; it often is preferable, too. Passers-by are poor but generous, the garbage cans are never empty, the children do not throw stones. Accidents are few and far between, but the authorities are concerned about hiding what is now considered the "disgrace of our modern cities."

The village and the family

Every village has its madman. In traditional circles there is a widespread notion that for all to be in order in the village, there has to be a madman. What function of the madman or of madness does this notion refer to? The scapegoat, glory, or, somewhat more surprising to us, the function of mediator and bearer of a transcendental message? Children occasionally throw stones at him, but the community vaguely perceives that he is of some use and he therefore has his place, a language, and a right to be listened to.

If he becomes a nuisance, he is tied up or chained. There sometimes arrive at the mental hospital patients who have been chained up for several years, either in a hut inside the concession or within the family community. How do these patients come to be brought to the hospital? The community has tried many healers and spent a great deal of money to no avail. Weariness does not lead to exclusion immediately; years can go by before they get to the solution whereby the sick individual is transferred to outside facilities. It would be a mistake to take at face value the apparent conviction, often forcibly expressed, that the Western institution—whatever its therapeutic intent—is a place where cures are actually accomplished. The real conviction, held by everyone, and which dictates a family's action, is that "At the hospital they are quieted down, but nobody gets cured." When patients leave the hospital—if they ever do

—they have to go back to the traditional healers who are the only ones with the power to reestablish the order, or set up a new order between the patient, the spiritual powers, and the community of the living.

The place of cure is the space of the healer. This is the hut where he makes a diagnosis during the course of his meditations or his dream; in other words, he reveals to himself and to the patient, as well as to the group, the entity responsible for the attack. It is also the patient's hut, where the healer and his aides go to invoke the ancestral spirits and find out, through the mouth of the patient, which of them is inhabiting him and causing the trouble. The place of cure can also be the healer's concession, where the disturbed people live in community, sharing the same meals, the same huts, and the same existence with those "treating" them. This is a more complete form of the traditional therapeutic village, governed by the more or less liberal reign of the marabout[1] or the biledjio,[2] the holder of power attributed to him by consensus.

The Psychotic and Society

The different places where the psychotic expresses himself, regresses, lives, or dies, have certain characteristics involving other people, such as (1) those treating the subject— whether they are of the traditional order of psychiatrists— and (2) the community, whether the family, the village or the public authorities.

It is easy to distinguish here a number of different situations measured in terms of isolation, rejection, adaptation to traditional circuits, or culture loss.

The image of the asylum where the universally rejected insane huddle to die, on one hand, and that of community life in the healer's concession or village on the other, present good material for comparison. Even when the sick individual's feet are fettered to a tree-trunk, people around him, his "therapist" and the others, still consider him as a person. A marabout told us that "someone who comes here does not stop being considered as a person (Nit in Wolof); he is like me, he shares my life."

What is more interesting and also more difficult, is to see what factor precipitates rejection at a particular given time. The question could be put this way, still with reference to the traditional attitude towards the mentally sick: At what point and for what reason does the sick person stop being sick and become the madman?

The reply to this has to refer to the nosography in question, the sufferer's symptoms and behavior, the tolerance of traditional societies, social changes (in the direction of technical and so-called "consumer societies") which leave no room for burdensome and useless subjects or the failure of therapeutic attempts. These factors have different weight according to the specific case, social class, and the degree of urbanization and schooling.

Approaching the meaning of psychosis, one can also identify the types of request which help to determine what becomes of the sick person.

Who formulates the request for therapy or the other, unadmitted request, for exclusion? What is the significance of the request for exclusion as opposed to the request for therapy?

In traditional cultures not yet contaminated by Western models the request for exclusion is rare. The request is essentially for therapy, and is formulated by the patient, the family, and the group. The sickness concerns the community. An evil act has been committed against a member of the community, and the community is troubled by it. The "etiological" possibilities are limited and clear. It is either a spirit or a human who is responsible. The healer—in the broad sense of the term—who possesses the knowledge and the power, is appointed by the group to find the solution for the group. It could be said here that the sick person is secondary, almost accessory to the situation; what is important is his significance as a symptom of some troubled relationship within the group itself or between the group and the transcendental environment (ancestral spirits of the traditional religions or spirits of imported religions). As long as the patient remains within the circuit of healers this request on the part of the community is responded to. It should be noted that this request, made more for the sake of the group than of the sick person, maintains the latter's full place in the community. It matters little what treatment is applied to him or what kind of restraints are imposed on him.

As soon as the request is formulated on a less communal basis, either by the family or the public authorities, and addressed to the hospital, its significance changes. It becomes a request for temporary or permanent exclusion; or at least, that element is present to some small extent. This small extent probably gives way to the renewal of the original significance, in some cases. Even then, an adequate response has to be found. Indeed, there is a great risk of the exclusion being reinforced by a poor attitude. Whatever the case may be, it seems certain that the hospital "leaves its mark," whereas even very long periods spent with healers leave no trace.

Identifying the change in the request's significance has still not clarified the reasons for the separation. Logical or rational seeming references are inadequate: one agitated or aggressive subject will be tolerated indefinitely, while another who has recovered will be permanently rejected because he is considered bad for the group. This presents an unsettling problem with regard to discharges.

In the big towns the request sometimes comes from the patient himself, who finds himself rejected by everyone and seeks a refuge in the hospital. This situation is a result of the phenomenon of urbanization, which scatters communities and isolates individuals. In these conditions the problem of discharge is again a very thorny one; the hospital tends to become the permanent shelter.

More often than not, it is the family who can stand the situation no longer or who feel ashamed; the police also bring patients in. Whatever the case may be, there is a higher occurrence of requests for elimination or expulsion than for taking care of the sick individual. The latter, condemned to his solitude, has no alternative but to entrench himself in his madness or his freedom. Altogether, the request is misplaced, ambiguous, and contradictory. In circumstances such as these, which are quite customary in Europe, the task of the medical practitioner is no easy one. If he is to fulfill his role he simply has to stifle his aspirations, satisfy his narcissism, and fall back upon an institution where he will attempt, with varying degrees of success, to organize a place with a therapeutic function. We shall come back to this later, and first try to encompass the significance of psychosis and traditional cures for it.

Psychosis and the Traditional Cure

As far as its significance is concerned, traditional African psychiatry makes little distinction between psychosis and other disorders. The madman, the "döf," is perfectly well defined on the level of description of behavior; the significance of psychosis is merged together with that of neuroses, and somatic and character disorders.

The one factor acknowledged in all of these categories (even including organic disorders where, in fact, the physical or biological mediator can be admitted) is that of an aggression or a conflict. As a first step, the healer has to recognize, or make known, the "cause" of the sickness.

The procedure leading up to this identification can involve not only the patient and one healer or a group of them, but also the family group. At any rate, whatever the case may be, there is explicit (divination) or implicit (dream, intuition) reference to the spiritual forces who incessantly interfere with the lives of humans, either to help them or to attack. This initial bringing into focus of "what is going on," for which an agreement has to be reached, is itself a therapeutic act. Since the cause is thereby identified, it also indicates the treatment modalities to be adopted.

The explanatory systems can be reduced to two basic types, which our insistence upon classification separates from each other:

1. Systems which relate to aggressivity or competition between individuals with no superhuman intervention; and
2. systems referring to religious law, ancestral or Islamic, and relating to transgression and the conflicts arising from the desire to transgress.

These systems can only be summarized here, with gross oversimplification; they have been described and interpreted at length elsewhere.[3]

The first type concerns sorcerer cannibalism and marabout activity. The sorcerer cannibal (a man or woman of the patient's immediate circle or transferred, on the parental image basis, onto other people) is accused of symbolically devouring the patient, who begins to die or go insane as he loses one or several parts of his person. It is easy to identify the mechanisms of projection of aggressivity and guilt involved here. This oral, unconscious, intentional, desired, suffered, or feared attack corresponds to archaic modes of relationship contained in the pairs devour/be devoured, incorporate/be incorporated, possess/be possessed. The sick individual experiences above all devourment and destruction. The attack of the sorcerer cannibal is aimed at producing the death of its victim. The sick people sometimes assume responsibility for the death of villagers, and either confess to sorcery or are accused of sorcery by the group. The therapeutic techniques used here for both the patient and the sorcerer involve an expulsion. The patient rejects the sorcerer by confessing the latter's name to the community under sometimes brutal pressure from the witchhunter. The sorcerer who himself wishes to be cured, that is, to become a human like all the others, surrenders the "substance of witchcraft," sometimes in material form. This system is a widespread method of explanation provided by the patients. In the Islamic countries it is often concealed beneath other systems and is more difficult to bring out because it is contrary to the beliefs of Islam.

The system using the marabout introduces a third party between the aggressor and the victim. In general he intervenes in situations where the aggressor and the victim are in competition with each other. The aim here is not to destroy but to reduce the strength and power of the other. This aggression does not end in death, but causes sexual impotence, the loss of intellectual or physical strength, or mental illness. The person of the marabout (the fetisher in non-Islamised countries) is the neutral point through which the aggressivities pass and meet. He is neutral because he is never attacked by humans, but he is the instrument directing the aggressivity of others. He derives his power from the spirits whom he can question, consult, and manipulate. His work can always be undone either by himself or by another marabout. Although with the introduction of a third party this system goes back to a less archaic relationship than the other, it is often mentioned as being at the origin of psychoses.

The second type of model refers to spiritual forces, the spirits of traditional religions, the Wolof "rab," or spirits of Islam. The sickness is the result of an attack by the rab, the jinns or the seytani.[4]

The interpretation of mental illnesses caused by the

rab—the ancestral spirits—has been approached fairly sati-factorily through the observation of the complicated cura-tive techniques used, especially the "ndöp." In this therapeutic ritual the sickness appears as signifying bad relations between the sufferer and his "rab," in other words the law or his family. The rab or rabs who possess the sick person belong to either the paternal or the maternal line or to both. The job of the therapist and his numerous assistants is to reestablish relations between the patient and his line or lines of ascendants (family or ancestors), through the symbolic intermediary of the ancestral spirits.

There could be a temptation to find among the variety of different representations and the therapies through which their meaning is clarified, conceptual models which are familiar to us. The risk here would lie in trying to interpret according to our own models a reality which our desire for possession prompts us to dominate.

This risk has not been any discouragement to ethnolo-gists, anthropologists, and psychoanalysts. There too, each one can probably find what he wants to.

For example, the sorcerer cannibal system has been found to be the expression of a pathology with an oral significance or genesis, and the marabout element a re-joinder to difficulties at the genital level. If the witch-hunter is asked who can be attacked or who can be a sorcerer, he answers "as many people are attacked by sorcerers as there are sorcerers," or "there is a sorcerer and a victim in each of us," or again, "the parents are sorcerers to their chil-dren, brothers to brothers, the co-wives to the wife, neigh-bors to neighbors, one family line to the others. . . ."

The field spreads out from the original relationship and the danger changes direction, even though it retains the same form and is manifested by very different symp-toms. One might even conceive of possession, the most frequent expression of the rab system, as an attenuated form of devourment: who carries out this attenuated devourment? The father and the mother, since the rab is connected with the paternal ancestors as well as those on the maternal side.

When the rab is difficult to identify, in other words, when no one (the therapist, the patient, or the family) knows which line of ancestry is involved, does this have something to do with the Kleinian fantasy of the combined or merged father and mother? In this case it could be felt that what is interpreted as disharmony, preventing recovery and justifying the therapist's refusal, is in fact representative of disorganization at a deeper level.

In the rab system the "ndöp" cure, with which some of you are familiar, has also been the subject of different interpretations:

1. A rite of reintegration into the group of the individual who strays from it by not conforming to the ancestral law. This reintegration is brought about through the intermediary of an imaginary relationship with the person of the rab of the individual and the rabs of the group as a whole.

2. A rite of weaning and separation referring back to the dual mother-child relationship which has not been able to "beget" a multiple socialized relationship. During the curative process the patient would get rid of his maternal inclusions or submission to his mother and attain sufficient autonomy to permit social relationships in his own name.

3. A rite of parturition. Under pressure from the ndöpKat, which is somewhat reminiscent of the pressure of a midwife, the patient gives birth to the rab. Who is expelled or born? The parents, the ancestors, the group. Is it in fact an expulsion or a birth? The rab "gets off" the patient and enters a sacrificial animal; the animal is then mounted by the patient, put to death, offered up, and shared. In the meantime, an altar is set up for the rab in order to settle it in one place and at the same time pay it the duties necessary to establish an improved relationship.

Giving birth to the parents is a theme frequently encountered in puerperal psychoses. The reversibility of time facilitates the regressions and inversions of the movement of procreation. The patient is her own mother as well as the child. She reverses the procedure of procreation and gives birth to her own mother.

4. A sexual rite. What happens when the patient is buried beneath the loin-cloths and hidden from the view of the assembled people, with his body "stuck" to or separated from that of the animal by the horns? Is it the unspeakable fault that is consummated here?

5. A ritual murder. Can the ensuing sacrifice be considered the realization of the impossible murder? Who is killed in the animal? The father or the son? Everyone can see in it what they want, and the question is that of Abraham. Who is destroyed in the ram?

6. A rite of alliance. For alliance to be possible there has to be separation, autonomy. The patient separates himself from the rab and can then consecrate the alliance. But who is the patient and who is the rab?

The rab-bearing patient is as much the person of the sufferer as his family, society, and its values: the ancestors, the gods. Why is he sick? Is it because of this difficult cohabitation which gives rise to antagonisms, conflicts impossible to cope with, and loss of identity? The complicated procedure of the "ndöp" might make possible a separation in order to establish new positions with the same elements, in a relationship of alliance.

Expulsion, separation, recognition . . . recognition of one's parents in oneself, recognition of others in oneself; giving them their proper place; not allowing oneself to be invaded or possessed, but nonetheless allotting them their rightful place. Recognizing others, forgiving them for existing, for being me, for being in me, for not wanting to go away . . . this is the attainment of adulthood.

This would make of the ndöp ritual a rite of ordinance or maturation. Each sequence is a whole in itself, articulated with the others to form a composite whole. But each sequence or phase, through its particular place and structure, has a more specific significance allowing individual conflicts to be expressed and eliminated or overcome.

Can we, for present purposes, have forgotten certain characteristics or a place specific to psychosis in African cultures?

This seems difficult, and to close this chapter I shall confine myself to a few remarks which could be taken as a stand on the matter and which are closer to the subject of psychoses.

In traditional cultures the genesis of mental illnesses is both psychological and social. They signify bad relations or absence of relations among humans, either immediately and directly, or more often in an indirect way, through the mediation of the transcendental beings who share the universe of humans and protect or threaten them. In comparison with the genesis of psychosis in the "Western representations" it has been said that in the African cultures psychosis is more recent, less historical; in other words, more closely related to the "here-and-now" than with the history of the subject. This point of view could explain the richness of psychotic pathology in societies undergoing rapid processes of change.

The traditional cure, whatever modalities it assumes, is organized around four poles which each have diversified roles and clearly defined functions:

1. The healer and his aides, the bearers of strength and knowledge often acquired after long apprenticeship, and recognized as such by the community;
2. the sick individual and his family. No patient is

accepted on his own, and the request must always come from a group;

3. the mass, or the entire community which constitutes the patient's human environment; and
4. the spirits (ancestors and gods) without whom no therapy is possible.

The active participation of each of these poles is apparent in varying degrees at different points in the treatment. The patient can be mothered to excess and become the center of the group for a time and then be forgotten. The spirit might possess some participant or another who would then express his own conflicts or those he has perceived in other people; the crowd might dance; the therapeutic movement takes its course.

Despite appearances, drugs and medicinal preparations have little part in this. Drugs, "levied" upon trees, plants, or roots, have no virtue unless the necessary power is imparted to them by ritualized word and gesture.

The techniques used are varied, and can be simple or complicated; we could discern here the form of cures developed and conceptualized by Western cultures. What can be seen quite obviously is:

1. the importance of community participation;
2. the importance given to physical techniques (massages, caresses, mothering, physical exchanges);
3. the use of the basic myths, such as symbolic birth and death; fusion, possession and separation; killing and giving life; begetting and being begotten; and
4. the importance of dancing, rhythm, and celebration which confirms the participation of everyone together in community and liturgical life.

All in all, it is an equilibrium between the "therapeutic techniques," personality, and culture, and also a religious and community psychiatry.

Psychoses and the Psychiatrist

The function of the psychiatrist still remains to be defined.

It is very difficult for the psychiatrist to get away from the realities of his environment and indulge in attending to his own narcissism or aspirations, which take on different dimensions in the cross-cultural situation.

The environmental realities consist, on the one hand, of this traditional psychiatry whose content and equivalence we have outlined, and, on the other hand, the request for treatment, for the patient to be taken in charge or for his removal by confinement.

The request addressed to the healer and that addressed to the psychiatrist are not at all the same. In most cases, even when there is a genuine request for treatment, it goes without saying that the procedure implies calling upon a different culture, or in other words, a different system of values. How can a dialogue be started and with whom? When the patient and his family talk about sorcerer cannibals, the rab, marabouts and their activities, jinns and seytani, the psychiatrist may well be able to see beyond the symbols and perceive the underlying mobilizing force. Does this imply his integration in a therapeutic circuit in the same way as the healer? Certainly not. His function is an ambiguous one.

The images he receives are very ambivalent. He can effect a cure, but he does not know the world of the African, his culture, his ancestors, and his gods. Then what is the value of the cure if the sickness is seen as a disruption of order among all those who exist, living or dead, humans or spirits, and if recovery means an order giving rise to better relations among them? And what basis can there be for a psychotherapy which fails to mobilize either the ancestors or the myths?

This psychiatrist is also the one to whom the patient is given: "Keep him for ever, we don't want him any more." Such a gift of a son or a brother has nothing in common with the pact of alliance sealing friendship with a reciprocal identification or recognition, upon which the traditional cure is based. The "We don't want him any more" represents final, irrevocable rejection, and the medical practitioner becomes its guarantor.

This type of request is becoming increasingly frequent. Social change, urbanization, schooling, the technical administrative take-over are all weakening the traditional family structures and faith in religious beliefs, representations, and myths. The sick individual is no longer considered the bearer of transcendental significance, of a message from the ancestors; his sole remaining value is that of a symptom translating some disorder within the group. In extreme cases, he is no longer of any interest to anyone. He is thrown out by his family and wanders about the streets until the police bring him in to the hospital. The public authorities want hastily built premises to cope with the need. Under these circumstances there is no possible chance for any dialogue to get beyond the hospital walls.

It would be unfair not to recognize one less negative consequence of this inevitable evolution. This is the fact that adherence to Western models attributes a role to the psychiatrist, and what is asked of him is the same as everywhere else. Should his action be directed toward facilitating a maturation which would give greater autonomy, greater responsibility or individual care, or should it attempt to restore order at the community level? To what extent is he capable of this, since he cannot perceive this community order?

Some can get around the difficulties by prudently remaining within the bounds of a symptom and drug psychiatry. This position can be a solid one. What are the patient and his family looking for when they abandon the healers? Something different, of course, a scientific side of psychiatry which corresponds to the image they have of the white man's science, with all its complicated instruments, its vocabulary, the names of illnesses, and the injections and pills to make people better. The attendants' request is on the same level, because it too is reassuring. The relationship cannot be manipulated with impunity, for it also implies transcendency. And so there is a tendency for an organic psychiatry or psychopharmacological model to be set up, supported as much by a clinging to the power of "science" as by a defensive organization.

The psychiatrist can try to allay his discomfort by becoming accessible to this other culture, which puts him in question, but where he can also find inspiration for his desire to act.

This is in some ways what has happened in the Dakar institution at the Fann Psychiatric Service, with all its trials and errors. Here there is permanent questioning of our action and its "legitimacy," an attempt at community psychiatry where each one makes an effort to recognize the other's right to speak out. The institution has become a public place without clearly defined limits. Everyone can come and sit down, talk and listen, outline his knowledge or ideas about mental sickness, discuss with everybody else the problem of a particular patient, or the problem of authority or food or whatever. Is this institutional therapy, or sociotherapy? The medical practitioner fades into the background; his role is to listen, to let everyone express his thoughts in front of the others, to bring about the "collectivization" of therapy, along the same lines as the healers. However much he may want to, it is hardly possible for him to make use of a symbolic universe and myths which are not his own.[5]

The therapeutic village, either a fantasized model of an institution or a copy of the healer's village, has not yet come into existence. The discussions the idea has provoked have taken all meaning out of it. The few individual or family huts which have been built in the institution opposite the classic modern main building are no more than a pale off-shoot. They have, nonetheless, helped to change the atmosphere in what we like to consider a therapeutic manner.[6]

The treatment of "long-term psychoses" is never an easy matter anywhere. The Western psychiatrist working in Africa may have somewhat more favorable circumstances in some respects, namely, the possibility of communication between subjects, less distance between therapist and patient, less fear, greater freedom of action, less rigorous administrative constraints. And from another standpoint, the advantage of a cultural confrontation which holds up values, models, and practice to challenge.

However, the difficulty also resides precisely in this challenge. Is there a place for the Western psychiatrist, can he be considered a reference? This question oversteps the limits of psychiatry and leads on to the critical examination of "technical cooperation."

NOTES

1. Marabout is an Islamic priest with curative powers due to his ability to intervene in the world of the spirits.

2. Biledjio is the hunter of cannibal sorcerers, i.e., the man in the community who devour the sick individuals in a symbolic or fantasized way.

3. In particular by A. Zempleni, *L'interprétation du désordre mental chez les Wolof et les Lébou (Sénégal)*. Ph.D. thesis, University of Paris, 1960.

4. Jinn is a neutral spirit, but whom it is dangerous to meet if the interdicts are not respected. Seytani is always an evil spirit (corresponds to the Western concept of a devil).

5. The question has arisen over the Moslem ceremonials (the sacrifice of the ram), and the ritual circumcisions carried out in the service. What is the significance of our participation in them?

6. The function of the hut for a single patient, two patients, or one patient and an accompanying person is complicated. It is both a socializing and a security-providing element opening out on to a public place and also giving the possibility of withdrawal and isolation. The patients and accompanying persons showed immediate and enthusiastic preference for this type of hospital arrangement.

Chapter 5

CHRONICITY, COMMUNITY, AND CULTURE

H. B. M. Murphy, M.D., Ph.D.

It is usually assumed, particularly in Europe, that the psychoses fall into two natural categories, the acute and the chronic, each requiring different treatment. The acute, deriving mainly from organic or emotional traumata, are seen to require prompt, short-term, and curative treatment. The chronic tend to be seen as deriving from some basic deficit or irreversible damage, requiring long-term handling mainly to keep their symptoms under control. The acute are often seen as preventable; the chronic are rarely seen as such, at least after the first episode, and there has been virtually no mention of prevention in the previous papers at this symposium. Yet, if some prevention of chronicity were possible, part of what has been said about long-term treatment might need changing.

In recent years, the antipsychiatry movement[17] has been arguing that the chronicity of the psychoses is perhaps less inevitable than we have assumed, and that it may be either iatrogenic or sociogenic. The orthodox answer to this is that although doctors and institutions have certainly been guilty at times of promoting dependency and institutionalism, or of failing to give the best treatment, the basic psychotic process is not affected by such matters and hence remains essentially unpreventable by social action.

The purpose of the present paper is to question the latter assumption. I will do this by reference not to individual case histories and subjective impressions, but to epidemiological data on the course and outcome of schizophrenia in different populations. In the past, when differences in the outcome of schizophrenia have been observed as between one population and another, it has usually been possible to attribute this to differences in diagnostic or outcome criteria, or, as in the case of the New Haven surveys,[6,15] to inadequate treatment. Not all instances can be so accounted for, however, and my own research studies happen to have yielded several challenging examples. These studies yield data much more general than those which other speakers at this symposium can cite, but I am addressing myself to a general problem: how to assist millions with some simple steps rather than a few with a whole elaborate battery.

CULTURES AND SUBCULTURES

The first instances concern paired comparisons of societies that differ with respect to their cultural traditions and seem also to differ with respect to the chronicity which affects their schizophrenics. One cannot make such comparisons without first knowing something about the criteria used for labeling the cases as schizophrenic, and also about the criteria for assessing outcome, but this does not mean that these criteria need be precisely equivalent. I believe that in the examples which I will be summarizing very briefly here

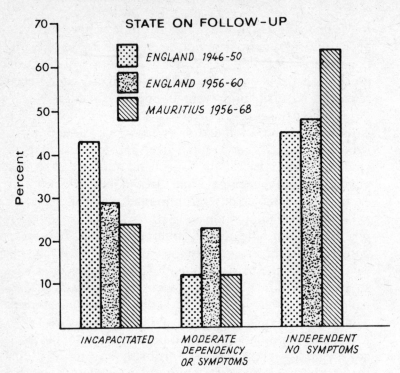

Fig. 5.1. State of schizophrenic patients at follow-up five
or 12 years after first admission; data from
two British studies and one Mauritian

there has been sufficiently good correlation to make the
results significant.

Figure 5.1 presents data derived from two follow-up
studies in England and one in Mauritius. Sample A was
treated at the Maudsley Hospital before the advent of
phenothiazines and before the social reorganization of hospitals took place, and the researchers thought the patients
to be slightly less severely affected but otherwise representative of first admissions for schizophrenia in England at
that time.[5] Sample B was drawn from three hospitals cho-

sen to be representative of the range of British hospitals after the change in social climate and soon after the introduction of the phenothiazines.[3] Sample C comprises all first admissions diagnosed as schizophrenic during the index year, a year in which the phenothiazines were not yet in use in Mauritius. As I have argued in the paper from which these data are taken,[13] I believe that the diagnostic and follow-up criteria were quite similar in all three studies, and that the incidence of hospitalized schizophrenia in the societies from which the samples were drawn was also quite similar. The difference between the A and B results seems to represent what had been achieved by improved social and pharmacological treatment, but the difference between B and C is not as simple. The phenothiazines were not yet in use when the Mauritian patients were hospitalized and although the social climate in the hospital might have been favorable, this cannot be attributed to a higher level of professional care, since the Mauritian hospital at that time had fewer trained staff than the British hospitals and lacked outpatient aftercare facilities. The Mauritian criteria for diagnosis and follow-up evaluation were less strict than those used in Britain, and there seem reasons for thinking that the better outcomes in Mauritius were obtained *despite* the formal treatment rather than because of it.

The data in Fig. 5.1 referred to the state of the patients at time of follow-up, but a slightly different picture is obtained when one compares the courses of illness which the two 1956 samples present. As Fig. 5.2 shows, the two samples had very similar percentages experiencing chronic disablement but quite different percentages experiencing episodic relapses and partial disability. In the British sample the incomplete recovery is the commoner picture but in Mauritius one apparently meets either full social recovery or almost full disability, with few cases experiencing an episodic course. Taken by themselves or linked to reports

COURSE OF ILLNESS

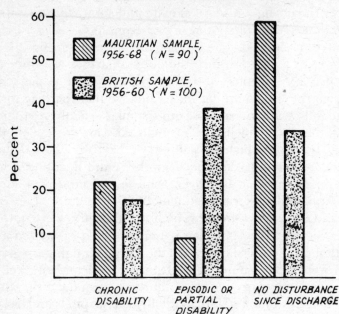

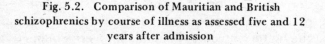

Fig. 5.2. Comparison of Mauritian and British
schizophrenics by course of illness as assessed five and 12
years after admission

from Africa by workers such as Tewfik,[16] these data might
suggest that there is a hard core of severe schizophrenics
which is much the same in all societies and is unaffected by
social conditions, but that the remaining majority is
affected by social conditions, which oppress the patient in
a highly developed country such as Britain and are relatively benign in less-developed societies. This inference
would harmonize with Laing's ideas. However, data from
another underdeveloped part of the world, the Caribbean,
discourage such a simple interpretation.

During a mental health survey of St. Thomas, the most

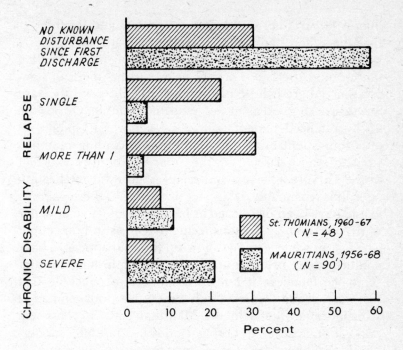

Fig. 5.3. Course of disorder of schizophrenic patients in
St. Thomas, Virgin Islands, and in Mauritius,
over three to seven and 12 years, respectively
(diagnostic and outcome criteria are not
necessarily the same)

populous of the U.S. Virgin Islands, Dr. Hugh Sampath and
I found that there had been 48 cases of schizophrenia,
excluding visitors and nonresidents, diagnosed during a
five-year period, and we were able to trace their subsequent
history over an average of five years, making home visits to
a quarter of them for an independent assessment of outcome.[10] Fig. 5.3 classifies the course of illness which these
patients showed and compares them as closely as possible
with the Mauritius sample to show a striking difference.
The St. Thomas outcomes, even after allowing for more

liberal North American diagnostic criteria and for the fact that the island had a neuropsychiatric ward in a general hospital instead of a mental hospital, are again better than one would expect in a European or North American sample, since there is little continuous disability; but they are not nearly so good as in the Mauritian sample. Out of the 45 hospitalized patients (three were never hospitalized) only four spent more than 13 weeks, including readmissions, on the ward, but on the other hand only about half of the 45 were able to avoid relapse and rehospitalization later. It is reasonable to suspect that some of these patients would have been diagnosed as having an affective disorder in Britain or an acute nonspecific psychosis in France, but when cases were seen on follow-up they did appear to have conformed to British criteria for schizophrenia. In consequence I believe it not unreasonable to conclude that there is a genuine difference between the modal course of schizophrenic illness in the Mauritian and St. Thomian populations, although both societies can be called underdeveloped and a substantial proportion of both populations are descended from African slaves.

The advantage of citing these data from Mauritius and St. Thomas is that one cannot easily attribute the better results to better formal treatment, but they have a disadvantage also, namely, that one may think the differences attributable to racial resistance to the disease. For this reason, I wish to finish this section of my paper with some less satisfactory data—they relate only to duration of hospitalization and not to results on follow-up—which concern people of European origin. In a previous paper I had shown that the incidence of hospitalized schizophrenia in Canada varied significantly between groups of different European national origin and that in every one of these groups the Roman Catholic males had higher incidence rates than the Protestant males.[12] What I did not mention in that paper

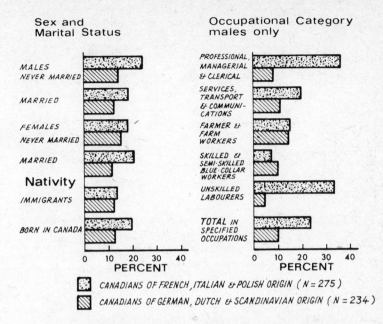

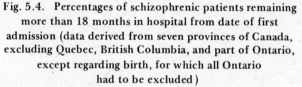

Fig. 5.4. Percentages of schizophrenic patients remaining more than 18 months in hospital from date of first admission (data derived from seven provinces of Canada, excluding Quebec, British Columbia, and part of Ontario, except regarding birth, for which all Ontario had to be excluded)

was that groups with a predominantly Catholic tradition tend to have a higher incidence rate and a higher chronicity picture, judging by the percentages of patients remaining more than 18 months in hospital, than groups with a predominantly Protestant tradition. The latter is shown in Fig. 5.4, where one can also see that the difference is not attributable to the relative percentages of immigrants in each group, or relative social class, or to a difference in marriage patterns.

Since age structure and educational levels have similarly been excluded as explanations and since there are no

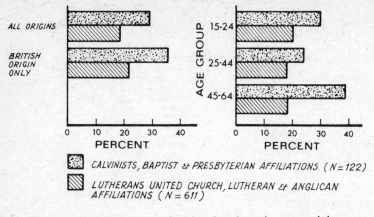

Fig. 5.5.   Percentages of schizophrenic patients remaining
more than 18 months in hospital at first admission;
Canadian data as in Fig. 5.4, members of certain
Protestant churches only

strong racial differences between the two groups, it seems probable that the greater tendency of the Catholic group to remain long in hospital is related to their religious cultural background rather than to anything else. This probability becomes stronger when one sees in the final data which I propose to cite in this section (Fig. 5.5), that even within people of a single national origin, the British, and within the broad mantle of Protestantism, religious affiliation appears to make a difference as to how long the schizophrenic tends to stay hospitalized. (Incidentally, these differences, which like all the other main ones reported are statistically significant, were only uncovered after the theory to be explained below had predicted that they would be present.)

RURAL COMMUNITIES

So much for statistics. They have been presented here to show that schizophrenics from some social backgrounds

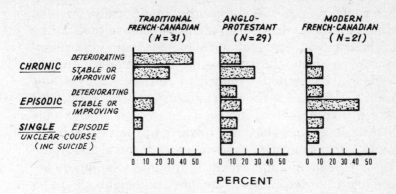

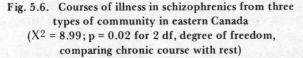

Fig. 5.6.   Courses of illness in schizophrenics from three
types of community in eastern Canada
($X^2 = 8.99$; $p = 0.02$ for 2 df, degree of freedom,
comparing chronic course with rest)

almost certainly have a greater tendency towards chronicity
than schizophrenics from others, but they do not by themselves offer many clues as to the reasons for such differences. To find more meaningful clues one needs to move
away from the realm of numbers to the realms of clinical
impressions and social judgements, realms which are more
susceptible to subjective distortion and from which I would
have been hesitant to bring observations, had they not
been preceded by independent material of the foregoing
type.

The source of these more subjective observations is a
mental health survey of rural communities in Eastern Canada, three of which were traditionally oriented French-
Canadian, three French-Canadian of a more modern
orientation, and four predominantly Protestant with a British or German background. Details regarding these communities have been published in an earlier paper
concerned more with the incidence of schizophrenia
among them than with its chronicity,[11] but Fig. 5.6 shows
that there were considerable and probably significant

differences in the ratios of episodic to stable courses. Schizophrenics belonging to the traditionally oriented communities tended to run a chronic course both in the hospital and at home, though sometimes with gradual improvement, while those belonging to the modern French-Canadian communities tended to run quite an episodic course with violent flare-ups alternating with substantial returns to normal functioning. The cases belonging to the Protestant groups showed a mixture of the two patterns, some patients moving in and out of the hospital and attaining independent employment in the intervals, others becoming a burden on their families and neighbors, and a third group aiming too high, failing, becoming violent, and deteriorating in the hospital. The reason why I believe that this material offers more clues than the previous studies is not that my colleague and I could assess the patients better but because we studied the communities, their treatment of these patients, and their attitudes towards mental illness in general. Between these attitudes and the clinical courses which the patient followed is a clear link, I believe, and this link offers a guide to the understanding of the other differences I have been citing.

In the traditional villages the essential attitudes towards mental illness were that it could be a trial sent by God, that the people so afflicted should be supported by society as long as they tried to be good Christians, that there was a proper way for every sick person to behave, and that there was not much that man could do against such an affliction. Accompanying these attitudes were social reinforcers, efficient means of supporting those who were seen as needing support, rewarding those who were conforming to their traditional ideals, and expelling or ostracizing those who were too deviant. The patients were thus supported and confirmed in their sickness as long as they fitted into the approved sick-role, but effectively expelled or rejected if they did not fit in, particularly when they behaved in such a way as to challenge the community's rather inconsistent belief system.

In the Protestant villages the essential attitudes were that mental illness was something to be fought, that it was conquerable, that social support of the sick was dangerous except in the short run since it encouraged dependency, and that the person who succumbed without putting up much of a fight was despicable whereas the patient who was struggling to maintain his independence was to be tolerated despite other forms of deviancy which he might show. The patients, therefore, were encouraged to seek early treatment and were accepted after treatment as long as they could earn their own living, were allowed to behave quite bizarrely or to remain in isolation if they were independent, but were led to despise themselves if they could not maintain that independence.

The "modern" French-Canadian communities held nominally the same attitudes as the traditional communities, but did not have the social reinforcers and had absorbed something of the Anglo-Protestant's views regarding independence. Their patients and other members could thus tolerate the idea of being mentally sick much easier than the Protestants could and there was not the same pressure to conform to a prescribed sick-role, but, on the other hand, there was not much community support either, and little guidance to restrain the patient from physical violence.

Social Factors

These links between community attitudes and clinical courses should enable one to predict the tendency towards chronicity in patients from similar backgrounds, and thus it is not at all surprising to find in a Quebec mental health region which runs in a narrow corridor from a more modern, industrializing zone to a more traditional farming and forestry zone, that the readiness of patients to accept or to desire long-term dependency in the hospital or boarding foster care increased as one progressed from the modern to the traditional sector.[18] But do the links help explain the differences cited previously or guide one toward an understanding of social factors affecting chronicity in a quite different society? I think they do. Underlying the suggested links are two broad variables, the one relating to value orientations and the other to social integration. The same variables can be detected in the situations discussed earlier.

The value orientations which most affect attitudes towards sickness and the persons who suffer from it are those concerning the relationships of man to man and of man to nature, with God and the supernatural seen as part of nature. Following the ideas of Florence Kluckhohn,[7] one can recognize three broad views of the man-nature relationship, namely, man-over-nature, man-with-nature, and nature-over-man. Similarly, though here I part company with Kluckhohn's formulations, the man-man value orientations can be broadly classified as competitive, cooperative, or hierarchical, the last meaning where the majority of men are conceived to be acting in their own best interests when they live under the guidance or direction of individuals who are better endowed than they. The orientations are linked, for when men view nature as something to dominate and exploit they tend to view their fellowmen in the same light, competitively, whereas a hierarchic orientation tends to be associated with the idea of submission to the gods or supernatural powers.

The chronic tendencies in mental illness are likely to be resisted more strongly where the patient and his society share the idea that man is the conqueror of nature, than where they share the man-with-nature or the nature-over-man orientations; and up to a point, therefore, patients with the first of these orientations should show less chronicity than other patients. However, where this man-over-nature orientation exists, there usually also exists an overevaluation of individualism and a sense of defeat if the disease or other natural agent is not overcome, and this sense of defeat or the overstraining to succeed may in the case of schizophrenia reactivate the disease. The patient in such a society has to account to himself and to his associates for the fact that he has been crazy, and the effort to provide a logical, nonsupernatural explanation for this incomprehensible fact may make him crazy anew. While the course of the illness is not so likely to be a quiet settling into chronicity with patients from such a background, therefore, it is quite likely, if this theory is correct, to take the form of deteriorating episodes in rapid succession, something which, in the long run, is not really different from chronicity.

Where the nature-over-man or God-over-man orientation is stronger the patient can accept his own weaknesses much more easily, but he does not have the same motivation to overcome them. Only when some extraneous factor stimulates him is he likely to struggle; otherwise he will accept the sick-role and the support which his society provides, and since that society is likely to have a hierarchical orientation with the better endowed accepting to guide and care for the lesser endowed, this support is likely to be forthcoming. Chronicity is thus encouraged. Only with the third orientation is the schizophrenic relatively safe from either trap. If he and his society believe in finding compromises with nature and their fellowmen, he will not struggle very hard against his disease but he will not automatically sink into a sick-role either. His society will not support him as thoroughly as if they believed that God ordered them to do so, but they will tolerate him and find a partial use for his healthy capacities rather than demand that he compete in life and show himself as independent as the rest of them.

This is, I believe, one of the broad social factors which

affects the course of schizophrenia, and one can see that it offers a possible explanation for some of the differences cited earlier. The Roman Catholics and the Calvinists, with their shared image of God dominating man, show more chronicity than the Lutherans and vaguer Christians who think more in terms of man dominating nature. But the Calvinists with their added emphasis on each man proving his own worth show the strongest tendency towards continued hospitalization. The Mauritians and the inhabitants of St. Thomas, who have more of a man-with-nature orientation than most Europeans have, show less chronicity than the British samples, and one can also argue that the Mauritians, who migrate relatively little despite economic pressures, have a less competitive and man-over-nature attitude than the inhabitants of St. Thomas who are mostly either immigrants from neighboring islands or people who have sought their fortune on the mainland and returned. However, there are features in the rest of the data which cannot be so well explained by reference to value orientations alone, notably the episodic character of the histories of St. Thomas and the "modern" French-Canada, and one must therefore make allowance for at least one further factor, that which I am calling "social integration."

By integration I am referring not to the organization of relationships or the place of individuals within a society but to the efficiency with which a community or society supports and controls its members. Where integration is high, as in the traditional French-Canadian communities, and also in much of Mauritius and much of Europe, one finds that prescribed modes of behavior are largely adhered to, rewards and support are provided for those whom the society thinks should be rewarded or supported, escapes such as the sick role are provided for members who wish to conform but find this too difficult, and those who do not accept the prescribed roles and standards are somehow eliminated. Where integration is low there is much more variation in the behavior shown by individuals and small groups, rewards and support may be promised but not provided, escapes from social pressure are easier and not so institutionalized, and although steps are taken against deviants they tend to be inconsistent or ineffective. In St. Thomas there was broad tolerance for idiosyncracies but little community support or guidance. In the "modern" French-Canadian villages there was a general belief in the same orientations as held by the traditional communities (though with more emphasis on man dominating nature), but the leaders complained that they could not achieve conformity and the ordinary member complained that proper behavior was not rewarded. Accordingly, the schizophrenics in these less integrated communities showed a wider variety of symptomatology and a more erratic course of illness than the schizophrenics in the more integrated, for there was no clearly defined sick-role into which they were pushed and little guidance on how to avoid a relapse.

Low integration tends to result in a greater inconsistency between what is preached and what is possible than is found with high integration, and if the preachings are believed in, then this inconsistency can be expected to increase the risk of schizophrenia, but regardless of whether incidence is increased the course of illness is more likely to be episodic than if integration is high.

Practical Applications

Since this is a conference on the treatment of the chronic psychoses, the exposition of the above theory remains incomplete unless something is said about how it could assist in the handling of our patients. There are two ways in which I think this might be done.

First, the theory would seem to predict that it will

usually be better to place the exschizophrenic in a section of society that believes in the man-with-nature orientation rather than in a section which holds either of the alternatives, and it suggests that if he has grown up absorbing either of these alternatives, an effort should be made to change his orientation. By this is meant not merely that the patient or expatient should be placed among people who will tolerate his peculiarities and that he should be taught to tolerate them himself, for if such attitudes are specific to himself or to patients as a category but not to life in general the sense of being not a full human being will persist. Rather, the inference means that attention should be paid to the general philosophy of life which the patient and his associates accept, not merely to their view of sickness. Also it means that if there is a well-integrated image of the sick-role, this should be attacked (or if you like, sabotaged) not simply within the walls of the treating institution, as has frequently been done, but in the society around that institution. What this first application of the theory proposes is not very different from what many people are already attempting, but the relation of their activities to the theory may make these attempts more systematic or inclusive.

The second use of the theory is more specific. It involves examining the sociocultural context of the patient in order to identify the available escape roles, the aspects of social interaction which are important if the patient himself is to accept the roles that demand too much subtlety, and the idiomatic twists which every culture gives to the value orientations which otherwise it would share with much of mankind. Some years ago I attempted for teaching purposes to do this empirically with respect to the types of Canadian community covered by our rural survey, keeping in mind the commoner questions that tend to arise when a treatment team attempts to plan a patient's rehabilitation. Figure 5.7 shows the result and illustrates the fact that measures that would be appropriate for patients from some

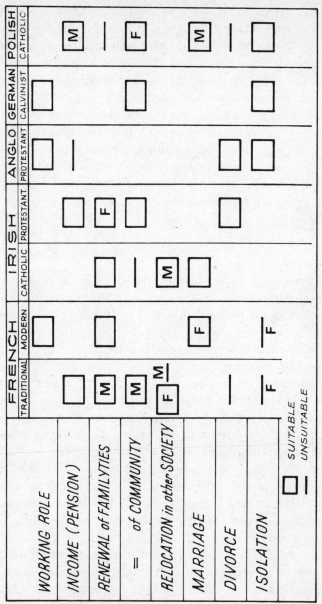

Fig. 5.7.   Suitability of rehabilitation measures in different
Canadian subcultures

backgrounds might be quite inappropriate for patients from others. With the aid of an anthropologist or anyone with a good knowledge of the society from which one's patients come, I think that it is possible to carry out a similar exercise anywhere, an actual study of the interactions between patients and their communities being theoretically unnecessary. I would like to recommend this exercise as a means of introducing oneself to the question of how far one's own society has elements in it which may be contributing to the chronicity or relapses from which one's psychotic patients suffer.

CONCLUSIONS

In a previous paper addressed to medical geneticists, I attempted to estimate the amount of variation which social factors can contribute to the risk of developing schizophrenia.[14] I would like to do the same now with respect to the influence which social factors have on the risk of the schizophrenia remaining chronically disabling, but the evidence is still too slight to permit this. Yet there is such an influence, and we have every reason to think that it is much greater than the psychic influence of the therapeutic team, for the latter has contact with the patient for only a small part of his life whereas his society is in contact with him at all times unless he can find some escape. The traditional mental hospital provided such an escape, but an escape that was a trap. Other types of escape are being explored at present, but they can be expected to accept only a very small proportion of patients. A more logical approach to reducing the adverse social influences is to identify their nature by comparing settings where chronicity is high with settings where chronicity is low, and applying the lessons from these comparisons to preventive practice. This paper has attempted a few steps in that direction.

NOTES

1. Basaglia, R. (1970), *L'Institution en Négation.* Paris: Edition du Seuil.
2. Boyers, R. & Orrill, R. (1971), *R. D. Laing and Anti-Psychiatry.* New York: Harper & Row.
3. Brown, G. W. et al. (1966), *Schizophrenia and Social Care.* Oxford: Oxford University Press.
4. Cooper, D. (1966), *Psychiatry and Anti-Psychiatry.* London: Tavistock.
5. Harris, A. et al. (1956), Schizophrenia; a prognostic and social study. *Brit. J. Prev. Soc. Med.,* 10:107–113.
6. Hollingshead, A. B. & Redlich, F. C. (1958), *Social Class and Mental Illness.* New York: Wiley.
7. Kluckhohn, F. R. & Strodtbeck, F. L. (1961), *Variations in Value Orientations.* Evanston, Ill.: Row, Peterson & Co.
8. Laing, R. D. (1967), *Politics of Experience.* New York: Pantheon.
9. Mannoni, M. (1970), *Le psychiâtre, son "fou" et la psychanalyse.* Paris: Editions du Seuil.
10. Murphy, H. B. M. & Sampath, H. (1967), Mental Health in a Caribbean Community; a Mental Health Survey of St. Thomas, V.I. (Report to the Government of the Virgin Islands, U.S.A., unpublished.)

11. Murphy, H. B. M. & Lemieux, M. (1967), Quelques considér-
     ations sur le taux élevé de schizophrénie dans un type de com-
     munauté canadienne-française. *Canad. Psychiat. Assoc. J.*, 12, No.
     Spécial, S71–81.

12. Murphy, H. B. M. (1968), Cultural factors in the genesis of
     schizophrenia. In: *The Transmission of Schizophrenia*, eds. D. Ro-
     senthal and S. S. Kety. London: Pergamon Press.

13. Murphy, H. B. M. & Raman, A. C. (1971), The chronicity of
     schizophrenia in indigenous tropical peoples. *Brit. J. Psychiat.*,
     118:489–497.

14. Murphy, H. B. M., The schizophrenia-evoking role of complex
     social tasks. In: *Genetic Factors in Schizophrenia*, ed. A. R. Kaplan.
     In press.

15. Myers, J. K. & Bean, L. L. (1968), *A Decade Later: A Follow-up of
     Social Class and Mental Illness.* New York: Wiley.

16. Tewfik, G. I. (1958), Psychoses in Africa. In: *Mental Disorders and
     Mental Health in Africa South of the Sahara.* CCTA/CSA-WFMH-
     WHO meeting of specialists on mental health, London.

17. See the writings of Laing,[8] Mannoni,[9] and Basaglia[1] and the
     reactions which they have elicited.[2,4]

18. The actual figures are shown in Table 5.1. "Long-term preva-
     lence" refers to the rate of cases more than six months in the
     hospital or placed in foster care. "Short-term prevalence" re-
     fers to patients less than six months in the hospital or attending
     a sheltered workshop, rates being per ten thousand adults. It
     can be seen that except at the zone in which the hospital is
     situated, the first rate increases as one moves from the modern
     to the traditional end, while the short-term prevalence shows
     only random variation.

Table 5.1. **Long- and short-term prevalence**

Zone		Long-term prevalence	Short-term prevalence
Modern	1	11	30
	2	23	23
	3	24	30
	4	30	32
Location of hospital	5	(57)	(54)
	6	37	27
Traditional	7	33	23

Chapter 6

AGING IN PSYCHOTICS

Christian Müller, M.D.

INTRODUCTION

The increase in the number of old people in the average population has forced psychiatry to deal with mental health problems of this particular time of life. Geronto-psychiatry has existed for a long time, but has met initially with lack of interest; today, however, it has gone beyond what we could call the "justification stage," and we no longer have to "justify" our dealing with the nosological and pathogenetic aspects of the psychic disturbances of old age. On the contrary, requests come in from all directions for exact information, figures, and forecasts in this field.

In this context, reflection is called for upon the influence of age on adult psychoses. Indeed, not only is it important to know what are the consequences of aging for normal persons, but in connection with the study of the development of long-term psychoses there also arises the question of the interaction between these psychoses and various new elements which appear with the approach of old age.

Writers have emphasized the distress of the elderly; King Lear, who sinks into depression, is a conspicuous example. However, we do find accounts describing the soothing and restoring effect of senescence. Don Quixote, for example, who after the vicissitudes of an existence marked by delusions and the projection of his fantasy wishes into reality, recovers his lucidity towards the end of his life, recognizes his mistakes, and dies in peace. There is also a marvellous story by Laxnes, winner of the Nobel prize for Literature, where a peasant leaves his village, convinced he is another Napoleon; he lives out his delusion to the full and leads a double life for years, until as an old man he goes home cured, his delusional conviction abandoned and with no further desire to transform reality to fit the exigencies of his desire for grandeur. We have also found examples, of course, of chronic schizophrenics finding their lucidity again on their deathbed, and a few very rare works give exact descriptions of this. The theme of physical illness which "destroys the body but cures the soul" is one we occasionally come across here and there.

Clinical practitioners are not the first to have had the impression that old age sometimes blunts the keenness of pathological phenomena, and that diminishing vital energies are accompanied by greater calm and harmonious serenity. Old people turn toward their past and live in retrospect, which is often a movement of introversion. If they continued to live in an extravert mode, they would lose themselves in a futureless perspective and be in a constant state of anxiety, therefore running the continual risk of decompensation.

We shall examine here to what extent this impression can be clearly defined and controlled by scientific methods. What happens when two long-term illnesses interact, with no acute stress being involved and with no etiological connection between the two? This constitutes a real interference and the interaction between old age and preexistent psychosis is one of our main fields of interest. Close observation of the resultant of two processes can possibly lead to valid conclusions as to the nature of one of these processes. For research of this kind to be carried out according to valid criteria, a whole series of conditions have to be present. For example, the first illness—or the first factor studied—has to intersect the second sufficiently often for statistical evaluation to be possible. The second factor also has to be frequent enough in the average population for it to be recognized on its own. Finally, the two processes have to intersect at the same level, which in our own case means that both modify psychic functions.

It seems to me, that these criteria are met where there is a combination of adult psychic disturbances with alterations resulting from senescence. The psychological and neuropathological phenomena of old age are in fact sufficiently well known and are not exceptional. They are regularly found among the average population and can intersect virtually all known adulthood disorders.

If we start with the hypothesis that there is a real interaction between senescence and preexistent psychoses and that, for example, a chronic schizophrenia can be modified with the appearance of old age phenomena, then we can formulate hypotheses with regard to the nature of these modifications.

The first of these would be a hypothesis of psychogenetic action. From the psychological point of view the period of senescence is characterized by a narrowing of interests and by a regression manifested in the appearance of bodily preoccupations, often of an oral or anal type. Can one talk of a real and objective reduction of libido in senescence? Together with Ciompi, we have tried to clarify this point of view. The action mechanism of a tardive improvement in the psychosis would then lie in an easing off of libidinal conflicts, withdrawal of cathexis from pathological object relations, abandonment of certain narcissistic positions— in short, an abatement of instinctual conflict. The id would present a mitigated opposition to reality.

The second hypothesis would focus on the importance of changes in reality which occur in old age. The old person has had a certain number of real losses which he had to accept such as, the death of members of his family; changes from the professional point of view; the emergence of a physical dependence which obliges him to establish new contacts; the obligatory surrender of dominant positions; and a real lessening of the need to fight for survival. Given the major importance of environment, sociocultural factors, and family on the symptomatology and course of schizophrenia, for example, it would not be unjustified to assume that these same factors can to a large extent explain a modification in a prior psychosis.

Finally, a third hypothesis, which is by no means the least interesting, could be one which attributes predominant importance to the organic factor in old age. Mental slowing down, the basic phenomenon of old age, the appearance of mnemonic disturbances, major changes in hormone and metabolic balance, modification of neuron activity as a result of humoral transformations, could all be suggested as factors capable of influencing a preexistent psychosis, such as schizophrenia, for example, but also depression or any other adult psychosis, with or without an organic component.

This latter hypothesis would certainly be of interest above all to the organicists and especially those who accept the existence of a somatosis underlying the group of psychoses known as endogenic.

It would certainly be premature as yet to try to be dogmatic and take any one of these hypotheses as exclusively valid. A great deal of research still has to be done and the available literature gives only very vague information.

In fact, a glance at the literature on schizophrenia shows that most of the major monographs dealing with its evolutions—studies using prolonged catamneses—make no mention of old age at all. Only a few authors, such as Riemer, Bychowski, Barucci, Wenger, and others have attempted to go deeper into this field. More or less the same can be said with regard to depression. Many authors have examined either the course of depression during adulthood, but without taking into account the changes occurring with senescence, or else the involutional tardive depressions; the latter are already intimately linked with the problem of growing old. It is only as a side issue that we find information on patients observed from adulthood up to advanced old age in the works of Kinkelin, Matussek, and Angst, and in works of the English and Americans (Post, Roth, Kay, and others). While some authors, such as Bostroem, consider that attacks of depression tend to become particularly serious in old age, Weitbrecht, Bronisch, and others uphold the contrary, that the symptomatology becomes less pronounced with old age.

We could also try to summarize the data in literature dealing with other psychoses, such as general paralysis, alcoholism, drug addictions, epilepsy, and so forth, but once again we would find that there is a lack of systematic works on these subjects too.

OUR OWN INVESTIGATIONS

With a view to filling in the gaps mentioned above, we undertook eight years ago a series of systematic studies examining a population of former psychotics as they entered the period of senescence. As with any catamnestic work, we had to overcome a certain number of methodological difficulties. I do not propose to go into these in detail here, as we have described our procedures at length elsewhere.[26] Let me simply repeat that our "Lausanne Survey" dealt with the 907 survivors out of a total of 5661 subjects born between 1873 and 1897. These 907 former patients were reexamined either at home or in a hospital, with a semistructured interview, the examination of records, and third-party information. We established our own scales for evaluating the degree of change in symptoms, improvement or deterioration, social adjustment, etc.

Let us begin with schizophrenia. Fifteen years ago, I had examined 101 chronic schizophrenics already in old age, but all hospitalized. From the point of view of overall social adjustment, I had found 14 patients whose condition had deteriorated, 55 cases who had improved, and 32 who showed no change. With regard to changes in the symptomatology proper, i.e., delusions, hallucinations, autism, and depersonalization phenomena, I had found an improvement in 27 percent of the cases, no change in 47 percent, and deterioration in 26 percent. So we had already by that time observed a contradiction between improved social adaptation and the presence of a schizophrenic symptomatology. In our present survey we have managed to include among the subjects nonhospitalized schizophrenics who have reached senescence, thus making a total of 304 subjects. The average length of catamnesis is 30.7 years as from the first admission, and the average age of these patients is 76.5 years. We found 26.3 percent of them living in a family, 12.8 percent living alone, 39.9 percent in nursing homes, and 20.1 percent hospitalized in psychiatric establishments. As far as schizophrenic symptomatology is concerned, we observed its complete disappearance in 21.4 percent of these cases, an improvement in 42.1 percent, and deterioration in 5.6 percent of them; there was no change in 29.3 percent. Only in 1.6 percent of the cases was information insufficient to warrant any judgement. To summarize then, it can be said that old age brought about an improvement in two-thirds of the patients and that only one-third of them showed no change or deteriorated with old age. Social adaptation was good in 16.1 percent, satisfactory in 17.1 percent, fair in 35.2 percent, and poor in 29.4 percent of these cases. The proportion of actual senile dementiae was more or less the same among these 304 subjects comprising both hospitalized and nonhospitalized schizophrenics as it was among the 101 hospitalized schizophrenics in the first group studied, i.e., approximately 8 percent. This confirms that senile dementia appears to be no more frequent among former schizophrenics than in the average population. We have, of course, attempted to analyze a certain number of variables in relation to these overall observations concerning the evolution of schizophrenia and psychic adaptation in old age, and in particular factors such as heredity, constitution, childhood family milieu, intelligence levels, professional qualifications, premorbid personality, age at the onset of the disorder, length of hospitalization, treatments received, physical health at the time of catamnesis, the extent of psychoorganic deterioration and, of course, sex, to quote but a few. Some interesting results emerged from the examination of correlations between these variables; first of all, we found no differences according to sex. Neither did heredity or constitution appear to play a determinant part in regards to the type of development in old age. What we did find surprising was the observation that intelligence has only a relative influence, in the sense that as far as overall adaptation in old age was concerned only identified oligophrenia had any statistically significant correlation with an unfavorable condition. Professional qualifications were a favorable element in overall adaptation in old age. Low professional qualification at the time of first admission had a significant effect upon general psychic adaptation in old age. Premorbid personality seems to have little influence on the modalities of growing old in schizophrenics.

How should these data be interpreted? First of all, I do not think that these results can be used to support a single etiological hypothesis. In any case, they provide no evidence of the predominant importance of an organic process, metabolical for example, for if this were present it would be only logical to expect progressive deterioration of the disorder in old age. In actual fact, the contrary is the case, as we have just shown.

With regard to the psychodynamic aspect, we were also surprised to observe that the period of senescence, with all its consequences, such as increased isolation, loss of contact through disability on one hand, and the environment on the other, inherent tendency to regression, and so on—brings an improvement, whereas one would more readily expect to find deterioration. Indeed, should one not consider the psychological situation of old people as schizophrenogenic, favorable to the loss of all vital contact with reality? Hence our observation of an objective improvement of schizophrenia in old age remains something of a mystery. We can only suppose that with some very real frustration a new equilibrium has been established, more favorable than before precisely because of the increasing remoteness in time of the original family conflicts, the lessening of social pressures which require the individual to adapt and integrate into a group, and also the allaying of guilt feelings at the appearance of regressive needs. So here we again find the essential elements of our first two hypotheses with regard to the nature of the changes which occur.

Now let us go on to another major group of psychoses, depression. In our research this was dealt with especially by my colleague, L. Ciompi, who examined 127 patients whom he saw on an average of 25 years after their first admission to a hospital as a result of severe depressive episodes. We were both struck by the same phenomenon: for the majority of our subjects, depressive disorders tend to improve in old age. About one-third of them had no further relapse after the age of 65; in approximately one-third of these cases the attacks diminished in frequency and intensity, and in the remaining third only we observed a condition unchanged or deteriorated by comparison with their former state. While authors such as Post, Taschev, Matussek, etc., have shown that the critical period for depression is the climacteric and involutional age, we can now state that once the point of 65 is passed not only does the appearance of new depressive phases become less frequent in a given population, but formerly depressive phases tend to become more infrequent; if the depressive symptomatology does persist, it becomes less sthenic, more flat and monotonous, and tends to shift from the ideo-affective plane towards the somatic level, with hypochondriac complaints, tiredness, weakness, and psychosomatic disorders. We have also often noted that new affective disorders, of a less blatantly depressive kind, come into play. This is an aggressive and vague discontent. Once again we come back to the question of the role of psychoorganic deterioration. Its frequency is no more marked among depressives or schizophrenics than in an average population. In fact, we found established dementia in 7.1 percent of those of our former depressives whom we reexamined. Examination of the statistical relations between the evolution of depressions and psychoorganic deterioration shows that there is no progressive aggravation of depressions with accompanying intensification of psychoorganic disorder. There is an initial phase where the two disorders are superimposed or follow one another with no apparent particular interaction. On the other hand, where there is some degree of psychoorganic deterioration but not to the extent of a dementia properly speaking, the subject often enters a critical phase during which depressive disorders can be accentuated. This can easily be explained by the fact that the subject is already well aware of the loss of his intellectual capacities; he feels a deep loss of security and reacts to this by accentuated depression. It is only when the capacity for self-criticism disappears with dementia that the depressive disorders also tend to fade out. As in the case of schizophrenia, we also noted in the study of depressions that, statistically speaking, there is a significant correlation between good physical health and the state of mental health.

We should also like to mention briefly the other categories of patients we examined, although they do not belong to the group of psychoses in the strict sense of the term. In alcoholics who have reached old age, we naturally observed a high mortality rate. However, among those who have survived and reached the age of 70 or 80, we found that a considerable percentage showed an improvement in their alcoholism, not in the sense of abstinence, but of moderation. There has been considerable debate as to whether a chronic alcoholic can, theoretically, return to "normal" consumption—a question of great practical importance. We think we have provided a positive answer, and in this connection I would refer you to Ciompi's work recently published in *Psychiatrie sociale.*

With regard to drug addicts, we found more or less analogous results, namely, a definite tendency to improvement in old age; they had either completely dropped all misuse of drugs or had reduced their consumption.

There were too few adulthood psychoses of an organic order in our study for us to draw any valid conclusions from them. It is nonetheless interesting to note that among our syphilitics we found no real correlation between senile dementia and paralytic dementia. This is an interesting point, because it could well have been supposed that general paralysis might be a predisposing factor to senile or arteriosclerotic dementia.

Finally, as far as the large group of oligophrenics is concerned, we found no grounds for confirmation of the opinion widely expressed in the literature that this group undergoes premature psychic and physical aging. Once again, we demonstrated in this group the capital importance of social adjustment and milieu.

To conclude with, our "Lausanne Survey" has enabled us to clarify on a statistical basis the general tendency of psychopathological symptoms to improve in old age. We are, of course, aware of the weak points in our argument: first of all, we were dealing only with a population of surviving patients, and we cannot tell what the old age of our former psychotics who died before the age of 65 would have been like. This objection has only a relative value, though; the fact is that any study dealing with people in the period of senescence is a survivor study.

Secondly, the objection could be raised that this is a retrospective study. It is almost certain that no definitive answer could be given to the questions we asked unless we were in a position to follow the patients with repeated examinations up to old age according to previously established assessment criteria.

NOTES

1. Angst, J. (1966), Zur Aetiologie und Nosologie endogener depressiver Psychosen. Monograph. *Neurology und Psychiatrie,* Heft 112. Springer, Berlin-Heidelberg-New York.

2. Barucci, M. (1955), La vecchiaia degli schizofrenici. *Riv. pat. nerv. ment.,* 76:257; La vecchiaia degli schizophrenici (reperti necroscopici). *Rass. studi. psichiat.,* 64:1.

3. Bostroem, A. (1938), Die verschiedenen Lebensabschnitte in ihrer Auswirkung auf das psychiatrische Krankheitsbild. *Arch. Psychiat.,* 107:155–171.

4. Bronisch, F. W. (1962), *Die psychischen Störungen des älteren Menschen.* Stuttgart: F. Enke.

5. Bychowski, G. (1952), Schizophrenia in the period of involution. *Dis. Nerv. Syst.,* 13:150–153.

6. Ciompi, L. & Eisert, M. (1971), Etudes catamnestiques de longue durée sur le vieillissement des alcooliques. *Psychiatrie sociale,* 6:129–151.

7. Ciompi, L. & Lai, G. P. (1969), *Dépression et vieillesse. Etudes catamnestiques sur le vieillissement et la mortalité de 555 anciens patients dépressifs.* Bern: Huber.

8. Ciompi, L. & Müller, C. (1969), Katamnestische Untersuchungen zur Altersentwicklung psychischer Krankheiten. *Nervenarzt,* 40:349–355.

9. Gillieron, M. (1968), Etude catamnestique sur la vieillesse des anciens toxicomanes. *Schweiz. Arch. Neurol. Psychiat.,* 102:457–480.

10. Kay, D. W., Beamish, P., & Roth, M. (1964), Old age mental disorders in Newcastle-upon-Tyne. Part I. A study of prevalence. *Brit. J. Psychiat.,* 110(465):146–158.

11. Kay, D. W., Roth, M., & Hopkins, B. (1955), Affective disorders arising in the senium. I. Their association with organic cerebral degeneration. *J. Ment. Sci.,* 101:302–316.

12. Kinkelin, M. (1954), Verlauf und Prognose des manischdepressiven Irreseins. *Schweiz. Arch. Neurol. Psychiat.,* 73:100–146.

13. Matussek, P., Halbbach, A., & Troeger, U. (1965), *Endogene Depression. Eine statistische Untersuchung unbehandelter Fälle.* München:Urban & Schwarzenberg.

14. Moser, A. (1977), *Die Langfristige Entwicklung Oligophrener.* Berlin: Springer.

15. Müller, C. (1959), Ueber das Senium der Schizophrenen; zugleich ein Beitrag zum Problem der schizophrenen Endzustände. *Bibl. Psychiat. Neurol., Fasc.* 106. Basel: Kargel.

16. Müller, C. (1969), Manuel de géronto-psychiatrie. Paris: Masson.

17. Müller, C. (1970), Katamnestische Beobachtungen zur Entwicklung der progressiven Paralyse bis ins hohe Alter. *Arch. Psychiat. Nervenkr.,* 213:149–165.

18. Post, F. (1962), *The significance of affective symptomes in old age. A follow-up study of one hundred patients.* Maudsley Monogr. 10. London: Oxford University Press.

19. Riemer, M. D. (1950), A study of the mental status of schizophrenics hospitalized for over 25 years into their senium. *Psychiat. Quart.,* 24:309–313.

20. Roth, M. & Kay, D. W. (1956), Affective disorders arising in the senium. II. Physical disability as an aetiological factor. *J. Ment. Sci.,* 102:141–150.

21. Roth, M. & Kay, D. W. (1962), Social, medical and personality

factors associated with vulnerability to psychiatric breakdown in old age. *Geront. Clin.,* 4:147–160.

22. Taschev, T. (1965), Statistisches über die Melancholie. *Fortschr. Neurol. Psychiat.,* 33:25–36.

23. Villa, J. L. & Lai, G. (1966), Difficultés méthodologiques dans la recherche géronto-psychiatrique. *J. méd. Lyon,* 47:153–167.

24. Weitbrecht, H. J. (1960), Depressive und manische endogene Psychosen. In: *Psychiatrie der Gegenwart,* Band II, Berlin-Görttingen-Heidelberg: Springer, pp. 73–118.

25. Wenger, P. (1958), A comparative study of the aging process in groups of schizophrenic and mentally well veterans. *Geriatrics,* 13:367–370.

26. See notes 6–9, 14–17, and 23.

Part IV

THE PSYCHIATRIST IN THE COMMUNITY

INTRODUCTION

Psychiatrists today are moving away from the mental hospital and drawing their patients out of that milieu too. Even though, contrary to the antipsychiatrists, they believe in the existence of mental illnesses, they still battle against any conception of sickness which leads to the segregation, rejection, and alienation of the "insane." To this end, not only must they be installed geographically outside the hospital and set up an increasing number of outpatient departments, day institutions, and other facilities which avoid the patients' separation from their family and social milieu, but they must also work with and in the community to bring about a change in its attitude to mental sickness.

The role of the psychiatrist in the community, within the city itself, is the subject of the three texts comprising the final chapters of this symposium, which are based on experiments carried out in Lyon (France), the Bronx in New York, and the 13th District of Paris, respectively.

Hochmann gives a good example of what can be done

to avoid hospitalization. He gives consultations and therapeutic sessions in an outpatient department, visits the patients at home and, as one might say, "accompanies" the
patient in his personal development, his discovery of the
outside world, etc.

The utility of this "home hospitalization" work no
longer has to be demonstrated. It can only be carried out
by a multidisciplinary team, and lends itself to innovation
without reference to a formal or traditional model of the
individual roles. In both Lyon and Paris the existence of a
permanent reception group proved essential.

Contrary to the impression sometimes given of catchment area psychiatry as "police checking," as Maud Mannoni chooses to call it, we see that Hochmann makes no
attempt to force care on people at all costs and shows no
tendency to therapeutic activism. He and his team are
present and available and have made it possible to organize
a reception place, which is something extremely rare in the
modern metropolis where each individual rushes about in
a great hurry, preoccupied with his own worries, and shut
off in the little box of his apartment. Hochmann and his
team also work at reducing the anxiety of the patient's
family and neighbors, who learn to call up the team rather
than the police when a crisis appears. They encourage and
facilitate the renewal of natural relationships with his surroundings.

Israel Zwerling demonstrates the advantage of creating diversified therapeutic programs "à la carte" to respond to patients' needs. He also shows the difficulties
involved. One cannot wait for the patient to adapt to institutions, but must get him at whatever his current stage of
capacity for functioning and give him a chance of social
reintegration. The picture of the "network" of resources
set up in the Bronx appears as a more structured experiment, which corresponds to the North American "pro-

gram" policy, and contrasts with the more flexible, more improvised French manner.

Philippe Paumelle goes from the forcefully written defense of a psychiatrist's presence in the city to the examination of statistical data and the illustration, with case descriptions, of the daily success of the Paris 13th District Mental Health Association's pledge of getting out of the rut that the traditional mental hospital, or the "asylum" was sinking into. Paumelle emphasizes the three fundamental principles of *therapeutic continuity, staff responsibility,* and the *nonrejection of the mentally sick.*

We join René Angelergues, whose thought we summarize here, in saying that the arrival of the psychiatrist in the city constitutes an unprecedented change in the evolution of the psychiatric *praxis.* Unless great care is taken, psychiatric action is liable to be radically changed by it. With the loss of his traditional institutions, the psychiatrist could easily tend to consider the community as his institution in their place. The activity he would then carry out through the intermediary of a caring team, however much the hierarchical structure may be minimized, would lead to a twofold negation: firstly, denial of the reality of the mental functioning of the individual, which remains the sole legitimate preoccupation of the psychiatrist and in which he can hope for some competence; and secondly, negation of the political and social content of human phenomena, which, despite models borrowed from psychodynamics and psychosociology, would turn the psychiatrist into an instrument of order and control in the city.

C. C.

Chapter 7

SIX YEARS EXPERIENCE IN COMMUNITY-BASED PSYCHIATRIC ORGANIZATION[1]

Jacques Hochmann, M.D.

Once the protective straitjacket of asylum walls and routines is thrown off and the fascinating identification with the model of highly specialized and remunerative liberal medical practice is put aside, and once the "public health" ideology of early screening and administrative pattern is removed, the psychiatry of psychotics has to look, if not for an object, at least for a method. Whereupon contradications arise on all sides, and the pendulum swings between the community view and the psychotherapeutic aspect; support for the patient's circle by means of analysis of the tensions running through it and individual treatment; the precedence given to prevention or therapy; intensive outpatient work or home visits and, at a deeper level, tolerance of regression or concern for mobilizing the patient by proposing various forms of activity.

Our practice developed within an outpatient team based in a multidisciplinary medicosocial center and composed of psychiatrists, psychologists, part-time speech therapists, two secretaries, three full-time and two part-time nurses, all of whom as a team worked in close cooperation with the community social services. This report deals only with that part of the team's activities in which the author participated directly. As a reaction against the totalitarianism fashionable in psychiatric institutions, we were inclined to favor a "fragmented" system with a set of people working independently and autonomously in relation to each other, rather than an organization with any real structure. Within the team there is no link of actual subordination between one person and another (fantasies are another matter altogether), and if two or three people frequently work together this is determined by personal affinities, mutual interests, or simply habit, and not in conformity with any previously established hierarchical arrangement.

Over a period of six years we had our ups and downs and our battles too. Today we feel that the contradictions experienced by the organization as a whole and perhaps also in the subjectivity of each of its members, reflected:

1. the internal contradiction of the psychotic, split in his ego and projecting his splitting outwards;
2. the no less apparent splitting revealed in others by the confrontation with psychosis; and
3. finally, and especially, the double exigency we are faced with, namely, that of the patient and that of his circle.

We shall depart from custom here and deliberately confine this circle to the patient's immediate environment, his family, his neighbors, and the various social entities in *direct* contact with him. Of course, we are well aware of the fact that those with whom the patient is in communication do convey a certain number of values and standards related to the infrastructures of our society, and particularly to relations of production and economic alienation. Although we have little talent for science fiction, and with clinical observation as our only tool of analysis, we nonetheless have to recognize the fact that the nature of the link between the insanity of one or several persons and the particular form of a society—even if we accept the existence of this link—is still too obscure for it to be used as a basis for either our theoretical efforts or, especially, our day-to-day practice. We do not deny that we who are committed simultaneously to providing treatment and maintaining order are living out social contradictions far more fundamental than the psychological ones of the patient or those in contact with him. This is borne out by the witch-hunt for drug addicts which some people would like us to join in, with all the ambiguous arsenal of a repression given a rosy glow of assistance. As far as those who pay us are concerned, our job is more to submit the individual to the exigencies of production and consumption and fit in with the tranquility of the public at large rather than to restore what we can of his capacity for happiness. But this tension between the individual and society, public and private concerns, the reflection of the division of labor and class antagonism is in no way particularly ours. We share it with all the citizens of this society, and especially its officials. So let us avoid "Freudian-Marxist" verbiage and concentrate on insanity, which constitutes the specificity of our profession and which, in our view, goes beyond the economic and cultural characteristics of a particular form of society, however debatable that may be.

The psychotic is someone who, for numerous reasons related to the particular form of his individual drives or to the inadequate response of his maternal environment, has failed to establish during the first few weeks of his life a fusional relationship with his mother. Had this fusion been possible, it would have allowed temporarily the magical and transitory meeting of fantasy life and the outside world, the partial overlapping of desire and reality which Winnicott calls "illusion." To acquire the capacity for disillusion, emerge from the vague fusion with the other and accede to object relations, to accept the irrevocable separation between self and nonself, the narcissism—or so we believe—has to have been sufficiently bolstered up by a prior transfusion of energy, a "narcissistic contribution" (Grunberger). If this contribution is inadequate then it leads to a "basic fault," as Balint so aptly puts it, a permanent flaw in the basis of one's being, giving rise to a particular kind of dynamism which drives the psychotic on in an unending search for the symbiotic links which would enable him to establish what he lacked.

Like anyone else, the psychotic goes simultaneously through a process of biological and instinctual as well as psychological maturation. And this maturation incites him to seek autonomy and to dread absorption by someone else, although this is precisely what he is desperately looking for.

There is an ensuing clash of forces which brings about distorted development, a kind of scoliosis of the ego, to which his only solution is projection and splitting.

As for the circle of family and friends itself, which is first and foremost the mother but gradually extends to a whole set of people, all more or less merged together and all of whom have a maternal connotation for the psychotic, it too undergoes a course just as contradictory, torn between a desire to make amends via some form of symbiosis, and the mass rejection of the patient.

In the end, there sets in a circular process which we should like to call "confirmation." The patient finds confirmation of his fears and delusions in the attitudes of people around him. In his turn, he does all he can by his behavior to confirm the projections of his circle. This confirmation is, so to speak, the negative of the illusion. It is the overlapping of fear and outside reality just as the illusion arose out of a temporary equivalence between desire and its realization. It too leads into a magical universe whose keynote is omnipotence. In this sense, it is also a substitute for the missing illusion and therefore has at once a reassuring and a terrifying function, which explains the combination of fear and joy the psychotic finds in it. This confirmative process is catching. Initially confined to the psychotic's relations with his mother, it spreads to those which alternately oppose and bring him closer to the other members of his family, his neighbors, his colleagues, and employers. In particular, it penetrates the functioning of residential institutions whose job it is to look after the mentally sick.

The latter, since they establish an arbitrary break between the patient and his circle, can in fact only have abstract individuals to deal with. Cut off from the bases upon which his existence is built, and apart from which, since he has not managed to attain autonomy, he cannot be a person by himself, the psychotic will not rest until he succeeds in reconstituting the fragile and painful equilibrium which formerly enabled him to keep going. No amount of nursing training is enough to keep this reconstitution at bay. The psychotic is only one half of a pathology; the other half, situated outside the institution, is very cruelly lacking. So much so that he has to force the institutional staff to reconstitute it, if only to enable himself to exist again. Insanity cannot remain something secret and personal. It crystallizes around the projection and disavowal of reality, and drags others along in its wake—all the more easily so in that it finds confused echoes in each one of us. It makes itself known and always has a political dimension, in the real sense of the term.

It is therefore essential to get away from the pattern of segregative institutions as well as the isolation of psychoanalysis and into a place where madness remains free to develop in an interhuman space, where it can unfold in a collective history.

It necessarily follows that there has to be a radical change in the position of the caring staff. In residential institutions the patient is, by definition, taken into *total* care. This means that he has no possible avenues of communication other than with his companions and the staff of the institution, with whom, as we have already said, he tries to reconstitute the psychotic universe which for him is the only one possible.

The caring staff can be very quick to detect the signs of this institutional "transference"; they will find that they are alternately "good" and "bad" and, applying the psychoanalytical pattern, try to interpret what they see. But their procedure will be flawed from the very start by the confusion between interior and exterior, and despite themselves they will find that they are drawn into a *real* process of confirmation of psychosis which will disqualify all their interpretations.

Community-based treatment is, on the contrary, characterized by its *partial* aspect. The patient still has the usual people around him, all those who participate in his suffering. Those caring for him come face to face with the whole tragedy of insanity, a drama with many characters and no longer a monologue interrupted by his responses.

The caring staff can then confine themselves to their essential and specific task, which is to provide the patient with the possibility of a reparative symbiotic relationship with an ill-defined "other," practically unseparated from him, malleable and indestructible, "like water and the sand," a real primary substance at the disposal of fantasies of omnipotence, and whose only limitations are those of their own narcissistic resistance.

At the same time, they can facilitate by their presence and their "solicitude" a renewal of the narcissistic economy of his circle, sorely tried by the patient's avidity and aggressions.

This puts us, as we said, in the uncomfortable path of a two-fold request, each of whose terms are equivocal, and which gives rise to our contradictions, themselves the reflection of those experienced in and among themselves by the people who call on us for help. The majority of the social responses to insanity simply reject these contradictions. They are firmly set in a one-way direction which forbids any dialectization in the internal space of the patient and those close to him as well as in their interpersonal space.

Thus we have seen the blossoming of all kinds of institutions based on the complete break. "A place to put them" if one is in a mood for rejection and identifies with the request of family and society, or "a shelter for them to go to" if one feels sorry for the insane and identifies with their request.

We wanted to listen to people, however halting or jarring their words might be, and to hear everyone, the patient and his family and friends. We wanted to hear them as though listening to a symphony (which excludes neither dissonance nor atonal forms), in other words, like a succession of acts and words from different sources but which taken together form a general sense. We tried to understand what was said and also to make it easier for people to talk. Not by means of a hypothetical breakdown of resistances with a great array of interpretations (they very quickly began to sound silly and our clients themselves laughed at them, preceding us in the art and making a parody of it), but rather through an active and totally reliable presence. In short, through reparative care of our patients' narcissism *and* that of his family and circle. It is no easy matter to stay put in this place where reason and unreason confront each other. Since Aristotle, corroborated by Sganarelle, it has been common knowledge that it is better not to put one's finger between the tree and its bark.

Let us make it quite clear that we are not trying to impose any fallacious equilibrium. We have no intention of encouraging the homeostasis of a system doomed to death in the resolution of its tensions.

Ideally, our concept is not even to "care for" the insane, if by this one means to reduce the "abnormal" to silence and make conformity "normal." It would rather be to allow words, however crazy they may be, to keep circulating, to let the irrational meet the rational without either one attempting to impose its law of repression, to enable the madman to give voice to his reason and those possessed of reason to speak their insanity out loud.

It was accurately summarized a propos of his insane child by a father who, I think, had understood what we were getting at: "For me what he says is not madness any more; it's poetry I try to make out and understand."

After these general considerations, we should like to give a few illustrations.

The Case of Alain: "Outpatient" Psychotherapy of a Psychotic Child and His Parents

Alain was six years old, a psychotic child with practically no language ability whose fantasies of destruction and falling into pieces were expressed in the form of inarticulate yells which racked his whole body like a piece of clockwork about to explode, acts of self-aggression (he punched his own nose and set off nose-bleeds at the slightest frustration), and stereotyped games in which he would incessantly break up and mend toy cars. His mother considered him as a kind of repellent parasite, an evil, curse-bearing organ whose mere contact could damage her, and had projected a whole serics of hypochondriac preoccupations onto him. The father had established a sort of symbiotic relationship with him, which may have been reparative, but in any case excluded the mother. With regard to the child, the father oscillated between depression, during which he declared he wanted to break him, and a state of fusional exaltation in which—"as if he were crazy," according to the mother —he denied the existence of any pathology and was satisfied with such a manageable prolongation, the vector of all his dreams, which he almost seemed to carry in his bosom.

There had been established between Alain and his parents—especially between Alain and his mother—a system of projection-introjection, with the fantasies of one of them finding immediate confirmation in the behavior and speech of the other.

The team, which entered the scene as a third party, consisted of a medical practitioner, a nurse, and a speech therapist,[2] and had set itself the objective of (1) providing the child with a substitute maternal object to enable him to renew relations with a body other than his own, limit his own body, and, through the symbiotic relationship which— we assumed—he had lacked, move on to individuation, language, and the dialectic of castration; and (2) supporting the parents' narcissistic economy to help them, on one hand, to respond to Alain's regressive desires without any harm to him or to themselves, and on the other, to accept and understand his emerging language.

With five approximately two-hour sessions a week, the nurse set out to establish with Alain a relationship founded first of all on physical contact and occupation of the same space. As Alain's real "auxiliary ego," she was to facilitate his gradual grasp of the outside world by accompanying him from his home to the clinic, from the clinic to the swimming pool, to the park or the shops, and so on; she let him take over her car as a two-person space, protective and mobile at the same time, through whose windows the outside world went by, menacing at first but gradually becoming increasingly familiar. Through the nurse's encounters, Alain went on to discover others. Meanwhile, she was also attentive to the mother, who took part in some of their activities. Through the nurse, Alain and his mother were able to discover a previously impossible physical contact.

Twice weekly, by means of free play and drawing, the speech therapist tried to encourage structuration of the human body, time and space. To the parents as well as Alain, and also the nurse, she was that other—the beginnings of a process of symbolization—who set limits to a relation of fusion otherwise doomed to fall irremediably into the realm of the imaginary. Little by little she focused her attention on language.

Every two weeks the doctor and the nurse went to see the parents in their home. Although at first they were received with awkwardness as dangerous and frustrating inspectors (because of their nonadvice and nonguidance), they later became friends taken in to the family. They had to detach themselves from this and get back to the role of interpreting the child's faltering speech, which the parents have now become expert at understanding. They now accept the irrational dimension without reducing it to a handicap or insanity, and can recognize—according to the father's expression quoted above—its "poetry." It is indeed a poetry of death and castration that Alain expresses today in words, and not in the brute form of his screams and classic activity. His body now encases the fantasies he relates to us and is no longer the same empty and permeable space, the ravaged intersection of the fears of his mother and father. With their own narcissism restored, his parents have in turn become our interpreters in a group of parents of psychotic children who occasionally join us with the children for a day in the country.

Our function in this case-history, which is now in its third year, is difficult to describe in any but negative terms.

It is easier to say what we are not than what we are. Perhaps this ascetic exercise, this stripping-down, is what psychiatry is all about.

We are not educators, neither for the child nor for his parents. We have never replaced them in bringing up their child, and have never given them advice, however peculiar some of their practices may have seemed. Neither are we acting psychoanalysts here, for we have never interpreted, either to Alain or his parents, anything that emerged from their unconscious.

All we do is to be there, each in his or her place, with no attempt to fill in the internal emptiness of our clients or the void between them by assortments of supposedly pedagogical activities, advice, practical solutions, and so forth. Not that we refuse our help in various ways when it is asked for in some undertaking or another, or doing some small service (driving Alain and his mother to a hospital appointment, for example), our major concern being to provide the possibility for verbal dialogue within the family.

Family G.: Examples of Joint Action in the Home and the Outpatient Department

The G's are almost indescribable. The mother, an outrageously made-up round little woman is possessed by fantasies of omnipotence, of which she is capable of convincing other people. She is married to an old alcoholic on the brink of dementia, whom she continually calls upon to witness her complaints—a silent witness who is forbidden to open his mouth.

One of their two sons, Pierre, gave trouble from the moment he was born, screaming out when there was no milk left in his bottle. At age four he smashed everything in sight. After being put in various institutions for children with character disorders, he came back to live with his mother at the age of about 17. Ever since, their relationship has been one of envy and hatred. It was one long series of yells and insults, blows and blood, interspersed with huggings and embraces and patching up. Pierre's short-lived marriage with a psychiatric hospital patient hardly interrupted this pattern. Taken on his own, Pierre can give the impression of a psychopathic alcoholic who fills his internal emptiness and long frustration by more than generous helpings of drink laced with barbiturates. In relation to his mother, he appears to be bogged down in the unending search for a symbiotic link which neither of them can manage to create to make up for the initial failure, but which neither can overcome. This explains the mirror-like behavior, with its sad repetitiveness: when the son proposes a rupture, in the form of noisy bouts of drunkenness, the mother reacts in her "all-powerful goddess" register and calls in the police emergency service or the local doctor. There follows internment and a separation which is imposed and unacceptable. Pierre calls his mother to come to his aid, she comes running and snatches her son out of the institution, which she sees as a rival. Pierre sinks for a while into tormented dependence, never leaves the house, obeys his mother to the letter in everything, becomes an obsessive house-keeper and mends everything he has broken. The mother has him sleep in her room, "the better to keep an eye on him" (did I mention that he is 24 years old?) and Pierre's anxiety becomes increasingly acute. There is talk of incest in the house. The mother reacts to this proximity with incessant railing and whining and dark prophecies . . . which soon come true (whence confirmation of her omnipotence) and the whole thing starts again.

The second son, Maurice, who is 19 years old, does no worse than have occasional bouts of delusional drunkenness and plunges for a while into a depression from which he emerges to tell—savagely and scathingly—the truth about his family. It is through him that the outside world enters the duo formed by his mother and brother. He brings home pet animals, his friends, girls. It was he who brought Pierre to the clinic for consultation. He too is confined from time to time on the initiative of his mother, who thus attempts to get rid of an awkward witness of her relationship with Pierre, when this again becomes symbiotic (she cannot tolerate the two together).

Around the two boys there has formed a group about which a word or two should be said here.

The patients used to sit in the Center waiting-room, for an injection or a consultation with a medical practitioner,[3] a psychologist,[4] a nurse, or more recently a male nurse.[5] There are several doors opening into this room from three consultation rooms, a small infirmary, and the secretary's office. The various members of the team come in one after the other during the course of the day, between two home visits, meetings with the social workers, consultations in schools or other clinics, visits to inpatients at the mental hospital or, more and more frequently, the general hospital's emergency service. Only the secretary[6] is there the whole day, and she provides a nonstop reception service and ensures transmission of information among the different members of the dispersed group. It had become customary to give coffee to those who were waiting. The patients knew where the pantry was and used the kitchen, taking over this space as their own, and also cathecting the time spent, which went well beyond that of the actual consultation.

Today this has become a sort of welcoming reception place, created by the patients; it is their property and they manipulate within this, at their own measure, both the form and the duration of their participation. The staff take turns, with no previously set plan and according to their availability, their sole function being to be present and available.[7]

Maurice G., his brother and an inseparable pal, Hervé, represent the permanent background against which the fleeting forms of more transitory participants are silhouetted. It is difficult to talk about this group and, in fact, little talk takes place in it. We thought of calling it the "group without a name," in parody of Ernst Wiechert's *Missa sine Nomine,* an admirable novel relating the story of a narcissistic recovery. And this is precisely what is primarily involved in a fusional "one" where the psychotic's cry can come to the surface and be heard, without any artificial constraints of timetables, limitations of a spatial order or of imposed activities butting in to fill the void he expresses and redcucing him to silence. In fact the sole limitation is a narcissistic one, that of the presence of me and the other together and our respective tolerances—a limitation which cannot be pushed back indefinitely. Thus each one, staff or patient, is free to stay or to leave, to remain isolated or to merge again with the group. When tensions or numbers become too much to cope with, the fact of there being several unoccupied offices make it possible for the group to split up into several subgroups. Often private conversations start up within the group between patients, among staff, or between staff and patients. Sometimes one client or another asks to go aside into an office with one of the staff to talk or to ask for a prescription. In the latter case, it is usually the patient who dictates the prescription. In this way there unfolds a dialectic from the "We to the I-You" which is carried on outside the clinic through the special relationships established between some patients, and also through the occasions where they might run into one member of the team or another, in a restaurant, a café, a shop, when there is some activity they do together, or during the home visits.

As far as the G's are concerned, a therapy program was gradually and quite spontaneously established which includes not only participation in the "group without a name" and individual talks on request with one of us, but also a weekly visit by the doctor and the nurse[8] to their home at a time when the mother is often alone there. The brothers attach a great deal of importance to this visit and reproach us if we ever miss one. Yet they very rarely take part in this encounter, which they consider as being for the mother's benefit. At that particular time they usually go to the Center or out for a walk, or more often to a hostel set up recently in a small house in the neighborhood where a caring team[9] and a group of psychotics meet and which they run jointly.

Mrs. G. is certainly convinced that we are totally incompetent. Since she cannot manage to bend us to her all-powerful will and is also unable to use us as an active extension of her desires, she has declared us useless. There is no point in trying to galvanize us into action by pressing some button or other, as she does with the police, the family doctor, or the district attorney, since in any case we take no action, make out no prescriptions, and lock nobody up. Rather than acknowledge our resistance or opposition, which would be a curtailment of her omnipotence, she adopts the supposition that if we do nothing it is because we are incapable of doing anything anyway. In virtue of which, she accepts us as people to confide her troubles to and as her sons' therapists—therapists who are so inactive that she does not feel they can be considered as her rivals.

What the brothers say they get out of the Center is rather difficult to define: a calm and restful place which contrasts with the tension kept up at home by their altercations with their mother, a place where they are to some extent the masters, a space and time to themselves, where they can live. "You can't forbid things here," they say, in reaction to the "legalistic" intervention of a doctor who refused to see them one day when they were drunk. Any interference on our part—this is increasingly rare, though —which gives the slightest impression that this place is more ours than theirs, that we are more responsible for its upkeep than they are, is taken very badly. But so is any outbreak of violence, the violence they all contain to the brim but leave outside, as though to protect an ideal matrix. And if a patient starts a fight they—who are themselves so ready to quarrel—experience a dramatic moment of mourning: "... if we get to killing each other here too. ...."

They have established a symbiotic relationship with the institution rather than with any one of us. Even if there are one or two people they prefer talking to in particular, they confide fairly easily in all the members of the team they may encounter. And although we, in turn, might transmit these confidences to the others when we meet in an office, a restaurant or somewhere, we find no necessity for doing so systematically. Actually, we dropped the general team meetings in favor of numerous informal contacts, and real cohabitation, leaving more structured meetings for moments of paroxysmal tension or for the examination of a particular problem, as a more or less permanent working group. These meetings are only for those directly involved in the problem in question.

Furthermore, we respect the client's need for a number of different interlocutors to each of whom he gives a glimpse of certain facets of himself, without these people necessarily getting together and sending him back the reflection of a schematic composite portrait, alienating and distorted. It seems to us essential for the patient to be able to set up compartmented relationships with and amongst us in different sectors. What have they not done in hospitals, in the name of institutional psychotherapy and under pretext of putting the pieces back together, to enforce transparency and forbid all private relationships!

With a relative lack of structure, the institution is as manageable as a whole as it is in each one of its members. The patients can belong to it without any sense of intrusion, can dominate it and find a place that fits their own dimensions, without having to submit to being reduced to a given obligatory form, and without any adaptation being required of them. A number of problems arise here which' are far from being solved yet. How can we analyze and control our inclinations to constitute an exclusive "body" of specialists with its own rituals and jargon, which would appropriate space and therapeutic time as *its own* extension (whereas it is just as much theirs as ours, if not more so)? How does one reconcile the necessity for each patient to have among the team a "sponsor" who feels personally and especially concerned about him, with the no less essential all-embracing versatility of each individual therapist? How can we prevent the patient from becoming the exclusive concern of one given person without this entailing his condemnation to abandonment and anonymity?

The group's lack of structure and absence of exclusive "team spirit" makes for easier contact with other members of the community. There are no clear-cut demarcations between them and us. Perhaps the ideal thing would be for us, in turn, to merge into the surrounding community and maintain with it too a symbiotic type of relationship. We have not reached that point yet, but one cannot fail to be struck by the increasing resemblance between the relationship of the psychiatric organization and the community on one hand, and on the other hand that which we try to establish individually with our psychotics (or which the psychotics ask us to establish with them). Our last example, which has been going on for nearly two years now, and which we shall only outline in its major points, will show how these relationships are established.

Mrs. R., Her Family, Her Neighbors, and We

Mrs. R. suffers from chronic delusions and lives alone in an attic room with her two children. A relational network has been set up around her in which we can list a married sister, a grandmother, a neighbor (an elderly spinster who dabbles in charities), the latter's female cousin, who is a doctor, and one of her friends, a clerk. Mrs. R's parents live in the south of France and are in touch with her only on infrequent occasions. Mrs. R. is also supposed to have a lover (or several) who are rejected by the people around her.

Relations between Mrs. R. and all these people are not simple, and are characterized alternately by extreme proximity and violent rejection.

Other tensions gradually worked their way into the system and a rift appeared between the neighbors and the members of the family. The family accused the neighbors of meddling in Mrs. R's business, while the neighbors accused the sister and parents of abandoning the patient. The conflict crystallized upon the children, Nelly, aged 12, and Jean, aged 2. The older is a legitimate child and became a center of contention. Mrs. R's friends were in agreement on the point that she was incapable of bringing her up. She was taken in by a neighbor and then temporarily placed in a home by the authorities, who had been notified of the case. The younger child, the result of a fleeting affair with a North African, was wanted by no one—except the mother, whose wishes were in any case totally ignored by everyone—and ended up in an orphanage.

Quite understandably, this manipulation, the battle ground for conflicts whose source lay elsewhere, gave Mrs. R. food for her delusions. She was being spied upon, people were out to get her, she was not being allowed to eat, to heat her room, or get dressed and so forth, and in fact she virtually let herself die of hunger and cold, shut herself up at home in a state of terror, watching the street from behind closed shutters. Her stove was cold and her pantry empty; finally, she would no longer get out of bed. Neighbors and family became sick and tired of this and gave up coming to see her. Winter arrived and the situation became critical. Alongside the "natural" network, a therapeutic team was constituted between the social worker of the place where Mrs. R. worked occasionally, two nurses, and a medical practitioner[10] from the Mental Health Center.

Our action was to cover three different directions:

1. With regard to the social agencies, we had to deal with Mrs. R's Social Security rights, which she had allowed to lapse for lack of the necessary papers, to maintain her contact with her work, prevent her dismissal and, once she was able to work again, to facilitate her reintegration and acceptance by her colleagues. She also had to be helped to keep up a relationship with her children in homes.

2. As far as her circle was concerned, we tried to build a system free of rivalries between neighbors and family, the whole group and ourselves, and to avoid competitive actions. Telephone conversations with each of them and meeting them at the Center helped to set up a cooperation which manages to limp along fairly well and is reassuring. Thus by the mere fact of our existence we have become a kind of lucky charm, an antiphobic object which forestalls the rejecting acting-out.

3. With the patient, there began a long drawn-out "taming" process. The social worker, the two nurses, and the doctor took turns at her home, and although sometimes met with violence or suspicion, and at other times by a locked door, they were gradually accepted and acknowledged. We did small services for her. The doctor would light the fire while the nurse prepared a meal, and we were considered friends rather than therapists. This explains why Mrs. R. obstinately refuses to sign the Social Security papers which attested to our capacity as therapists but which would at the same time therefore force her to consider herself sick. Nonetheless, she regularly asks to pay her membership fee to the nonprofit-making association we have formed (under the law of 1901). In this relationship, money, gifts, and services rendered have an important and complicated role. Mrs. R. refuses to collect her pay so as

not to draw upon her the wrath of her mysterious persecutors who, she says, forbid her to do so. Yet she sewed a dress for the nurse and asked an appropriate price for doing so, a price which apparently represents for her her own value in the eyes of the nurse. She accepts with ambivalence what we bring her to eat and will eat our provisions when the nurse tells her that she personally cannot bear to let her die of hunger. The lit fire or the food brought are thus an expression of our own narcissism, and represent our intolerance of her death as well as our own. At the same time, she gives us coffee and insists that she is going to buy us a drink in a local bar one day. It seems to us that she is really trying hard to make us lose interest, in other words, to shake off a concern which is becoming too close and too demanding for her, and to reestablish a distance between us.

So to her money and gifts are not a mediation, a neutral element representing an external law governing exchanges. In her case we are not (yet) dealing with a system involving law. This kind of triangulation is still inaccessible to her. In the dual relationship we form with her, money (or the gift) is a part of herself which she gives us in order to keep us at a distance, or the symbol of her importance to us that she tears away from us.

We can compare this attitude with that of Maurice G. who demanded a salary for his activity in the "group without a name" where, as he quite rightly pointed out, he does the same work as we do: talking, listening, and welcoming the others. This manifests his desire to occupy the active pole in the therapy, which seems to us the best possible indication of cure in the psychotic.

Mrs. R. has not yet reached this stage, and can only be perfused by us or, occasionally, when she wants to shake off a proximity and passivity which have become a source of anxiety, perfuse us in her turn.

It was in fact this type of relationship that existed for a long time between her and those around her, but it produced such a degree of anxiety and gave rise to such tension that hospitalization—i.e., recourse to a law of exception—seemed the only possible way out. Now we do not believe that this imposed law can have any therapeutic function whatsoever. It merely enables people around her to let their wounds heal, in a vague feeling of guilt, itself the source of further rejection and sometimes final abandonment of the patient who has by then become a chronic asylum inmate. It gives the patient the opportunity to clothe himself in a borrowed identity, that of the socially acceptable insane.

We do not think that the limits so cruelly lacking in psychotics—who are incapable of containing within themselves their inner life while they are at the same time permeable to all the projections of others—can be manufactured from an external source. They have to be cathected gradually, from the inside, on basis of a narcissistic enrichment and the simultaneous discovery of the narcissistic reality of others outside himself.

This enrichment and discovery take their place in a symbiotic relationship where the psychotic can experience himself more or less merged with the caring person in a universe which surrounds them both (the universe made concrete by the car in Alain's case). Contacts with the surrounding world are for a time established through this particular universe; it is only at this price that the psychotic might possibly one day reach the stage of triangulation, the symbolic and law, permanently accept the separation, and emerge from the imaginary. To enable the psychotic to undergo this privileged experience while creating around him sufficient tolerance for the symbiosis to be more than a fleeting moment in his life, a particular place, a specific response, and not a total intake conducive to chronicity is, or at least should be, the therapeutic ideal of a community psychiatric team. This ideal seems to us related to that of the "institutional care" described and theorized by P.-C. Racamier.

The difference, however, is that we confine ourselves to a partial response, addressed to the patient as much as to the people around him, and try to organize their contradictory and ambiguous requests into a dialectical relationship while having no pretentions to representing all the relational poles necessary to the one or to the others. Above all, we do not attempt to replace for the patient what, however meagerly, his parents, his neighbors, or others, give him. We do not substitute ourselves for the family or local facilities, but simply support them in a narcissistically exhausting task and provide the patient with the possibility of narcissistic recovery. To this end we use everything available and therefore do not duplicate existing institutions by creating specialized structures. We find a workshop sufficiently tolerant of the sick to be preferred to a so-called "therapeutic workshop" and to a day-hospital we prefer a class where, thanks to frequent meetings between us and the teacher, a psychotic child is accepted for half-days.

We have only provided, and only expect to provide, what appeared to be lacking; a minimally structured web of reception places which are easy to manage and where both the length and the form of stay can be made to suit each one concerned. We do cooperate with existing specialized institutions, mental hospitals, and medicopedagogical institutions, but remain independent of them (even though some of us also work in the institutions and have some of the same clients in both places). Hospitalization in particular is considered by us as of limited duration, occasionally essential but with no therapeutic value in itself.[11] Hospitalization provides a barrier against the patient's destructive instincts directed against himself and others, and temporary relief for the people around him when the danger-point is reached. It is sometimes the unavoidable means of constraint necessary for a crisis to be managed. However, the number of people and different capacities in the community psychiatric team, its greater cohesion and sounder experience make it less and less necessary to fall back upon this solution, or its replacement by a short period in a general hospital (made easier by regular visits from the members of the team in the service concerned), or again, by a stay in a nursing home.

To conclude with, we should like to emphasize the modesty of our aims and the economy of our means. The former seems to be in line with our profound ignorance as to what exactly insanity is—an ignorance which, as Gendrot remarks is sometimes decked out in the falsehoods of an artifical nosography or an ideology which is more para- than antipsychiatric. The latter we feel is indispensable if we are to avoid what are properly speaking social problems being turned over indiscriminately to psychiatry. It provides our specific clients, psychotics, with the means of insertion in a web flexible enough for them to be able to dominate it and remodel it in their own way and according to their own needs.

NOTES

1. A more detailed description of this organization and the principles governing its constitution is given in: J. Hochmann and M. Sassolas, Le traitement des psychotiques dans le cadre d'une expérience de psychiatrie communautaire. *Revue d'Epidémiologie, de Médecine sociale et de Santé Publique*, 1971, 19(7):641–660. See also, J. Hochmann, *Pour une psychiatrie communautaire,* Le Seuil, 1971.

2. J. Hochmann, A. André, and M-N. Redon. This observation has been published in detail and under the title "Alain foutu, à propose d'un cas de psychose infantile suivi à domicile." *L'information psychiatrique,* December 1971.

3. M. Sassolas, P. Safar, I. Fouletier, J. Pellet, J. Hochmann.

4. J. Dill, R. Iattoni.

5. A André, N. Thivisol, D. Michaut, A. Royannez, J. Devaux.

6. F. Renaud.

7. This type of functioning will be recognized as similar to that of the "permanent group" so creditably set up by Woodbury in the 13th District of Paris. Our sole originality here is that instead of deliberately creating it, we simply watched it grow

almost spontaneously out of the staff-patient interaction within the time and place of the clinic.

8.   A. André.

9.   Centred around M. Sassolas.

10. Miss Dessale, A. André, N. Thivisol, and J. Hochmann.

11. We do not, of course, exclude the possibility of therapeutic relations in the hospital. What we do dispute is the idea that a hospital stay is therapeutic *in itself.*

Jean Guyotat, M.D.

I should like to complete Hochmann's report by a few considerations of both a practical and a theoretical order.

On the practical level, I should point out that the experience he has reported developed out of a hospital psychiatric service, contrary to what happened in the 13th District. It was quickly structured to counter the hospital and its administrative delays. Naturally we did not all share the attitude of exclusion of hospital reality, but the fact remains: the extra-hospital team functions as a split from the hospital team.

We have come to accept that in actual fact such splitting with all its painful implications for the caring staff, does have a structuring value.

This split system involved an organization of narcissistic economy different from that obtaining within a more structured and apparently less split institution. It is essentially on this point that I should like to focus my analysis, but before doing so I should again emphasize the fact that *officially*, in the departmental organization of the battle against mental disorders, all these care systems still come under the aegis of the hospital ward. This represents a planning agency acting over the heads of the others, and seen as presenting the risk of enemies being parachuted into the community.

I shall now go into a few far more technical points.

1. Fragmented structure: The fragmented care system Hochmann referred to at the beginning of his report is not a bad one, as one might think. We gradually came to be accepted at the hospital itself, both among and inside care units.

Indeed, like many others, we felt that it was first of all necessary to organize the treatment of the caring team's own scissions if we were to give proper treatment to our psychotics. Little by little we came to realize that this cure of scissions, in fact, appeared more than anything else as one manifestation among others of the caring staff's omnipotence, or rather the intellectual omnipotence so easily instilled in the mind of the psychiatrist by the psychotic himself.

Obviously this is not what those who prompted the cure had at all in mind, but it is how things develop in any lightly structured institution.

One correlation has to be pointed out: at the time when we accepted this fragmentation among care units and between intra- and extrahospital elements, we realized that we were incapable of preventing certain psychotics from committing or attempting suicide. Since that time, we have had far fewer psychotic suicides.

2. We now find these increasingly autonomous outpatient care units in different form, with spontaneously formed groups of caring staff and those they care for, little islands of mutual narcissistic recovery, open, linked together by the necessity to produce, for if there are no patients nobody gets paid. This means that energy is polar-

ized in a different way in the extrahospital system. Inside the hospital there is a far greater distance between the caring staff's financial survival and the presence, the existence of the psychotic. We are therefore under less obligation to produce in the hospital, but on the other hand we have a greater tendency to conservatism and cathect the hierarchical structures, the overlapping of roles and statuses, rather than the psychotics themselves. In the hospital we do not spend our time cathecting our patients and leaving them no margin for thinking of people other than ourselves. Treatment is, in fact, just as partial, in Hochmann's sense of the word, in the hospital as in the outpatient system.

I agree with his criticism of some—though only some —experiences of community-based therapy in intensive care at the hospital. We hold the same view on this point. We feel that the patient has to be left to establish his own economy as he wants, or as he can. Group or intensive community experiences more often than not involve intense erotization between caring staff and patients, which frequently puts the patient in a position of indebtedness toward the caring staff. The psychotic's jump, in the hospital, from excessive withdrawal of cathexis to overstimulation is experienced as an attempt at seduction, which leads either to sacrificial conduct on the part of both caring staff and patients, satisfying the narcissism of one and the other, or else to sadomasochistic behavior which satisfies the instincts.

3. I think that leaving the patient to establish his economy as he wants means, above all, providing him with the possibility of organizing his splittings as he thinks fit; in other words, to ensure as best he can the separation between the good and the bad object. But this has nothing to do with "inside" or "outside," or intra- or extrahospital matters. It should be borne in mind that families and friends come to visit as much at the hospital as outside. So

the patient can organize his splittings himself in favorable conditions in the hospital itself. Let me give a simple example:

A patient was hospitalized for a subacute psychotic attack; it is obvious that he is caught between a mutually eliminating separated father and mother. The father, a former racing cyclist, sets a racing cyclist ideal and our patient had himself, in fact, been a racing cyclist at the cost of a certain number of head injuries. The patient finally had enough, and left his father in order to go and live with his mother, thus himself organizing a splitting, since there is no longer any communication between the father and the mother.

The mother was herself a low-key psychotic who had previously been hospitalized, and our patient, taking the ideal of this mother, himself gradually became psychotic.

At the hospital he could not bear being separated from his mother at the will of the caring staff, and this led to fugues, rehospitalization, etc. He therefore countered the caring staff's split-inducing will by organizing his own system of splitting to suit himself. After a few weeks the father, whom we had notified, came to the hospital to see his son; the latter then organized a confrontation between the father and the mother. But he could only do this in his own room at the hospital, where he was alone, and only after locking the communicating door between his room and the rest of the ward. After this procedure he improved and was finally able to leave; he is now followed up by hospital and outpatient staff. As you see, all of this is a problem not of inside and outside, but of separation of objects sometimes cathected as good and sometimes as bad.

What seems to me the important thing in the experience recounted by Hochmann is that in the system of extrahospital narcissistic islands the patient organizes the splitting in his own way. A patient can go from one island to another, with one functioning for the moment as good and the other as bad. There can also be psychotics in the hospital who use it as a means of getting away from what they feel is intensive care on the part of an extrahospital group.

On this subject I should like to outline briefly what I see of splitting between good and bad objects in my practice.

I agree with Green that one has to distinguish between splitting and falling into pieces or rather, between multisplitting and bisplitting.

When a psychotic is treated he goes from a system of multisplitting to a system of bisplitting with the depressive position imminent. He therefore needs to find reassurance in another object which he sees as antagonistic to the previous one; if he can make use of this, it is a structuring factor, but if the movement is imposed by a calculated system, whether intra-or extrahospital, then it is destructive. However, this risk is much greater in the hospital either because of its sclerosed structures or, on the other hand, because of overintensive institutional therapies.

4. I have several times used the word "production"; I am not referring to production of work here; indeed, there is no evidence that the patient treated within the community produces work any more easily than those treated in hospital.

It is above all a matter of production of imaginary energy, of which psychotics consume so much. In this sense community-based therapy, as Hochmann describes it, appears to be far more productive than that carried out in the hospital. And here again, what seems important to me, and upon which note I shall conclude, is that the psychotic can use this in any way that suits him, for he badly needs to maintain his omnipotent control over distances for a long time.

Chapter 2

COMMUNITY-BASED TREATMENT OF CHRONIC PSYCHOTIC PATIENTS

Israel C. Zwerling, M.D., Ph.D.

INTRODUCTION

The Problem of Defining the Problem

A story which recently enjoyed wide currency in academic circles in the United States concerned a newly appointed, ambitious chairman of a university department of behavioral science who was determined to win national prominence for his department as a research center. He convened his staff and announced that henceforth all promotions and other academic rewards would be won only through research publications, and that reviews of research in progress would be conducted every six months, on the basis of which the merits of each faculty member would be judged. A professor whose scholarship was most widely respected, and who was acknowledged by the students each year to be their most effective teacher, was not, however, gifted as an investigator. He puzzled and suffered over the demand of his new chairman, and at the time of his first six-month review submitted the following:

Research
Area: Conditioning of the Flea to Verbal Stimuli
Procedure: A flea was conditioned to jump in response to the verbal command, "Jump!" Subsequently, the legs of the flea were removed one by one, and observations made after each amputation.
Results: 1. A flea *can* be conditioned to jump in response to the verbal command, "Jump!"
2. As the legs of the flea are removed, the distance jumped diminishes.
3. When all six legs have been removed, the flea becomes deaf.

This story comes to mind because it seems to me that there is the greatest uncertainty about the "flea" who is the concern of this symposium—i.e., the chronic psychotic patient—and why he does not "jump" as we all do. It is crucial at the very start to recognize that we are confronting vastly different problems if we perceive psychosis to be the consequence of an organic defect, than if we see it as a disequilibrium of psychodynamic forces and counterforces, or a maladaptive learned response pattern to a disturbed family, community, or larger social unit. The old-fashioned, rather simplistic eclecticism proposed that all three levels of integration were involved equally, and lineal, causal relationships were posited as essentially independent and parallel sequences. Current systems approaches offer a more sophisticated structure for relating the events in any behavioral subsystem to those in other subsystems or larger systems; while we are as yet far from our colleagues in the physical sciences in their ability to express determination in mathematical generalizations, and while articulating concepts which bridge subsystems are still quite scanty, it is at least clear that any behavioral event—including any therapeutic intervention—at any systems level has immediate representation in all systems. At our hospital meetings during the week these remarks were written, a case was presented in which a patient showed a dramatic improvement immediately subsequent to a marked *decrease* in medication. When the material had been presented and the floor opened to discussion, "explanations" were offered in rapid succession by three members of my staff: one, that the limbic system had been released from overcontrol; the second, that the patient had interpreted his heavy medication schedule as confirmation of his self-image as being helpless and crazy and, in turn, understood the decrease in dosage as a signal that he was now capable of rational behavior; and the third, that the ward nursing staff and the patient's family understood the new prescription to mean that he was getting better and his improved behavior was in response to the expectations of others that he would now conform more closely to social norms. My own bias is that all three were right—indeed, that if any one was right, all had to be right, if not in the particulars of their formulations, then certainly at least in their generic areas of concern.

A corollary bias is that, given the range of behavior potential in the mixture of determinants—genetic endowments, individual biological and psychological developmental experiences and opportunities, and sociocultural forces—the classification of persons at the extremes of the spectra of coping disabilities as "sick," with all the traditional implications of the medical model of "sick" and "well," is at the present state of our knowledge a tragic and costly error. We recognize continua in virtually all human properties—and we accommodate to the ranges we expect in body length and weight, in intelligence, and in various skill areas among people by appropriate ranges of goods, services, and activities. It seems to me that until we know more about each system level concerned with the determinations of human behavior, and know more as well about the articulating bridges connecting the several systems, we would do well to concentrate on a functional classification of coping capacities and to replace our present absorption with psychiatric diagnoses. This brings me to state my basic philosophy concerning community-based treatment of the chronic, severely disabled mental patients: the goal must be the provision of the widest range of vocational, social, residential, intellectual, and recreational resources, to the end that each person can be provided with opportunities to cope successfully in all areas. The logic of the medical model has driven us relentlessly to the identification of disabilities, to a sharp separation of the "sick" from the "well," and to programs of "treatment." What appears to be indicated is rather a process of identifying abilities, and programs which offer opportunities for effective and gratifying functioning to persons at all levels of ability.

The Problem of Evaluation

A second prefatory bias must be explained before attempting to present a description of the programs of the Albert Einstein College of Medicine for the treatment of chronic psychotic patients in the community, this concerning the question of evaluation. It is difficult to assess psychiatric programs of treatment, and the evaluation of community-based long-term treatment of chronically ill mental patients poses several difficulties over and above the familiar obstacles to definitive outcome research in psychiatry. First, the criteria which immediately present themselves—namely, readmission rates, and duration of hospitalization during exacerbations of illness—are highly sensitive to a host of factors unrelated to the conditions of the patient. For example, if few beds are available, readmission rates will necessarily decline; if ample beds are available, and if outpatient alternatives do not exist or are inaccessible, readmission will frequently serve as a solution to a crisis in community-based treatment. A large-scale natural experiment in the United States over the past 25 years illustrates this point sharply. The two largest states, California and New York, have approximately equal populations (19.9 million and 18.2 million residents, respectively in 1970.) There are currently about 11,000 mental patients in hospitals in California, and about 47,000 in New York State. This extraordinary discrepancy hardly reflects the advantages of the California climate. In the immediate post-World War II period, both states invested substantially in expanding their mental health services. California developed an extensive network of outpatient clinics, and filled all available places; New York built a network of gigantic hospitals, and filled all the beds. Other powerful forces also work to make hospitalization a very unsatisfactory criterion for evaluating community treatment programs. The capacity of a family to care for a patient varies; in a recent incident in my experience, Mrs. F.'s death precipitated the hospitalization of her marginally adapting schizophrenic son and her mildly senile husband—both had been statistical "successes" of the community psychiatric services provided to them, and their hospitalization then represented statistical "failures" in a program whose quality had, of course, undergone no change. In some instances, inpatient services urge patients being discharged to return to the hospital on the occasion of the first faint evidences of difficulty, on the theory that it is more economical to have a larger number of very brief admissions than a smaller number of very extended admissions. The rate of hospitalization for these and other reasons, is an extremely unreliable index of the effectiveness of community treatment programs, and yet is probably the single most widely used criterion.

Still further on the difficulties of assessing community-based treatment programs for psychotic patients, it is evident that criteria based exclusively on the behavior and on the fate of the identified patient do not take into account the burden placed upon the family and community in extramural care of the patient; a family willing to replicate a hospital ward to retain one of its members at home can obviously keep a much sicker patient out of the hospital than a family unwilling or incapable of tolerating any measure of deviance in the behavior of the identified sick member. The more I have studied families with a psychotic member, the clearer it has become to me that at some juncture in family life the *family*—and not the admitting psychiatrist—makes the decision that the patient is to be committed to the mental hospital.

And finally, if a program is judged, by whatever criteria, to be successful in maintaining equilibrium in psychotic patients living in the community, the elements of the program responsible for its success cannot readily be sorted out because of the many variables at work. By the same token, no matter how carefully a successful program is described, it is virtually impossible to duplicate it with precision in a new setting. For all these reasons, community-based long-term treatment programs can only be recommended with caution, and conclusions drawn from the results observed must be tentative.

The Setting

The mental health programs which I shall describe are elements of a network of services in the Bronx, New York City, with approximately 1,500,000 residents. The major facilities include a 1000-bed state hospital; a children's psychiatric hospital currently staffed, because of budgetary restrictions, for 25 inpatients, but capable of admitting 200; two community mental health centers; two departments of psychiatry in municipal general hospitals, one with a 100-bed inpatient unit and the other with 12 beds; and three departments of psychiatry in voluntary general hospitals, one with 25 beds used principally for private patients and the other two with only outpatient services. The Bronx State Hospital serves as the center of the regional program for the care of chronically ill psychotic patients. It is "unitized"—i.e., clusters of wards are organized as semiautonomous services or units, each devoted to a specific geographic area of the Bronx. Quite diverse liaison programs between the hospital services and community-based facilities exist, varying with the amount and quality of care and treatment provided by the latter facilities.

Except for the smallest of these facilities—a voluntary hospital with a newly created department of psychiatry and with only a small outpatient service—all the major psychiatric services are affiliated with the Albert Einstein College of Medicine. This fact is critical to an appreciation of the programs to be described. Much as is in the United Kingdom, the administrative structure of public mental health services in New York State has built in a separation of the mental hospitals from the local services at the very top, with a deputy commissioner responsible for each, and with functionally separate budgets supporting the hospitals on the one hand, and the community-based services on the other. The result is an entirely predictable struggle between local and state supported facilities as to who is responsible for which patient. The principal factor, which has made possible any success we may have enjoyed in developing liaison models, has been the ultimate control of the Executive Committee and the Chairman of the Department of Psychiatry of the medical school over the directors of each of the affiliated facilities. What may appear in the descriptions to follow to be acts of nobility on the part of some participants in sharing their staff, space, and equipment resources was as often as not the result of a decision of the medical school rather than an agreement based on an appraisal by each facility director of what might be best for patients. This is not an incidental point—again, my central thesis is that a range of vocational, residential, social, and recreational resources must be available in the community to accommodate to the range of abilities of all the residents, including those with chronic psychoses, and if clusters of specialized facilities are administratively sequestered from each other without responsibility to one overall regional authority, the probability is that competitive, overlapping, and fragmented services rather than comprehensive and coordinated services will be available.

RESIDENTIAL PROGRAMS

The gap between life as a patient in a hospital ward and life as a member of a fully independent household in a community is indeed great. The range of intermediary facilities that we have developed is incomplete, but does include some components which merit description.

To begin with, the hospital does not represent a sharp and total separation from family and community. It is located in the community. The wards are open, except for scattered locked areas. Visiting in the hospital is allowed every day, and patients are encouraged to spend evenings and weekends at home at the earliest feasible time. Deliberate efforts have been and are being made to encourage community use of the hospital grounds and facilities; football and baseball fields have been set aside for community teams, and meeting rooms have been provided to a number of community organizations. It is hoped that hospitalization should represent a brief move from one locus to another *in the community.*

Second, therapeutic community programs within the hospital and the earliest use of day-hospitalization are encouraged, in order to maximize the retention of responsibility for self and to minimize dependency and the loss of social skills. These are familiar devices and widely described in the literature. A particularly valuable predischarge residential component within the hospital which we have used extensively is the "Hotel Ward," a ward operated with no, or token, staff, where patients take full responsibility for medication, activity programs, and leaving and returning to the hospital. The nursing stations on these wards are, deliberately, sparsely furnished—there is a telephone table, a chair, a phone, and a directory of the principal offices in the hospital relevant to life on the ward. Patients go to the pharmacy with prescriptions provided by the doctor who referred them to the Hotel Ward and obtain medication for a week at a time. They see their therapist on schedule, much as though they were outpatients. If they voice physical complaints to referring ward staff members —an almost universal occurrence during the first day or two on an unsupervised ward—they are told they are free to call the Medical Clinic and make an appointment, much as they might call a neighborhood doctor when they are out of the hospital. In most units, there are inadequate provisions for cooking for the entire Hotel Ward, so that patient groups take turns; some cook while others have regular hospital meals delivered to the ward.

Perhaps the most useful application of the "Hotel Ward" has been the opportunity provided to the staff to form small patient groups for discharge as units to our "Apartment Program." Chronically ill patients notoriously are abandoned by their families in significant numbers: in a group of 151 chronic patients recently transferred to our hospital from another state hospital because their legal residence was in our district, 58 patients had no relatives whom we could locate. Among those whose family members could be located, 83 made clear that they did not intend to accept the patient into their household upon discharge; only 10 families indicated a willingness to work with the hospital staff towards the patient's recovery and to accept the patient into their household. Our impression is that these figures are representative for the population of chronic patients. The problem of establishing a residence in the community for these patients is then considerable; it is complicated by the shortage of low-cost apartments, by the reluctance of landlords to rent to tenants discharged from mental hospitals, and by the fear patients have of purchasing furniture and undertaking a long-term lease in the face of their experience of recurrent hospitalizations. In order to deal with these problems we have organized a nonprofit corporation, the "Pibly Fund" (an acronym for the initials of the founder who donated the starting sum of money) that rents and furnishes apartments and leases them to discharged patients. They, in turn, pay rent to the Fund, so that only a small sum of money is required, once past the initial endowment, to maintain the Apartment Program. Patients are generally discharged in groups of from two to five, depending upon the size of the apartment. Since its inception in 1963 with a half-way house, the Pibly Fund has grown to acquire a total of 13 apartments, in which 68 discharged chronic patients currently reside. A total of 182 discharged patients have been served by the apartment program to date. Occupancy rate in the apartments has been 87 percent. Filling a newly acquired apartment involves the selection of suitable patients (suitability being judged on the basis of freedom from acute psychotic symptoms, capacity for some degree of interaction with others, interest in employment, and absent or problematic family relationships), and their participation as a group in a variety of activity and therapy programs, preferably on a hotel ward. When a single vacancy occurs in an apartment, the remaining residents participate in the selection of a replacement and have veto power over recommendations made by the staff.

A community housing resource which has been particularly useful to us with geriatric patients is a variety of group residence which provides essentially hotel services—i.e., meals and minimal room housekeeping—with little additional supervision. These residences are licensed by the Department of Health of New York State, though the safety and staffing requirements are considerably less stringent than for nursing homes or chronic-care hospitals. They are private, profit-making facilities, and since demand for accommodations far exceeds supply, and personnel costs are high, these residences offer little in the way of programs for their tenants. Greatest use of these residences is made by our state mental hospital, which for years was a "no-exit" repository for all the aged whom the families in our communities would no longer care for. The initial experience had been that discharging patients to such residences generally resulted in a very short stay in the community and early return to the hospital, because of the lack of services available to residents. Consequently, hospital staff were deployed to provide social services, regular medical checkups, and organized group activities on the premises of the residence; the result was a decided improvement in patient behavior and a much slowed rate of return to hospital. Currently, 16 discharged geriatric patients are in such residences; all of them have been out of the hospital for over one year.

Because half-way houses are familiar devices for starting chronic patients into community living, only passing mention will be made of this resource. Our experience has led us to maintain a high expectation for patient independence, and to rigidly limit the duration of patient stay, lest the half-way house become a small open-door hospital in itself.

Foster home placements, nursing homes, and of course return to the patient's own family, complete the range of residential resources we have available for housing chronic patients in the community. It is important to emphasize that any point along the continuum of autonomy and independence may come to represent a resting place for a chronic psychotic patient; to insist on an all-or-none division into hospital vs. fully independent community life is simply unrealistic. This may appear to be a pessimistic note, implying a recognition that the chronic psychotic patient will never be totally "cured" and rendered capable of living like the rest of us. If I may repeat my theme just one more time, I rather see this as *our* problem—the problem of the *observers*—rather than that of the chronic psychotic patients we are observing. It has been demonstrated that the presentation of a wooden facsimile of a monkey will terrify a colony of monkeys. In a related experiment, a fish trapped in a plastic bubble and released back into his school to swim his wobbly course will scatter the other fish in apparent terror. I am suggesting that much of our behavior is like that of the monkeys and the fish; we cannot abide the more wobbly swimmers and more wooden ones among us, and our panic becomes translated into an urgent need to make them just like ourselves. I have the feeling that if we make provision in the community for a range of wobbliness and woodenness, we will in the end, paradoxically, move further toward our present goal of "cure" than insistence upon polarizing humanity into the "sick" and the "well" will permit.

I would propose the same general perspective with regard to vocational rehabilitation, socialization, and recreation programs. To the extent that we can establish a full range of opportunities, we can gradually move patients to their own optimal levels of functioning; to the extent that we insist upon an all-or-none dichotomy between total dependence and total indepencence, we condemn chronic psychotic patients to repeated failures in their attempts to jump the gap. Some of our discharged patients, living in a variety of community settings, continue to work in the hospital "Work-for-Pay" shop; others can succeed in sheltered workshops located in the community; still others can retain jobs with private employers able to make provision for special areas of disability; some, of course, can enter into the competitive labor market on their own. In this general regard, I prefer the goal of "productive participation" for chronic psychotic patients to the goal of "productive work"; the former somehow suggests a more loose array of acceptable activities and a less rigid insistence on totally independent functioning.

Liaison Programs

Equal in importance, in our experience, with the principle of graded adaptational opportunities for the community treatment of chronic psychotic patients is the principle of continuity of care. I mean by this the organization of mental health service delivery in such a manner that patients are cared for by a unified and cooperating group of mental health workers, whatever the modality or locus of treatment. It is remarkable that institutions, and I know many, can continue for years to "refer" patients to alternative treatment programs (e.g., from an inpatient ward to an outpatient clinic), fully aware that only 15 percent of the patients so referred keep the appointment made for them. Our experience has been, for example, that the simple device of making a specific appointment with a specific, named therapist increases this figure to over 50 percent, and the added step of having the clinic therapist or even a clinic representative meet the patient prior to discharge, discuss the necessity for aftercare, and make a specific appointment increases initial attendance at the clinic to over 90 percent.

I have earlier referred to the fragmentation of service agencies in the Bronx; city, state, federal, and private funds support a variety of institutions, established without the benefit of centralized planning for the region and acting in essentially competitive ways. Territorial disputes are virtually built into such a conglomerate and the chronic psychotic patient, along with the aged, the addict, and the mentally retarded—and most particularly if the chronic patient is black and poor—is the target for exclusion from all: conversely, the young, white, college trained, articulate neurotic patient—and most particularly if she is attractive —often can find a number of agencies competing to provide her with treatment. This is perhaps not the appropriate occasion for a detailed sorting out of the many elements involved, such as the continued preeminence that psychoanalysis holds in American psychiatry, the racial and class biases, the reluctance of mental health professionals to risk failure in treating conditions which tend not to respond to current approaches when so many potentially responsive patients continue to be available, all these and other forces and counterforces constitute the matrix within which the community-based treatment of the chronic psychotic patient must be carried out.

Our concern has therefore, of necessity, been directed to the establishment of liaison arrangements among the component elements in the mental health network so that continuity of care may be provided to chronic psychotic patients. A variety of patterns have emerged, some of which merit description.

Liaison between Hospital and Community Mental Health Center

Over the past 12 years the principal thrust of the public mental health effort in the United States has been the development of community mental health centers. Stimulated by federal support for construction and, initially, for staffing as well, over 450 such units have been created throughout the country, each assigned to provide community-based mental health services to a geographically defined catchment area with from 75,000 to 200,000 residents. To qualify for federal support, a Center must provide five essential services: inpatient, outpatient, partial hospitalization, day-and-night emergency care, and indirect services (i.e., community consultation and education). Two such Centers are located in the Bronx, one of which approximates a model liaison arrangement with a state mental hospital. The Director of Inpatient Services of the Center (it is the Soundview-Throgg's Neck Community Mental Health Center) is responsible for the 50-bed unit operated by the Center in the community, and is also the Chief of Service for the 100-bed Soundview Service at the Bronx State Hospital, which is responsible for patients in the same geographic area. He uses a single admissions room—in the community hospital—from which patients may be admitted to either unit; generally, patients requiring longer hospitalization are admitted, or transferred, to the state mental hospital. One of his wards at the state hospital is a hotel ward, and patients from the community hospital may, before discharge, be transferred to the state hospital if it is felt that the experience of minimally supervised living offered by the hotel ward would be useful. Case conferences are held at which staffs of both the community and state hospitals attend. The Center operates three "town clinics," one in each of the three demographically distinct communities which comprise the Center's catchment area, and each town clinic has a liaison staff which literally escorts patients into the hospital, maintains contact during hospitalization, and participates in discharge planning, including the very specific scheduling of initial visits to the town clinic, when the patient is ready to leave the hospital. Over 90 percent of these clinic appointments are kept.

Liaison between Hospital and Comprehensive Health Center

A more recent development in general health care, unmistakably modeled after the community mental health center, is the "HMO," the Health Maintenance Organization. This device, which is likely to be the central agency in the national health program clearly on the horizon in the United States, provides general medical, pediatric, and prenatal care on an ambulatory basis to population groups of from 20,000 to 40,000 in defined geographic areas. As is the case with mental health centers, the HMOs attempt to develop health consciousness and to establish preventive as well as treatment programs. A further similarity is that, in both, extensive use is made of nonprofessional or paraprofessional health workers.

One of the units at the state mental hospital, the Montefiore Service, is a cluster of wards providing hospitalization for psychiatric patients from a large area also served by a voluntary hospital, the Bronx-Lebanon Hospital; the Mental Hygiene Clinic of this latter hospital provides outpatient treatment to chronic psychotic patients discharged from the Bronx State Hospital, through a quid pro quo, in return for which the Bronx State Hospital pays the salaries of a psychiatrist and a psychiatric social worker employed at the Mental Hygiene Clinic. Parenthetically, our experience, contrary to that reported by others, is that the chronic psychotic patient does better when treated in a general psychiatric clinic than when segregated in a separate aftercare clinic. Almost twice as many patients from that area treated in the state aftercare clinics were returned to the hospital in a year as compared with the Bronx-Lebanon Mental Hygiene Clinic (38 percent, as against 20 percent); more significant, *twenty* times as many patients in the Mental Hygiene Clinic continued in treatment after two years, as against the segregated aftercare clinic.

To return to the theme of this section, imbedded within the Bronx-Lebanon district is the Martin Luther King, Jr., Comprehensive Neighborhood Health Center, and HMO providing general medical, pediatric, dental, and prenatal care, but exclusive of psychiatric care, on an ambulatory basis to a population of about 45,000 persons. Very recently we have begun to discharge patients from the subarea served by the King Center to the family care teams of that center, and to provide a psychiatric consultant to each family care team to attend the weekly meetings of the team and to serve as advisor on the psychiatric care, not only of the discharged chronic psychotic patients, but of all patients with emotional problems seen by the family care workers and the team professionals. An evaluation study of this program has just begun, and our impression is that this pattern of supervision of aftercare treatment by a team providing comprehensive *medical* care is a more effective and far less costly approach to community care for chronic psychotic patients than either an aftercare or a mental hygiene clinic.

Liaison between Hospital and Staffed Aftercare Clinic

One state hospital service, the Jacobi Service, consists of a cluster of wards responsible for the psychiatric hospitalization of patients from a geographic area served by a municipal hospital which refuses to accept chronic psychotic patients into its mental hygiene clinic. This service, after a trial of the state aftercare clinic which proved highly unsatisfactory, organized its own outpatient department, using professional and nonprofessional staff members from the wards as clinic therapists, rather than a separate, discontinuous clinic staff. Some patients, deeply involved in group therapy on the ward at the time of discharge, may have their outpatient appointments initially made to the wards to coincide with the ward group meetings. The results have been salutary; the percentage of rehospitalization has dropped from 51 to 33 and is still declining, and the percentage of retention in treatment after two years rose from close to zero to about 50. The Jacobi Service Outpatient Department (OPD) is located on the grounds of the mental hospital, but near the entrance and some distance from the wards of that service. Ideally, the service would like to locate its OPD entirely off the hospital grounds and in the community to emphasize for patients their changed status, but it plans to retain the practice of using the same treatment staff for inpatient and outpatient phases of treatment.

In each of the three liaison arrangements described, the dispute between the inpatient unit as to who is responsible for the patient has disappeared, and the rate of patients keeping initial clinic appointments after discharge has risen to 90 percent or more. This directly reflects the high degree of continuity of care achieved. Much more remains to be accomplished in this regard. Much more, also, may be expected in the future in the way of developing more specific and effective psychopharmacological, milieu, family, group, and individual therapeutic approaches. I have not dealt with the actual treatment approaches practiced by our community-based units because of the limitations of time, and because of my feeling that we have made a more valuable contribution in the areas I have described. Progress in therapeutic approaches will surely come, and may dramatically change the problem of the care and treatment of chronic psychotic patients. In the meantime, the twin goals I would urge upon any mental health service delivery system are first, a full range of rehabilitative, residential, social, and recreational facilities to accommodate to the full range of abilities and disabilities of these patients, and second, liaison arrangements between treatment resources which provide optimally for the continuity of patient care.

Chapter 3

PSYCHOTICS AND PSYCHIATRIC PRESENCE IN THE 13TH DISTRICT COMMUNITY (PARIS)

Philippe Paumelle, M.D.

PSYCHOTICS AND PSYCHIATRIC PRESENCE IN THE 13TH DISTRICT COMMUNITY

Justification of Psychiatry within the Community for all Patients

The two most frequently used terms, "catchment area psychiatry" and "community psychiatry," have never seemed entirely satisfactory. They sound suspicious.

The former can mean abusive psychiatric power over a territory and the people in it, and the latter pretends to have knowledge concerning the resolution of conflicts between people, and even among nations. Does not the word "community" here presuppose the existence somewhere in the world of a society free of conflicts and social struggles?

The word "catchment area" evokes the idea of strategy. "Community" has a megalomanic ring to it, a social life which is by definition happy or, on the contrary, a psychiatry whose aim is to "change life."

In order to give a better idea of what we aim at, we prefer to use the word "presence," counter to everything that might mean abusive power or knowledge, and to avoid using the adjective "community" or "catchment area" in this sense so as to make it quite clear that what we hope to carry out is all psychiatry and psychiatry for all. This presence is active above all in the community, but we prefer to say in the city or in the common society. We are not dealing with a psychiatric subspeciality of interest to only a few subjects.

As we wrote as early as 1959 (*Congress of Psychiatry and Neurology,* Tours), on the objective and spatial level, psychiatry in the community means "the transfer of the meeting place" for all patients. "The encounter will take place between a known 'subject-in-situation' in his normal environment, and a doctor as much inserted in the world as possible."

Briefly, it is clear that such a project entails some very profound reflections on the image of ourselves with regard to the many temptations and comfortable positions which might be waiting to lure us:

1. that of the doctor attracted by the security of the act of diagnosis which objectifies and categorizes while it differentiates;

2. that of the asylum doctor who would risk losing the security of the closed-in world and perhaps also the so-called "revolutionary" satisfaction of protesting in the name of and in chorus with the insane against the exclusion imposed upon them by Society; and

3. that of the psychoanalyst who would lose the advantages attached to the form of neutrality necessary for the treatment of neuroses, even if the treatment of psychotics should logically lead him to abandon it, to expose himself,

let himself be seen, in short, to be "present" while still remaining neutral in a different way.

Let me just mention what those who call themselves "antipsychiatrists" could lose if they decided to become psychiatrists in the common society.

It is no easy matter to abandon a position according to which one can only be "with the insane against society" or "with society against the insane."

This initiative on the part of the caring staff to get out of the closed mental hospital is justified by the recognition of a double "no-exit" situation:

With regard to care structures there is the observation of asylum sociopathology and its constant renewal, and of the barriers which any reform from the inside comes up against.

Daumezon used to say that "since the patients could not be cured individually, the mental hospital itself had to be cured," and later on Goffman showed how any closed world, like it or not, secreted pathological and pathogenic relations among those shut in it.

Foucault pronounced unqualified condemnation of the position of the psychiatrist in the hospital: "The science of mental disorders such as it can progress in asylums will never be anything more than a matter of observation and classification."

The second "no-exit" we have to recognize concerns ourselves. Is it not true to say that since the last war, each time one of us tries to approach a traditional psychiatric ward as chief medical practitioner, the contradiction between the therapeutic and the segregative function evokes some kind of inauthentic tragedy?

Words go in pairs: flight or insurrection, discouragement or irritation, and, to talk "psychiatrist," we could say: from the depressive to the paranoid attitude.

The resolution of this double impasse on the structural

as well as the individual level supposes as a starting position that there is "no communion possible" between those who are deprived of their liberty and those who take it from them. This project of presence in the community takes on all its truly tragic significance here. Might this not fundamentally be the psychiatric team's "re-representation" of its noncomplicity with the established order, given first to the patient but this including also the participation of the nonpatients, the families, and neighbors?

The tragic value of the idea of the psychiatrist's presence in the common society is first and foremost the radical challenge of scientism. "The tragical," writes Jean-Marie Domenach,[1] "is the face-to-face encounter, getting a man out from hiding, making him talk not in the abstract cybernetic way of the technician, but by direct confrontation and dialogue."

In the footsteps of Nietzsche and Hegel, this position signifies that there is no such thing as a "human science," that this is a senseless pretention, and that there is only the history of mankind.

Parallel to this, "it is no longer possible to separate the man who knows from the one who is known"; such was Freud who could affirm the universality of the Oedipus tragedy only by being the first to recognize that he was experiencing it in his own inner reality.

The personal presence of the caring people in the city means that we can no longer talk about the sick or the criminal in general. Each case appears in its uniqueness. In the final analysis, everything is played out, as in tragedy, on a person-to-person basis.

Thus, psychiatry in the community has no pretentions to changing man through science nor to changing society for mankind, while it is nonetheless fully aware of the extent to which the concrete person it approaches is determined by the world around him.

The psychiatrist present in the community is dealing

with "men of flesh and bones" (as M. de Unamuno sees it),[2] people who are born, suffer and die—die, especially—who eat, drink, take their leisure, sleep, think, love: the man one sees and hears, the brother, the real brother . . .

For there is something else also called "man" and which is the subject of many a wandering of a more or less scientific bent. The mythical featherless biped . . . a man from neither here nor there, not of this age nor of any other, with neither sex nor homeland; in short, a mere idea, or in other words, something that is not a man at all.

Our man is the one of flesh and bones.

Such an approach surely protects us both against our own temptations in the direction of omnipotence and against the omnipotence which is so readily attributed to us; "tragic wisdom is a wisdom of limitations" (Lukacs).

This presence, whose specificity can be found in both knowledge and research on what some call the "psychic apparatus" and others the "intrapsychic reality," while also involving us as the "ordinary man," can only be justified through the transmission of a specific request.

We do indeed propose the hypothesis that he who is considered, or considers himself sick, is the bearer of at least an implicit request and certain suffering to which the psychiatric team can and must respond more specifically. Here we feel it necessary to lean on an existential philosophy which can be shared whatever one's ethical options or scientific outlook.

Heidegger's notion of "assistance to others" seems, for the time being, to provide the most satisfactory answer to our question.

This conception of encounter and coexistence is the antithesis of Sartre's stance when he gives us to understand that there is no such thing as interhuman meeting without objectification and therefore alienation of the other.

Heidegger identifies two antagonistic forms of assistance:

1. One of them can be compared with what in terms of psychiatric assistance seems open to challenge, if it means putting into a state of dependence, organization in the asylum neoworld, chronicization. This, according to Heidegger, is the attempt to unburden the other of his cares to be concerned with him to the extent of substituting oneself for him.

2. What he proposes, on the contrary, is the possibility of an assistance which attempts less to substitute oneself for the other than to precede him in the potential of his existence; not to dispossess him of his troubles, but to restore them to him in their authenticity. This assistance relates essentially to the authentic concern, that is, the existence of the other.

THE REASON FOR TREATMENT OF PSYCHOTICS WITHIN THIS FRAMEWORK

Although we feel that our presence in the community a priori concerns the entire field of psychiatry, it does seem to be particularly important to psychotics for two reasons:

1. Their negation of reality and the rejection so often forthcoming from their families and friends are mutually reinforcing and bring them more frequently than other patients to the closed mental hospital.

2. From the quantitative point of view and for all of France, nonalcoholic psychotic states represent 45 percent of the present male population and 55 percent of the female population in the mental hospitals.

The fate of psychotic patients and the number of them in mental hospitals does seem to have undergone little change in countries where a certain form of so-called "community psychiatry" was addressed solely to those who were capable of formulating a clear request, instead of covering the entire psychiatric field.

When confronted with psychotics, the psychiatrist, in his traditional role, is faced essentially with three types of situation:

1. The psychoanalyst in dual therapy receives the impact of a transference so tremendous and unrecognized that his attempt at therapy often ends with rupture.

2. The private psychiatrist, if he is isolated and shut up in his consulting room, after a few attempts at treatment with neuroleptics or supportive psychotherapy, is often led to certify the patient for confinement thus justifying, with no possibility of mobilizing it, the rejection cast upon the patient.

3. The Mental Hospital medical practitioner, both master and prisoner of his establishment, in spite of all his efforts to open up its structures to the outside and to get out himself, finds over the years a particularly marked sedimentation of the psychotic group. If this group represents 50 percent of all hospitalized patients, it means that more than half of them have been there for more than five years; the objective length of confinement can hardly be called "long-term treatment," but rather indefinite or atemporal, which is well indicated by the label often applied to these patients—"chronic."

Thus the situation imposed upon both caring staff and patients in the classic structures can be summarized in three words: *therapeutic discontinuity, nonresponsibility* of caring staff, and social *rejection* of patients.

When the caring staff decides to go into the community, the research hypothesis experienced and put into practice tends to be centered around three totally contrary objectives: *therapeutic continuity, responsibility* of caring staff, and *nonrejection* of patients.

In other words, if psychotics are in the majority in mental hospitals because they are both attached to them and rejected there; if they are the "real insane" in the eyes of the population and also of psychiatrists to the extent that they are more successful in resisting their "desire to get better," then it seems to me that the possibility of transforming their situation conditions hopes of a psychiatric revolution that is valid for everyone.

Going into psychiatry in the community means trying to find the answers to three major questions of particular significance for psychotics, for whom the mutual reinforcement of the mechanisms of social and mental alienation are of central importance.

1. Does there exist a position in the space of the caring staff, an institutional concept where the patient is not shut up in a closed world signifying rejection and absolute power of those around him?

2. Does there exist for caring staff a way of being and of making contact whereby the patient is not reduced in our eyes and our everyday attitudes to an immobile object, frozen and incapable of evolution?

3. Finally, what new therapeutic horizons emerge from the answers to these two questions?

But there the research worker has to step beyond the laboratory. The answer to these questions directly concerns the questioner personally. The fact of formulating these questions denotes, from the start, acceptance of the idea of getting away from the traditional positions.

This is a real "giving birth" for the psychiatrist, and is something that cannot be done painlessly.

The forms of presence proposed by psychoanalyst-psychiatrists vis-à-vis psychotics are based on a preliminary observation: the impasse frequently runs, by exclusive conformity, into models of the dual relationship either in reference to the person-to-person dialogue of the medical practitioner or to the traditional analytical position.

In concrete terms they are translated by:

1. *The presence of the community* in any individual or collective therapeutic initiative; the team is faced at once with the request of the patients, their families, and the collectivity. It exists in full view of the user, and the dialogue is established with him.

Reciprocally, the caring-staff's presence in the community, i.e., sharing common social reality with the patient and his family and friends, makes them familiar characters, not strangers, and thus makes it easier for a request to be expressed.

2. *The caring staff working as a team:* this makes it possible to calculate the right amount of specific and differentiated interventions and to coordinate them constantly within a coherent therapeutic project.

The silent neutrality of some, and the consistent presence of the others; the superego function of some and that of ego-auxiliary of others; the concomitant representation of external reality and of intrapsychic reality; that of "inside" and "outside," can all be assumed constantly by the team or by several coordinated teams for any given patient.

The flexibility of relationships among the members of the caring team and the mutual support this can represent make it possible to perceive and deal with the effects on the team of the patients' splitting projections which, in a dual situation, are often carried through with the therapist unable to mobilize the massive transference of which he is the object.

3. *The technical and administrative responsibility for the creation and day-to-day functioning of the whole range of nursing institutions lies with the entire community of psychiatrists responsible*

for the catchment area. In this way the institutional neoreality constantly lies open to modification according to necessity as it arises, for each individual case as well as for the whole cohort of patients.

The institutional neoreality remains interlinked with common reality, and the catchment area team is in a position to assume the function of "outside," "before," "after," and "beyond" the institution, while maintaining the continuity of the therapeutic program.

Medical practitioners responsible for creating and running the care institutions also, like the doctors dealing with each individual case, must be aware of the dangers of confinement in an institution and have to set in motion a real "antiinstitutional" function as soon as they see that the institution is becoming pathogenic.

SOME STATISTICAL AND OPERATIONAL DATA CONCERNING THE PSYCHOTICS TREATED AT THE 13TH DISTRICT CENTER

These figures concern the years 1962 to 1970, inclusive. Some of the patients were taken in for treatment before then, but at that time we did not have a research service to record exact data on patients.

First Admissions Between 1962 and 1970, Inclusive

It is worth noting that overall the admission curve rises gradually from 1962 to 1970, see Fig. 3.1. There is always a slightly lower proportion of psychoses than neuroses at the point of admission.

In relation to total annual admissions the percentage of psychotics varies within the range indicated by the following maximum and minimum: from 22.18 percent in 1963 to 29.74 percent in 1968.

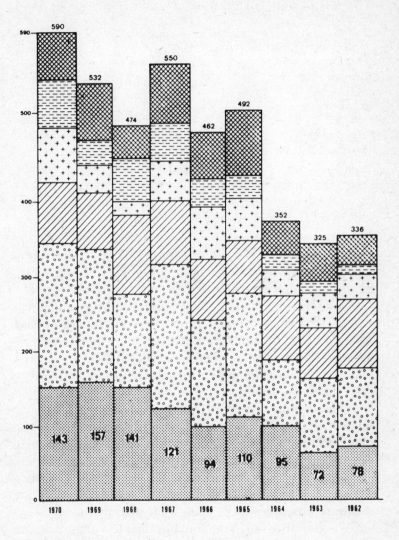

Fig. 3.1.   13th District Mental Health Association,
Department of General Psychiatry: Distribution of admissions
from 1962 to 1970, inclusive, according to year and diagnosis.

Table 3.1.   13th District Mental Health Association,
Department of General Psychiatry: Diagnostic distribution of the
functioning file (1970)

Diagnosis	Total	Percentages
Psychoses	629	34
Neuroses	489	27
Psychopaths	138	8
Alcoholics	246	14
Organic, senile	150	8
Others, retarded	168	9
Functioning file	1820	100

Patients in the Functioning File in 1970[3]

The diagnostic distribution shows 629 psychotics out of 1820 patients in the functioning file, i.e., 34 percent of the total number of patients treated (see Table 3.1).

Comparison of data in Table 3.1 with those in Fig. 3.1 concerning admissions shows an increase in the percentage of psychotics in the functioning file while the percentage of neurotics decreases. It therefore seems that long-term treatment is far commoner for psychotics than for any other diagnostic category.

Observation of patients in the functioning file as of December 31, 1970, whose admission dated further back (1962, 1963, and 1964), indicated in Fig. 3.2, shows that the total number of these patients over those three years is 188, of whom 99 were psychotics. These patients represent 52 percent of those still under treatment at present and who were admitted in the same year with them.

We therefore see in the functioning file a phenomenon of sedimentation particular to psychotic patients.

It is interesting to note how close the percentages are. On the average, psychotics represent:

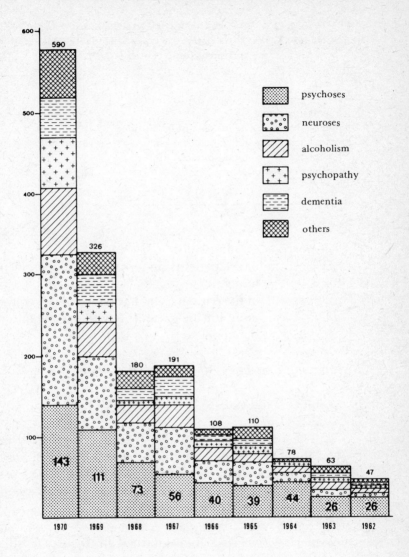

Fig. 3.2. 13th District Mental Health Association,
Department of General Psychiatry: Distribution according to
diagnosis of patients still present as of December 31, 1970

Table 3.2.   13th District Mental Health Association,
Department of General Psychiatry: Therapeutic modalities adopted for
the treatment of psychotics (1970)

	Totals	Percentage
Catchment area team	236	38
Catchment area team and outpatient institutions	125	20
Catchment area team and hospitalization	154	24
Catchment area team and hospitalization and outpatient institutions	114	18
Total	629	100

25 percent of admissions

34 percent of the patients under treatment at a given moment

52 percent of the patients who have been under treatment for the greatest length of time (after seven years)

Therapeutic Modalities Adopted for Psychotics

Table 3.2 indicates:

1. The very high proportion of psychotics treated in 1970 (236 or 38 percent) *with no recourse to hospital or other institutions, and using only the resources of the catchment area team;*

2. The use of hospitals for psychotics in comparison with other diagnostic categories.

Table 3.3 concerns patients in the 13th District Hospital as of December 31, 1970: out of 156 patients, 83 (53.20 percent) are psychotics and 66 (80 percent) of these had been under treatment for less than one year. Only six patients remained hospitalized for more than two years.

Table 3.3.   13th District Mental Health Association,
Department of General Psychiatry, Catchment area mental hospital,
Soisy-sur-Seine: Duration of hospital stay for those
present on December 31, 1970, by diagnostic categories

Diagnoses	1 year	1–2 years	2–3 years	3–5 years	5–10 years	10 years and over	Total
Psychotics	66	11	3	1	2	—	83
Neurotics	11	—	—	—	—	—	11
Alcoholics	11	2	1	—	—	—	14
Psychopaths	4	—	—	—	—	—	4
Senile disorders	11	3	2	2	—	—	18
Defectives	11	1	—	1	—	—	13
Others	6	1	—	—	—	—	7
Unclassifiable	5	1	—	—	—	—	6
							156

Thus we see that although there is a sedimentation of psychotics in the functioning file, this phenomenon does not appear in the hospital.

It is worth comparing this observation of the absence of hospital sedimentation in the 13th District catchment area facilities with the latest known and published INSERM data for the year 1968 and covering all French mental hospitals (see Table 3.4).

Thus, the psychotics under treatment at the 13th District Center constitute the diagnostic category with the highest frequency of long-term treatment, but this type of treatment does not involve a high degree of inpatient sedimentation, contrary to the French mental hospitals as a whole, although paradoxically the cohort of psychotics in the 13th District catchment area hospital represents 53 percent of the total number of patients there in 1970.

In the statistics covering all the French mental hospitals, the cohort of psychotics represents only 46.61 percent of all patients hospitalized. Out of 112,789 patients hospitalized as of December 31, 1968;

Table 3.4. Extract from mental hospital statistics (1968)

Diagnoses	1 year		1–2 years		2–3 years		3–5 years		5–10 years		10 years and over		Total	
	Male	Fem.	Male	Fem.	Male	Fem.	Male	Fem.	Male	Fem.	Male	Fem.	Male	Fem.
Psychoses	5,655	7,498	2,213	2,466	1,630	1,608	2,280	2,348	3,558	4,084	7,755	11,480	23,091	29,484
Total	13,153		4,679		3,238		4,628		7,642		19,235		52,573	
Neuroses	1,085	1,963	271	351	138	154	124	178	134	200	123	183	1,873	3,029
Total	3,048		622		292		322		334		306		4,904	
Alcoholics	4,485	1,280	1,071	416	618	224	701	308	777	350	731	292	8,383	2,870
Total	5,765		1,487		842		1,009		1,127		1,023		11,253	
Psychopaths	1,247	863	429	269	236	165	296	196	326	282	404	452	2,938	2,227
Total	2,110		698		401		492		608		856		5,165	
Organics, seniles	2,105	3,589	971	1,559	639	1,043	723	1,231	925	1,117	1,355	1,510	6,718	10,080
Total	5,694		2,530		1,682		1,954		2,042		2,865		16,806	
Retarded, others	2,001	1,365	680	728	960	577	1,449	912	2,508	1,732	4,913	3,761	13,011	9,075
Total	3,366		1,408		1,537		2,361		4,240		8,674		22,086	

Source: National Institute of Health and Medical Research (INSERM).

52,573 were psychotics,

26,877 had been in hospital for more than five years (over 50 percent)

13,153 had been hospitalized for less than one year (25 percent)

Examination of Data

A specific study with longitudinal data on the cohort of patients taken for treatment at the 13th District since 1965 enables us to formulate an approach as to the forms and hypotheses significant of these long-term treatments.

In 1965, of the 492 patients admitted, 98 were psychotics; 63 left the functioning file in less than six years, 35 were still under care on December 31, 1971, i.e., between six and seven years after the beginning of treatment.

Here we will deal only with the particular aspects relating to the 35 patients still under treatment after six years, and leave it to Dr. Balier's and Mme. Faure-Dayant's paper to give a more in-depth study on the fate of the total cohort treated since 1965.

We shall present our data in two tables.

Table 3.5. Study of the cohort of patients admitted
in 1965 and evaluated in 1970:
Average number of days per year spent in
institutions, by diagnostic category

Diagnostic categories	*Number of subjects*	*Days in hospital*	*Days spent in hospital and outpatient institutions*
Manic-depressive psychoses	1	10	32
Schizophrenias	14	79	120
Chronic delusions	14	12	49
Acute psychoses	8	24	70

Table 3.6.   Cross study of admission prognosis, therapeutic outcome, and use of institution for the 35 psychotic patients under treatment for six years (from 1965 to 1971)

Therapeutic outcome	Admission prognosis			Average number of days spent per year	
	Favorable	Undetermined	Unfavorable	H^a	$H+I^b$
Good	4	4	6	22	53
Fair	7	8	5	75	112
Poor	—	—	—	—	—
None	—	—	—	—	—
Deteriorated	—	—	—	—	—
Undetermined	—	—	—	—	—
No response	—	—	—	—	—
	H *H+I*	*H* *H+I*	*H* *H+I*		
Average number of days annually	30 41	44 94	70 105		

[a] Hospital.
[b] Hospital and institution.

Table 3.5 gives the average number of days per year spent in institutions by diagnostic categories.

It appears in particular that the schizophrenic syndromes account for a far greater number of institution days than all the other categories and that the chronic delusion category, which is numerically high, makes very little use of institutions, since these patients are often given outpatient treatment by the catchment area team.

Table 3.6 shows a cross-study of the admission prognosis, therapeutic outcome, and number of days per year in the institution for 35 psychotic patients under treatment for more than six years.

It should be noted first of all that the average number of days per year in the institution for every one of these 35 patients was less than one-third of the year (maximum number of days spent in hospital and institution was 112).

Another paradoxical result is that after six years of

uninterrupted therapy, 34 of the 35 patients are considered
to have attained a good or fair therapeutic outcome. The
remaining case was not able to be evaluated by a new doctor at the time of the study.

Naturally, when the admission prognosis is favorable
and the therapeutic outcome evaluated after six years is a
good one, the use of institutions is lowest. On the other
hand, however, when the admission prognosis is unfavorable, as was the case for 11 patients out of the 35, the
therapeutic outcome is found to be good or fair even with
very high use of institutions. The least one can say is that
as a general rule the frequency of recourse to institutions
does not, in our system, mean abandonment or rejection.

Consideration of the Treatment Profile

Consideration of the treatment profile for the six years will
give a good idea of the effects of the permanent dialectic
established between the catchment area teams and those
responsible for the institutions.

We will give particular attention to two questions
raised by:

1. the four psychotic patients out of 35 who had no
    need of institutions for six years, and
2. the 11 subjects with unfavorable prognoses and
    high use of institution, and yet who do not seem
    to have been abandoned by the agent of continu-
    ity, i.e., the catchment area team.

Of the four patients who were followed only at the
Mental Health Center during the six years, three had an
unfavorable prognosis and the other were undetermined.
Three were chronic delusion cases, the fourth a fixated
schizophrenic.

For all of these patients, the catchment area team has simply a supportive role, with no attempt at in-depth mobilization. The team is often the only place of refuge from the hostility of the outside world. In these cases, mediatory action, through the presence of the nurse in particular and neuroleptic treatment, is essential. The rhythm of contact with the team is not negligeable: for these four patients over a period of six years it was on an average six times a year.

Apart from the three patients mentioned above, the eight others with unfavorable admission prognoses were given a considerable amount of treatment time in institutions. Only one case, an extremely early infantile psychosis who prior to his admission at the 13th District had been hospitalized for 12 years in a ward for severely retarded patients in a state mental hospital, was hospitalized without interruption from 1965 onwards.

This patient arrived in a state of complete mutism other than screaming, totally incontinent and racked with continual motor stereotypies; he has shown a considerable improvement and now speaks, eats without help, and goes to a workshop. He is still being very closely followed by the catchment area team, and especially by the kinesitherapist.

The seven other cases never stayed more than a total of 18 months in the hospital out of the six years, and they presented two types of development:

1. The first type includes a maximum of one and one-half years of hospitalization during the six years, associated only with intense psychotherapy from the catchment area team (five cases). For these patients the annual average number of team actions is 28, which represents the interventions appropriate to each case on the part of the medical practitioner, the social worker, and the nurse.

2. In two cases, after a relatively short period of hospi-

talization, increasingly light forms of nonhospital institution treatment, day hospital, and then the therapeutic
workshop or foster home were proposed. Here too, the
catchment area team is still very much present, with an
average of 18 contacts a year.

It is impossible from these quantitative data in terms
of actions or days spent in institutions to draw a qualitative
picture other than the impression of a great variety and
therefore an individualization of therapeutic projects and,
inside each of these therapeutic projects, the image of patient mobility within the institutional network.

The catchment area team still remains a sufficiently
continuous reference throughout the years for it to be significant for the permanent opening of any institution onto
an "outside" and a "beyond."

To conclude this reflection on the figures, one cannot
fail to be struck by the fact that the therapeutic outcome for
all 35 of these patients remaining under treatment for six
years is invariably *good or fair*.

True, we have stressed the aspect of the nonrejection,
nonabandonment, particularly within the framework of a
single institution, of the 35 patients in question, but the
objection might perhaps be raised that these follow-ups of
patients and teams throughout the years could be the result
of an abusive and questionable desire to cure at any cost.
But the existence of cases given only very light team support, and the variety and mobility of institutional care
seems to counter this objection.

The observations we shall present later will give better
support than figures to the fact that this stable and constant
accompaniment of patients by the team is only possible,
and takes on any meaning, through their sharing what I
shall simply call a hope and a fate, which has to be through
the gradual formulation of a more clear request by the
patient.

THE CONTRADICTIONS EXPERIENCED BY A CARING STAFF WORKING WITH PSYCHOTICS

Placed in communal society as a team responsible for a differentiated network of institutions, psychiatric workers have to live throughout the whole period of treatment through conflicts and contradictions which neither the psychoanalyst in his consulting room nor the chief medical practitioner of a hospital ward ever come up against. We shall illustrate with clinical cases the situations which seem to us today the most difficult to deal with.

The psychiatrist, according to the different cases and the given moment in the treatment of the individual patient, has to establish and coordinate forms of presence which are apparently contradictory and irreconcilable, that is, from the ordinary mortal to the psychoanalyst-psychiatrist, the specialist shuttles between presence "like" and presence "as."

We are always groping to find the difficult and delicate articulation of the technical and the tragic.

The Treating Team's Confrontation of the Patient's Double Request

Colette[4]

She is 33 years old. We have known her since 1965, but ever since 1957 another catchment area team had tried everything to establish a psychotherapeutic relationship with her. For a long time she was thought to present a neurotic structure.

One day in July 1957, the medical practitioner dealing with her case referred her to one of our best psychoanalysts at the institute. The latter found her in what he described as "full-scale emotional crisis" (probably in an anxiety stupor) and wrote: "I was unable to assess her intellectual and verbal capacities. I rather fear that a psychoanalysis would be hampered by too low a level."

Her biography contained affective factors which were considered to have been traumatic. One means after another was tried in an attempt to avoid social maladjustment. Those caring for her seemed to be undertaking a systematic denial of Colette's psychotic development until the day, in November 1959, when Dr. M. wrote that she had for the first time expressed delusional convictions: "I can see an enormous black spider in my head; it's real, as long as it doesn't move." In the sheltered workshop she had just entered, Colette had the impression that the instructors were talking about her.

Her entry into psychosis was a dramatic time for the caring staff; they kept a close watch out for the brief periods of internalization of her conflicts. Then there were successive periods of hospitalization, initially in an open ward and later in a closed ward, and she was given increasingly high doses of neuroleptics.

These were the circumstances, with the patient living in a small room in the 13th District, when one of our catchment area teams made their first visit to her at home.

Colette asked for nothing. She had a violent feeling about outside action. She lived alone in a miserable room, in a state of intense autistic withdrawal. The neighbors wanted to rape her, they were insulting and infecting her. She felt absolutely besieged. Yells, obscenities, and scuffles interspersed phases of virtually total imprisonment in a room with neither heat or running water.

The two fears, the patient's and that of the people around her, reached such intensity that there started a repetitive cycle of emergency police calls, ending up with forcible hospitalization. In fact everything fell into place in such a way that the concrete procedures of the people around her, provoked by fear, simply confirmed Colette's delusions. She was in fact quite genuinely persecuted and rejected. The psychiatric team had only two alternatives: either be there to meet the patient when the police brought her to the hospital, or get to her first. The idea was not to do the same thing, wearing white coats, that those in uniform do perfectly well themselves, but something quite different. With Colette, everything happens through her eyes. It is through her eyes that others attack her, and take over her brain and her mind, but these same eyes also express simultaneously a complaint, an intense request for help for which she cannot find words.

We very soon discovered that no man ever got her to open the door. She would *only* open it to the nurse and no one else—and even for her Colette was very difficult to approach.

At first it was only clinical knowledge that made it possible to maintain any contact. The terms "safety perimeter" and "critical distance" immediately sprang to the caring people's mind. In the beginning no one was to get any nearer than three yards or so. Then we had to try to understand her look, to hold her gaze without feeling it as menacing, even if we were well aware that Colette was on the brink of acting out. It was a real process of taming and familiarization, Saint-Exupéry's "taming," that began. Eventually the nurse's hand could touch Colette's hand or shoulder and almost without a word they left together for the hospital. But the neighbor's fear was to touch off an impulsive call to the emergency police two or three times more and all would have been lost had the caring team not been capable of receiving her, of understanding the fear of those around her, and of considering it, a priori, quite genuine.

After two years of contact there was no longer any question of the neighbors' verbalized anxiety being addressed to anyone but the caring team. As soon as Colette shut herself in, or they were afraid of her violence, or, on the contrary, that she was letting herself die of hunger or cold, they automatically called the nurse.

Meanwhile at the hospital, the caring staff was learning to expect the continual alternation between a request for exclusive protection and aggressive reactions at the slightest hint of abandonment. Colette gradually began to show herself capable of an increasingly clear awareness of the intrapsychic nature of her conflicts. Instead of shutting herself in her room or withdrawing into mutism, one day she was able to say: "I nearly died from being separated from my mother."

A psychoanalyst was then able to enter into contact with her. For months the analyst had to deal with a relationship which was neither a real face-to-face encounter nor the analytical position neither; Colette remained three-quarters facing, at a distance of more than two yards. Her head would turn to cast a piercing and fixed gaze which penetrates one in order not to be penetrated.

In the beginning Colette could only stand the "trial of strength" for between one and three minutes at a time, but she still came alone each week or asked her nurse to accompany her and little by little "inside" and "outside" began to settle into place. After three years of treatment, Colette was cathecting positively the catchment area therapeutic possibilities as a whole.

In her relationship with the team doctor, the critical distance phenomenon disappeared completely. Each time she felt she was about to go into a paroxysm of fear she would on her own initiative ask to go into a home or be admitted to the hsopital.

At the present time she is hospitalized, but rarely spends more than 48 hours a week in the hospital, which has become her refuge at the very moment she is multiplying her contacts with her mother, with employers, and at the same time, she goes each week for a three-quarter-hour session with her psychoanalyst.

For Colette, the catchment area's set-up of people and institutions reconstitutes temporarily a mediating world which can both accept and withstand the intensity of her annihilating anxiety and put a definite end to the real fear and hostility of those around her.

If a three-person team, a doctor, a social worker and a nurse, had not dared to put itself between Colette and her surroundings at the time and place of the maximum degree of tension, and if this team had not been able to work in close cooperation with a hospital team and then with a psychoanalyst, Colette would without doubt today be immobile and mute, enclosed in an irreducible autism.

The Analyst, Provider of Time and Milieu[5]

Mr. S.[6]

Today aged 70, Mr. S. was born near Turin in Italy and came to France illegally at the age of 23; he worked as a digger or construction laborer and at 27 he married a girl from Brittany in Paris. The couple had only one son, who is now married and has five children.

In 1955 he was confined against his will because he expressed delusional ideas of persecution, ruin, incurability, and incapacity for work, and especially ideas of suicide; he claimed that the various general hospital services he had been to had "destroyed him, made him go to seed, made him ill."

He was in the same mental hospital for 14 years without interruption. Then three years ago, it was realized that he was domiciled in the 13th District and he was transferred to our hospital ward.

All the observations we gathered indicated that over these long years Mr. S. had become the perfect asylum patient. His space was reduced to the walk between his bed and the hospital linen room, and he never seemed to have any ideas of leaving the hospital. He had found an equilibrium in a withdrawal excluding any project for the future; on the symptomatic level, hypochondriacal complaints had replaced his former complaints of persecution. His sole contact with the outside world was regular visits from his wife.

The catchment area treating team, like the Soisy hospital team, found themselves faced with a form of wholesale regression which could no doubt have continued until the patient died, but which was also maintained and cultivated by the walled-in form, the enclosed space, and the atemporality of the asylum.

On a certain level, this patient who had found his equilibrium for 14 years in that situation represented a kind of "successful sickness," and this was going to be challenged by the inevitable exigencies of a more dynamic therapeutic system.

For several months Mr. S., who did not verbalize his anxiety at all after this transfer, to which he appeared indifferent, presented the caring staff with a sort of caricature of his asylum character, thus manifesting his deep anxiety. Desperately attached to his old regulation mental hospital suit, and refusing to take it off even to sleep, he would wear a large hat and a flower in his buttonhole and go for walks, talking to himself and gesticulating energetically, picking up cigarette butts and old newspapers with which he would fill his pockets. But behind this mask—I was going to say this explicit language—he organized for himself, in acts, a whole secret life which was made possible only by the hospital's openness onto the outside world. He would get up at dawn and leave without permission by the main gate when the first cars went through, and go and have coffee in the village, walk around for a while outside, and then return to the hospital building at the time everyone was supposed to be getting up.

The catchment area team's contact with his family enabled him to take a second very decisive step towards the outside world. He was told that his wife, whom he had not seen for several months, was on the point of death (terminal cancer) at the Hôpital Cochin. Only the social worker's presence enabled him to go twice to see his wife before she died, and then go to his apartment to clean and air it.

At this point the team was astonished by the capacity for autonomy demonstrated on this occasion by the patient, whose own behavior made the team begin to see him as someone perhaps recovering the possibility of a future and, on the level of actual reality, that of leaving the hospital.

In the hospital, over a period of about four months, Mr. S. slowly changed. He dropped his eccentric mode of dress and his asylum habits of picking up cigarette butts and old newspapers, his circle of acquaintances enlarged, and he went to the woodwork shop and developed deeper relationships with the caring staff, although remaining totally indifferent to anything concerning the other patients.

What was going on was a matter between himself, the caring staff, and the outside world. He began to read, watched the television news every day and, as always, went for solitary walks in the gardens.

Outside the hospital a further contact was established with the son, who no longer had anything to do with his father and showed tremendous hostility towards him. When he was 15 years old, his father had nearly killed him in a bout of alcoholism. The son's development made its way through the complex interplay of a constant relationship with the social worker. During an interview with the team doctor it became apparent that the son had a real capacity for resolving his manifest ambivalence regarding his father. They were able to renew contacts when concrete problems arose.

For some time the patient showed a considerable degree of hostility and occasionally plainly persecutive reactions towards the social worker. Finally, however, he began to rely on her for support toward a potential autonomous existence outside.

Today, Mr. S. is in an aftercare home. He was able to

express clearly his anxiety at leaving the hospital, but is getting along without any major crises.

He has been living in this home for eight months now, goes regularly to his apartment, and is about to go back to live there, as long as he can go each day to the Old People's Day Center.

This history is presented as a counterpoint to the previous one. Here the team, while constantly assessing the patient's possibilities for cathexis, simply gave him the opportunity to move about in an extended space. The team itself acted only as a kind of bridge between the enclosed space and the open space outside. It first represented and then presented, in a mediating role, the people—his wife and his son—who, so to speak, roused him out of a long period of blank forgetfulness.

From the human point of view, in the tragic register, Mr. S., who forgets or is forgotten, in a kind of psychic death, touches us as deeply as Colette, who could only bear the hostility she felt from others by shutting herself up at home and letting herself die. On the technical level, however, a new style of presence had to be assumed, as a team. It was essential to be able to wait, to recognize the capacity the patient manifests for cathecting new objects, and to do this at the latter's own speed. The most difficult thing was to stop oneself from using an excess of "words for adults" as Balint would say, to avoid untimely and omnipotent interpretation and mobilization which could have made us unable to tolerate Mr. S.'s deliberately provoking exhibition of the old asylum of which he was still a part.

Presence and Neutrality

François[7]
Born in 1932, François is an only son and lives with his mother, who is a secretary. The father left their home in 1948 when François was 16 years old.

He is a tall blond boy, with a rather babyish but intelligent face which contrasts with his gangly frame; bowed head, rounded back, loose-hanging arms, he always seems to be about to keel over, ready to be blown down by a breeze. He is immediately winning, and arouses a general desire to protect him . . . an intense desire to help him out, to cure him! . . . He was treated at the Center from 1960 until a few months ago.

We, who had come from the classic mental hospital in 1960, found ourselves affected by very intense feelings about him, tinted with suspicious shades of omnipotence!

Between 1954 and 1959 he had been admitted on three occasions to a private clinic and a general hospital psychiatric ward for repeated insulin and electroshock treatment.

Agitated by motor sterotypies, he would hit his own head, tear out his hair and, when he went out into the street he could only do so by performing a complicated ceremonial: two steps forward, three backwards, and rocking back and forth on the spot. He was considered the local madman: passersby would stop and take him by the hand, and give him sweets as though he were a child.

This extremely disturbed behavior contrasted strongly with his lively intelligence, remarkable insight, and astonishing capacity for verbalization. He described with touching intensity his first experience of depersonalization: when he was 14 years old, at his grandmother's house, he heard "You've got a narrow forehead . . . You'll never get anywhere in life . . . ". He immediately looked at himself in the mirror, and at once everybody in the street and all the newspapers were talking about this strange creature, different from the others.

Finally, and above all, we allowed ourselves to recognize his mother as the typical pathogenic schizophrenic-type mother. François slept in a twin bed in her room, holding her hand. She had to dress him and make him eat following an interminable ceremonial procedure.

This latter perception, which was shared but not clearly acknowledged by the catchment area team and the team at the day hospital where he had just been admitted, caused the interruption after a few sessions of the dual psychotherapy indicated by the team and embarked upon by one of us.

The patient responded to our massive countertransference by an equally intense transference: "... dazzled right from the first session of psychotherapy, he had the overwhelming feeling of being understood, of being able to be met on his own ground . . . ." He was to pay dearly, and so were we, for this initial reciprocally psychotic exchange.

His mother took him away for three months, without any warning, and took him to another psychiatrist, who gave him a series of electroshocks.

It was only as a team that we were able to recover the necessary neutrality in Racamier's sense of the word, i.e., the "capacity to perceive objectively, without suffering from or becoming overinvolved in all the aspects of an interpersonal relationship."

This resulted in the stronger contact with each member of the team, but each one according to his or her own specificity, modulating interventions both differentiated and articulated.

An instructor gave help and support to François and his mother every morning to get him to the Day Hospital.

With the help of the catchment area psychiatrist the mother was ready to recognize her own inner difficulties, and she herself began taking group therapy with other mothers.

She readily accepted, without breaking either with us or her son, the latter's hospitalization for a brief spell.

It was at the beginning of 1962, after a year and a half of dual psychotherapy, that a decisive event occurred. François' therapist was expecting a child and had talked with him about it; shortly after the birth, she suggested to him that he continue some of his sessions with her at her home.

There she showed him the baby, and it was then and only then, that a certain distance became possible and the transference was able to be mobilized.

In the workshop, François' autonomy was quite spectacular; he produced earthenware objects on his own, did drawing and woodwork, and was able to leave his mother for a while to live in a home.

In 1963 François was able to leave the day hospital. He began working again part-time at the social security job he had dropped five years ago, and a year later was working there full-time.

Mother and son each continued with their respective psychotherapists, while maintaining close contacts with the team and the Patients' Club. Both were very active.

His social circles widened; he would go to the swimming pool with his colleagues, and joined a choir.

It was François himself who, in 1967, detached himself from the surroundings and the members of the caring team. The team and the psychotherapist were now only onlookers. He returned only to the Club, not for his own benefit, he said, but to show the others his progress, to give them support; he identified with the caring staff and considered himself the Club leader.

At the beginning of 1971 he definitively dropped his sessions, shortly after having taken his analyst to see the new apartment he had just moved into with his mother, and had shown the analyst that the twin bed had been dismantled and could not be set up again in his new independent room.

His mother and his psychotherapist met each other without incident in front of him. Neither one nor the other was destroyed.

In January 1972, following the return after a year's absence abroad of a doctor whose illness had caused him anxiety, François came both to verify the latter's existence and to outline his inner development.

"Before," he said, "everybody else could get into my mind. . . ." He then named one after the other all the workshop and Club counselors, the nurse and social worker, his psychotherapist and the psychiatrist. "Because of them I can live better inside my own body. I am inside an impenetrable fortress . . . I'm not afraid any more"; as though the person of each member of the caring team named had made it possible to reconstruct the dividing lines between inside and outside. Before leaving, he told me about his secret love for a work colleague.

François is not cured, but he lives a lot better. He still maintains contact, a sort of straining wire with a member of the team whose role intervenes, precisely, at the limits of the body, the dividing point between inside and outside, the kinesitherapist, whom he actually meets outside the Center.

This long history shared with François and his mother taught us, by experiencing them to recognize the massiveness, the violence, the exclusiveness and the megalomanic omnipotence of our feelings towards François. We were only able to find a real neutrality through the organization of an intense, flexible, and team presence vis-à-vis not only François, but François and his mother.

Conversely, in the subsequent phase of François' history, was it not the pregnancy of his psychotherapist that constituted the ground, the terra firma on the basis of which the transference was able to be mutually recognized and acknowledged? After this the presence of the caring staff became daily more and more discreet, on the initiative of the patient himself.

It is an understatement to say that the caring team is faced with contradictions when it decides to accompany psychotic patients over the long term. "The patient," Balint writes, "says that he feels there is a fault within him, a fault that must be put right . . . there is a feeling that the cause of this fault is that someone has either failed the patient or defaulted on him ... a great anxiety invariably surrounds this area, usually expressed as a desperate appeal that this time the analyst should not—in fact must not —fail him."

Rosen advises the analyst treating a psychotic to behave as though he were a member of his family, personally and humanly committed and involved in the patient's existence and fate.

Lebovici, Diatkine, and myself—the initial nucleus of the 13th District team—would like to tell you here the same thing the opposite way: what a tremendous influence in our existence was exercised by the history we experienced with another patient (Guy), from the point when one of us diagnosed him as an infantile psychotic at the age of eight.

Through the years he forced us to intensify our research, to become aware of the significance of many of our conflicts, and to experience ourselves the demands imposed by real team work where flexibility is as imperative as the certainty of duration and indestructibility. As early as 1949, he and children like him caused us to reflect upon the 23 other hours, which in a traditional ward can wipe out the good effects of the best of sessions of analytic therapy. He forced us to rediscover and experience the risks involved in the subversive function of analysis faced with the rigid aspects of discipline, hierarchy, and administration in therapeutic settings. These risks were taken and led to the expulsion of two of us from the ward they were working in. Step by step, the three of us subsequently created the conditions for a new practice. It would take a whole book to tell this story, of which Guy and ourselves were both authors and beneficiaries. Guy has now been elected by all the patients treated at the Center as President of the Club, even though he as never lived in the 13th District. This is the very image of the absolute necessity in some cases for a continuity kept up despite administrative obstacles, and despite the discontinuity and number of institutions. "It was," said Guy, "a matter of life and death. . . ." "There is no intellectual translation for everything," Nietzsche would say.

NOTES

1. Jean-Marie Domenach (1967), *Le retour du tragique,* Paris: Editions du Seuil

2. Miguel de Unamuno (1913), *Del sentimiento trágico de la vida,* Obras completas, Madrid: Afrodisio Aguado.

3. The term "functioning file" is used at the 13th District Center in preference to "active file." It includes all the patients who have had at least one therapeutic consultation during the year.

4. Observations: P. de Grado, J. Loriod, Ph. Paumelle, and M. Rovarino.

5. M. Balint.

6. Observation: J. Azoulay, Mme L. Guillou, and Mme Vallée-Vignot.

7. Observation: N. Cassens, P. de Grado, Ph. Paumelle, S. Paumelle, G. Pous, and M. Rovarine.

CONCLUSION

In conclusion, let us present some reflections on the relations between research work and clinical practice.

In the psychiatric field as a whole, we can distinguish two lines of research.

One of these consists of a more in-depth study of individual cases; at the case-work level, insight, presence, and clincial experience are important factors. Reflection on practice and consequent enrichment of theory is in itself research, and a number of examples of this have been given by the papers collected in this book.

The second line of research is that of statistical and comparative studies.

In order to attain complete accuracy of clinical description together with the clear identification of the numerous variables which show such complexity in the etiology and treatment, it is important for these two types of research to be carried out by the same team, and not by different ones.

H.B.M. Murphy mentions the importance of psychiatric research in the general population, and he considers that community-based psychiatry opens up new possibilities in this respect. Sylvie Faure-Dayant voices her misgivings at this idea, on the grounds that studies on the general population would run the risk of increasing the demand for care, which is already high. It is known that as soon as a new source of care is set up, this demand immediately increases.

General population studies raise major questions for us, for they demonstrate the existence of psychotics who are not known and not treated. This does not mean that we should go and look for them and subject them to treatment whether they like it or not, nor should there be a general screening, "neither of adults or of children" (here we do not go along with L. Bellak). Some people have compared catchment area psychiatry with police checking and we, who are not doing any such thing, are taken to task for this. In a general population study we observe that there are psychotics who are not known and not treated. We have to ask ourselves and understand why and how, despite disorders which are obvious to the clinician and analogous in all respects to those of psychotics who have become patients either of their own free will or under constraint, either these children or adults are not identified as sick by their families and friends, or are simply considered as peculiar but tolerated.

Something could certainly be learned from a comparison between psychotics who receive long-term treatment and long-term psychotics who receive no treatment at all.

Certain talents—artistic, for example—afford an alternative route side-stepping psychosis, a solution which leads to a type of professional activity and an unconventional kind of life. There should, of course, be no confusion between unreason and richness, insanity and genius. One can be a genius though insane but one is not necessarily a genius because one is insane. Despite the poetic value of some works produced by some psychotics, the most striking thing is the gradual impoverishment and inexorable barrenness brought on by many long-term psychoses.

With regard to children, what emerges is on one hand that those the school complains about are not always the ones whose future mental health seems to us most seriously jeopardized, and on the other, the great number of children whose childhood is spent in what can only be described as unfavorable conditions, from any point of view. There are children whose obvious insufficiency of neurotic mechanisms, their lack of neurotic richness, gives cause for concern as to their future. These are the ones whom some of us call prepsychotics, and who are in danger of developing in the direction of psychosis or severe character disorders, or are headed toward the impoverishment, the psychological poverty referred to by André Green.

As a result, the psychiatrist, and especially the catchment area psychiatrist, is faced with the problem of primary prevention. In order to avoid putting matters on a psychiatric level and being sent ever-increasing numbers of patients, he has to work hand in hand with the community institutions, for example, with the school for a transformation in pedagolgical thinking.

This is how psychiatric work, while maintaining its own specificity, is articulated with social problems such as the functioning of schools and the team which teachers should constitute and do not, and also with political problems arising from the question: what does our society expect from its schools? What is it prepared to spend on them? What is true for schools, for children can also be applied to other social organizations at the adult level. Greater expenditure has to be made for those children who come from underprivileged sociolcultural backgrounds, and also for adults who are disabled because of their insanity. This is a sound economic proposition in the long term, but is it taken into consideration?

C. C.

INDEX

689